The Joy of Knowledge
GENERAL EDITOR: JAMES MITCHELL

The Illustrated Reference Book of
The Ages of Discovery

WINDWARD

Preface

How to use this book

The Ages of Discovery consists of one section of *The Joy of Knowledge*. It contains all the general knowledge my editors and I think most important in world history during the years between the middle of the thirteenth century and the close of the eighteenth century – a period of major discoveries in every field of human endeavour, including the arts, exploration and science.

The spread system
Every topic in *The Joy of Knowledge* takes the form of an article that occupies two facing pages of text and pictures; what we call a "spread". Each two-page spread in the book is organized in the same way. It is the heart of our approach to explaining things.

The spread system is a strict discipline but once you get used to it we hope you'll find the structure to be systematic and reassuring. You should start to feel at home in all sorts of unlikely areas of knowledge with the spread system to guide you. It works like this.

Each spread in this fascinating book, as throughout *The Joy of Knowledge,* tells a self-contained story. It explains all the essential facts you need to know about its subject in as efficient a manner as possible. We believe that the discipline of having to get in all the essential and relevant facts in this comparatively small space actually makes for better results than a rambling essay could achieve – text that has to get straight to the point, pictures and diagrams that illustrate the salient points in a clear and comprehensible fashion, and captions that really work and explain the point of the pictures.

The spreads are, in a sense, the building blocks of knowledge. Like the various circuits and components that go to make up a computer, they are also systematically "programmed" to help the reader find out things more easily and remember them better. Each spread, for example, has a main article of about 850 words summarising the subject. This article is illustrated by an average of ten pictures and diagrams, the captions of which both complement and supplement the basic information in the main

article. Each spread, too, has a "key" picture or diagram in the top right-hand corner. The purpose of this picture is twofold: it summarises the story of the spread visually and it is intended to act as a memory stimulator to help you recall all the integrated facts and pictures on a given subject.

Where to start
A good way to begin acquiring knowledge from this particular part of *The Joy of Knowledge* series is initially to read the Introduction. The Introduction provides a useful framework for the information contained in the following pages. If, however, you prefer to plunge straight into the book (but don't have much basic general knowledge on the subject) I suggest you look first at the spreads "Feudalism" beginning on page 10, "European society 1250–1450" on page 12, "The world Europe set out to explore" on page 22 and "The age of exploration" on page 34. Once you have absorbed the information on these spreads you can build up a more comprehensive general knowledge by exploring the rest of the book.

Here is a highly informative book about the brightest eras of human imagination, innovation and inquiry. I hope you will find it both stimulating and helpful.

Contents

The Illustrated Reference Book of The Ages of Discovery

Editor's introduction

The giving of descriptive names or titles to periods of history can seem, at first sight, to be an arbitrary business. After all, time flows on at a steady pace and all events, regarded scientifically, have an equal importance in the universal scheme of things. But man is, by his nature, unwilling to and incapable of regarding all things with an omniscient impartiality. We attach more importance to some things than to others. It is perfectly respectable, and is indeed essential, for an historian to reconstruct the past in his imagination in such a way as to make a pattern out of apparent chaos. Part of that imaginative construction of patterns, which is the very business of the historian, is the division of the past into historical epochs – periods in history that appear to us to have exhibited certain outstanding characteristics which mark them off from preceding and following ages.

The Illustrated Reference Book of The Ages of Discovery deals with world history during the years between the middle of the thirteenth century and the close of the eighteenth century – years which can justifiably be called the Ages of Discovery. In this period, men made discoveries of great moment in every field of human endeavour: geographical exploration, the arts, the physical sciences, warfare and politics. There is justification for looking upon these few hundred years as one of the brightest eras of human discovering because for so many centuries preceding them, human imagination and spirit of innovation (the attitude of inquiry) seemed to have slumbered. A languor had descended upon what historians once called the Dark Ages.

At the very centre of the years spanned by this volume stands the Renaissance.

The word is not the invention of historians who came after; Italians of the fifteenth century used it to describe their own age. They felt that they were taking part in a rebirth. And they called it a rebirth precisely because they were conscious that, after long years of dormancy, the values and attitudes of the pre-Christian Greek and Roman societies were once more lodging themselves in men's minds. What was the cardinal quality of the Greek attitude, the distinguishing mark of the Greek cast of mind? The Greek attitude was not, strictly speaking, a secular one, because the Greeks were worshippers of their gods. But it was certainly a less mystical, less comprehensively religious attitude than the Christian one which followed it. Mammon and the gods were accorded their separate due. The physical world held its own, independent interest, and its workings called out for investigation. Above all, the Greeks took pleasure in exploring the world in order to discover how things worked. It was that inquisitiveness, that readiness to explore all worlds, which was taken up afresh by the men of the Renaissance. Their investigations were carried out in the seventeenth and eighteenth centuries, themselves commonly known as the Age of Reason and the Age of the Enlightenment respectively.

Men had long been interested in regaining Paradise, in actually rediscovering the lost Eden which they believed to exist somewhere. But when Columbus caught sight of America, men rejoiced at finding a *new* world. Columbus' achievement, being accidental, was a far more exciting event for his contemporaries than the landing on the Moon was for us – we, after all, knew that the Moon was there. The age of overseas exploration was forced upon the nations of western Europe when the Ottoman Turks captured Constantinople in 1453 and sealed off Europe's traditional trading routes to the East. The centre of Europe's economic and financial gravity shifted from the Italian ports to Spain, Portugal and The Netherlands. The early navigators set out in search of gold and wealth. They sought a new route to the rich spice islands of the East. They rounded the southern tip of Africa and made their way to India and China. But it was the discovery of America that mattered in the long run. At first dismissive of the value of the Indians' land which they called "virgin", the European monarchies soon awoke to the rich potential of the new world. The sixteenth century was not far advanced before Spain, Portugal, Holland, France and England had begun their empires.

Not all the discoveries were geographical. No more important change occurred in early modern Europe than the one heralded by the invention of movable type (individual, reusable characters) in the middle of the fifteenth century. The turbulent political history of the years between 1600 and 1800 – years marked by the rise of national monarchies and the attendant decline of the Holy Roman Empire, marked also by the proliferation of radical Protestant religious sects and the Reformation's assault upon the universal authority of the Roman Catholic Church and Papacy – owed a great deal to the fact that for the first time in history revolutionary notions in politics and religion could be broadcast by means of the printed word. One of the first printed books to be published was a translation of the Bible in the German tongue. At a stroke, direct access to the revealed word of God ceased to be the exclusive enjoyment of the educated, clerical elite who knew Latin. The Gospels became the property of nations. At the heart of the Protestant Reformation of the sixteenth century lay the assertion that each individual was capable of a direct relationship with his creator: the elaborate (and corrupt) edifice of the episcopal hierarchy was not essential to eternal salvation. The Reformation re-asserted, or re-discovered, the worth of the individual. And that rediscovery naturally insinuated its influence into social and political affairs, producing, in the latter part of the eighteenth century, the American and French Revolutions. Ever since that time the belief in the sanctity of the individual and of certain fundamental individual human rights has been the foundation of Western political and social thought.

Coincident with the political revolutions of the late eighteenth century was the beginning, first of all in England, of the Industrial Revolution. In a similar way to the geographical explorations of the early Renaissance, the Industrial Revolution was forced upon men: an agricultural economy was running out of the means to supply the food and energy requirements of a rapidly expanding population. To that great historical necessity, European man responded with abundant ingenuity. Just as the sixteenth and seventeenth centuries had witnessed a scientific revolution (the overthrowing of medieval cosmology and physics by the work of Copernicus, Galileo, Kepler and Newton) so the eighteenth century witnessed a revolution in engineering, symbolized above all by the steam engine and the power cotton loom. The Industrial Revolution represented a fundamental break with the past, a change in man's way of living as dramatic as the agricultural revolution of the eighth millennium BC. The Italian economist and historian, Carlo Cipolla, has argued that those two revolutions were the most decisive moments of change in human history, events which utterly and irrevocably transformed men's economic environment and which thereby "created deep breaches in the continuity of the historical process".

It is natural that we should be most keenly interested in that part of history which touches us most nearly – the events that took place in western Europe and the Americas. But even by a more objective appraisal, Europe would dominate the history of these centuries. It is not mere fiction to describe the pre-modern societies of China and Japan as stagnant. The stimuli that spurred Europe on to great achievements seemed lacking in the East, where a good deal of scientific and technical knowledge lie dormant. The discovery of gunpowder by the Chinese, for example, served them merely as a diversion in pyrotechnics, leaving its great potential to be realized by Europeans. The modern world, seen at any rate through Western eyes, was shaped by events that took place in Europe. For four hundred years Europe led the world in science, philosophy, engineering, and the development of democratic political and social institutions. Europe's overlordship of the world has now come to an end, and whether it will ever again come to exercise such sway in world affairs is a matter for conjecture. Yet in its hayday Europe had no rivals: the Ages of Discovery were also the Ages of European domination in trade, industry, culture, military might and colonialism.

Town life in medieval England

Town life in England re-emerged in the tenth and eleventh centuries after being practically non-existent since the departure of the Romans in the early fifth century. The medieval towns, especially London, were important as centres of trade and production and were also the cradles of a sophisticated non-feudal political consciousness.

The earliest towns

There were a number of towns in England before 1066 which formed part of the tenth-century kings' coherent plan of local government and defence. They were often planned towns: excavations at Winchester have revealed the grid plan of the tenth-century streets, and it seems that Oxford was consciously populated in about 910 by drafting villagers in from nearby communities. Although they were really fortified villages rather than towns, with agriculture far more important than industry, towns were nevertheless the means by which a measure of peace and government was imposed.

Some 52 "towns" were described in the Domesday Book (1086). In the twelfth century, growing international trade and a rising standard of living combined to multiply their number and to give birth to new crafts. The *negotiatores* (general traders) of the past gave way to specialized occupations organized in guilds. The purveyors of luxury goods, the vintners, goldsmiths and pepperers, were the earliest specialized trades in London. By 1191 representatives of a score of different trades witnessed a charter at Oxford, only a middle-sized town. Guilds [7] enabled the towns to maintain their supplies and markets: smaller towns began with a single "guild merchant" of all the trades, but during the thirteenth century humbler craft guilds [6], of weavers, bakers, fishmongers or smiths also emerged to claim their share in city government. These craft guilds looked after their members' interests whereas the guilds merchant organized the fundamental trading and market privileges of the towns [3].

Life in the towns

Crowded sites soon made necessary a new style of life: closed street frontages, houses with their narrow ends to the street stretching far back into their gardens, created the town house and the modern townscape [Key, 1]. Warehouses, counting-houses, shops and living-rooms shared many cramped sites in burgeoning towns such as Southampton. The streets themselves were narrow, because space was valuable: ordinances frequently forbade householders to encroach upon them. Open gutters in the middle of streets carried much refuse, although nearly every house had a cesspit as well. By 1300 town authorities were beginning to improve sanitary conditions: paviours were engaged to restore the surface of the streets, and butchers were generally forbidden to slaughter livestock except in "shambles" situated safely beyond the walls [9].

The new communities where men could suddenly rise to great wealth and which had relative political freedom were naturally conscious of their difference from the more static rural society. At first they were dominated by small oligarchies made up of men in the luxury trades who had great influence at court. In their confident hands London and Oxford tried in 1191 to become communes

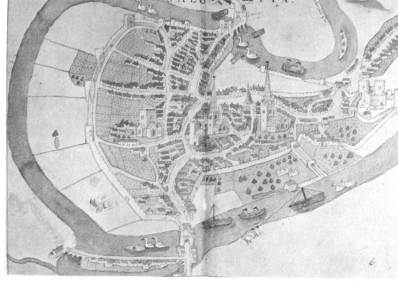

1 Shrewsbury, in a 16th-century map, appears crowded round its market square. The castle was first built in 1070 and the town obtained its first charter in 1189. In the great period of medieval town life, before 1350, many towns outgrew their walls. The walls in most English towns were not built until the middle of the 12th century.

2 John granted a charter of incorporation to London, England's largest town, in 1215. From the mid-12th century, London's citizens, who claimed even the right to elect the king, were seeking and winning privileges of self-government. John's charter confirmed the citizens' liberties and permitted the election of a mayor.

3 Markets were the life-blood of a medieval town, and they provided an outlet for peasants from the surrounding countryside to sell their own goods, as well as being the centre for the inland distributive trade in more luxury products. They were situated in regular places in each town, often marked by a market cross or a covered hall. Markets could be violent places, and there were strict regulations governing them, particularly on the standards of the goods sold. Towns hired officials such as the assayers of ale and bread, and offenders suffered heavy fines. A successful market could be an important source of profit for the town or the baron who set it up. The great period for the creation of market rights was the late 12th century.

4 Southampton was an important town for both imports and exports in the Middle Ages. The network of roads was used to take these goods to inland towns. Goods from Southampton were found as far away as Leicester, 220km (137 miles) to the north. Only valuable and easily carried goods were taken so far. The quality of the roads, particularly in winter, was not good, and although the trading towns tried to ensure that bridges on the vital routes were kept in good repair, responsibility for road upkeep was in the hands of each parish. As a result, many goods were carried by water whenever possible.

Furthest distribution of:
- Dyestuffs
- Wine
- Household goods, iron, fish
- Tile, stone, slate, coal

— Main trade routes

Leicester · Coventry · Gloucester · Oxford · Abingdon · Bristol · Newbury · Reading · London · Basingstoke · Guildford · Andover · Salisbury · Winchester · Southampton · Exeter · Honiton

0   80km

independent of the surrounding shires, and many towns had mayors, aldermen, a common council and a town clerk by the middle of the thirteenth century [2].

But just as remarkable as the emergence of these towns was their vitality and tenacity in the face of radical social change. In the late thirteenth century the great urban oligarchies in London, Lincoln, York and other towns were swamped by the practitioners of the lesser guilds, many of whom were immigrants from the country. But although they displaced the old families, sometimes violently, these new families everywhere maintained and developed the old privileges, traditions and organizations of the towns.

Social unrest in the towns

Urban upheavals were common, especially after 1300. Many towns such as Louth and Stamford, dependent on their production of cloth, declined into small market towns when the introduction of the fulling mill made it more practical to make woollen cloth in the villages. The Black Death (1348–50) hit especially hard at the densely packed towns.

A general movement of wealth and population from the Midlands to East Anglia and the south-west left behind the shells of once prosperous communities: at Oxford falling house rents after 1325 attest the declining population [8]. English towns were spared the violence of fourteenth-century Ghent or Florence, but the rising of the peasants in 1381 found allies in York, Norwich, and especially in London. And thieves at all times could find a ready refuge in the slums outside the city walls.

Only London could muster a mob with the violent potential of the urban masses in Paris or other European towns, but on several occasions in the late fourteenth century that London mob proved able to frustrate the government. For a few days in 1381, in association with the peasants led by Wat Tyler (died 1381), it managed to render the government completely powerless. Urban life in England was precarious, yet it remained attractive. Trade, law, and government itself could not function without towns, and by 1500 they had become a vital element in all other English institutions.

English medieval towns were often as crowded as this illustration of Paris suggests. The shops were little more than market stalls, and each trade was concentrated into a specific street. Most stable towns grew out of markets; others, relying on single industries, were liable suddenly to expand or disappear.

5 The export of wool was vital to the economy of many towns in the early Middle Ages, because the Flemish cloth industry came to rely on English wool in the 13th century. But when the English cloth industry itself grew up, based largely on the villages, many towns contracted. In the 15th century several towns, such as Bradford in Yorkshire and Devizes in Somerset, prospered on cloth, but most of the towns that had grown in the 13th century now stagnated. Their political importance declined as the economy faded after 1400 and political hegemony reverted to the nobility. Henry VII tried to revitalize town life after 1485 by stimulating trade overseas.

6 The craft guilds held examinations for apprentices before they were admitted to the guild as master craftsmen. Apprentices were required to learn their craft for seven years, and after qualifying they served as journeymen, travelling the country until they could afford to set up in business permanently. One of the most important functions of the craft guilds in the early 14th century was to maintain the standard of workmanship, and they adopted the concept of examinations from the universities. During the 15th century, when many towns were in decline, guilds generally tried to limit the number of apprentices by restricting entry to the sons of existing craftsmen.

7 The Guildhall of the Merchant Adventurers at York was built in about 1360 and served as a meeting place for the guild. The Merchant Adventurers became one of the greatest guilds in York as the trade in cloth overtook that in wool in the later Middle Ages. Cloth exports, unlike wool, were not bound to any staple and a merchant community emerged, ousting the foreign traders from their control of the business. Like most other guilds, the Merchant Adventurers was not purely economic in function, but had a partly religious and charitable purpose, because it undertook to support any of its members who became destitute. By the 15th century, the guild had many branches throughout the Low Countries.

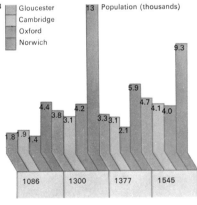

8 The population of medieval towns is hard to determine exactly, but it is clear that most towns lost between a third and a half of their population in the Black Death. This fall was only slowly reversed in the later Middle Ages.

Gloucester
Cambridge
Oxford
Norwich

Population (thousands)

13
9.3
5.9
4.7
4.1 4.0
4.4
3.8 3.1
4.2
3.3 3.1
2.1
1.8 1.9
1.4

1086 | 1300 | 1377 | 1545

9 The Shambles, York, is one of the few remaining medieval streets in England. It was originally devoted to butchers' shops. Despite legislation that butchers should only work outside the towns, the regulations, as here, were often ignored.

The Church in medieval England

The medieval English Church, like the Church elsewhere in Europe, had little spiritual or organizational unity, but was a tangled association of virtually independent bodies. It included monasteries and cathedral chapters, bishops and their officials and individual clergy, great international orders such as the friars, all catering more or less directly to the spiritual welfare of the country, and all under the general jurisdiction of a distant pope. It was a tinder-box of conflicting rights and privileges, careerism and spirituality.

Shrines and monasteries

To the layman in the Middle Ages the Church was a collection of shrines such as Canterbury, which had relics of St Dunstan and St Thomas Becket [1], Bury, with the body of St Edmund, and St Paul's, London, where the image of St Wilgeflot ("St Uncumber") was invoked by women who were tired of their husbands. Powerful monasteries [8] or cathedral churches grew up round these shrines, served by clerks or monks jealous of their privileges and profiting from the pilgrimages made to them.

Church authorities respected these popular cults but also attempted to impose order upon them and to raise the spiritual quality and education of the clergy. The first attempt, in the tenth century, was monastic. By 1200 the older monasteries were no longer the powerhouses of spiritual renewal, but they remained the most distinctive and often the best-loved of English religious institutions. Although varying greatly in size, they all shared a strong vested interest in their landed rights and, as a result, kept a weather-eye on political affairs. They had a slow, agrarian pace of life, and a conservative dislike of religious enthusiasm and novelty. In the twelfth century, many austere houses including those of the Premonstratensians, Carthusians and especially Cistercian orders were founded to regenerate spiritual life [3].

At first the monasteries maintained their corporate discipline. The monk's day began before dawn, and was devoted primarily to prayer, with labour in the fields taking up the rest of the time. According to the chronicler William of Malmesbury (c. 1095–c. 1143), monks abstained from meat, ate only one meal a day in winter, never wore fur or linen garments, and were sparing in speech. The abbot observed the same austere customs as his monks, although he dined separately from them, "with the strangers and the poor". In the later Middle Ages many orders of monks acquired a reputation for avarice, and although monks were rarely guilty of the debauchery portrayed by Protestant and anticlerical propaganda, comfort gradually replaced austerity after 1200.

The bishops and reform

The second attempt to organize the Church for pastoral work was episcopal. It began in the late eleventh century in the atmosphere of reform engendered by Pope Gregory VII (reigned 1073–85). Archbishop Lanfranc (c. 1005–89) of Canterbury and his successor St Anselm (1033–1109) set up a regular organization of the English dioceses, and by 1150 the forms of diocesan organization, were clearly established. The beginnings of the canon law of the Church made possible stricter control of the various offices.

A spate of parish church building be-

1 Thomas à Becket (c. 118–70) was killed by followers of his former friend Henry II (r. 1154–89). As Archbishop of Canterbury, he defied the king's attempt to set up a centralized legal system that would cover members of the Church as well as the laity. Becket had served previously as chancellor to Henry; throughout the period the rulers of Church and state were often linked personally, even though their interests were kept carefully separated. Henry underwent many penances for the murder of Becket, who was canonized in 1173, and whose tomb in Canterbury Cathedral became the object of pilgrimages until the Reformation.

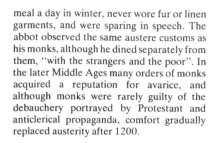

2 The friars came to England in the 1220s with the intention of revitalizing spiritual life by preaching and living in poverty. They were bound to no particular convent (although friaries were set up soon in many towns) and stressed pastoral work. Encouraged by Bishop Grosseteste, they were pioneers of philosophy and theology at Oxford University and included two of the finest medieval philosophers, Duns Scotus (c. 1264–1308) and William of Ockham (c. 1300–47). They also transformed the art of preaching and used a vivid outspoken style to attract large congregations. They were prepared to attack injustice and defend the interests of the poor.

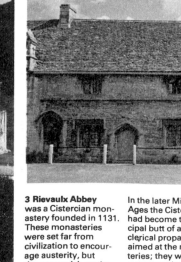

3 Rievaulx Abbey was a Cistercian monastery founded in 1131. These monasteries were set far from civilization to encourage austerity, but they grew rich on the profits of wool production, which financed their great building programmes.

In the later Middle Ages the Cistercians had become the principal butt of anticlerical propaganda aimed at the monasteries; they were seen as an overtly political and wealth-seeking organization, whose original puritanism had become entirely lost.

4 Almshouses, such as this one at Burford, Oxfordshire, became common in the 14th century, when the rural economy ceased to grow and urban poverty became a palpable problem. Charity had always been a charge upon both monasteries and bishops, and now hospitals, almshouses and religious fraternities were set up specifically to care for the victims of destitution and disease. The founders were often secular and ranged from the high nobility to permanent guilds of prominent townsmen.

tween 1100 and 1250 [Key] provided most communities with at least the rudiments of religion, and in the early thirteenth century the first attempt was made to regulate the religious life of the laity. Stephen Langton, Archbishop of Canterbury (1207–28) and Robert Grosseteste (c. 1175–1253), Bishop of Lincoln (1235–53), proclaimed that the laity should take common and private confession at least once a year.

An ambitious and wide-ranging attempt to provide an educated clergy was necessary: the ignorance of many parish priests was an evil often bewailed by Grosseteste. The new universities at Oxford and Cambridge became, under Grosseteste's influence, the breeding ground of a small group of highly educated churchmen [2]. These men naturally came to occupy the commanding heights of the Church; by 1400 nearly all the bishops had attended a university and many parish priests, too, were educated there. The stream of educated graduates came to occupy posts of responsibility in the state as well as the Church and throughout the Middle Ages high promotion in the Church often

depended upon previous service to the Crown [9], and vice versa. As a result, the question of who had ultimate authority to appoint the higher officers of the Church, whether it was the king or pope, was a major source of contention, as was secular infringement on clerical jurisdictions.

Wycliffe and Lollardy
Many of the graduate clergy, as well as laymen, were uneasy about ecclesiastical wealth [5]. The most determined of the later movements of reform was the work of the fiery Oxford theologian and royal clerk John Wycliffe (c. 1328–84). Wycliffe saw the organized Church as a creation of Antichrist and proposed a return to "simple" Christianity, free of both hierarchy and superstition, dependent on the Bible, and led by the Crown. His followers, known as the "Lollards", attracted much influential support, and their translation of the Bible (c. 1388), although officially condemned, was widely read. Their attack on established traditions, however, eventually brought down on them all the force of the Church.

Henry III (r. 1216–72) organized the rebuilding of Westminster Abbey. Church-building was an important activity in the Middle Ages, uniting all classes in a common endeavour.

The results of this building programme are still obvious. The great period of parish church building began after the Norman Conquest and continued into the 13th century. Most of the

"decorated" or "perpendicular" churches of the later Middle Ages were alterations or additions to older buildings. Local guilds or landowners often bore the building and maintenance costs.

5

5 This image of a "greedy friar" occurs in an early manuscript of the poem *Piers Plowman* (1362–92). There were many attacks on the Church for its corruption for many parish priests were badly educated.

6 Sacraments such as marriage brought the Church to the centre of the life of many people. The priest was often the only available doctor, marital adviser, teacher and lawyer for the village poor.

7 Tithe-barns, such as this one in Tisbury, Wiltshire, were built to receive the tithes or taxes payable to the Church, comprising ten per cent of each parishioner's gross earnings. Lawyers insisted that the poor, like the rich, had to pay tithes, but they added that priests were equally bound in charity to reprieve the very poor. At tithe-gathering, the village haywards used to ring the church bells and then go from house to house; but tithes were hard to enforce, and excommunications for nonpayment were common. It was generally assumed that everyone owed a debt to the Church for protecting their spiritual interests, but not to be spent on worldly ostentation.

8 Monasteries were found in almost every part of England. These institutions, which were central to medieval Christianity, were often established as shrines and as centres for the dispensation of charity, as well as being land-owning corporations. Each monastery was more or less independent of any superior authority, and the main problem of any prospective reformer such as Grosseteste was to battle with the abbots and cathedral chapters who were jealous of their privileges and local autonomy. As a result, much of the history of the English medieval Church is littered with obscure legalistic wrangles, with moral issues submerged. Benedictine monasteries were the oldest, dating from the Anglo-Saxons.

- ● Benedictine monasteries
- ▲ Cistercian monasteries
- ✝ Bishoprics
- ■ Archbishoprics

Carlisle
Durham
York
Lincoln
St Asaph
Chester
Lichfield
Coventry
Norwich
Ely
St Davids
Hereford
Llandaff
London
Dorchester
Bath
Wells
Exeter
Salisbury
Winchester
Canterbury

0   100km

Scholars (8)
Monks (4)
Magnates (10)
Diocesan clergy (3)

9 The episcopacy in England in 1275 comprised men from different backgrounds, but there was a higher preponderance of scholars and university-educated bishops than at any other time in the Middle Ages. During the next 50 years,

the number of civil servants, or royal administrators, sharply increased, reflecting a more secular outlook in the Church. At the same time, the rise in factionalism among the nobility made the Church – an important source of patronage and power – a more

attractive object of baronial ambition, and many bishoprics came under the direct control of the barons. After 1350 encroachment of secular politics on those of the Church (as opposed to a secular attack on clerical privilege) was common.

5

Rural life in medieval England

The structure of the English village originated in a deliberately chosen pattern of settlement. Brought to England probably by the Anglo-Saxons, it was characteristic of the open landscape of northern Europe. Except in the west and north, where Anglo-Saxon settlement was less complete, it generally replaced the isolated farmsteads of the Celts, and was well suited to the cultivation of the open or "champion" country of the Midlands and southern England.

The medieval English village

In the eleventh century villages acquired the characteristic shape and size that survives today, clustered around a church and often a green. Little essential has changed since *Domesday Book* (1086), in which were recorded almost all the settlements and village structures that now exist: the large village greens typical of north Yorkshire and many other areas, the straggling villages of much of East Anglia, the hamlets of Dorset. By 1100 the idea of several families living in close proximity and co-operating in the agricultural tasks had wholly taken root.

The peasant's house usually stood in its own vegetable plot. Many peasants also owned a pig or a few fowls. The whole family took part in the struggle for survival: the women looked after the garden and made the normal leather clothes (and, after 1350, the woollen clothes that slowly replaced them) while the men worked in the fields. The primitive implements included the ox-drawn plough, but backbreaking work from sunrise to sunset was still necessary [1] both in the peasants' own fields and in those of the lord to whom they owed labour services. A monotonous diet of bread and ale (not yet flavoured with hops) was only partly mitigated by vegetables and fruit, although the plentiful livestock of most parts of England made meat-eating reasonably frequent for all classes.

The social system of the village

In any village there were men of many different social degrees. In the eleventh century there were *geneats* (a lord's free retainers and messengers), *cottars* (who in theory owned five acres but owed labour services to

the lord) and *geburs* (who had more onerous services than cottars); landless labourers and slaves also existed in some areas. By 1200 these various distinctions had been simplified into *freemen*, who could sell their land and leave the village, and *villeins* (bondmen), who were hereditarily tied to their lord. These classes, however, were not exclusive or separate. The extensive records of Ely show that free peasants, villeins and labourers intermarried, and by the early fourteenth century some villeins could buy and sell property without hindrance and amass considerable personal wealth. Whatever the importance to landowners of the legal status of peasantry, it was certainly less central to peasant society itself than the ties of kinship and membership of the village community.

The village community demanded organization, and most villages of the thirteenth century were "manors", or estates owned by a lord (whether resident or not) and composed partly of *demesne* (fields directly cultivated for him) and partly of fields held by peasants in return for rent or

1 Most of the tasks of the agricultural year were done by hand. The agricultural writer, Walter of Henley (*fl.*1260) advised that seed should always be brought from other manors at Michaelmas, because it grew better than the home-produced product; and similar lore surrounded other jobs. Agricultural output was at its medieval peak in the 13th century when many improvements to estates were introduced and virgin land was cultivated.

3 Hunting was an overriding passion for King John (*r.*1199–1216), as well as many other kings. William II (*r.*1087–1100) died in a hunting accident and the itineraries of many rulers' journeys through the realm were tours of their hunting lodges, some of which, such as Woodstock in Oxfordshire, developed into sizeable towns. Forests were richly stocked with bear, wolves, boar and all kinds of deer. Falconry was also practised.

4 The reeve was the local agent of the landowner, and he was often a native of the village in which he officiated. Despite this he was frequently depicted as a tyrant. Here a reeve is shown directing peasants as they reap on the lord's demesne.

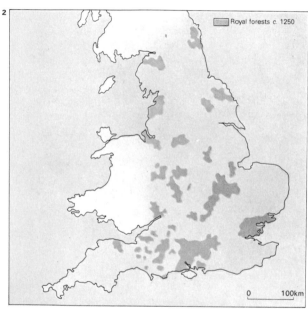

Royal forests *c.* 1250

0   100km

2 Royal forests took up a significant proportion of the land of England in the 13th century. Woodland was as important to the medieval economy as open country for it yielded not only timber and charcoal, but served as a reserve for game and provided pasturage for pigs. After the Norman Conquest the Crown began to assert its authority to gain control of the woodland, designating areas (and sometimes whole counties) as royal forests in which rights of hunting, farming and gathering were severely restricted. These controls were often resented by local inhabitants, and disputes over encroachments by farmers seeking to extend their estates were common throughout the Middle Ages.

5 The postmill, an elaborate version of the windmill, was introduced into England in the 1180s and quickly became common. The whole mill turned to face the wind. A monopoly of milling was an important part of a feudal lord's authority in his manor.

6 The birth-rate in the 13th century was higher than today, but infant mortality varied between 15% and 20%. Once a man reached the age of 20, he might expect to live to 50. The Black Death, however, severely reduced life expectancy, even in the countryside.

week-work [7]. Labour services varied widely, but they generally included up to six days' ploughing or reaping [4] for a few weeks of every year (perhaps two days at other times) and additional "boon-work" at harvest time, as well as carting, tending the lord's garden, and marling (fertilizing).

Declining feudal obligations

These obligations were often taken lightly; in theory milling at the manorial mill [5] or baking in the manorial oven, for a small payment, were heavy duties upon unfree peasants, but in practice the absence of many landlords could render them obsolete. In some instances, as at Wigston Magna, Leicester, the village was divided between two manors, and the peasants ploughed together the common fields of both manors; feudal obligations there can have amounted to little more than a few customary dues. From the twelfth century, labour services were increasingly commuted to money rents. The manorial lord controlled justice amongst his villeins, but villagers could apply to hundred or shire courts, in which they might hope for a greater degree of impartiality in cases involving their lords.

By the fourteenth century the life of the peasant was changing rapidly. The pressure of population before 1300 [6] led to great distress, exacerbated by the great famine of 1315–17; but the Black Death of 1348–50 and its recurrences in the next half-century dramatically reduced the number of mouths to feed. It brought about a shortage of labour and so forced up wages, despite attempts to hold them down. While prices remained stable, the wage for a farm labourer doubled between 1350 and 1415. At the same time the great estates were less often directly farmed, and instead the demesne was rented out. Thus the distinction between free and unfree came to be irrelevant in practice, and the yeoman farmer, with consolidated fields and wage-earning farm labourers, began to dominate the rural scene. Numerous solid and prosperous fifteenth-century yeoman farmhouses separate from the village are a feature of much of the English countryside, a symbol of the decline of the manorial system.

Wool provided one of the most important sources of English wealth in the Middle Ages. The Flemish and, later, the English cloth industries were almost insatiable, and after the 12th century when the numbers of sheep as farm live-stock overtook pigs, sheep-farming brought great profits to many areas. In the late Middle Ages, peasant-owned flocks became as important as those belonging to the lords, as peasants' estates grew in size.

7 Peasant farming generally took place in open fields. Signs of these fields can still be seen in some places, as here in Crimscote, Warwickshire, where the patterns of medieval furrows, undivided by hedges or fences, can be detected by aerial photography. Fields were divided into strips, which were measured by the amount that could be ploughed in a day. They were distributed by lot, annually at Michaelmas, so that a man's fields changed each year. A primitive system of crop rotation, with one field out of two or three lying fallow while wheat alternated with oats or barley, was usually operated; but without adequate manure, the yield was only half that of modern agriculture.

8 Stokesay Castle, Shropshire, was built between 1260 and 1300 and was a fortified manor house in the characteristically expansive and lavish style of the age of "high farming" and booming agricultural rents. Its wide halls without aisles, and its tall traceried windows, seem to represent a new standard of comfort for the provincial landowner. The solar wing with small chambers indicates a growing inclination for privacy. But the polygonal tower and gatehouse serve as reminders that Stokesay was in the unruly Marches, or border areas with Wales; the whole enclosure could provide protection for the village from raiders.

9 The centre of wealth in medieval England shifted dramatically after the mid-14th century from the champion, or open, country of the Midlands, that concentrated on crops, to the sheep-runs and cloth-production areas of southwestern and southeastern England with their flourishing entrepôts of Bristol and London. The map shows the percentage increase in wealth of each county over the period 1334–1515. Village cloth-making, which depended on the fulling-mill that needed clear, fast-flowing streams, probably accounts for the growing prosperity of Somerset and the Cotswolds. The wealth of Kent and Essex was more broadly based, as the wealth of London reached the home counties. The north stayed relatively backward.

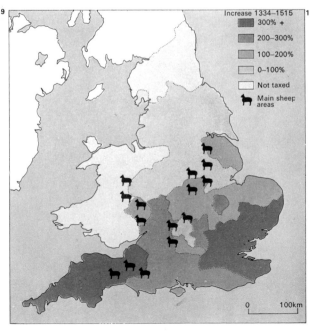

Increase 1334–1515
- 300% +
- 200–300%
- 100–200%
- 0–100%
- Not taxed
- Main sheep areas

0   100km

10 Lavenham, Suffolk, was one of a series of East Anglian towns that won great prosperity in the 15th century, arising from the production of wool and a certain amount of cloth. As well as boasting an extravagant "wool-church" financed by this industry, Lavenham's wealth was seen in the elaborate timber-framed houses, which have been preserved almost intact. In such houses the art of domestic living was perfected, unassailed by the pressures of town life that prevailed in more urbanized boroughs. The old central hall was divided into several units, including a solar or small hall, and probably a kitchen. The fireplace was an original part of such houses, and was situated on a wall instead of in the centre of the hall. Glazed windows were another luxury.

The emergence of France

The beginnings of the French nation can be traced to the medieval house of Capet. Hugh Capet, a feudal lord whose lands centred on the middle Seine, was elected king of the west Frankish domains in 987 and reigned until 996 (superseding the Carolingians). France was then only a part of Gaul, which stretched from the Pyrenees to the Rhine and had been, since the Frankish invasions of the fifth century, a conglomeration of Germanic, Celtic and Romance elements. The French-speaking peoples came to the fore and were united only with the slow extension of Capetian authority. The Capetians initially controlled only a small area around Paris and Orléans and for 200 years were given only nominal allegiance by the many more powerful feudal lords in France.

The Capetian kings
The Capetian kings had almost no contact with Aquitaine and the south, while in the north powerful dynasties of the nobility in Normandy, Anjou, Flanders and Burgundy were their equals in wealth and influence. But the real source of Capetian strength was

the popular veneration they were increasingly accorded. The kings, although at first powerless, gradually emerged as sacred figures, consecrated by the holy oil first used by St Remy (c. 438–533), the "Apostle of the Franks", in c. 497 at the baptism of Clovis. This oil was thereafter kept at Reims in an ampoule that never emptied [Key]. The royal touch was also believed to cure scrofula (lymphatic tuberculosis). In 1297 the kings added a halo to their inheritance with the canonization of Louis IX, whose spirit became the focus of both religion and patriotism.

Gradually the French kings built up their political power too. This had a solid base in the growing prosperity of France – in the thriving city communes, which were actively encouraged by the twelfth-century kings, and which became foci of loyalty. A dramatic expansion of authority beyond the royal patrimony took place in the reign of Philip II Augustus (1165–1223); he took advantage of the unpopularity of King John of England to regain English-ruled Normandy and bring his own vast territories extending to the Pyrenees under direct royal rule. His son,

Louis VIII (1187–1226), introduced royal power into the heartland of southern France (Languedoc), after the Albigensians there had been crushed by a papal crusade against their heretical view of the world as a creation of the Devil. The power and prestige of Louis IX (St Louis) (1215–70) were so great that he was able to act as the arbiter of all Europe. The apogee came in the reign of Philip IV (1268–1314), who advanced the frontier far to the east and subdued even the Papacy.

The change in government
With this advance came a new kind of government. The thirteenth-century kings attracted formerly independent lords into their service and, with the help of educated men from the University of Paris [5], began to establish a "civil service" of local officers who judged cases and collected revenue in the provinces. At the centre were the parlement of Paris, the highest court of the kingdom, and the Chambre des Comptes, a financial department, staffed by lawyers of high calibre who made French royal justice widely sought. By 1314 the French king was

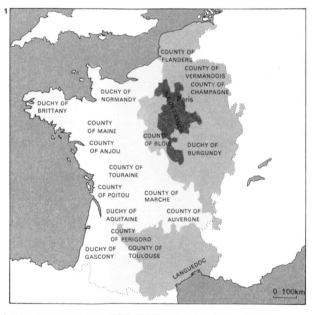

1 By 1180 the map of France included parts of modern Belgium but excluded Franche Comté, Dauphiné and Provence, which were ruled by the emperor. But even within the confines of the Capetian dynasty's formal authority, many provinces were almost wholly beyond royal control. The real centre of the king's power was between Paris and the Loire. To the west lay the dominions of his Plantagenet rivals. Almost all of these were gained by Philip II Augustus (r. 1180–1223).

■ Royal demesne 1180

□ Fiefs held by English king 1180

▨ Other fiefs 1180

0   100km

2 By 1328 France had expanded beyond her borders of 1180, and in 1349 she gained the Dauphiné. Internally the Capetian dynasty had established its hold on the former Plantagenet lands, and

all the feudatories in Burgundy, Brittany and Languedoc acknowledged it, as did the English king in Guyenne. But the many enclaves and noble houses indicate how shallow were the roots of royal author-

ity, which often merely confirmed the positions of local magnates. In ensuing wars, many nobles played off the English and French crowns against each other, to gain almost complete independence.

■ Royal demesne 1328

▨ Territories of royal princes 1328

□ Fiefs held by English king 1328

▨ Other fiefs 1328

0   100km

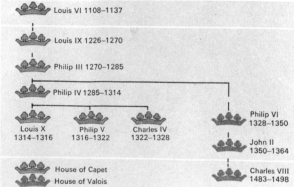

3 Louis VI 1108–1137

Louis IX 1226–1270

Philip III 1270–1285

Philip IV 1285–1314

Louis X 1314–1316

Philip V 1316–1322

Charles IV 1322–1328

Philip VI 1328–1350

John II 1350–1364

Charles VIII 1483–1498

House of Capet

House of Valois

3 The French monarchy descended in the male line from 987 to 1848. The direct succession of son to father was carefully preserved until 1316. The elder Capetian line died out altogether in 1328. The Valois line then ruled until 1589.

4 The ambulatory of the Abbey of Saint-Denis was one of the earliest inspirations of Gothic architecture and it represented the cradle of French national sentiment. It was built in the mid-12th century during the reign of Louis VII.

5 The seal of the University of Paris was made in 1215. The university began as a corporation of scholars in the 12th century and in the 13th century trained many of the most useful servants of the Crown as well as great philosophers.

richer, more respected and better served than any other European ruler.

That his power was nevertheless limited was shown by the crises of the fourteenth century. Up to 1314, by a remarkable chance, power had passed uninterruptedly from father to son; but the direct line of Capetians ended in 1328 and the crown passed to their Valois cousins [3]. The Valois claim was challenged by Edward III of England (1312–77), to whose court flocked all the dissidents of France: in Flanders, in Brittany and above all in the south, local noblemen hoped to increase their patrimony by playing off Philip VI (1293–1350) against his rival. Edward crushed the French arms at Crécy (1346), while France became the prey of war-bands who made their fortune from the profits of ransom, pillage and terror. At Poitiers (1356) [7] King John II (1319–64) was himself captured by Edward's son, the Black Prince, and released only for an enormous ransom. English successes were not continuous, but during the reign of Charles the Mad (1368–1422) a murderous factional struggle between the rival houses of

Burgundy and Orléans exposed France to a renewed attack from England. With the help of the Duke of Burgundy, the Lancastrian King Henry V was able to conquer Normandy, occupy Paris and induce Charles VI to disinherit his son in his favour.

Joan of Arc, the Maid of Lorraine

At the lowest ebb of the Valois fortunes, when the English and Burgundians ruled northern France, the popular and religious aspect of kingship reasserted itself in the extraordinary events involving Joan of Arc (c. 1412–31) [6]. Joan, a humble girl from Lorraine, went to the court of the disowned heir, Charles VII (1403–61), [10] and by claiming the miraculous intervention of the saints in his cause endowed it with a popular fervour. She herself was burnt by the English but a reconciliation between Burgundy and Charles VII at the Congress of Arras (1435) made the English position hopeless.

As the English withdrew from France, the monarchy found itself firmly established in the affections of its subjects. The unity of the nation was never again in doubt.

The Coronation Chalice at Reims Cathedral is the symbol of a sacred kingship. The French monarchy made up for its lack of physical power by the prestige of its religious sanction. Kings were anointed with the oil said to have been used at the baptism of Clovis, the first king of the Franks; the oil was kept in a phial miraculously refilled for each coronation. The king was regarded by many as a religious figure. The lilies on his shield were said to have first appeared supernaturally on the shield of Clovis, and his banner, the oriflamme, was said to be the mythical flaming lance of Charlemagne, King of the Franks.

6 Joan of Arc was captured at the battle of Compiègne in 1430. She had appeared at the court of Charles VII when his fortunes were at their lowest in 1429. Her adoption of the dress and manners of the mercenaries shocked some but inspired many more and she eventually turned events in Charles's favour. She was tried by the English in 1431 as a heretic and burnt at the stake.

7 The Battle of Poitiers (1356) (from a 15th-century manuscript) was a great defeat for the French army. The English, led by Edward, "the Black Prince", were heavily outnumbered, but at the height of the battle they launched an attack from behind the French lines and the French king, John II, fled, only to be captured with his son Philip. He was taken to England, where he died.

8 Charles V of France is seen here entertaining Emperor Charles IV on the latter's state visit to Paris in 1377. Charles V (1338–80), who came to power at the age of 19, became one of France's most successful kings in her darkest days. After heavily reducing English power in France he sought European allies to drive his enemies from his country.

9 A miniature by Jean Fouquet (c. 1420–80) shows the trial of John, Duke of Alençon, for treason in 1458. The duke fought with Joan of Arc and was loyal to her even during the court intrigues of the time. However, as an outspoken rebel who had made no secret of his loathing for the king, he was still given a fair and formal trial and did not die until 1476. French judicial institutions, which enjoyed a high prestige throughout Europe, had been perfected in the 13th century. They were based on Roman law.

10 Charles VII was painted by Jean Fouquet in 1445. This much-abused monarch is the least understood of French rulers. He overcame appalling misfortunes which began with his disinheritance by his father Charles VI in 1420 in favour of Henry V of England, the victor of the Battle of Agincourt. Yet he became the focus for all enemies of English rule in France and gradually succeeded over 30 years in expelling his opponents from the realm. However, revolts of the nobles disturbed the last years of his reign.

Feudalism

In a civilization like Europe's in the early Middle Ages, with no civil service, police, or legal profession, the only stable institutions were the family group and especially – since wealth and power could result from it – the warrior band with its lord. The bond between lord and warriors was the basis of "feudal" society, in the Germany, England and France of the eleventh and twelfth centuries. The ethic of the medieval warrior demanded fierce loyalty from the retainer and unstinting generosity from his lord.

Land tenure

The personal bond between the warrior and his lord, or later the tenant and the king, which was expressed in fealty, vassalage and homage (increasing grades of obligation), became translated into the sphere of property relations. Absolute ownership of land was unknown in the Middle Ages; instead the king granted estates or fiefs, in return for definite services, often military, which were supported by oaths. The king's tenants-in-chief, too, granted out land to knights in return for oaths of loyalty to themselves. The ceremony of homage [1] did not necessarily imply either a permanent or an exclusive tie, and it was common for a knight to owe homage for an estate to several lords, or even to a social inferior. Feudal terminology was therefore simply a way of describing the complexities of land tenure: society was not in any hierarchical "feudal pyramid".

Nevertheless, the period from about 950 to 1250 is properly called "feudal" because of the dominant position of a warrior aristocracy in Western Europe and in Crusader Palestine. This aristocracy shared a common training and fighting technique, that of the mounted knight, and a common code of conduct, the ideal of "chivalry". Its basis was the technological superiority of mounted men over foot soldiers, which emerged about the time of Charlemagne. In antiquity the stirrup and the horseshoe were unknown; introduced from central Asia about 750, stirrups, in particular, had revolutionary consequences: they made it possible to charge effectively with a lance carrying the full impetus of a galloping horse without the rider being unhorsed on impact with his target [2].

This placed great value on mounted warriors [Key], but before about 950, horses were scarce; the Franks' relative wealth in them partly explains Charlemagne's successes.

Rise of the knights

There is evidence that the number of horses increased rapidly after 950 and in the next century mounted men everywhere decided the fortunes of war. Their numbers were small, their equipment expensive and their training long. But this increased their pride and prestige and by 1100 mounted warriors would symbolize their corporate spirit by the initiation ceremonies of knighthood.

Local society was thus dominated by the knightly classes. They served in various capacities: many, without a permanent master, sold their services as mercenaries to the highest bidder. Others, especially at the start of their careers, took service as the household knights of a great lord. Still others, particularly the Normans, were bound by the conditions of their tenure to fight at specified seasons; "knight-service" was the most important obligation for landowners.

1

1 The ceremony of homage is shown in a metaphorical context in this 12th-century illustration of Theophilus paying homage to the Devil. The Devil carries a charter or written record. But the original ritual of homage was designed to register the contract in public in a memorable way without the need of documentary record. Because few men were literate in the earliest period of feudalism, it was essential to make legal contracts before witnesses whose memories could be relied on. Submission was represented by the lord taking the hands of his man between his own; afterwards they kissed to symbolize friendship.

3 Functional armour was characteristic of Norman knights. As the sword [G] and axe [F] became longer, protection had to be increased with heavy shields [D, E] and the 10th-century helmet [A] gave way to a helmet with visor [B] and a fitted coif of chain mail [C].

2

2 A 14th-century knight, Sir Geoffrey Luttrell, receives his helmet and lance (from the Luttrell Psalter). Knights were regarded as heroes and their combats were invested with glamour. The impetus of their charge depended on the innovation of stirrups; the high saddle also acted as a lever. The lance, intended to unseat opposing horsemen, could be used properly only with these aids. Few lords had many horses but evidence exists that careful breeding was increasing the number. An important stud at Corvey, Saxony, supplied the German imperial armies.

4

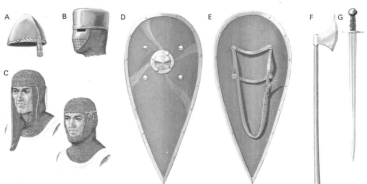

4 Langeais Castle was one of 13 built by Fulk Nerra, Count of Anjou (987-1040); from them the House of Anjou, which later ruled England, began its formidable rise to power. In each, a castellan and garrison controlled roughly as much country as could be traversed in a day. Although fortified towns had existed before, the stone keep, which was the oldest type of castle, was an invention of the tenth century. Keeps, such as that at Langeais, stood on an artificial mound with a stockade. Internally they might have only one big room and a store, but they were focal points of feudal power and by 1100 had spread throughout Western Europe.

The most formidable of knightly warlike skills was probably the charge in close formation, which was used devastatingly against the Turks in the First Crusade. But as professionals, knights also learnt defensive skills, the most spectacular of which was the development of the castle, from the simple eleventh-century keep to the elaborate bastioned castles of the 1200s [5].

Chivalry and landowning

The knightly ideal of chivalry demanded that knights should fight to avenge the oppressed, to vindicate the honour of ladies – the theme of romantic love first appears in knightly circles in southern France in the twelfth century – and to advance the Christian religion against the Muslim Saracens [7, 8]. The Templars and Hospitallers combined knightly prowess with monastic chastity in the defence of the Holy Land.

A knight's fighting career, unless he became a lord's military official, a marshal or a constable, was comparatively short, and his ambition was usually to acquire and cultivate an estate. Once on the land most of them lived simply in keeps with one first-floor room for living and sleeping and, below, a storehouse. Although knights had customary rights over the tenants who held plots by their grant, villagers did not live entirely in the shadow of their lords. The spread of a "three-field system" of farming with its complex organization, and the appearance of village communes in France, suggests that many villages [6] while paying dues had an independent corporate life, to which the knight contributed by providing leadership and protection and often by taking the lead in cultivating neighbouring wastelands.

Feudalism thus maintained a series of obligations which linked the peasant with his immediate lord and, indirectly, with royal power. Although the dominance of a warrior caste was crumbling by the fourteenth century through the competition of other groups of a less military nature, the disappearance of feudalism was gradual and the knight would constitute a social ideal for centuries. The material remains are with us still, as are the vestiges of chivalry as a guiding principle of Western European civilization.

The knight, armed and mounted, was at the centre of feudal society. Only an élite could afford the costly equipment.

5 Caernarvon Castle, Wales (1283–92), was one of the massive castles built by Edward I after he conquered Wales. By 1300 the primitive keep had developed into a fortified community large enough to house, and strong enough to protect, a provincial government behind technically innovative bastions.

6 An English village [centre, left], dating from feudal times, was created on uncultivated land at Chelmerton, Derbyshire. It shows a pattern implying a planned settlement, either through the enterprise of a lord or simply peasant co-operation. Each house has a garden and narrow strip extending into the waste land.

7 Ekkhard and Uta, a thirteenth century Crusader and his lady sculpted in Naumburg Cathedral, represent the highest ideal of European nobility – the Christian warrior – towards the end of the feudal period. From the First Crusade (1096-9), warfare found an idealized form in the defence of Christendom against the Saracens. Great numbers took part in expeditions to Jerusalem and enthusiasts united in the military orders of the Templars and Hospitallers. Besides the great international Crusades, many knights went individually to win a reputation or expiate an offence, to fight in Palestine, in Spain, or in pagan Lithuania.

8 Chivalry is exemplified by St Louis IX, King of France (1226–70), rescuing a Saracen lady and her child in battle. The feudal knight evolved a code of conduct transcending even his Christian allegiance, and chivalry was a central theme.

European society 1250–1450

By 1250, the material basis of Europe as it is now known was established; most of the towns and villages that exist today were already inhabited. Although forests were more extensive than now, the area under cultivation had passed the period of most rapid expansion. The next 200 years were characterized by crises of population and production, alternating boom and slump, and by the development of the techniques of finance [Key, 3], business and trade. The underlying crisis was probably the high population of the thirteenth century. Tax records show that in southern England and Provence the number of inhabitants doubled during the century. Older towns such as Florence [2] pushed out beyond their walls and multiplied their parish churches, while new towns were founded in every part of Europe.

The increase in urban populations

In 1250 the population of Europe had reached about 70 million and evidence from several sources suggests that the rate of increase was about one per cent a year. In consequence the food resources of the conti-

nent were stretched. Migration from Germany into central and eastern Europe reached its height in the thirteenth century, while the poor soils and marginal lands of the alpine and Apennine uplands came under the plough [1] for the first time. A higher expectation of life combined with a higher birth-rate to push European society into a slowly maturing demographic crisis.

This process created new social forms, above all the large towns that profoundly modified European civilization. Since classical times, probably no town with more than 40,000 inhabitants had existed; now Venice Naples, Barcelona, Bruges, Paris and some others far exceeded this limit. Immigrants, often from distant places, crowded into them, to work in the textiles of Bruges or Florence, or the more diversified trades of London and Paris. Two great ports, Venice [4] and Genoa, provided Europe with the products of the East, and among the first Europeans to visit China was the Venetian merchant Marco Polo. The Baltic trade was monopolized by the Hanse – a powerful league of North German cities.

In the urban centres, more specialized ways of life could develop. The skills of the accountant and the banker (developed first in Pisa and Florence) and the practice of marine insurance (a Venetian speciality) made possible the first international companies; the Bardi of Florence, through their agents in London and Bruges, were the greatest creditors of the English crown, for instance. Courtiers, civic patrons of art and people of fashion flourished in the midst of a new, degrading poverty. The friars adapted religion for the urban masses, while poverty and disease were mitigated by burgeoning charities. Whatever the crises, the great cities continued to grow.

A century of catastrophe

Undernourishment left the teeming population of the thirteenth century a prey to a worsening climate, hunger and disease. In 1315 persistent rain inaugurated a series of harvest failures and two years of famine throughout northern Europe. The high prices and booming business of the previous century now proved unstable; the economy had

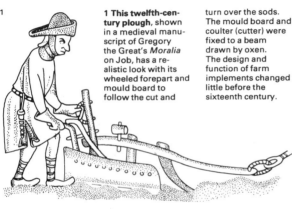

1 This twelfth-century plough, shown in a medieval manuscript of Gregory the Great's *Moralia* on Job, has a realistic look with its wheeled forepart and mould board to follow the cut and turn over the sods. The mould board and coulter (cutter) were fixed to a beam drawn by oxen. The design and function of farm implements changed little before the sixteenth century.

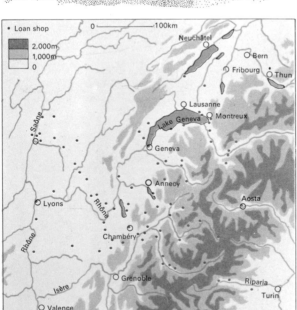

2 The fortified Roman town of Florence was reduced during the stagnation of the Dark Ages but grew rapidly in the twelfth and thirteenth centuries. Its expanding size and power were marked by the wider walls of 1172 and 1284–1330. In spite of internal factional struggles the city's position as a centre of cloth-making and the wool trade led to an era of prosperity and cultural achievement, particularly after the rise of the Medici merchant family in the early 1400s. Florentine bankers were the most influential in Europe and the florin, minted in the thirteenth century, became a monetary standard.

Walled city in Byzantine period
Walled city in 1172
Walled city in 1330

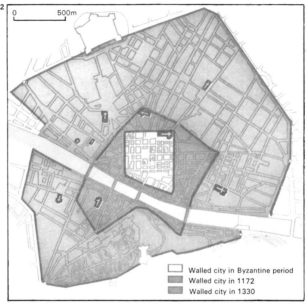

3 Loan shops or *casane* of Lombard moneylenders were a feature of the alpine valleys of Savoy in the thirteenth century. In many parts of Europe country life was transformed by money at this time, especially in Italy. The rise in the population made necessary the rapid development of different soils. Peasants obtained the required capital to a large extent from loans. Moneylenders operated from shops set up in rural areas.

4 Venice at the time of Marco Polo's departure for Asia in 1271 (depicted imaginatively in this book illustration) was the busiest port in the world. The city was also a centre of shipbuilding and a leader in ship design.

advanced too fast. The boldest venturers, the Italian bankers, were hit hardest of all and in 1343 repudiation of the English royal debt precipitated a crash in which the house of Bardi and many others collapsed.

In 1348–50 came the terrible Black Death, the first of the recurrent bubonic and pneumonic plagues that were to beset Europe until the 1730s. Carried by both rats and humans in ships from the Crimea, the plague was immediately fatal and spread rapidly from southern to northern Europe. Its effects were catastrophic: probably about 50 per cent of the total population died, but some towns in Provence lost four-fifths of their inhabitants and many villages were finally deserted. In many parts of Europe there was some recovery, but the plague returned in 1361, 1369 and 1379, and by 1400 the population had shrunk to about a half or two-thirds of its total a century before. This was reflected in the all-pervading theme of death in late medieval art [6].

One of the effects of these calamities was social disorder, in towns and in the country. For the first time peasants and townsmen took violent action against bad government, in the Jacquerie rising [7] of northern France (1358) and peasant rebellions in England (1381) and Catalonia (1409–13). Governments everywhere were fearful of such movements and tightened their control wherever they could. These revolts were led by men of enterprise, peasants, farmers or artisans who resented the legal limits on their activities. The fall in population led to a demand for labour and labourers demanded the right to sell their services to the highest bidder.

The standard of living

The revolts reflected the rising expectations of the peasantry; in England, wage rates doubled while prices remained stable between 1350 and 1415. They were a sign of the vitality and independence of humbler men [8]; for them, the demographic decline meant a higher standard of living and the opportunity to turn peasant holdings into small farms. After a century of catastrophe, the fifteenth-century peasant followed the bankers and merchants of the pre-plague age into a measure of prosperity.

KEY

Coins proliferated in the late Middle Ages with the development of economies based on trading. A gold coinage, almost unknown since the seventh century, was restored in the thirteenth. Pioneers of the new money were the republics of Venice with the ducat and Florence with the florin. These coins are of roughly standard appearance and were issued in 1357–67 by Pedro I of Castile [A]; in 1399–1413 by Henry IV of England [B]; in 1419–34 by Conrad III of Mainz [C]; in 1368 by the republic of Florence [D]; in 1350–64 by John II of France [E]; and in about 1420 by Tommaso Mocenigo representing the Venetian republic [F].

5

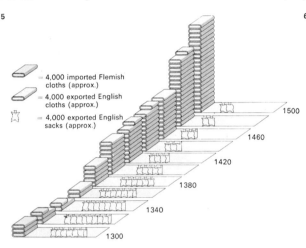

= 4,000 imported Flemish cloths (approx.)

= 4,000 exported English cloths (approx.)

= 4,000 exported English sacks (approx.)

1500
1460
1420
1380
1340
1300

5 The English wool trade expanded rapidly after 1200. Raw wool was at first sent for processing to the established cloth makers of Bruges, Florence and other centres in France, Flanders and Italy but their monopoly was broken by the growing export of English-made cloths.

6

6 "The Triumph of Death" by Andrea Orcagna (c. 1308–68) was painted shortly after the Black Death of 1348. It depicts with terrifying realism the sufferings of the sick who beg to be released from the torments of plague. The theme of death and the instability of human fortune pervades the literature and art of the later fourteenth century and it is likely that this was an effect of the dramatic carnage of the plague. "No one wept for the dead", wrote a Sienese chronicler, Agnolo di Tura, "because everyone expected death himself". Survivors surveyed their shrunken world in a sombre mood.

7

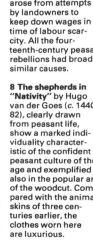

7 The Jacquerie, a peasant rising which engulfed the Paris region in 1358, resulted from the disorder in France after the English captured King John II in 1356. The main grievance arose from attempts by landowners to keep down wages in a time of labour scarcity. All the fourteenth-century peasant rebellions had broadly similar causes.

8 The shepherds in "Nativity" by Hugo van der Goes (c. 1440–82), clearly drawn from peasant life, show a marked individuality characteristic of the confident peasant culture of the age and exemplified also in the popular art of the woodcut. Compared with the animal skins of three centuries earlier, the clothes worn here are luxurious.

8

The origins of Parliament

The English Parliament has no definite origin; but it clearly came into existence during the thirteenth century. At that time, the word "Parliament" meant a special session of the king's Council with the judges present to hear petitions to the king from his subjects. Early "parliaments" were largely occasions for judicial business in the presence of the king's councillors or barons, where great matters could be decided more solemnly than could be done by the judges alone. In the reign of Henry III (reigned 1216–72), whose judges actively opposed baronial privileges, this was a widely popular precaution; and the greater the number of earls and barons, bishops and abbots present, the more definitive the settlement of the business. In this sense Parliament was a variation of the ancient king's Council.

Parliament and taxation

Parliament was not only judicial in function: it also provided an occasion for the king's subjects to give their consent to taxation and their advice on important matters. This function implied representation of the various interests and communities by men with power to bind their constituents to their decisions. Taxation with the consent of such representatives was the general rule in the "Parliaments" called by Simon de Montfort (c. 1208–65) [1] to show the broad support for his rebellion of 1258–65.

Edward I (reigned 1272–1307) [2] defeated de Montfort's revolt in 1265, but during his reign all the various functions of Parliament came together: a session of the Council with as many councillors, barons and bishops present as possible; and representation of the shires by two knights, of the boroughs by two burgesses, and the clergy of the northern and southern provinces by proctors, all armed with plenipotentiary powers to grant taxes.

Advising the king

Although Edward I summoned representatives to only a few of his early parliaments, their presence became increasingly common as his need for funds grew, for without their consent taxes proved difficult to collect. By 1307, it was normal for individually summoned lords and representatives of the "Commons" to meet each year. Parliament was the creation of the government for its own purposes, but it was also a call to the propertied classes to participate in the processes of government. This call was accepted with reluctance by shires and boroughs that were preoccupied with local affairs. Nevertheless their representatives came, and in a fourteenth-century parliament the "Commons" were generally represented by men who had experience on the countless local commissions of the peace, for the collection and assessment of taxes and so on, that shouldered the executive work of government. For instance, a certain John Morteyn, who was a large landowner, several times serving in the wars of Edward II (reigned 1307–27), a frequent member of commissions, and a strong partisan who evidently made enemies, acted nine times as Member of Parliament for Bedfordshire. Such men naturally had independent views, and their voice, joined with that of the lords, became increasingly influential.

Parliaments continued to hear petitions

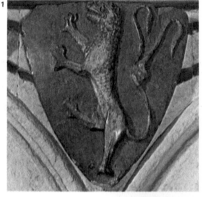

1 Simon de Montfort, whose shield is shown here, is sometimes said to have invented the English Parliament. To bolster his revolt against his brother-in-law Henry III he summoned a representative "parliament" in 1264. He genuinely believed in corporate, legal government, with frequent sessions of parliament to act as a bulwark against untrammelled royal or bureaucratic power. His ideas were later taken up by Edward I.

2 Edward I sits in Parliament with the kings of Scotland and Wales in this contemporary illustration, but in fact they never attended together. Behind them are royal princes and the archbishops. Barons and the other bishops sit down both sides, and in the centre are the judges, the councillors and the legal advisers of the Crown. The Commons and the proctors of the clergy (who must have outnumbered the rest) stand before the king.

3 The structure of Parliament was fairly settled after 1350. After a peer had been summoned once, he was usually automatically called to later parliaments, and many knights and burgesses were chosen regularly. Some shires and boroughs did not bother to send representatives; as a result, the size of the Commons might vary. The royal councillors were a reminder of Parliament's original function.

4 The Chapter House at Westminster was the venue when the Commons first sat separately from the Lords. This was during the "Good Parliament" of 1376 when impeachment was first used against royal ministers for allegedly embezzling taxes for the war. The step marked a clear realization that the Commons had a different role from the Lords. By this time they had already evolved a formal procedure and elected a speaker. The Chapter House was used by the Commons until the mid-16th century.

5 Thomas Hungerford (d. 1398) was one of the first recorded speakers of the Commons. A client of John of Gaunt, one of the main objects of the Good Parliament's attacks in 1376, Hungerford represented the Commons the next year when Gaunt managed to reverse many of that Parliament's decisions. The speaker was elected by the Commons to be their spokesman, and also served as chairman of their debates. The institution of Speaker crystallized the rising confidence of the Commons: in the 1400s it felt able to oppose the king himself, asserting that Parliament was more competent in administrative matters than the king.

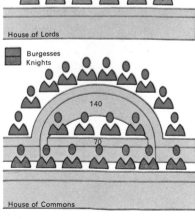

3
Bishops
Abbots
Lay magnates
Royal councillors
The King

10   20   30
60
House of Lords

Burgesses
Knights

140
70
House of Commons

and act as courts of justice, and to make grants of taxation to the Crown. But many parliaments did neither and it seems that it was their advice and on occasion their consent to legislation that was sought by Edward II and Edward III (reigned 1327–77). By 1370 statutes had to be promulgated by the king in Parliament, and the kind of business on which they legislated broadened in scope: the Statute of Labourers, 1351, arose from petitions by landowners to Parliament to control labourers' wages.

The Lords and the Commons

During the period 1370–1450 Parliament evolved its classical structure and procedure. The representatives of the lower clergy broke away to form their own "Convocation", and by 1376 Lords and Commons met as separate bodies. Both Lords and Commons developed as political bodies able to put pressure on the king's ministers. Their weapon was "impeachment", a judicial process in which the Commons as a body "appealed" or accused a minister before the Lords who acted as judges of the case.

Under Richard II (reigned 1377–99) and Henry IV (reigned 1399–1413), parliaments were keen to experiment with ways of influencing the processes of government: in 1377 they appointed special "war-treasurers" to supervise taxes granted for military purposes; in 1401 they proposed to grant no taxes before redress of grievances. In these demands, the Commons were led by a new kind of member: the national figure, often himself a member of the Council, independent, outspoken and politically experienced, such as Arnold Savage, Speaker in 1401 and 1404. In the hands of such national "front-bench" politicians Parliament was ready to assume a central role in the politics of the fifteenth century. Its elections became the arenas for factions to assert their authority, and many leading noblemen acquired sizeable groups of supporters in the Commons. Henry VII (reigned 1485–1509) used Parliament to legitimize his dubious claim to the throne [7], but tried to reduce its incursions on the royal authority by cutting his expenditure so that Parliament would not have to be called so often.

The three estates, the division of society into knights, priests and labourers, was basic to the concept of Parliament, but was not directly expressed in the structure of the Lords and Commons.

6

7

6 Westminster Hall, an 11th-century building, was reconstructed between 1394 and 1402. As the central hall of the king's palace, it was the usual place of formal sessions of Parliament in the Middle Ages. But sometimes, as in 1388, Parliament was held in the "White Hall".

7 Henry VII formally declared his claim to the throne in Parliament in 1485, and recorded it in the Statute Roll, in the already antique "Norman-French" of legal documents. Unlike the long acts of Richard III and Edward IV declaring their titles upon intricate legal arguments, Henry's title rested simply on the declaration of Parliament in this quite short bill. It marks not only the succession of an entirely new dynasty, but also the recognition of the sovereign efficacy of Parliament. This foreshadowed the Parliamentary declaration of royal supremacy in 1534.

8 Henry VII opened Parliament in 1485 and tried to ensure that it acted as an ally of the Crown. His policies were well suited to the interests of the merchants who were prominent in the Commons; he significantly reduced the power of the Hanseatic League in England and in 1496 passed the *Magnus Intercursus* to improve trading relations with The Netherlands. But when Henry had consolidated his income, he called Parliament only in cases of abnormal expenditure.

8

The Hundred Years War

The conflict between the Plantagenet and Valois dynasties, lasting from 1337 to 1453, was marked by short campaigns, longer truces and periods of stalemate. Known as the Hundred Years War, it dominated the history of both England and France in the fourteenth and fifteenth centuries. Even after 1500 the threat of its resumption was a potent weapon in the hands of the English.

The start of the war

The origin of the war lay in the Norman Conquest itself: an Anglo-Norman empire was a reality up to 1204 and its shadow was pursued with energy by Henry III (reigned 1216–72). Gascony, which the Treaty of Paris (1259) left in English hands but effectively in remote dependence on the French Crown, proved a source of constant dispute. It would have remained merely a legal issue had Edward III (reigned 1327–77) not laid claim to the French throne [1] after the death of Charles IV (reigned 1322–8).

Although Edward's mother was a sister of Charles IV, the French nobles ruled out succession through females and decided that Philip of Valois (1293–1350), as a cousin of Charles, had the best claim. He therefore became king as Philip VI. Despite this setback, Edward did not press his claim until public opinion had been sufficiently aroused by constant pinpricks over Gascony and French support for Scottish independence.

After war began in 1337 and the English won a naval victory at Sluys (1340) Edward relied on the traditional method of recruiting huge armies through subsidies to the princes of Germany and the Low Countries, which cost the English taxpayer enormous sums. Although his clumsy invasion of France ended in disaster through the deceit of his continental allies and shortage of money, the adaptable Edward learned quickly.

After 1340 he employed what could almost be called guerrilla tactics. He acquired footholds on the French coast, strongly fortified, which served as bases for devastating raids on the countryside. This had the advantage of requiring smaller forces than usual. More important, the profits of prisoners' ransoms and the plunder of the country [4] made the expeditions largely self-supporting and attracted the nobility and ambitious but impoverished knights.

His tactics relied on speed and flexibility against the more numerous but rigidly arrayed mounted knights of France. His archers [7], although less accurate than the French crossbowmen, were highly effective from carefully chosen positions. At Crécy (1346) [Key] Edward inflicted a crushing defeat with a rain of arrows; at Poitiers his son, Edward the Black Prince (1330–76) [6], routed the French cavalry and captured John II (reigned 1350–64). Perhaps even more important was the capture of a base at Calais (1347) which remained as an English colony for two hundred years. By 1360 both sides were exhausted, and in return for peace at Brétigny the French agreed to abandon Gascony to Edward. From the English point of view the war seemed to have ended in victory.

Fighting for fortunes

Peace, however, proved illusory. The war was not really a conflict between nations: it had become a highly organized business

1 **The fleur-de-lys** was incorporated in the newly designed royal arms of England when Edward III assumed the title of King of France in 1340. He acted only after securing the support of the Flemish and discontented subjects of France. The arms and the title "King of France and England" lasted to 1801.

2 **The English campaigns** in Gascony and France consisted of plundering raids on most of western and northern France. Except for a few captured strongholds, from which ambitious and profitable expeditions could be launched, there was little attempt to conquer French territory until Henry V invaded Normandy early in 1417.

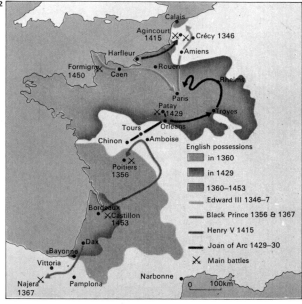

English possessions
- in 1360
- in 1429
- 1360–1453
- Edward III 1346-7
- Black Prince 1356 & 1367
- Henry V 1415
- Joan of Arc 1429–30
- ✕ Main battles

0   100km

3 **Control of the Channel** gave a decisive advantage in war and up to 1340 the French, with the help of the Genoese admiral Barbanera, had been able to raid Southampton and show their flag at the mouth of the Thames. The decisive Battle of Sluys in which English vessels won the first important naval engagement in their history, marked the turning point. At the Battle of La Rochelle (shown here), fought in 1372, the Castilians, who were allied to the French, surprised an English fleet taking reinforcements to Gascony. This defeat ended the English domination of the Channel and was followed by defeat for the army in Gascony, marking a decline in the military fortunes of Edward III.

4 **Plunder** was one of the main reasons why ordinary soldiers took part in the war, regularly supplementing their wages. It could be acquired in two ways: by ransom or by capture of a place by storm. When a whole village or town was taken the usual practice was to plunder it and subject the inhabitants to fire and the sword. When the Black Prince took Limoges in 1370 he not only permitted looting but put the entire garrison to death, and after Calais fell it was said that "every Englishwoman was wearing its booty". The profits of war, especially for the victors, were great. When Henry V wanted to gain the good will of captured towns he managed to restrain his men from looting, but this was exceptional for the times.

enterprise for the exploitation of France. Individual captains such as Walter Mauny (died 1372) and John Chandos (died 1370) recruited soldiers by "indenture" or contract with pay for a limited period; they themselves signed similar contracts with the king which committed them to bring a specified number of soldiers [9].

Expeditions or cavalry raids such as that of the Black Prince in 1355-7 or of John of Gaunt (1340–99) in 1373 were designed to make a profit for the participants through plunder, levy of tribute from the countryside, and especially through prisoners' ransoms. Such ransoms were divided between the king and the captain who took the prisoner, and they could amount to huge sums. The ransom for King John of France was set at £500,000 (but was never fully paid) and even the humbler prisoners of Mauny were sold by the captain to Edward for £8,000.

The resumption of war

As the war was fought on French soil the English made far more profit than their enemies, and they resumed hostilities in

1369. English victories were less common in the years before a "twenty-eight years' truce" was agreed in 1396.

The most spectacular phase of the war followed the accession of Henry V (reigned 1413–22). Henry was a military genius who could organize and discipline a large army for years on end, and his renewal of the war was immensely popular. His victory against superior forces at Agincourt (1415), followed by the systematic occupation of Normandy in 1417, was made possible by the feud between the Armagnac and Burgundian factions, and Henry's alliance with Burgundy. By the Treaty of Troyes (1420) Henry married Catherine, the daughter of Charles VI, and was made his heir with the intention of inaugurating a single Anglo-French monarchy. Although he died before this was fulfilled, Henry controlled the whole of northern France with his Burgundian allies, and his infant son, Henry VI (reigned 1422–60; 1470–71) held sway in Paris until 1435. By 1453 the revival of the House of Valois finally deprived the English of Normandy and even Gascony.

The Battle of Crécy was the first great English success of the land war, fought when the superior and larger French army overtook Edward's forces who were making for Flanders. English archers checked the French cavalry raid with concentrated fire and the French were almost totally destroyed.

5 Sieges dominated warfare in the later Middle Ages and were accompanied by strict conventions. Formal siege began when a herald of the besieging party demanded entry in his master's name. Once this was done the besieger could not retreat without dishonour.

The Duke of Burgundy excused his failure to take Calais in 1436 by claiming that he had never formally besieged it. If there was no hope of relief for a besieged castle or town, the honourable practice was for the captain to surrender. Mining the walls was the most common form of assault; by 1400 cannons had largely replaced siege engines. The command of a captured garrison was one of the greatest rewards that could be offered to a benefactor of the king, and, like other positions of responsibility, might be highly profitable.

6 Edward, the Black Prince, the most notable knight of the age, and victor of Poitiers (1356), took his name from the black armour he wore. This effigy lies on top of his tomb in Canterbury Cathedral.

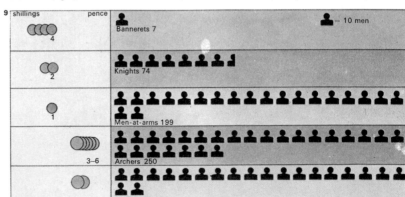

7 The skill of the English archers paved the way for several victories. The crossbow [right] was an effective weapon that had been used to deadly effect in the Crusades. It was more accurate than the longbow over short distances and had greater force, but it could not fire more than one arrow every 30 seconds. The longbow, 1.83m (6ft) long, could fire as many as six arrows in the same time.

8 Caister Castle was built by Sir John Fastolf, the successful captain of Henry V and VI, about 1432–5. Made of brick, crenellated and surrounded by a moat, it cost several thousand pounds and indicates the wealth that Fastolf won in war. After the aggression of Henry V, English policy became more defensive, to preserve the profitable estates and towns from being recaptured. Charges of governmental mismanagement of the war became common in the 15th century.

shillings	pence			
4		Bannerets 7		= 10 men
2		Knights 74		
1		Men-at-arms 199		
	3–6	Archers 250		
	2	Armed men 200		

9 The armies of the Hundred Years War comprised companies recruited and trained by indentured captains who were noblemen or soldiers distinguished by their military ability. Captains contracted with the king to muster their men and fight in return for wages. They usually led their men in specific military operations, designated in the contract. Captains subcontracted for men-at-arms. The foot soldiers and archers were often volunteers, but many were recruited by "commissions of array" which were appointed for each county. The offer of good wages and free pardons stimulated recruitment, and often there were more volunteers than the king could employ. This diagram shows the retinue of the Earl of Northampton in 1341. The system proved more flexible than the old system of feudal obligations; the short-term contracts were soon applied to peacetime relationships between lord and servant, and were instrumental in the growth of "bastard feudalism".

The age of Chaucer

Thanks to the poet Geoffrey Chaucer (c. 1345–1400) [Key] the late fourteenth century is more vivid than any other period of medieval English history. In his *Canterbury Tales* (c. 1385–1400), he describes the pilgrimage, which was a social event that united all classes, and through his immortal sketches of the various pilgrims and the tales they tell along the way he unfolds an ironical, dispassionate but profoundly sympathetic vision of English society [3].

Chaucer's chequered career

Chaucer himself, with his many-sided experience of life, was perhaps uniquely placed to interpret his age. The son of a London vintner, he learnt the world of the court through his service with Lionel, Duke of Clarence (1338–68), and later with John of Gaunt, Duke of Lancaster (1340–99). He served in the French wars and as a diplomatic agent of Edward III (reigned 1327–77); he was a Justice of the Peace in Kent, sat in parliament for the shire, and was a controller in the port of London. He was several times both creditor and debtor, suffered robbery from high-

waymen and was perhaps guilty of rape. London and the court were his special province, and Chaucer the poet probably had in mind a sophisticated court audience. This did not limit his appeal because he was widely known by all classes in his own lifetime.

The growth of a court culture

The age of Chaucer was distinguished by the emergence under Edward III and Richard II (reigned 1377–99) [4] of a "court", in the sense of a luxurious and fashionable cultural centre. It was sustained by London's new role as the unchallenged metropolis of England, and imbued with the delicate tastes of the rival "court" in Paris. The transformation of a somewhat provincial aristocracy into worldly, elegant courtiers can be observed in many innovations of Chaucer's lifetime: the luxurious appointments of Edward III's new palaces at Eltham and Sheen; the changing fashions of court ladies; the new, subtle style of cuisine; the taste for witty songs and elegant dances, and for poems and stories of delicate refinement, such as Chaucer's *Book of the Duchess* (1369), a lament for the

Duchess of Lancaster, or with a touch of irony, such as his philosophical tragedy *Troilus and Criseyde* (c. 1385) [Key].

Court culture, however, was not simply exquisite or exclusive. At its heart was the broad experience of the world given to men of all classes by the Hundred Years War. This tough but liberating experience gave the nobility an extrovert interest in the ordinary life and character of the ploughman as well as the prince. Chaucer's *Canterbury Tales* with their rich, earthy realism, or the scenes of London low life by Thomas Hoccleve [2], were not only for the nobility but also a much wider audience – the now literate middling townsmen and countrymen.

The Peasants' Revolt

The period of Chaucer's maturity, from the resumption of the war with France in 1369 to the deposition of Richard II in 1399, was the testing-ground of a new popular attention to the activities of government. It was punctuated with eruptions of opposition, sometimes in parliamentary form as in 1376 and 1386, sometimes in a violent defiance of

1 The England of the Canterbury Tales was mainly confined to the southeastern part of the country, and was dominated by London and, of course, Canterbury, to which the pilgrims were journeying to visit the tomb of St Thomas à Becket (c. 1118–70). Even though the population of every other town in the country had fallen since 1330 because of the ravages of the Black Death, London's continued to rise because of constant immigration, and it stood at more than 50,000 in 1400. South-east England was the richest and most populous area at that time and the dialect of the south-eastern Midlands was becoming accepted as standard English in the court.

2 Thomas Hoccleve (c. 1370–c. 1450) is shown presenting his book, *Regement of Princes* to the Prince of Wales, who later became Henry V (r. 1413–22). As in this case, a "patron" was often merely a potential benefactor of the poet who hoped to gain favour by presenting the book. Patronage from a notable member of court was necessary to win a poet recognition, and perhaps a job to enable him to live. Hoccleve was a clerk of the Privy Seal, where his duty was to clothe royal orders and proclamations in elegant prose. His poetry is notable for its realistic and acute observations of life in the London taverns, and centres on his own involvement in that life.

3 Chaucer's pilgrims were depicted on the Ellesmere manuscript, an authoritative illuminated text of c. 1400–10, which may have been written for Chaucer's son Thomas (c. 1367–1434). Shown here are [A] the merchant "with a forked berd, in motelee". As a customs officer, Chaucer was familiar with such great international merchants. The Nun's Priest [B] is not described in the Prologue, but the tale of the Chante-

cleer reveals a distinctly witty cleric, even if riding a "jade", a horse "both foul and lene". The Wife of Bath [D] is one of Chaucer's most vivid portraits; a middle-aged Venus with a huge amorous ap-

petite who had had five husbands, she was outrageously dressed. The brawny miller [F] was, like most of his type, enterprising and thrusting, benefiting from his lord's monopoly of milling; and the squire [C] was an apprentice

in the arts of war and love. Chaucer himself had been a squire in the household of Lionel Duke of Clarence. The Prioress [E], "ful simple and coy" was an exquisitely ironic sketch of an over-refined lady.

4 The portrait of Richard II on the Wilton Diptych, probably painted for the king himself c. 1395, is by far the best portrait of a medieval English king, and exemplifies the finest achievements of the court culture of his reign. On the back of

the diptych the king's emblem – the white hart – is depicted with refinement, probably by John Siferwas, and on the front Richard is seen being ushered into heaven by his patrons Edward the Confessor and Edmund the Martyr. Its painter is unknown.

royal authority, as in 1387–8, when the "Lords Appellant" attacked the court favourites, and as in 1399, when Henry Bolingbroke (1367–1413) overthrew Richard II. Religious controversy, too, was heard at court, stimulated by John Wycliffe (c. 1328–84) and supported by John of Gaunt and the so-called Lollard knights.

The greatest explosion of all came from the humbler folk of town and country, in the "Peasants' Revolt" of 1381. The name is misleading, for it was really a movement of substantial farmers and tradesmen with a following of farm labourers, infuriated by the constant war-taxation and the arrogance of the officials who collected it.

This followed the social unrest caused by the Black Death [5] and its consequent recession and upheavals. The Statute of Labourers (1351) tried to restrict the rise in wages that followed the plague. The unrest was expressed by William Langland (c. 1332–1400) in his poem Piers Plowman (c. 1362).

Beginning in Essex in June 1381, when one village erupted and killed a tax-collector, the revolt spread as other villages heard of

the event [7]. It became a more serious threat when the men of Kent, led by a veteran of the wars, Wat Tyler (died 1381), marched upon London. The 14-year-old Richard II parleyed with them, first at Mile End and then at Smithfield, and promised to grant their demands – an end to serfdom and the dispossession of the nobility and the Church. At Smithfield, however, the Mayor of London, William Walworth, killed Wat Tyler [9], and Richard, with presence of mind and courage, forthwith persuaded the insurgents to disperse. Reprisals began once the rebels had returned home.

Although the revolt was against a government hated by most people, the excesses of the peasants and their demand for social emancipation alienated the landed classes; Parliament insisted on severe punishment.

Local riots were frequent in subsequent years; the government never again dared to tax the ordinary villager so heavily, and serfdom gradually disappeared in the following generations. In the increasingly complex society of the time, the peasants had shown that they too had interests to protect.

Geoffrey Chaucer regularly read his poems to his audience in the royal court. Troilus and Criseyde, which he is reading here, is a fine example of his narrative style, its plot being based on a story by the Italian poet Giovanni Boccaccio (1313–75). Such borrowing from a foreign culture was typical of the international atmosphere of the court; Chaucer may have met Boccaccio on a diplomatic visit to Italy in the 1370s. The theme of the poem is the traditional one of courtly love, treated with a new attention to personality and emotion. The seduction of high-born ladies was a favourite pastime of Chaucer's audience, and Edward III set an example with his mistress Alice Perrers.

5 The Black Death (1348–50) killed probably a third of the population and recurred throughout the next 50 years. The shortage of labour thus created led the peasants to more demands for higher wages.

6 John Ball (d. 1381) was an ex-priest who had been imprisoned for heresy in 1360. He voiced the most radical ideas of the rebels, demanding an end to ancient distinctions between lord and serf.

7 The Peasant's Revolt occurred mainly in the south-east; the rebels in Essex were in touch with those in Kent, from which the main march on London began, and townsmen were involved as much as countrymen. St Albans, Bury St Edmunds and

Leicester
Norwich
Yarmouth
Mildenhall
Cambridge
Bury St Edmunds
Ipswich
Sudbury
Dunstable
Colchester
Harrow
Billericay
Brentwood
Highbury
Mile End
London
Rochester
Twickenham
Blackheath
Maidstone
Canterbury
Winchester

✳ Riots
➡ Main peasant marches 1381
➡ Routes of Ball and Tyler

0   50km

towns in Norfolk all suffered violent movements: a Norfolk man even proclaimed himself king. Isolated incidents occurred as far away as York and Bridgewater, Somerset. In general, risings took place in the prosperous areas where legal restraints such

as villeinage no longer had any economic function and merely restricted the virtually independent farmer from pursuing his own fortunes. In addition the London mob was a particularly volatile element in English society, as it would be for many centuries.

8 The rebels burned the Savoy Palace of John of Gaunt, and the house of the Chancellor, Sudbury. After the king spoke to the rebels at Mile End, they entered the Tower unopposed and executed Sudbury.

9 Wat Tyler was killed by the Mayor of London two days after the rebels entered the city. His death ended such unity of purpose as they had possessed. He was described as "endowed with much sense".

The Ottoman Empire to 1600

The Ottoman Turks or Osmanlis (so called after their founder Osman, who died in 1326) began as Muslim warriors who patrolled the eastern borders of the Byzantine world. Osman's military genius raised them from nomadic tribesmen lacking any political institutions or national consciousness to become the formidable potential masters of a great empire by the mid-fourteenth century.

Osman's son and successor, Orkhan (ruled 1326–c. 1360) defeated a Byzantine army sent against him in 1329 and went on to capture Nicaea (Iznik) and other Greek cities. He annexed the neighbouring Turkish principality of Karasi. But his success in the holy war against the Christians attracted numerous other Turkoman warriors voluntarily to his lucrative service. Before 1453, the emerging Ottoman state held more lands of greater extent in eastern Europe than its considerable provinces in Asia Minor.

An era of expansion

By the time Orkhan's son Suleiman had set himself up in Gallipoli in 1354, the Ottomans commanded a large enough army to begin major campaigns against Europe. Murad I, Suleiman's brother and Orkhan's successor, took Adrianople and by 1365 had made it his European capital, thus establishing a pattern of conquest whereby the Turks took over a Greek capital and with it the machinery both of government and Church administration; they employed the local clergy as tax collectors and held them responsible for the behaviour of their charges. The average peasant was allowed as much freedom as he had enjoyed under Greek rule, if not more. Ottoman society was very flexible and the success of the Turks was in part due to the greater opportunities they offered to the peasant class.

The move westwards was halted momentarily during the latter part of the fourteenth century by the incursions into Anatolia of the Tatar ruler Timur (Tamerlane). Timur set up independent Turkoman emirates and although these did not survive long, their existence demonstrated the weakness of the empire. As long as the Ottoman objective remained the conquest of European territory (and the militarist structure of the state made constant expansion a necessity) Anatolia, so vital to the survival of the empire, would be vulnerable to attack and internal revolt.

The golden age

The golden age of Ottoman power occurred under Murad II (ruled 1421–51) and his son Mohammed II (ruled 1451–81). Murad was responsible for the creation of the Janissaries [Key], a corps of troops and administrators conscripted from among the Christians of the Balkans and raised to unquestioning obedience. This levy, called the *devşirme*, created a new social class whose fortunes were identified with those of the sultanate.

Mohammed II, called "The Conqueror", was responsible for the demise of the Byzantine Empire. In 1453, after a prolonged siege, he took Constantinople (now Istanbul) [3, 4], thus giving the empire the cultural and administrative centre it had lacked. Mohammed's achievement was to reunite the old Eastern Empire under a single sovereign. The translation of the sultan and his court to the new capital finally brought about the triumph of the *devşirme* faction over the old

1 The major east-west trade routes were taken over by the Ottoman Empire as it absorbed the old Greek world. Trading stations in the Peloponnese, along the Sea of Marmara and also in Cyprus, came under attack. But commercial interest was only one motive for Turkish aggression and trade profits were sometimes sacrificed to the overriding economic need for military expansion by the Ottoman state into the non-Islamic realms of Europe.

← Sea trade routes 15th century

← Land trade routes

▨ Ottoman Empire 1480

▨ Ottoman Empire 1600

2 Caravanserais were built as staging inns for the camel caravans that carried trade for the Ottoman Empire on a vast network of overland routes to and from the East. These routes declined when Portugal traded with India by sea.

The traditional caravanserai, following the Persian model, consisted of a two-tiered building with a lower floor that consisted of stables built round an open courtyard. The oldest of these buildings still standing dates back to about 1080.

3 When Constantinople (seen here on a 15th-century map) fell in 1453 a new phase opened in Ottoman history. The great city had long been the focus of Turkish ambition, but repeated attempts to overcome it had failed. When at last the old Byzantine capital was taken it became the Ottoman Empire's cultural and administrative centre.

4 The Topkapi Sarayi or Old Palace was built by Mohammed II, the conqueror of Constantinople, on the site of the old Acropolis. One of the earliest Ottoman buildings in the new capital, it was the sultan's official residence and also housed the harem. It was built round a series of courtyards and was conceived on a grand scale.

Stone frame around glazed brickwork

Glazed tiles

Stairs

Arcade

Turkoman nobility, but it also removed the centre of power away from Anatolia, which was to weaken still further the all-important eastern frontier.

The next major period of expansion occurred under Suleiman I, "The Magnificent" (ruled 1520–66) [5, 6], who took the empire still farther into Europe. The main force of the attack fell on Hungary, which in 1526 became a vassal state of the sultan. But the need to maintain a strong presence in Anatolia and the problems of supply and transport over such vast areas meant that no farther westward expansion was feasible. The siege of Vienna in 1529 [6] was a failure. The struggle by sea, however, continued, for the shipbuilding yards at Constantinople had made the Ottomans a major sea power. It was the Battle of Lepanto in 1571 [8] that reduced Turkish naval power and drove the Turks back into the eastern Mediterranean.

Decline and fall

Throughout the late fifteenth and the sixteenth centuries the two superpowers, the Ottomans and the Hapsburgs, faced each other menacingly. But by 1600 Ottoman power began to decline as a result of internal discord, factional struggles and harem politics at the centre, as well as constant pressure on the eastern frontiers. A revival occurred in the mid-seventeenth century but the second siege of Vienna failed in 1683.

The Ottoman Empire remained throughout its long history essentially tribal in structure. The divan, the sultan's administrative body, had only slight powers and although after the reign of Suleiman the grand vizier came increasingly to rule the empire, his position was always tenuous and provided no means for an easy succession on his death or loss of favour. The distribution of land in *timars*, quasi-feudal grants, never created a landed nobility that could identify itself with the sultan and although the *devşirme* gave the sultan a strong military power base, they also alienated him from the Turkoman nobility and became themselves in time a threat to his security. Despite its internal weaknesses the Ottoman Empire succeeded in knitting into a single race a group of scattered nomadic tribesmen.

The Janissaries were recruited from Balkan Christians taken at the capture of Adrianople and reared as Muslims with unquestioning obedience to the sultan. They were not only the army's best soldiers but, after they had received *timars* (land grants), they formed a social class. Because they had no links with any of the traditional tribal groups, they became the sultan's chief defence against the Turkoman nobles who resented attempts to curtail their autonomy. After the 1600s, the sultanate declined and the Janissaries, like the barbarians in the Roman army in the 3rd century, came to manipulate rather than uphold the government.

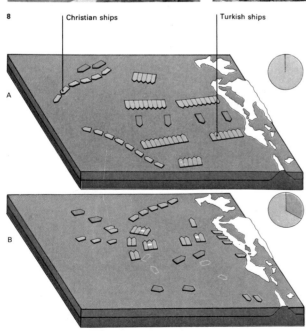

5 Suleiman I, called "The Magnificent", brought the empire to the height of its power. Here his workmen are restoring a castle in Egypt – a mark of the extent of his military power and authority.

6 The first siege of Vienna, undertaken by Suleiman the Magnificent in 1529, marked the limit of Ottoman expansion in the west. The Ottoman supply lines were already stretched too far from Istanbul.

7 The Cathedral at Famagusta symbolized the magnificence of Cyprus in the 1500s. Under the Venetians it had become the wealthiest island in the Mediterranean. The Ottoman conquest of the island in 1570 was the main event in the reign of Sultan Selim II, an otherwise unworthy successor of Suleiman the Magnificent. It marked the beginning of a new phase of hostilities between Christians in the west and the Turks. The war was fought out largely at sea and culminated a year later (1571) in the Battle of Lepanto.

8 | Christian ships | Turkish ships

8 The Battle of Lepanto, between the allies (Spain, Venice and the papacy) and the combined Ottoman fleet was fought off the Greek coast. At the start [A], both navies were grouped in two advance lines and one rearguard. The Christians had both galleasses (dark blue) and galleys (light blue). Four hours later [B] the Turkish fleet lay scattered with most of its ships beached, sunk (white outlines) or boarded (white-barred vessels between blue).

9 A miniature painting of Suleiman from the mid-1500s shows the borrowing of foreign styles typical of Turkish art. The Turks adapted the skills of their subjects and there is little original Turkish art except for carpets and other textiles.

The world Europe set out to explore

At the end of the fifteenth century Vasco da Gama (c. 1469–1525) sailed round the Cape of Good Hope to India and Christopher Columbus (1451–1506) stumbled upon the Americas. So began an age of discovery in which Europeans were to navigate the seven seas, make their landfall in most of the inhabited regions of the globe and come to think of the world as a whole. The voyages east, however, were simply new ways of going to places already, if imperfectly, known.

Alexander the Great had marched the Greeks through Persia into India; Rome had bought Asia's silks and peppers and had bequeathed Ptolemy's geography to medieval Europe; Byzantium had long been a bridge between Europe and Asia. But the hostile crescent of Islam had hemmed in Christian Europe, until the extensive conquests of Genghis Khan (1167–1227) [4] gave it a brief respite from Islamic pressure.

The achievement of Marco Polo
The Mongol empires, stretching from Russia to China, straddled the land routes between Europe and Asia and allowed the two conti-

nents to trade directly with each other. In 1271 Marco Polo (1254–1324) travelled via Bokhara to Kublai Khan's court at Peking [2], and in the mid-fourteenth century an Italian handbook for merchants, la Practica della Mercatura, described the 140-day journey from the Black Sea to China [3] and listed no fewer than 288 spices and drugs that could be bought in the markets of Asia. But these tenuous contacts of traders and also missionaries were once again snapped by the hordes of Tamerlane (1336–1405) and the dynasties that emerged out of the wreckage of the Tatar empires. That is why discovering a route to the East by sea was so important for European commerce and trade.

The importance of China
At the end of the long journey east lay China; where the native Ming dynasty (1368–1644) expelled the foreign Mongols, cultivated its own empire, restored its economy and refined its bureaucracy. Threatened by offshore rivals and by the scourge of Japanese piracy, the Ming withdrew into partial isolation, broke off relations with some of

China's old tributaries, forbade its people to travel overseas, threw out foreign traders and prohibited private foreign trade. But the first Ming emperor had established relations with 17 different neighbouring states, and in 1502 more than 150 self-styled rulers from central Asia traded with China under the cloak of tribute relations. The maritime expeditions of Cheng Ho [6] hinted at a vast Chinese potential for seaborne expansion that was never to be realized.

By its self-denying ordinance Ming China did not fully exploit the valuable interport trade of the Indian Ocean, with its hub in the archipelago. This was left to the merchant principalities of the East Indies and to a motley crew of traders – Arabs, Persians and Indians. Ever since the time of the Cholas, India's mainland empires, expanding from their bases in Hindustan, were more concerned to defend their northern frontiers and to acquire territory in the south than to probe overseas. Babur, the first of the Moguls, began his conquest of India soon after Vasco da Gama reached Calicut. But the empire he founded remained land-based, and was

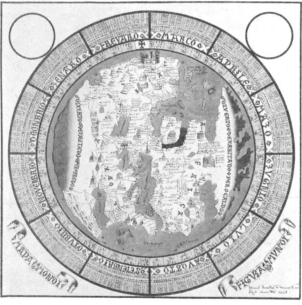

1 This Venetian map of 1448 shows how the typical medieval "wheel" map of the world was beginning to change. The medieval *mappamundi* was biblically inspired, with Jerusalem at the centre, the terrestrial paradise at the top and systematically disposed continents. By the mid-15th century the conventional medieval map was being influenced by contemporary marine charts and enriched by incorporating some of the information from travellers. It was also modified by the recovery of classical writing about the outside world, in particular the geography of Ptolemy and Fra Mauro, as evidenced by this map.

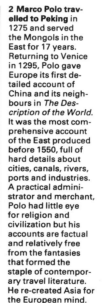

2 Marco Polo travelled to Peking in 1275 and served the Mongols in the East for 17 years. Returning to Venice in 1295, Polo gave Europe its first detailed account of China and its neighbours in *The Description of the World*. It was the most comprehensive account of the East produced before 1550, full of hard details about cities, canals, rivers, ports and industries. A practical administrator and merchant, Polo had little eye for religion and civilization but his accounts are factual and relatively free from the fantasies that formed the staple of contemporary travel literature. He re-created Asia for the European mind.

3 In 1260 the Polos, Nicolo and Maffeo, travelled from the Crimea via Bokhara to Peking. Returning to Europe, they set out once again in 1271 with Marco Polo. His return journey, from 1292–1295, was along the Malay Peninsula, Sumatra and India. These journeys revealed how the Pax Mongolica had helped to connect Europe with Asia and enabled Europeans to learn about the East.

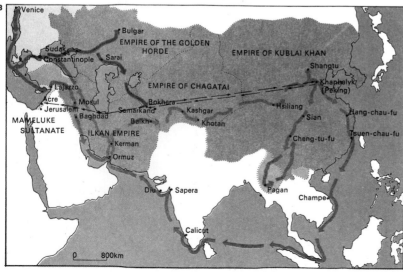

- Mongol Empire late 13th century
- Mongol tributaries late 13th century
- Christian world late 13th century
- Polo's known first journey 1260–69
- Unknown portion of first journey
- Polo's second journey 1271–95

4 Genghis Khan the Tatar conqueror, rode roughshod over the Chinese civilization, selling many people into slavery. The Chinese resented the Khan; and they did not appreciate the links that their conqueror forged for them with the outside world. For China, the imposition of Mongol rule meant the breaking point in the continuity of its tradition. The Mongols were looked upon as foreign overlords, and were finally expelled by the native Ming dynasty in the 14th century.

never to possess a deep-sea fleet of its own.

Europe's deadliest enemies were also its closest neighbours – the Ottoman Turks. By capturing Constantinople in 1453 [5], the Ottomans held the gateway between Europe and Asia; by taking Mameluke Egypt (the Mamelukes were originally Turkish prisoners of Genghis Khan who seized control in 1250) and Syria (1516–17), they severed the European trade route east and wrested much of the profits of the Eastern trade from the Venetians and Genoese.

The Ottomans move into Europe

Perhaps the most fateful decision in modern times was the Ottoman resolve to push westwards into Europe. This took the Ottoman armies through the plains of Hungary to the gates of Vienna and held their navy in the Mediterranean. By establishing their empire throughout the Balkans, the Black Sea region and the Levant, the Ottomans sealed off these areas from European expansion and gave the Iberian powers the incentive and the opportunity to find new outlets, whether by creeping round the African coast to the East

or by making their landfall in America.

In Asia, Europe once again came into contact with great Oriental despotisms, mainland empires, many of which were Muslim, which it did not dare to challenge and which it could not hope to penetrate. In getting to the East by the new sea routes, Europeans merely touched upon the western and eastern edges of Africa, a continent whose northern territories had long been influenced by Islam but whose interior was long to remain unknown to the outside world.

In the New World the story was different. Here the Europeans actually discovered a continent that was out of touch with the rest of the world. There were remote, isolated, civilizations that had wondrous monuments and strange customs, but whose technology lagged far behind that of Europe or Asia. America's discovery by Europe opened her swiftly to the full blast of European influence: conquest and exploitation, disease and religion. Here the result was a clash of two wholly different cultures, which had come into contact with each other for the first time in recorded history.

Until Marco Polo's return to Venice, Europe learned little new about Asia. In legend it was still a continent of monsters and demons. In the 12th century Christians debated whether the dog-headed men of India might be converted, and even as late as the 14th century Western manuscripts showed Indians with dog heads, fantasies which the discovery of direct sea routes to the East were at last effectively to dispel.

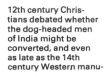

5 The siege of Constantinople in 1453 vividly illustrates how Europe in the 15th century was contracting, not expanding. The Ottomans had triumphed against the last Crusade from Europe. The capture of Constantinople (today known as Istanbul) meant that the Ottomans were in Europe to stay.

6 Cheng Ho's seven maritime expeditions, beginning in 1405, and visiting over 30 countries, were remarkable feats of seamanship. The largest of his ships was 121m (400ft) long and 54m (180ft) wide, with four decks and watertight compartments. The 62 ships of his voyage to India carried 28,000 men.

7 Nicolas Deslien's "upside-down" map of the world of 1567, based on lost Portuguese originals, shows how radically the European view of the world was changing as exploration continued. Whereas maps in the Ptolemaic tradition had often been drawn with east at the left and Jerusalem at the centre, this has north at the bottom and, as nearly as possible, France at the centre. Its accurate description of known parts of the world reflects the growing precision of navigational techniques, but when describing unknown parts – the land mass to the south of Java, for example – it is still seriously inaccurate.

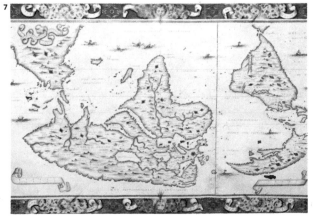

8 By the end of the 15th century, the vessels known as carracks were the largest merchant ships, at the other end of the scale from the small caravels. Portuguese carracks could be from 600-1,000 tonnes and were heavily built, with large castles, commonly three-masted with square rigging on fore and main and with lateen mizzens. The castle structures became more elaborate (as this 16th-century picture shows) and they were more often incorporated into the hull. These were the ships whose size, capacity for goods and men and solid construction made them the characteristic vessel used by the Portuguese in their Eastern reconaissance and trade, even though their bulk made them less well suited to carrying out the more detailed tasks of exploration.

Asian empires of the Mongols

The Mongol Empire, at the height of its power in the thirteenth century, was the largest land empire in history. It stretched from the Yellow Sea in the east to the Danube in the west and included areas of present-day Russia, China and Iran.

The origins of the Mongols are obscure. They were traditionally nomadic tribes who lived in felt tents called *yurts*, and followed their herds of horses, cattle, camels and sheep on an annual round of pasturage in the areas that are now Manchuria, Mongolia and Siberia. The numerous, loosely organized and constantly feuding Mongol tribes were first brought together as a unified nation under Genghis Khan (1167–1227) who became ruler of all the Mongols in 1206 [2].

Genghis Khan and the Mongol Empire

Genghis Khan's first move was to reorganize the major tribal groups in Mongolia as well as those on the Siberian borders. He then turned his attention to China. In 1211 he launched an attack on the Ch'in Empire, in northern China, an attack that continued until the whole of China finally came under Mongol domination in 1279.

But China was not the only target: the hitherto unknown Mongols also raided the west. In 1219–20 Genghis Khan defeated Mohammed Shah of Khwarizm, and as a result acquired Transoxiana and Persia. Two of his generals defeated successively the Georgians, the Kuman-Turks, on the Volga-Don steppe – later to provide the manpower reserve of the Mongol Golden Horde that dominated Russia – and the Russian armies themselves, on the Dnieper. The Mongol armies then withdrew to central Asia.

Genghis Khan's successors

Ogodei (1185–1241), who succeeded to the khanate after the death of Genghis in 1227, resumed the western offensive and Persia, Georgia and Armenia were overrun as far as the Black Sea. At the same time the eastern campaign led to the defeat of the Ch'in in 1234 and pressure against the Sung dynasty in South China increased.

Batu (died 1255), Genghis's grandson, drove north of the Caspian and the Caucasus into Europe, defeating the Bulgars on the Volga and capturing many cities, including Kiev, before splitting his army into two and initiating attacks on Poland and Hungary. Cracow and Breslau were captured and a German and Polish army defeated at Legnica in 1241. Batu himself devastated the Hungarian army at the Sajo, captured the towns of Pesth and Gran, and then led his forces to the Adriatic. No attempt was made to hold Hungary or Poland, but a Mongol base was established on the lower Volga to supervise the Russians and the Kumans.

Another grandson, Hulagu (1217-65) [6], the founder of the Persian Ilkhan dynasty (the title recognized subordination to the Great Khan), campaigned to the southwest. The Isma'ili sect, the Assassins, lost their great stronghold of Maymundiz in 1256; Baghdad fell in 1258 when the Abbasid caliph was killed. The conquest of Aleppo and Damascus followed, but in 1260 the Mongols met their first defeat, at Ain Jalut, at the hands of the Mamelukes under Baibars (1233–77), whose army had been battle-hardened against the Crusaders.

The Mongol army was commanded in this

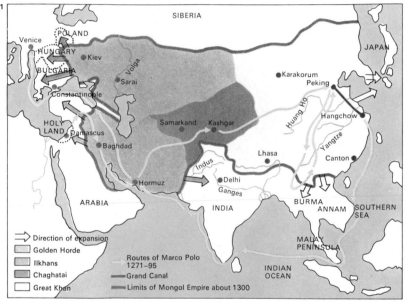

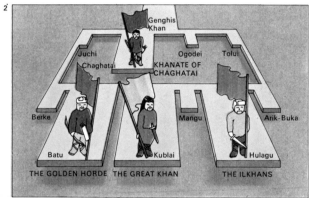

1 Despite the terror which the Mongols inspired, their domination of large areas of Asia and parts of Europe led to the development of trade routes used by traders of many nations in the 13th century. The Venetian Marco Polo set out for Peking in 1271. It was more than 20 years before he returned to Europe to describe the wealth and splendour of the Khan's court.

2 Genghis Khan united the Mongol tribes in 1206 under his leadership. After his death in 1227, the growing Mongol Empire was divided into four among his descendants, with Ogodei as chief.

3 Genghis Khan, portrayed here by a Chinese artist, was a politician as well as a warrior. He skilfully used patronage and alliances to further his aims.

4 A Yuan empress (from the dynasty founded by Kublai Khan) wears a medieval Mongolian headdress. Similar headdresses were still worn in this century.

5 Mongol troops are shown attacking a town with the aid of siege engines. These engines, called mangonels, were made by a German in China in 1273.

battle by the Christian Kitbogha, which illustrates the wide range of religions accepted by the Mongols. Shamanism, Buddhism, Islam and Nestorian Christianity were all practised, but in general the Mongols themselves were Shamanists. This tolerance explains the presence of various Christian priests at the Mongol court, and it encouraged and enabled Marco Polo (1254–1324) to travel across Asia to China. In fact the Mongol khans appear to have had a genuine intellectual interest in religion, and debates between experts of different faiths are reported by observers [8].

Kublai Khan conquers China
In 1260 Kublai (1216–94) became Great Khan, moving his capital from Karakorum to the site of present-day Peking in 1264. From there he conducted the campaigns that led to the annexation of all China, an area where the Mongol terror tactic was not general.

Although the campaign did not finish until 1279, the Yuan dynasty that Kublai founded is generally reckoned to run from the foundation of the new capital until the

last ruler fled before the Ming armies to seek refuge in the Mongol homeland in 1368. But the empire of which Kublai was the last ruler had broken up much earlier, for by 1295 the western Khans had accepted Islam and were no longer willing to submit to the overlordship of a non-Muslim Great Khan.

Nor did all Kublai's campaigns prove successful. In the north he was never able to subdue Kaidu (died 1301), the grandson of Ogodei. To the south, Burma surrendered but was not occupied, while in northern Vietnam disease forced a withdrawal. A seaborne campaign against Java was defeated, as was an attempted invasion of Japan. After Kublai's death there were nine rulers up to 1368. The dissolute rule of the last emperor, Togan Timur, saw revolts and chaos develop into open rebellion in 1348 and eventual defeat by the Chinese insurgents.

In the Middle East and in Russia Mongol dynasties continued to rule until 1502, although by that time they were little more than nominally Mongol because their various conquests had diluted the original Mongol groups to a considerable extent.

The horsemen who formed the élite of the Mongol armies were the key to their military success. They were trained to use the bow or sword while at full gallop.

6 Hulagu, invaded Iran in 1256, captured Baghdad and later defeated the Assassins, but was himself defeated by the Mamelukes in Syria. This was a turning point in Mongol history.

7 The Gur Emir, the tomb of Tamerlane (1336–1405) at Samarkand, was finished in 1434. This is one of the many magnificent buildings which this Mongol ruler, who was a great patron

of the arts as well as a warrior, had constructed in Turkestan, his favourite region, and elsewhere. With his Tatar supporters, he temporarily reunited the empire of Genghis Khan.

8 The prophet Jeremiah is illustrated in Rashid ad-Din's History of the World (1306). The author, a physician in the court of Abaga-Khan, the Mongol ruler of Persia, included biblical themes in his world history – an indication of Mongol tolerance of alien religions. This illustration also shows Chinese cultural influences – another indication of Mongol absorption of foreign ideas.

The empires of South-East Asia

The lands that lie along the maritime route between the Indian subcontinent and China [1] have been strongly influenced by both of these regions. Except in Vietnam, the major cultural influence has been from India, but for most of the Christian era the kingdoms of South-East Asia have recognized, to a greater or lesser degree, the ultimate political suzerainty of the emperors of China.

The first centuries AD
The involvement of India and China in the affairs of this complex region seems to have been the largely accidental result of a need to find an alternative route between them when the land journey was made difficult by political instability in central Asia. But the various parts of South-East Asia had already achieved considerable technological, economic and political development by the time they came under the influence of their larger neighbours in the first centuries AD.

Lin-i, with its capital near Hue, and Fu-nan in the Mekong Delta, are two of the best known states that existed to the south of China in the early Christian era. Lin-i became the kingdom of Champa, which dominated central Vietnam and parts of the south until the fourteenth century. Fu-nan grew into a substantial empire that dominated the greater part of the northern and eastern shores of the Gulf of Siam and their hinterland until the centre of power shifted, in about the middle of the sixth century, to a former vassal state, Chen-la, probably in the vicinity of the Tonle Sap. From this kingdom the Khmer Empire of Cambodia [Key] developed from the beginning of the ninth century onwards. To the west, in the seventh century, lay Dvaravati, near present-day Bangkok, and farther west again, in Burma, lay the Pyu kingdom of Shrikshetra, with its capital at Prome.

Southwards in the Indonesian archipelago, and on the Malaysian peninsula (parts of which seem to have been dominated by Fu-nan), a number of small kingdoms flourished, due in part at least to the development of trading routes between China and the West. These routes brought Buddhist pilgrims through the region and traders whose posts seem to have attracted teachers of Hinduism as well. These religions, originating in India, became the state faiths of the kingdoms of South-East Asia, a role that Buddhism has retained, but Hinduism [5, 7], except in Bali, has almost disappeared.

Buddhist and Hindu influences
By about the seventh century AD a Chinese Buddhist traveller, I-ching, was advising his fellows to spend some time in Sumatra studying Sanskrit and Buddhism before going on to India. He himself spent almost a decade there translating Buddhist texts into Chinese. The rise of this centre in western Indonesia, the beginnings of a state known as Shrivijaya which exercised commercial control in western South-East Asia for several centuries, followed a shift of power from the coast to the interior on the mainland. Meanwhile, elsewhere in the archipelago, in west Java (Taruma) and Borneo, Indian influences began to be detectable and a major dynasty, the Shailendras, Lords of the Mountain, who may have had links with Fu-nan, came to power in central Java. There, from about the eighth to the ninth centuries,

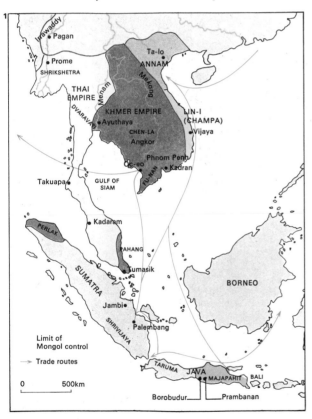

1 The geographic position of South-East Asia, lying between India and China at the centre of a monsoon system that facilitated sailing to and from both these countries, explains much of its cultural development and historical importance. The thriving commercial trade, carried inland along the great river systems, also brought a diversity of religious, political and cultural influences to the area.

2 Chandi Plaosan in central Java is a large Buddhist complex built in about the mid-9th century. Two apparently symmetrical groups have central shrines framed by rectangles of temples. Each main building is two-storied and houses a pantheon of Buddhas and Bodhisattvas. Inscriptions say that the images "shine forth the Doctrine" and windows were evidently arranged to create a radiant effect.

3 Borobudur, one of the world's greatest Buddhist shrines, was built in about the middle of the 9th century to a unique plan involving colossal resources – 570,000 cubic metres (two million cubic feet) of stone were moved from a river bed, dressed, positioned and carved with countless spouts, urns and other embellishments. The walls are covered with reliefs relating to Buddhist doctrine and there are altogether 504 shrines with seated Buddhas.

4 Chandi Mendut, a small temple of the Borobudur group, probably served as an antechapel. This relief, on the north wall of the porch, shows Kuvera, god of wealth, often associated with the merchant class who supported Buddhism.

Buddhism [2] appears to have flourished, its culmination being seen in the shrine of Borobudur [3, 4]. This, with its miles of reliefs expounding the faith, is one of the world's greatest religious monuments.

Hinduism was not neglected, however, and it was perhaps from this setting that Jayavarman II (c. 770–850), "returning from Java" as an inscription says, established in Cambodia the kingdom that dominated the central mainland from about the ninth to the fourteenth centuries. Hinduism, centred upon a lingam (phallic) cult located in a temple at the centre of the capital, was the state religion. The temples were of ever-increasing complexity, culminating in the magnificent structure of Angkor Wat [8] and the enigmatic Bayon in the centre of Angkor Thom. The economic strain of these ostentatious building programmes possibly contributed to the fall of the Khmer Empire under attacks from both the Thai, newly established as a power to the west, and the Vietnamese on the eastern borders.

Eastern Java, also perhaps for socio-economic reasons, saw the rise of the kingdom of Majapahit – a state whose maritime power enabled her to repel a Chinese fleet in 1293. Its influence extended as far west as central Sumatra and its blending of Hinduism and Buddhism was the culmination of a trend that can be detected in central Java as early as 782. The end of this kingdom seems to have been linked with the coming of Islam which, already established in northern Sumatra at the time of Marco Polo's visit in 1291, became important on the coast of Java a century or so later, although Majapahit's fall is usually dated to 1480.

Developments on the mainland

On the mainland, the Mongols, although unsuccessful in Java, had intervened with limited results in Vietnam. In Burma, the kingdom centred upon Pagan on the Irrawaddy, where some thousands of temples built over a period of two centuries testify to the power of Buddhism. It fell to the Mongols in 1287. At about the same time Rama Khamhaeng consolidated Thai power in what had been the western Khmer Empire to found the present state of Thailand.

Jayavarman VII (c. 1120–1215) became king of Cambodia in 1181 after driving out Cham invaders. Following his father, Suryavarman II, who built Angkor Wat, he embarked on an enormous building programme. In addition to temples and associated buildings he created hospitals and rest-houses for travellers and improved roads, with many stone bridges still in use today. Most of his predecessors were Hindu, identifying themselves with Hindu gods; Jayavarman was a Buddhist who seems to have had a special relationship with the god Lokeshvara (shown here), whose carved head dominates the towers and gateways of his buildings.

5 A terracotta head from southern Thailand depicts a manifestation of Shiva's wrath – a creature that ate its own body to satisfy its hunger after the demon it was born to eat had been pardoned.

6 The Lake Pavilion at the Summer Palace, Bangkok, with its elaborate carving and gilding, is a reminder that bamboo and wood have been used as the materials for most buildings in South-East Asia during the past millennium (as they still are today). Even shrines and their images were often wooden, so that much of the past has been lost from the archaeological record.

7 Garuda, vehicle of the god Vishnu, was a magic bird and enemy of snakes. In South-East Asia it became a divinity in its own right and was the centre of salvationist cults of various kinds.

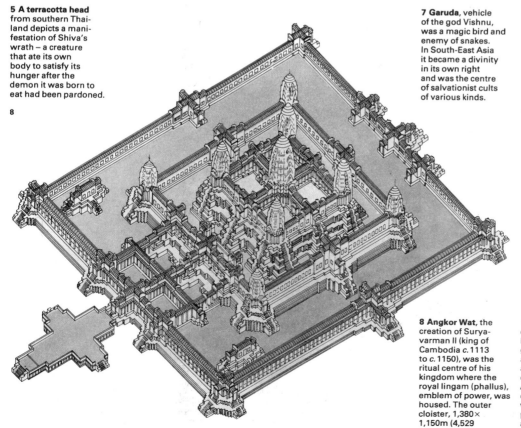

8 Angkor Wat, the creation of Suryavarman II (king of Cambodia c. 1113 to c. 1150), was the ritual centre of his kingdom where the royal lingam (phallus), emblem of power, was housed. The outer cloister, 1,380 × 1,150m (4,529 ×3,733ft), enclosed a complex of buildings, the main group arranged as a square of four at the corners and one in the centre. All were covered in exquisite low relief with divine dancers, plants, birds and animals. The many towers housed images. The walls of the central group were covered with reliefs depicting Hindu stories and battle scenes. In two, the king was shown. It was to be his shrine after death when he became identified with the god Vishnu.

African empires 500–1500

The most obvious sign of Africa's emergence from the primitive status of a "prehistorical continent" was the growth of political states [1]. The 1,000 years from 500 to 1500 saw the gradual emergence and then the great flowering of the black kingdoms that created such a rich and varied culture. By the beginning of the sixteenth century, much of the continent had entered this stage, evolving organized political societies with rulers, a soldiery under their direct command, and an administrative class. These were economically supported by the tribute that could be exacted from the mainly agricultural peoples considered to be either directly or indirectly the subjects of these states. Rulers often also controlled important trade routes.

The first black empires

The most ancient black African states were the empires of Kush/Meroë in the middle Nile valley (c. 800 BC– c. AD 400) and Axum in northeastern Ethiopia (first to fifth centuries). These were shaped by the influence of Egypt and south Arabia respectively and, although they had considerable effects upon later developments farther south, were rather special cases. These empires apart, the main African empires were in the Sudanic belt, that is in the area to the south of the Sahara and north of the tropical forests.

The earliest of these Sudanese empires was Ghana, which was founded by the West African Soninke people. The first reference to Ghana comes from a North African writer in AD 773, and by 800 it had emerged as a powerful trading state, ruling the whole of the country between the Senegal and upper Niger rivers. The prosperity of Ghana was based largely upon its control of the gold trade. The gold fields of West Africa lay well to the south and Ghanaian traders obtained the precious metal by a strange process known as dumb barter in which the gold producers never met these traders face to face. The Ghanaians then sold the gold to North African merchants, who gathered in the southernmost oases. These oasis communities on the edge of the Sudanic belt served as the termini for the caravans that braved the routes across the Sahara [3].

Sometimes the fierce Berber nomads who usually guided these caravans turned upon the settled trading empires. In the middle of the eleventh century, the Almoravids, a Berber confederation, led a Muslim holy war out of the desert to the north and to the south. In 1054 they invaded Morocco (later conquering southern Spain) and in 1076–7 seized the capital of Ghana.

The growth of the desert empires

Although the Ghanaian Empire fell, many smaller kingdoms survived and one of these grew into the spectacular empire of Mali [2]. Three great kings (who ruled between c. 1230 and c. 1340), Sundiata, Mansa Uli and Mansa Musa, so expanded Mali that it became one of the greatest empires in the world. It covered much of the western Sudan, and included the famous city of Timbuktu. The rulers had become Muslim (the religion travelled across the desert trading routes), and in 1324 Mansa Musa made the pilgrimage to Mecca, taking so much gold that he upset the Cairo money market en route. The successor state to Mali was Songhay, which had its centre on the middle Niger. The

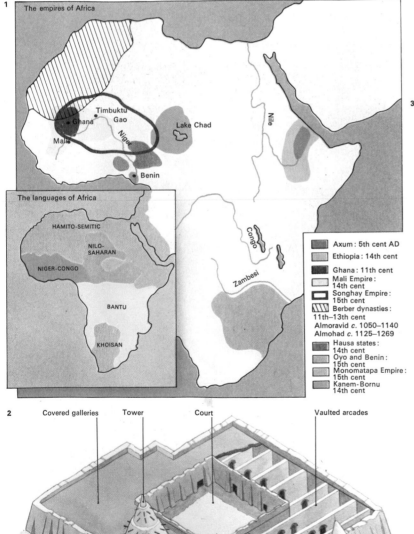

1 The empires of Africa

The languages of Africa

HAMITO-SEMITIC
NILO-SAHARAN
NIGER-CONGO
BANTU
KHOISAN

Axum: 5th cent AD
Ethiopia: 14th cent
Ghana: 11th cent
Mali Empire: 14th cent
Songhay Empire: 15th cent
Berber dynasties: 11th–13th cent
Almoravid c. 1050–1140
Almohad c. 1125–1269
Hausa states: 14th cent
Oyo and Benin: 15th cent
Monomatapa Empire: 15th cent
Kanem-Bornu 14th cent

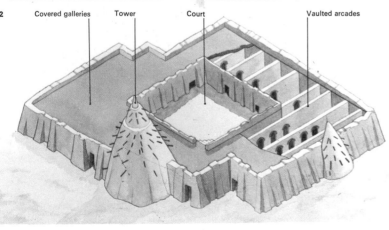

2 Covered galleries   Tower   Court   Vaulted arcades

1 The population of subsaharan Africa is mostly Negroid, although the Khoisan, in the south, are smaller peoples of different origins. The inhabitants of Africa north of the Sahara are paler – often Caucasoid in origin. Three main features distinguished the development of African languages: the long evolution of western African languages; the fairly rapid spread, after about 2000 BC, of an offshoot of them, the Bantu languages, over all of Africa south of the Equator; and the imposition of Arabic on the much more ancient Semitic languages, such as Berber, still spoken in northern Africa.

2 The great mosque at Timbuktu was designed in the 14th century by As-Saheli, one of the Egyptians brought back to Mali by the emperor Mansa Musa after his pilgrimage to Mecca in 1324. Timbuktu grew to be an important centre of commerce, religion and learning, producing many fine Muslim scholars.

3 Trade routes across the Sahara had developed in Greek and Roman times, but first came into their own with the introduction of the camel to Africa around AD 100 and the growth of the Islamic states six centuries later. This 13th-century picture shows a Muslim merchant of the kind that engaged in this ancient and hazardous commerce. He would have traded in West African gold, ivory, kola nuts, slaves and leather wares in exchange for salt, weapons and luxury goods. Control of the southern end of these trade routes made rich the great Sudanic states of Ghana, Mali, Songhay, the Hausa states and Bornu.

great rulers of Songhay at the height of its power were Sonni Ali (reigned 1464–92) and Askia the Great (reigned 1493–1528).

To the east of Songhay were the Hausa states, such as Kano and Katsina, whose origins are traditionally traced back to the eleventh century. By the fourteenth century they had become the domains of powerful kings and prosperous merchants, centres of population, crafts and trade. They were famous for their leather work, which was exported north across the desert. Europeans obtained it in North Africa, and knew it as Moroccan leather. In the central Sudan, on either side of Lake Chad, was the great state of Kanem-Bornu. From as early as the eleventh century its rulers had been Muslims. Kanem-Bornu was one of the oldest and largest African states, retaining its independent existence (although with changes of ruling dynasty) until it was overthrown by the European invaders at the end of the nineteenth century. In the mountains at the eastern end of the Sudanic belt, the Christian empire of Ethiopia [6] became the successor of ancient Axum.

In the woodland and forest areas to the south of the Sudan, kingdoms made a somewhat later appearance [4], but many, including Benin and the Oyo empires of Yorubaland (both of which produced some of the world's great sculptures, were in existence before the coming of the first Europeans in the fifteenth century.

The kingdoms of the Bantu nations

In other parts of Africa, especially in the vast regions south of the Equator over which the Bantu language family had spread rapidly during a few thousand years, states were beginning to be established. A cluster of kingdoms came into existence between the great lakes of East Africa, including Ruanda and Buganda. Another group, the Luba-Lunda kingdoms, grew up south of the Congo (Zaïre) forests, and the Kongo kingdom also emerged south of the river estuary that in colonial times bore its name. Much farther to the south were Great Zimbabwe and the empire of Monomatapa [7], on the Zimbabwe/Rhodesia plateau, which traded gold to the Muslims on the East African coast.

This bronze head with ivory headdress portrays an *Oba* (King of Benin). The splendour of the great African states was epitomized in the persons of their rulers. The headdress is carved with pictures showing the power of the *Oba*, which was, in the case of most African rulers, circumscribed; they were seldom absolute monarchs, being regarded instead as fathers of their people and personally responsible for their welfare. Many African kings were considered to be divine – their function in the world being to mediate between man and the gods. This high concept of leadership did not, of course, prevent corruption in ambitious rulers.

4 Powerful kingdoms had grown up in the forest regions of West Africa by the 1400s and were in trading contact with the older Sudanic states to the north. The former had a rich and ancient artistic tradition, especially in sculpture – Ife terracotta and bronze heads, and Benin bronzes have achieved world renown. This detail of a bronze head from Benin lacks the finesse of very early Benin workmanship but, although heavier, still exhibits considerable skill.

5 Knowledge of iron technology for producing tools and weapons was important in the history of African cultures and political systems, contributing to the ascendancy of many kingdoms that later became great empires. The spread of ironworking occurred over West Africa before the end of the first millennium BC and is linked south of the Equator with the rapid expansion of the Bantu. This picture shows the successive processes of smelting, forging and trading.

6 | Cross motif on roof | Dome over sanctuary | 7

Upper window

Lower window

Main entrance

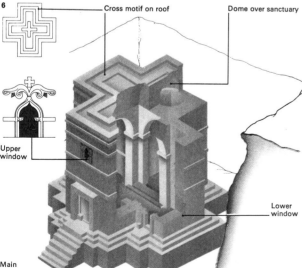

6 This church at Lalibela in Ethiopia was one of several hewn out of solid rock during the 13th century. The Middle Ages were a time of great church building and of general revival and expansion for this ancient Christian empire.

7 The Great Enclosure at Zimbabwe was built mainly in the 14th and 15th centuries on a site used for ritual purposes since *c.* AD 1000. The plateau area of Zimbabwe, the modern Rhodesia, supplied gold to Arab traders at Sofala (a coastal outpost of the rich trading city of Kilwa in East Africa). To the north of Great Zimbabwe, the Monomatapa kingdom was formed, probably in the 15th century, and by 1500 the Portuguese were supplanting the Arab trading links.

Mesoamerica AD 300–1521

During the greater part of the first 1,500 years after the birth of Christ there was a definable "Mesoamerican" civilization. This term was coined by the scholar Paul Kirchhoff in 1943 to describe the very similar cultures that occupied what are now southern Mexico, Belize, Guatemala, Honduras and El Salvador, extending eastwards through Nicaragua into Costa Rica between AD 1000 and 1500. These cultures shared temple-pyramids as religious centres; the sacred ball-game called *pok-ta-pok* by the Maya and *tlachtli* by the Aztec; a pantheon of deities including sun, wind and rain gods; and in the latter part of the period, especially, an iconography with a grisly emphasis on death.

Classic and Preclassic cultures

Many of these features had first appeared in the Preclassic cultures, and in the succeeding Postclassic period (from AD 900 to the Spanish Conquest in 1519) they reached their most complex form and widest distribution.

The first of the Classic cultures to attain great importance was that of Teotihuacán, based on the great city of that name in the Valley of Mexico. From AD 300–600 the city was at its maximum size, estimated to have contained about 200,000 people.

One of the surrounding cultures was that of the Maya. These people occupied the Yucatán Peninsula and the adjacent highlands of Guatemala and their area can be divided into three contrasting regions: the southern, consisting of the volcanic highlands and the short steep slope down to the Pacific shore; the northern, the arid scrub plateau of northern Yucatán; and the central, the jungle-filled basins of the Usumacinta, Belize and Hondo rivers. It was in this central area, that Classic Maya civilization emerged and flourished.

The appearance of this civilization is defined by the erection of stone stelae (upright slabs) with inscriptions in the complex calendar known as the Long Count, which combined three different calendars in one; by the building of massive stone temples and other public buildings in civic and religious complexes normally described as "ceremonial centres"; and by beautifully decorated polychrome pottery in new forms.

Oaxaca, a highland valley in southern Mexico, has one of the longest histories in Mesoamerica. The apogee of the culture of the Zapotec Indians who lived there came between AD 300 and 600 and was focused on the great hilltop city and ceremonial centre of Monte Albán [3].

The site has one enormous plaza laid out by levelling the hilltop, lined on all four sides by large buildings approached by broad sweeps of steps. The working of precious stones and metals was one of the notable characteristics of the Zapotec and of their successors as rulers of Oaxaca, the Mixtec. After Classic Monte Albán was abandoned in the seventh century, some of the tombs were re-used by the Mixtec nobility [7]. Mixtec expertise also extended to architecture and their capital at Mitla [6] has walls decorated with long, repetitive mosaics, of thousands of rectangular pieces of stone.

The Gulf Coast

No such spectacular manifestation of architectural brilliance existed along the Gulf Coast, the home of the Olmec. But the cul-

1 The Pyramid of the Moon at Teotihuacán is one of two massive structures that dominate the heart of this great city, the first major planned settlement in Mesoamerica. It flourished from about 100 BC until AD 700 in a small valley branching off from the Valley of Mexico. The pyramid and the great plaza in front close the northern end of the Street of the Dead.

2 There were three stages in the prehistory of Mesoamerica. [A] The cities of Teotihuacán and Cholula dominated highland Mexico (AD 500). [B] Toltec influence from Tula reached Chichén Itzá in the Maya lowlands. The Maya civilization began to collapse in about AD 1000. [C] The Aztecs ruled the highlands, and the Yucatán Maya sites were eventually abandoned (AD 1500).

3 The Great Plaza forms the core of the main Zapotec ceremonial centre of Monte Albán, on the hills overlooking the Valley of Oaxaca. The building in the foreground, Mound J, lies on a different orientation from the rest of the site, and has been identified as an astronomical observatory; it is also adorned with carved panels depicting the towns conquered by the lords of Monte Albán. A large population lived nearby.

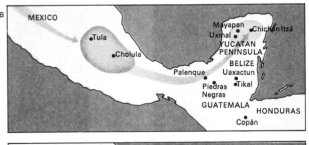

A
Maya Empire *c.*300-630
Maya Empire by 960
Teotihuacán *c.*300
Toltecs by 960

B
Maya Empire 960-1200
Toltecs 960-1200
Toltec expansion 10th-12th centuries
Aztec migration 12th century

C
Maya Empire 1200—*c.*1450
Aztec Empire by 1519
Aztec city alliance by 14th century

tures of Veracruz, and to the north that of the Huasteca, had their own distinctive characteristics. Veracruz sculpture was marked by panels filled with complex designs, many of them concerned with sacrifice, the ball-game, or both. The best-known site is El Tajín [Key], where five ball-courts have been uncovered. These panels are close in conception to those on the great ball-court of Chichén Itzá in Yucatán.

Chichén Itzá is a Maya site in origin. Its most spectacular ruins mark the occupation of Chichén and the domination of northern Yucatán by the Toltec, a warrior people from highland Mexico north of Mexico City. Many of the buildings at Chichén are derived from the architecture of the Toltec capital Tula. The most spectacular are the Castillo, a massive temple-pyramid with steps on all four sides, the Temple of the Warriors, and the *tzompantli* or skull-rack, where the heads of sacrificed victims were displayed [5].

The most impressive feature of the site is natural – the great circular Cenote (well) of Sacrifice, more than 18m (60ft) deep, into which victims were flung to bring rain.

The civilization of the Aztec was in full flower when it was destroyed by the European invaders and was the only Mesoamerican high culture to be observed and recorded as a living entity.

The cities of the Aztec

The Aztec had taken Teotihuacán [1] and Tula as models in making the central highlands of Mexico their base and like them had extended their way down into the coastal lowlands. Their capital, Tenochtitlán, was sited on islands in Lake Texcoco and had a population estimated at 300,000. It comprised two cities, the second being Tlatelolco to the north of Tenochtitlán, which acted as the commercial centre. Part of the marketplace and temples of this city have been excavated and restored, whereas the major part was demolished by the Spaniards during the conquest; the centre of the colonial capital was built on its ruins. Most of what remains of Aztec culture consists of grim lava sculpture, delicate turquoise mosaic work, and a number of manuscripts in picture writing, often with marginal notes in European script.

The Pyramid of the Niches at El Tajín is a large ceremonial centre on the Gulf of Mexico and one of the best-known sites of the Classic Veracruz civilization. It flourished through the first millennium AD contemporary with the Maya to the southeast and Teotihuacán to the south. There are 365 niches on the pyramid which have been interpreted as reflecting the days of the solar year in another aspect of the Mesoamerican obsession with the calendar and the passage of time. El Tajín also had a number of ball-courts, decorated with sculptures showing sacrifice, possibly of an earlier date than Chichén Itzá.

4 Famous for its stucco sculptures is the temple at the western lowland Maya site of Palenque. This was one of the first Maya sites to be explored in the eighteenth and nineteenth centuries, and work has continued there since. The most spectacular discovery came in 1952 when a stairway was found leading to a buried vault where a great stone sarcophagus contained the jade-laden body of a ruler. Recent study of the hieroglyphic tablets that give this Temple of the Inscriptions its name identify him as Pacal, first and greatest ruler of Palenque.

5 The Great Ballcourt at Chichén Itzá was the largest in Mesoamerica. This huge structure, about 83m (270ft) long, was erected by the Toltec conquerors of Yucatán in AD 1000. Stone rings in each wall were targets for the ball and sculptures along the base of the walls depict the decapitation of a ball-player, perhaps the captain of the losing team. A small temple stands at the end.

6 A room in the Mixtec palace at Mitla shows the complex stone mosaic decoration based mainly on the step-fret motif and built up of thousands of individually shaped stone blocks. The rooms, which were roofed in timber, lie round a series of closed courtyards accessible through narrow passages. There is also a pillared hall and tombs that lie below courtyard level.

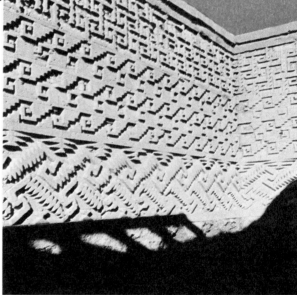

7 This head is one of the superb pieces of Mixtec gold work discovered in 1932 in the excavation of Tomb 7 at Monte Albán. This was a Zapotec tomb of an earlier period that had been re-used for the burial of a Mixtec lord. The tomb also contained carved bones, rock crystal, turquoise, mosaics and jades. This piece was probably worn on the chest and reveals a complex symbolism. The gold-working technique came from South America.

Colombia and Peru 300–1534

In South America one area has always led the rise to civilization – that of the Andes from Lake Titicaca northwards to Panama, and their flanking Pacific and Amazon slopes. There the earliest pottery, the first signs of agriculture and the first settlements and public buildings have been found. From AD 300 onwards, after 1,500 years of increasing momentum, a number of regional cultures of a diverse character arose. They were so strongly regionalized in their art as to suggest separate political units, with strongholds attesting to warfare between them.

The arts of Colombia

In the far north of the South American continent, in present-day Colombia, a gold-working tradition of great technical competence and artistic originality emerged [7]. Pendants and nose ornaments of sheet gold with added detail commonly survive, but there are also magnificent gold vessels for holding the drug coca and unique items such as the model raft with a god and his attendants in the Bogotá Museo del Oro. Techniques extended from the simple hammering of sheet metal to granulation, lost-wax casting and the creation of a gilt surface on a gold-copper alloy by removing the copper with acids from plants.

In southern Colombia the monumental art of San Agustín [1] flourished. The mounds in the area contain stone megalithic chambers, apparently both tombs and shrines, entered by stone tunnels decorated with painted designs. Huge blocks of the volcanic rock andesite were worked into box-like sarcophagi, and shafts of rock turned into menacing statues of warriors and demons. Some of them were double figures, with an animal alter ego looming over the man's head; others represented birds of prey wrestling with serpents. In the nearby Tierradentro region there are rock-cut tombs fashioned with domed roofs and equipped with stepped entrance shafts.

At the time of the Spanish Conquest, Colombia was occupied by large populations living in defended and palisaded settlements. Religion centred on sun-worship and the economy was based on potatoes and maize, and trade in salt, gold and emeralds.

The principal centre in northern Peru was the basin of the River Moche, the seat of Mochica, Chimú, Inca and Spanish colonial rulers. Moche civilization dates from about AD 200 to about 700 and the resources its rulers could command are demonstrated by the colossal Temple of the Sun [2], a terraced pyramid 228m by 136m (741ft by 442ft) and 41m (133ft) high, made of mud-adobe bricks, and the nearby Temple of the Moon, a palace complex adorned with wall paintings, as well as vast irrigation canals cutting across the desert. Some Moche cemeteries have been properly excavated, many others looted. The most notable furnishings are the stirrup-spouted jars [4], some with painted scenes of warfare, hunting and daily life, others modelled into three-dimensional portrait heads.

Palaces for life and death

From about AD 1000 onwards, the Moche valley held the capital of the kingdom of Chimor, the great city of Chan Chan, which covers more than 15.5 square kilometres (6 square miles) [8, 9]. The centre of the city

formed the ritual heart of the Mochica state during the first thousand years AD. Both palaces have suffered greatly from erosion and looting and the original form of the Sun Pyramid is now hard to discern.

1 Enigmatic and massive carvings are scattered on the hills round the present town of San Agustín in southern Colombia. Many depict men with spirit alter egos in the form of animals sitting on their heads and others combine human and feline features, with long fangs. There are megalithic chambers – possibly tombs – which are not unlike those of prehistoric Europe, with rock-cut basins and carved boulders.

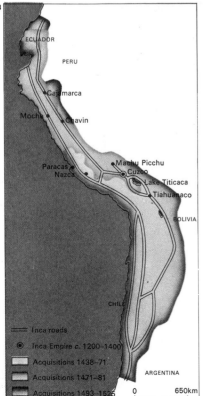

3 The Inca Empire at the height of its power reached from northern Ecuador to the centre of Chile, a distance of more than 3,200 km (2,000 miles). The capital was at Cuzco, the homeland of the conquering Inca nation. From there the Inca himself was linked to the distant parts of his empire by a network of roads and messengers in foot relays.

4 Stirrup-spouted pottery vessels were characteristic of the Mochica period in the first thousand years AD. These vessels were made by specialist potters. One type of vessel took the form of portrait heads, while another (an example of which is shown here) had plain, smooth bodies with painted designs. These often took the form of scenes from Mochica life and warriors in action. The spout shape changed subtly as centuries passed.

Inca roads
Inca Empire c. 1200–1400
Acquisitions 1438–71
Acquisitions 1471–81
Acquisitions 1493–1525

0   650km

ARGENTINA

2 Millions of mud bricks were used to build the Temple of the Sun (or Sun Pyramid) and the neighbouring Temple of the Moon at Moche, on the north coast of Peru. The Temple of the Sun

5 Nazca potters, renowned for the strong blocks of colour that give their work a cartoon-like effect, made this lifelike figure of a drummer. Nazca culture flourished in Peru at the same time as Mochica in the north.

consists of ten basically similar walled enclosures, each with a maze of rooms and open courtyards and once rich but now looted tombs. It has been suggested that these were the successive palaces of the Chimú rulers, the new king building a new compound while his predecessor's was maintained in perpetuity as a funerary shrine. The tombs are known to have contained gold and silver vessels and jewellery, pottery and textiles.

On the central coast of Peru the "Lima style" of pottery suggests a state similar to Moche with ceremonial centres such as Aramburu, near present-day Lima. But the most spectacular pottery style was undoubtedly that of Nazca on the south coast, with polychrome vessels [5], often in four or five colours, and a dominant motif of a cat demon.

The most influential culture in southern Peru at that time, however, was based on Tiahuanaco, south of Lake Titicaca. Vast areas of ridged fields have been identified along the lake, indicating a large agricultural potential and the labour to exploit it. Tiahuanaco is noted for its monolithic stone

carving, including the famous Gate of the Sun [6], which lies on one side of a large enclosure, and tall column statues in a stiff but detailed relief style. Tiahuanaco was preceded in the Andes by Pucará as a cultural centre and passed on some of its features to Huari, north of the lake.

Rise and fall of the Incas
Inca grandeur lasted for less than a century, from 1476 to 1534. Inca expansion began under the ruler Pachacuti Inca Yupanqui (reigned 1438–71) and continued under his successor Topa Inca. At its peak it reached from Ecuador in the north, into what are now Chile, Bolivia and Argentina, running along the cordilleras of the Andes and the coast for more than 3,200km (2,000 miles) [3], which left the Inca military over-extended. Much is known of Inca social and political organization – the system of recording information on knotted string *quipus* [10], the professional army, the communications by relays of runners, and the supreme authority of the Inca himself – the source of strength and ultimately the downfall of the empire.

Inca stone walls in the Peruvian Andes were constructed with quite remarkable skill, the hard stone blocks fitting closely together even though their outlines are irregular. One block in a Cuzco street has 12 angles, but such intricacy is not unusual. In Cuzco itself many Inca structures survive, including part of the Temple of the Sun. It now forms a section of the Dominican monastery. On the hills above Cuzco the great fortress of Sacsayhuaman presents its multiple ramparts to an enemy. Similar stonework is known at the mountaintop city of Machu Picchu and a version was used for agricultural terracing.

6

6 The Gate of the Sun, Tiahuanaco, Bolivia, is carved from a single block of stone and formed part of a great ceremonial enclosure. It is adorned with low-relief carving.

7 The art of gold ornamentation was highly developed in South America. The main centres of innovation were in Colombia and Ecuador, spreading northwards from there into Mexico.

7

8 A restored panel of decoration in adobe – mud brick – forms part of the outlying temple of El Dragón at the site of Chan Chan, the ancient city north of Trujillo in the Moche Valley of northern Peru. Moche was an earlier focus of civilization in this valley, as the colonial and modern city of Trujillo was after Chan Chan. The site consists of a series of great walled enclosures, altogether covering some 28 sq km (11 square miles).

8

9

9 Moulded adobe relief decorates the interior of a room at Chan Chan. The friezes are repetitive and consist of birds, fish or abstract designs. The rooms have niches in the walls and some have a U-shaped structure called an *audiencia,* which is thought to have been the seat of a clerk, who checked goods in and out.

10
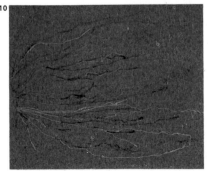

10 A *quipu,* a series of knotted cords, was used by the Inca as a counting and memory device. The knots were of different colours to denote different kinds of numerical information and are an eloquent testimony to the bureaucratic structure of the Inca Empire. For recording the constant payments of incoming tribute they were indispensable.

The age of exploration

The later fifteenth and early sixteenth centuries make up one of the most momentous periods in the history of Europe. In 1492 Christopher Columbus (1451–1506) sailed west across the Sea of Darkness and discovered the Americas. In 1497 Vasco da Gama (c. 1496–1525) embarked from Lisbon, sailed down the West African coast and around the Cape of Good Hope, up to Mozambique and Mombasa and then across to Calicut in India. In 1519 Ferdinand Magellan (c. 1480–1521) [3], seeking the route to the Orient that Columbus had failed to find, led a Spanish expedition around the southern extremity of South America and across the Pacific to the East Indies. Magellan himself was killed, but the survivors of his expedition, returning by way of the Cape of Good Hope, circumnavigated the globe for the first time.

The voyage of the Portuguese

Vasco da Gama's expedition [2] eastwards was less a voyage of discovery and more an armed embassy determined to open up Portuguese commerce with the East. It was the culmination of almost a century of tentative, hesitant exploration by the Portuguese in which their frail caravels (light Mediterranean sailing ships) had groped their way along the West African coast and finally rounded the Cape. Lured by the gold and ivory of Africa, and by the prize of Eastern trade which awaited Europeans who could reach India by sea, the captains of Henry the Navigator (1394–1460) [1] paved the way for da Gama by voyages to Madeira (1418) and the Azores (1431); by rounding Cape Bojeador (1434); the discovery of the mouth of the Senegal (1444); the sighting of Sierra Leone (1460) and eventually the discovery of the Cape of Good Hope by Bartholomew Diaz (c. 1450–1500) in 1487.

The motives of the explorers

The motives behind these early explorations, whether Portuguese or Spanish, were a combination of acquisitiveness and religious zeal. Barred by the Italians from the large prize of Mediterranean trade, deprived of the profits of the luxury commerce in Eastern goods which Muslims and Venetians together controlled, the Iberians sought new routes to the sources of supply. At the same time they were spurred on by their crusading zeal.

But not all the voyages during this period were by Iberians. Under Spanish patronage the Genoan Christopher Columbus sailed in search of a westward sea route to the Indies trade, and in October 1492 landed in the Bahamas, believing them to be an Asiatic archipelago. By 1504 he had made three more voyages to the Caribbean, but had come no nearer to proving that Asia had been found. Meanwhile, from England, the voyages of John Cabot (c. 1450–c. 1500) along the northeast coast of America, and the explorations of the Florentine Amerigo Vespucci (1454–1512) along the north coast of South America and Brazil on behalf of the Spanish, led to the belief that there was an uncharted land mass to the west between Europe and Asia, a New World [4].

The Portuguese had many advantages over other European rivals in the exploration of Africa and Asia. The Italians were bottled up in the Mediterranean; the Spanish were not united into one kingdom until 1479 (the

1 Prince Henry of Portugal, "the Navigator", was the most important of the precursors of the age of exploration. Placing gentlemen of his own household in command of his ships, Henry developed a systematic if intermittent programme of exploration beyond Cape Bojeador. By the time of his death his ships had advanced south by 2,415km (1,500 miles).

2 Vasco da Gama's voyage by which he reached Calicut in 1498 was an event of great significance, but his achievement cannot be ranked with that of Magellan or Columbus. In sailing east he completed what others had begun – Diaz had rounded the Cape of Good Hope in 1488 and in fact accompanied da Gama part of the way on his Indian voyage.

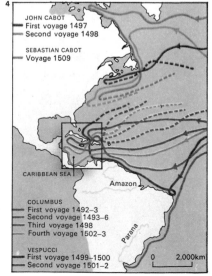

3 Ferdinand Magellan, a Portuguese employed by the King of Spain, embarked in 1519 from Seville on the voyage in which he sailed through the strait that bears his name. He then crossed the Pacific to the Philippines where he was killed. Del Cano completed the circumnavigation.

JOHN CABOT
— First voyage 1497
— Second voyage 1498

SEBASTIAN CABOT
— Voyage 1509

CARIBBEAN SEA

Amazon

COLUMBUS
— First voyage 1492–3
— Second voyage 1493–6
— Third voyage 1498
— Fourth voyage 1502–3

VESPUCCI
— First voyage 1499–1500
— Second voyage 1501–2

Parana

0   2,000km

4 Westward voyages, until Magellan's circumnavigation, were a gradual process of realization that an uncharted continent lay between Europe and the Indies. While the Portuguese sailed eastward to the spice trade, Spain and England were anxious to find a quicker, westward route.

expulsion of the Moors was not complete until 1492). By then the Portuguese had taken the lead.

A small seafaring nation, Portugal possessed a large fleet of ships, a seafaring population trained on ocean fishing, a well-organized system of marine insurance and investment and a royal family ready to back these maritime enterprises. Moreover, in the fifteenth century the design of European ships had developed rapidly and so had the necessary navigational aids.

Portuguese dominance in the spice trade
By finding a direct route to India by sea the Portuguese were able to gain an advantage in the spice trade. The architect of Portuguese supremacy in the Orient was Alfonso d'Albuquerque (1453–1515). In 1510 he seized the island of Goa; in 1511, Malacca. From the East Indies Portuguese ships went to China and sailed annually between China and Japan. Their twin commercial aims were to monopolize the spice trade with Europe and to get as large a share as possible of the inter-port trade of the Indian Ocean.

But in fact the Portuguese commercial empire of the sixteenth century – the result of the age of exploration – achieved less than its architects had hoped. The Portuguese succeeded in overawing but not in controlling their Asian competitors at sea. Until the coming of the Dutch they retained a monopoly of the sea route around the Cape which they had pioneered. But they never achieved a monopoly of the spice trade between Europe and Asia. The Venetians, supplied by the old land routes, continued to sell some spices in Europe, while the Portuguese did not achieve control of all the spice islands. Their Estado da India [7], a set of fortified trading-posts clinging sometimes precariously to the coast or to islands, never penetrated and certainly did not dare to challenge the empires of mainland Asia.

The explorations in the East were initially more important to Europe than for the countries explored. They indicate a shift in the centre of gravity of European trade from the Italian states to the Atlantic. The new routes to the East by sea permanently changed the mercantile map of the world.

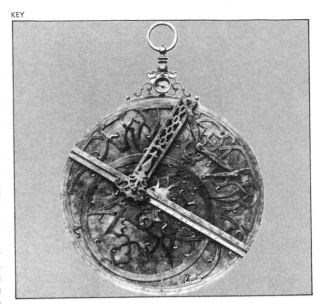

The astrolabe, together with the quadrant, was one of the chief navigational aids that made exploration possible.

5 Lisbon in the late 16th century, with a population of about 100,000, was the largest city in Portugal. It was the nerve centre of her seaborne empire where the spices of Asia were redistributed to the Mediterranean and Atlantic world in exchange for their goods. In the next century Portugal was to lose her commercial dominance in Asia and her political independence in Europe.

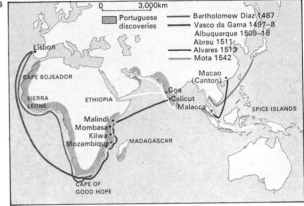

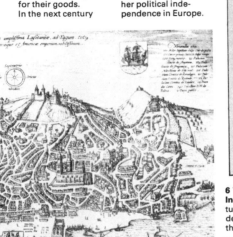

6 The route to the Indies took the Portuguese 50 years to develop from the time that Diaz rounded the Cape of Good Hope in 1488. The greatest single step was da Gama's crossing of the Indian Ocean, but it was the later venturers who gained for Portugal her central position in the trade of the Far East.

7 The Portuguese empire in the East consisted of a string of fortified trading-posts all the way from Sofala in east Africa to Macao in the China Sea. The headquarters of the Estado da India was Goa on the western coast of India. The grand forts, such as this one, that the Portuguese built in Goa were meant to overawe rivals from the sea and to dissuade attack from the hinterland.

8 The Dutch began to sail eastwards in 1595. Their innovation in getting to the East Indies was to leave India on their flank and sail direct from the Cape to the Sunda Strait and then turn north to Java. This new route had the advantage of by-passing Goa and Malacca, but it also meant that they had to carry bullion or European goods direct to Indonesia, without the support of local Asian trade.

Americas: conquest and settlement

By the early sixteenth century the Spaniards had established colonies in the Antilles and the Isthmus of Panama. The mineral resources of these islands, however, proved to be slender and, despite the name Golden Castile, the area had little to offer. Trading expeditions along the coast of Yucatán revealed a likelihood of greater wealth in the interior. In 1519, after two preliminary expeditions, the governor of Cuba, Diego de Velázquez (c. 1460–c. 1524), sent a fleet under Cortés to settle the region [1A].

The major conquests
Hernán Cortés (1485–1547) [2] and his expedition of 550 men landed on the coast of Mexico and founded the settlement of Veracruz. Cortés then threw over Velázquez's authority and placed himself directly under the crown. By a series of adroit diplomatic moves and superior military technology, Cortés took formal possession of the Aztec capital of Tenochtitlán. He was welcomed by its ruler, Montezuma, whom he promptly imprisoned. According to Cortés, Montezuma made a willing donation of his empire to Charles V in the mistaken belief that Cortés was the emissary of the god Quetzalcoatl. This widely circulated story is almost certainly a fable.

The conquest of Peru in 1532 by the adventurer Francisco Pizarro (c. 1471–1541) [4] was the result of the search for gold. When the Spaniards arrived on the Peruvian coast at Túmbez, the Inca Empire was divided by a civil war. Atahualpa emerged victorious shortly before Pizarro caught up with him at the fortress of Cajamarca [3]. Here the Spaniards succeeded in killing most of Atahualpa's retinue and capturing the Inca himself. Atahualpa offered to fill his cell with gold in exchange for his freedom. Pizarro accepted, but although Atahualpa kept his part of the bargain he was not released. The value of his ransom has been estimated at about 20 million dollars. It included the treasures of the Temple of the Sun and was all melted down for bullion.

Pizarro lacked Cortés's powers of leadership and after the subjugation of the Inca Empire, the conquerors began to fight among themselves. The civil war lasted until the death of Pizarro in 1541 and the execution of his brother Gonzalo in 1548.

With the conquest of Peru, the attention of the European explorers turned elsewhere. Expeditions were sent to Texas and Florida and some settlements were established. The colonization of New Mexico was slightly more determined but the area soon became little more than a military outpost.

Administration
The Spanish crown, fearful lest the more successful of the *conquistadores* (conquerors) should set up independent feudatories, rapidly took control of the government of the new colonies. The administration was complex. At the top was the viceroy, responsible only to the crown [5]. The distance between Spain and the Indies inevitably placed great power in his hands.

To maintain the balance of power within the colony, a separate court of appeal, the *audiencia*, was established. This had the right of direct representation before the crown and could suspend crown officials from their duties; it also served to represent the Indians

Aztec Empire

Route of Cortés 1519–20
Route of Cortés 1521
▲ Tribes who allied with Cortés
✺ Marshland

4,500 metres
4,000
3,500
3,000
2,500
2,000
0

0   60km

1 Cortés landed at Veracruz [A] on 22 April 1519. By forming alliances with the peoples of Cempoala, Jalapa and Tlaxcala, he maintained his supply line with the coast [B]. After some skirmishes, he persuaded the powerful independent "state" of Tlaxcala to join him, thus obtaining the much-needed base from which to launch his attack on the Aztec capital of Tenochtitlán. After the retreat of the "Sorrowful Night" on 30 June 1520, Cortés fled to Tlaxcala. With the help of local workmen he built a fleet of brigantines to harass the defenders of Tenochtitlán from the lake. These were carried in pieces and assembled on the lake shore, while the army, composed largely of Tlaxcalans, attacked the towns that seemed sympathetic to the beleaguered Aztecs.

2 Hernán Cortés was born in the province of Estremadura in Spain. He sailed for Hispaniola in 1504 and as Velázquez's lieutenant, he took part in the conquest of Cuba. His career subsequent to the conquest of Mexico was, like that of so many *conquistadores*, spent largely in an effort to secure from the crown due recognition of his achievements. He died in Spain in 1547.

Inca Empire at its greatest extent in 1525
Inca roads
Pizarro's expeditions 1524–8
Pizarro's expedition 1531–3
⊞ Spanish settlements
• Capital of Inca Empire

0   450km

3 A superb network of roads helped Pizarro to conquer Peru. Reaching Túmbez in 1531, he then marched inland to Cajamarca to find the Inca ruler Atahualpa. Following a surprise attack, the city fell, and Atahualpa himself was later executed. Pizarro founded a new capital at Lima, thus shifting the centre of Inca society from Cuzco to the coast.

4 Charles V gave his support in 1528 to Pizarro's third expedition to Peru. Pizarro had accompanied Balboa on his march across the isthmus of Panama in 1513 and later formed a partnership with Diego de Almagro and Fernando de Luque to settle Peru and seek out the riches of the Incas. The first expeditions (1524–8) were unsuccessful. In 1531, Pizarro and his brothers left Panama for Peru, joined later by Almagro. Pizarro lacked the diplomatic skills of Cortés and was unable to curtail the ambitions of his followers. Shortly after the subjugation of the Incas, Almagro broke away and during the ensuing civil war Pizarro was murdered.

before their overlords and to administer justice. The crown also imposed the system of *residencia*, whereby a crown official was examined at the end of his term of office and any misconduct punished. These cumbersome institutions were often ill-equipped to deal with the American situation.

The Indians were "granted" to settlers under the *encomienda* system. Theoretically this provided the colony with a salaried labour force; each settler was given a number of Indians (but not their lands) from whom he took tribute or labour. The position of the Indian was therefore rather like that of the European serf and the power that this appeared to give to the colonists forced the crown to make several efforts to abolish the system. By the Laws of Burgos of 1512–13 and subsequent royal decrees, the number of Indians held in *encomienda* was limited and their duties were to some extent lightened.

The wealth of the Americas

The great wealth of America lay in its silver deposits. The mines of Potosí in Peru and of Zacatecas, Guanajuato and the other Potosí

in Mexico were all discovered during the 1540s and their output soon came to dominate the European silver market. The colonists benefited little, however, and were forced to subsist on agriculture and trade in lesser commodities, such as silks, with the Philippines. Precious metals were shipped via Seville which enjoyed a monopoly of America's trade and where a clearing house, the *Casa de la Contratación*, had been set up as early as 1503. The Americas had always been a Castilian venture and the Castilian crown benefited directly [6].

The impact of Spanish colonization upon the New World was considerable [9]. The introduction of European crops and livestock destroyed the domestic life of the Indians and altered the ecological balance of central Mexico. The disruption of old tribal divisions and of the hierarchy of Aztec society produced an alienated, enfeebled community which rapidly succumbed to European diseases so that the population declined rapidly during the sixteenth century. Latin America thereafter was a mixed culture dominated by that of the Spanish settlers.

This 17th-century Inca wooden beaker shows Peruvian Indians and a European together. At first, the Spaniards tried to preserve the Indian social structure, using local chieftains as justices and tax-collectors. However, over the course of the 17th century, the native nobility inter-married and the Spaniards took Indian women as concubines, producing a mixed group known as mestizos. The Indian culture declined and was supplanted by that of a white, or near-white society.

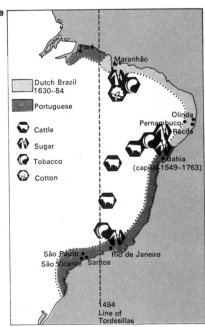

5 The Spanish crown rapidly replaced the *conquistadores* with its own officials, who set up a complicated government machine providing checks and balances to prevent any single individual from growing too powerful. There was also the *audiencia*, a court of appeal to which every citizen had recourse and which was responsible directly to Spain. This former governor's palace is in what is now Morelia, central Mexico.

6 Silver bullion from the Indies provided Castile especially with great wealth during the 16th century, but the influx slowed as the mines were worked out in the 17th. The massive inflation of 17th-century Europe may have derived from these imports of American silver.

Spanish territories
Other European territories

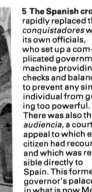

9·8
5·5
England
0·9
1·1
Dutch Republic
0·5
Poland
2
France
0·5
Savoy
2
Milan
1·5
Venice
0·5
Austria
3
Portugal
0·6
Aragon
Castile
Naples
4
Sicily
0·6
Ottoman Empire

Revenue in millions of Venetian ducats

7 Spanish cruelty towards the Indians was notorious. *Brief Relation of the Destructions of the Indies* by Bartolomé de las Casas, which became a best-seller during the 16th century, helped to foster and disseminate this "black legend". Its popularity, however, was due more to fear and hatred of Spain than to love of the Indians. This illustration by De Bry appeared in The Netherlands as anti-Spanish propaganda.

8 The conquest of America by Europeans in the 16th century meant that the indigenous cultures were almost wiped out. Because of the Spaniards' desire to convert the Amerindians to Christianity, the traditional features of the native way of life were absorbed into the dominant culture, although this process was uneven. The tribes that survived were the most primitive and they never developed, but the civilization of the Aztecs and Incas wholly disappeared.

9 By the Treaty of Tordesillas of 1494 the Spaniards and the Portuguese – at the instigation of Pope Alexander VI – agreed to a demarcation line between their territorial claims. When Brazil was discovered in 1500 by Cabral, Portugal naturally claimed it but did not seriously colonize it until 1530. Spain and Portugal were united between 1580 and 1640, so that Brazil was open to attack by Spain's enemies. In 1630, the Dutch seized a rich area in the north, which they kept until 1654 when they were driven out by wealthy land-owners. Throughout the 17th century, the Brazilian economy developed rapidly, based on sugar and tobacco together with cotton and cattle.

Dutch Brazil 1630–54
Portuguese
Cattle
Sugar
Tobacco
Cotton

Pará
Maranhão
Olinda
Pernambuco
Recife
Bahia (capital 1549–1763)
São Paulo
São Vicente
Santos
Rio de Janeiro
1494 Line of Tordesillas

The rise of banking

Between the twelfth and the fifteenth centuries Italy exercised a European supremacy in commerce and finance and was responsible for most innovations in business and banking. By the sixteenth century that supremacy was being eroded. In twelfth-century Genoa, banks accepted deposits, exchanged foreign coins for local currency and engaged in bullion dealing. Later the Florentines became the leading Italian bankers. Throughout this period banking and trade were invariably combined and the commercial contacts of the Italians throughout Europe necessitated the regular international transfer of money. The simple but commercially important bill of exchange [Key] was evolved in the fourteenth century and avoided the problems and dangers of transporting gold and silver coins.

Activities of medieval bankers

Largely as a consequence of the Church's ban on lending money for interest (usury), medieval bankers made exchange operations a key activity. Although the bill of exchange did involve a credit element until the money was paid out at a later date, it was not classified as a loan.

The banker's profit came from the exchange rate – the Medici averaged 15 per cent. The prohibition on charging interest may also have impeded the evolution of the basic banking activities of borrowing and lending at interest, although deposit banks did exist, mainly in Italy, but also in Bruges [1]. They offered non-interest bearing current accounts and the facility of making transfers between customers' accounts.

From the fourteenth century onwards some towns allowed written orders (the distant ancestor of the cheque) to make payments or transfers. These orders replaced the original requirement that such orders had to be made orally by the depositor in person.

A decline in private banking in the Low Countries and Italy in the fifteenth century is illustrated by the fall in numbers of large Florentine banks from 80 to eight between 1330 and 1526. The hazards of medieval banking are revealed in an assertion made in 1585 that over the years 96 out of 103 Venetian banks had failed, often through incautious loans to merchants and governments. Deposit banking recovered in the late sixteenth century, often in the form of municipally controlled public banks, as in Venice and later in Amsterdam [9], both of which accepted deposits and transferred money between customers' accounts.

Small banks and money-lenders

More widespread than the handful of great Italian merchant banks such as the Medici [6] were small local banks. These shared many of the functions of their large counterparts, accepting deposits, making loans on pledges and changing money, but avoided exchange and transfer operations.

Throughout Europe there were also the reviled but necessary money-lenders and pawnbrokers who made small, short-term loans to the poor [3]. Even in a largely subsistence peasant economy, money was needed to pay taxes and the poorest might seek a loan in hard times. Some of these money-lenders were Christians, but most were Jews to whom the usury laws did not apply and who could therefore charge interest. Some, such as

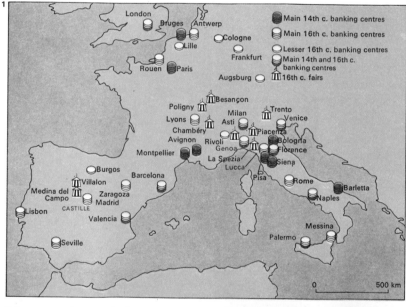

1 **Bruges,** whose financial activities were dominated by Italians, was the only permanent medieval banking centre outside Italy. The late 15th century witnessed the rise of the south German houses. The major 16th-century centres were Antwerp, Lyons and the seasonal fairs in Castille and at Besançon. The Genoese controlled the Besançon fairs which soon left and reconvened in Piacenza by 1579.

Map legend:
- Main 14th c. banking centres
- Main 16th c. banking centres
- Lesser 16th c. banking centres
- Main 14th and 16th c. banking centres
- 16th c. fairs

0 500 km

2 **The Papacy received dues** and taxes from all over Europe. Heedless of the usury prohibition, the Papacy also borrowed at interest from bankers. The great basilica of St Peter's, begun in the early 16th century, was partly financed by the proceeds from the sale of indulgences conveyed by the Fuggers, who had broken the Italian monopoly.

3 **Aaron,** a noted Jewish usurer, built this house in Lincoln in about 1170-80. He conducted business with the greatest families of England and financed part of the building of Canterbury Cathedral. On his death a special department of the Exchequer had to wind up his huge financial assets. The Jews were expelled from England in 1290, as the king hoped to take over their assets and debts from the nobility.

4 **Jacques Coeur** (c. 1395–1456), French merchant, money-lender and financier, built this palace in Bourges during his spectacular career. He lost his fortune in 1453 and was exiled until his death.

5 **This painting by Quentin Massys** (c. 1465–1530) shows the money-changer and his wife at work. For a small fee they would exchange gold for silver coins or the coins of one currency into another.

those in Florence in 1437, were officially invited to set up licensed pawnshops so that Christian souls should not be jeopardized through usury, although Christian money-lenders were not above charging disguised interest.

In mid-fifteenth-century Italy churchmen established non-Jewish pawnshops, the *Monti di Pietà*, to meet the needs of the poor. The charitable purpose of these pawnshops was perverted, however, when governments and the rich turned to them for loans.

Sixteenth-century banking

The sixteenth century saw no major innovations in banking practices but, as the European economy expanded, the scale of operations increased, credit became more extensive and other nationalities, especially the south Germans, adopted Italian methods. London remained a second-rank financial centre until the late seventeenth century. Methods of obtaining credit became more flexible as a result of the increasing use of endorsement and discounting, although until the seventeenth century these were rarely applied to bills of exchange. Interest rates fell and some Protestant states adopted a more liberal attitude towards usury. Expanding trade was facilitated by the evolution of an unofficial system of settling international trading debts and balances during the great seasonal European trade fairs. This lasted until the late sixteenth century when the fairs began to lose their importance.

The most spectacular development was the mid-sixteenth-century boom in government borrowing to meet the escalating costs of war. The French kings raised money in Lyons, the English and Spanish [8] rulers in Antwerp, the greatest centre for long-distance trade of the era. Fortunes were lost as the kings of France and Spain defaulted on their debts, just as Edward III of England had ruined two Florentine banks in the 1340s. Ordinary individuals as well as great banks such as the south German Fuggers [7] were hit. Although the Fuggers survived on a reduced scale, by the end of the sixteenth century the era of the international financier was over, although more mundane forms of banking continued to prosper and develop.

The form of the bill of exchange altered little from its evolution in the 14th century. To avoid the Church's prohibition on usury it had to instruct the recipient in another country to make payment in another currency to the person specified. Usually the rate of exchange was given. This bill, signed by Anton Fugger, required the Fugger agents in Rome to pay 2,700 ducats to the Dean of Elwagen.

6 The Medici family were the greatest of all 15th-century Italian bankers with branches in France, England, the Low Countries and Italy. Under Cosimo de' Medici (1389–1464), like his successors a patron of the arts, they reached the peak of their influence and wealth. Already in serious financial trouble, the firm finally foundered when the Medici were expelled from Florence in 1494.

7 In the early 16th century the Europe-wide commercial and financial empire of the Augsburg family, Fugger was the largest the Western world had ever seen. It rested on lucrative mining monopolies, extensive trade and loans on a vast scale. The most spectacular period occurred under the guidance of Jakob Fugger the Rich (1459–1525) (here painted by Albrecht Dürer). He learnt the banking trade in Italy.

8 Jakob Fugger's most famous loan was made to the Haps-burgs: 543,585 florins that helped to buy the votes of the Imperial Electors who made Charles V of Spain Holy Roman Emperor in 1519. The fortunes of the Fuggers and the Hapsburgs were thereafter closely linked. Charles V had to borrow unprecedentedly large sums from foreign bankers living in Antwerp to pay for his wars with the French, the Turks and the German Protestants.

9 The Amsterdam Exchange Bank (1609) was one of the most famous and successful of the municipally supervised banks set up after the financial recovery of the late 16th century. It received cash deposits of over 300 florins, transferred money between customers' accounts, traded in bullion and handled all bills of exchange over 600 florins. Like other municipal banks it did not make loans, grant overdrafts or discount bills nor did it issue bank-notes.

The politics of Europe 1450–1600

Medieval Europe was the *respublica christiana*, the universal world of Christendom ruled by two swords – the spiritual wielded by the pope, the secular by the emperor. But the sixteenth century saw the disintegration of this ideal and the growth of monarchical states whose triumph was at the expense of the Church and the nobility. The process was at its clearest in France [Key] where the crown gradually succeeded in converting lands held under the old feudal system into lands held by the crown, through a succession of accommodations between the crown, the papacy and the nobility.

Popes and kings

The disputed claim to the papal succession from 1378 to 1417 damaged the position of the pope as head of Christendom and the rival candidates became the puppets of secular rulers. Later popes retreated to play Italian politics while the princes of Europe exploited them to control the Church.

Monarchs of the sixteenth century attempted to increase their control over the nobility. The medieval king's real power rested ultimately on his wealth and the military strength that he could command. Towards the end of the Middle Ages a few noble families in many parts of Europe greatly extended their own power and fortunes. The Percy family, for example, had as much power in the north of England as kings. At times of weak kingship this situation produced civil war in France, Spain and England (the Wars of the Roses, 1455–85). But the disorder of war threatened the privileged classes as a whole and they looked to a strong king to restore stability. The princes set about re-erecting the former effective monarchical rule based on financial resources, powerful adherents, the centralization of the administration and the neutralizing of the power of the independent nobles.

In England the Lancastrian Henry VII (1457–1509), who won his crown in battle, attempted to establish personal control of government. Henry enjoyed the forfeited lands of the vanquished and was financially stable. He administered the affairs of the realm from his own household and was able to discipline a nobility weakened by wars and

to reduce the numbers of their military retainers. By marrying into the House of York he minimized the possibilities of dynastic rivalry. Henry rebuilt a strong personal monarchy in a realm that had seen nothing like it since Edward I (1239–1307). His son, Henry VIII (reigned 1509–47) [5], continued to strengthen the crown: he incorporated Wales within the kingdom and brought the wealth and authority of the Church into his hands.

Francis I and Charles V

Francis I (1494–1547) came to the throne of France facing a difficult situation. France had been rent by war, nobles such as the Bourbon family were powerful and the kingdom was large and divided. Francis exploited the royal rights of direct taxation, centralized the treasury and attempted to impose uniform Roman law codes on all the provinces.

There seemed some hope for a degree of unity and centralization in Spain when the kingdoms of Aragon and Castile were both inherited by the Hapsburg Charles V (1500–58) in 1516 [1]. Charles suppressed

1 The empire of Charles V was the product of dynastic accident. He succeeded his father Philip as Duke of Burgundy in 1506, and his grandfather Ferdinand as King of Aragon and of Castile in 1516. The territories of the Holy Roman Empire came with his election to the title in 1519. There was no logic to the empire and problems of communication made imperial rule almost impossible. Charles resolved these difficulties by handing The Netherlands (1555) and Spain (1556) to his son Philip II and the rest of his empire to his brother Ferdinand (1556).

2 The warring Hapsburgs and Valois dominated early 16th-century politics. Charles V, of the Hapsburgs, inherited disputed claims over parts of Burgundy and Italy [A]. Francis I, consolidating Valois rule in France, feared encirclement by the Hapsburgs. The conflict centred on Italy, important for its wealth and a vital hub of communications for the Hapsburg possessions in Spain and the empire. The route through the Italian passes was the only alternative to the Channel route, which was not under Charles's control. Most of the disputed areas came under imperial control by the Peace of Cateau-Cambrésis (1559) [B].

Key to map legend: Disputed areas in Italy 1519–59; Held by Francis I of France; Under Spanish (Hapsburg) rule; States under Spanish influence 1559

4 The "Field of the Cloth of Gold" is a painting that commemorates the historic meeting of King Henry VIII of England and King Francis I of France in June 1520 to conclude a long awaited peace. The encounter was marked by great festivity and elaborate preparation. Henry had built a temporary palace, all tents were embossed with gold and velvet and the royal interviews were occasions for jousting and other contests of chivalry, ceremonial banquets and firework displays. As each king tried to outdo the other in pomp and splendour, the occasion turned into a trial of strength. No alliance resulted and open war had broken out by 1522.

3 The life of Niccolò Machiavelli (1469–1527) coincided with the rise of the nation state and the beginning of the art of statecraft. Machiavelli outlined a guide for princes in his book *The Prince* (1532), and his *Discourses* on the first ten books of Livy, the Roman historian. *The Prince* shocked Christian Europe and earned for its author a reputation for devious and treacherous statesmanship. He became a leading figure of the Renaissance.

the "comuneros" revolt and sent royal officials (*corregidores*) to enforce his will. But the nobility remained powerful and jealous of their privileges and the two kingdoms remained separate. Charles was distracted by his imperial duties (he was also Holy Roman Emperor) from consolidating Spain. In order to obtain Castilian money, he recognized the privileges of the nobles. Philip II (1527–98) continued to rely on Castilian bullion for his campaigns and neglected Aragon, which voted little money to the crown. The kingdoms of Spain were never centralized and in the 1600s Aragon and Catalonia revolted against the crown.

When he became Emperor in 1519, Charles V tried to centralize his lands through imperial institutions and constant visits, but the task was impossible. The empire had no unity; large cities such as Nuremberg were proud of their independence, the princes were trying to assert themselves and powerful families such as the Wittelsbachs were anxious to stop the Hapsburgs from becoming too strong. The Reformation [8] finally divided the empire.

In the late sixteenth century the Hapsburgs gained control over their hereditary lands in order to provoke resistance in Bohemia.

Attempts by both Charles V and Francis I of France to increase control of their kingdoms led them into more than 40 years of war over disputed claims in Italy [2]. Instead of becoming more unified, Italy was completely fragmented by the war.

The need for a strong monarchy

Although more powerful monarchies emerged in Western Europe during the sixteenth century, there were serious limitations on their control. Without a paid civil service kings still depended on the nobility. Men thought of Catalonia or Provence before they thought of Spain or France; allegiance to family, locality or lord could still overcome allegiance to the king. In the late sixteenth century religious divisions threatened the monarchy in England and encouraged a return to separatism in France. But the chaos of war once again alerted the ordinary nobles to the need for a strong king as the guardian of law and order.

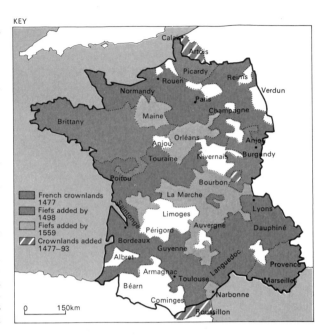

KEY

French crownlands 1477
Fiefs added by 1498
Fiefs added by 1559
Crownlands added 1477–93

0   150km

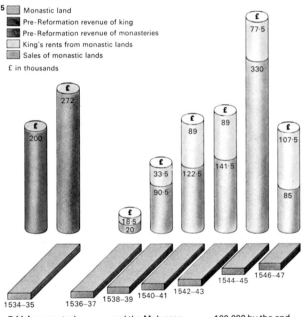

5
- Monastic land
- Pre-Reformation revenue of king
- Pre-Reformation revenue of monasteries
- King's rents from monastic lands
- Sales of monastic lands

£ in thousands

5 Henry VIII's increased revenue from his dissolution of the monasteries, with the proportion received from the rent and sale of the lands, is shown here. Henry took this action four years after his break with Rome and claimed that he did it to put an end to corruption. But his real motive was to acquire an extra income for wars to further his dynastic ambitions in Europe.

6 Christ Church (Cardinal's College), at Oxford was founded by Cardinal Wolsey (c. 1475–1530) in the 16th century. Its purpose was to train young scholars in philosophy, rhetoric, humanities and civil law. The educational foundations of the period owe much to the humanist belief in the relationship between education and the nobility of service to the realm.

7 Lisbon, central market for the spices of Asia, was the heart of a Portuguese empire that expanded east to the Indian Ocean and the Moluccas and west to Brazil. The population of this cosmopolitan city increased from about 50,000 in 1500 to more than 100,000 by the end of the sixteenth century. Similar developments in Amsterdam, Madrid, Antwerp, London and Paris were integral to the rise of the modern states. Capital cities, already centres of trade, also became the base of government and of court life.

8 Political propaganda in Reformation Germany is typified by this woodcut of a figure brandishing the banner of freedom. The development of printing, the growing respectability of vernacular languages and a period of religious and political conflict gave rise in the early sixteenth century to cartoons and broadsheets as a means of persuasion. Pictorial representation had the widest appeal in an age of limited literacy. Monks were depicted as wolves and the enemies of Luther were caricatured. The method of contrasting woodcuts in juxtaposition was employed frequently. In one the Ascension of Christ was shown next to the descent of the pope into hell.

England in the 15th century

The period from the deposition in 1399 of Richard II (in favour of his cousin, Henry of Lancaster) to the death of Richard III on the field of Bosworth in 1485 is among the most turbulent in English political history. The murders of Richard II, Henry VI and Edward V, and the violent death of Richard III, illustrate the inability of the Crown to establish the line of succession clearly enough and rule firmly enough to rise above faction.

An insecure throne

The claim of Henry IV (reigned 1399–1413) was powerfully supported by conquest and parliamentary title. Henry V's overwhelming popularity put the question of succession into abeyance while he lived and during his son's minority, but the feebleness of the adult Henry VI (reigned 1422–60; 1470–1) raised it anew. Richard, Duke of York (1411–60), popular as the enemy of the court favourites, had a strong hereditary claim to the throne. After his death his son succeeded in driving out Henry and reigning as Edward IV (reigned 1461–83) [9] – although not securely until he had extinguished the Lan-castrian dynasty after its short-lived restoration [7, 8] at the hands of the Earl of War-wick, "the Kingmaker" [Key], in 1470–1.

Factional dispute arose again during the minority of Edward's son, Edward V (1470–83), in 1483 and he was quickly imprisoned and almost certainly murdered as one of the "princes in the Tower" by his uncle Richard, Duke of Gloucester (1452–85), who reigned as Richard III (1483–5). The invasion of Henry VI's half-nephew, Henry Tudor (1457–1509), rallied the numerous enemies of the king but it was many years before Henry VII, his weak hereditary claim bolstered by marriage to the sister of Edward V, would sit securely on the throne.

Areas of consolidation

This political turbulence, although it bred insecurity, did not prevent solid progress and development of English wealth [1] and institutions. Parliament, by 1400 the essential organ of royal co-operation with the landed classes of the shires began by 1500 to command increasing respect. The courts of justice [2] were sustained by a vocal and pow-erful body of common lawyers. The traditional bodies that governed the counties and boroughs generally increased their autonomy: the counties in the hands of local gentry as justices of the peace (JPs) and the boroughs under their new charters of incorporation as independent legal entities. For the Church it was a time of peaceful enjoyment of traditional revenues.

The letters of the Paston family of Nor-folk reveal the intricate web of local and national institutions, secular and ecclesias-tical, and the need for patrons, connections and friends at court to use them effectively. Threatened by powerful neighbours in his inheritance from John Fastolf (c. 1378–1459), John Paston (1421–66) spent several months in London in 1465 seeking remedy from the law and help from patrons. The Wars of the Roses [6] did not seriously disturb the fortunes of such people.

The limits of ambition

Historians once attributed many of the polit-ical disturbances of the century to the over-whelming power of the nobility and their

1 Trade in northwest Europe increased markedly during the 15th century and England participated fully in the boom. The nation imported furs and corn from the Baltic, wine from south-ern Europe and spices from the East. Cloth was the main English export. The Hanseatic League of north German towns won trade concessions in several English ports in the 1370s and it dominated Lon-don's trade with the Baltic, where the League had a virtual monopoly. The Genoese dominated the trade with the south that was centred on Southampton. But Eng-lish merchant adven-turers gradually in-creased their share of the trade during the 15th century.

Major trade routes
- ▲ Cloth
- ■ Linen
- ■ Canvas
- ▼ Wine
- ▲ Silk
- ○ Spices
- □ Fish
- ◐ Timber
- ▲ Furs
- ■ Salt
- ▼ Fruit
- ▲ Glass
- ◐ Grain
- ■ Oil

2 At the Court of Common Pleas, the plaintiff spoke in a kneeling position. Although courts were subject to intimida-tion, the increasing influence of the legal profession and the independence of judges such as Chief Justice Fortescue suggests that on many occasions they re-fused to be corrupted.

3 A yeoman's cottage at Didbrook, Glou-cestershire, is typical of the stone or half-timbered houses put up in the 15th century which reflected the grow-ing prosperity of the independent rural land-owner. From the mid-14th century, land-lords increasingly rented or leased out the demesne since the fall in rural population made it hard to farm in the old way; the con-sequent new class of small farmers, freed from feudal obligations, strengthened their hold on the land and pro-vided a new basis for rural prosperity.

4 William Caxton (c. 1422–91) printed *The Game and Playe of Chesse* in Bruges shortly before he moved to London in 1476. Caxton was the first English printer and his books reached a far wider audience than could afford to buy manuscripts.

5 The Lollards regarded the Bible as the sole authority of religious truth and inveighed against the wealth and worldliness of the Church. They were the disciples of John Wycliffe (c. 1328–84) who had denounced clerical authority and the worship of images. After a "rising" in 1414 the Lollards were subjected again to persecution and public burning. This picture shows the prison chamber in which Richard Hunne, a rich merchant accused of holding unofficial religious services, was found dead in 1514.

hired henchmen, recruited to serve them for pay or political favour, without the moral or social obligations of earlier feudalism. "Bastard feudalism" – the short-term recruitment of military retinues and local agents from among the gentry by formidable political figures – was certainly practised, but these "empires" of patronage were never very solid. The great nobility might indulge in affrays like the Battle of Nibley Green (1469) between the Berkeley and Talbot families, but so did respectable gentlemen such as the Pastons. Moreover, "bastard feudalism" restrained potential troublemakers by associating them with great political factions.

For most of the century the nobility co-operated remarkably well to govern the country. Powerful captains such as Richard Beauchamp, Earl of Warwick (1382–1438), hoped the Lancastrian kings would lead them in victorious and profitable Continental war, and until the English were finally expelled in 1453 men such as Warwick had more to gain by exploiting the French than by civil war.

During Henry VI's long minority (1422–42) co-operative rule by the king's Council proved a successful and generally popular experiment, despite the rivalry of Henry Beaufort and Humphrey, Duke of Gloucester (1391–1447). The financial weakness of the Crown became an increasing problem however, and this, combined with the unpopularity of the queen and Henry's lapse into madness allowed the dormant claims of York to acquire genuine support during the 1450s.

The social progress and cultural achievements of the century were considerable. The rise of the independent yeoman farmer [3], the cloth-maker, the wool exporter and the small-town merchant encouraged a multitude of local enterprises, to the general profit. Such men were usually literate, increasingly so as printed books became more readily available [4]. English architecture, both ecclesiastical as in the magnificent King's College Chapel, Cambridge, or domestic as in Tattershall Castle, reached the zenith of its brilliantly distinctive Perpendicular phase. Whatever the troubles of the monarchy these achievements remained.

Richard Neville, Earl of Warwick (1428–71), called "the Kingmaker", supported the York claim to the throne. Upon the Yorkists' victory in battle he received vast tracts of land and important posts of state. At first a dominant influence on Edward IV, he then went out of favour, engineered the brief restoration of Henry VI and was killed fighting at Barnet.

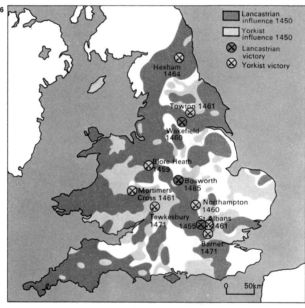

6 The Wars of the Roses were fought between descendants of Edward III. There was little consistent support from any particular area for either Lancastrian or Yorkist claimant to the throne, although from 1461 the Lancastrians relied on the support of the "reivers" of the Scottish borders.

7 The confused Henry VI was taken from the Tower and restored to the throne in a ceremony at St Paul's in 1470. His wife, Margaret of Anjou, was tenacious in keeping the Lancastrian cause alive in spite of his madness. Henry had become king in 1422, aged nine months. He was finally murdered in 1471 after the return of Edward IV.

8 At the battle of Barnet (April 1471), Edward IV defeated his former ally Warwick and cleared the way for his own victory the following month over the forces of Margaret of Anjou and her son, the Lancastrian heir, who was killed fighting. Although many of the leaders of the defeated side might lose their heads after such a battle, it was not impossible for their supporters from the gentry to survive by offering their services to their victors. The wars hardly affected the lives of the poor.

9 Edward IV had political as well as military talents, and despite his light-hearted manner he was an intelligent, determined king. His centralizing policies, particularly in the financial sphere, laid the ground for those of the Tudors.

10 The execution of Edward Beaufort, Duke of Somerset, followed his capture in the Battle of Tewkesbury (1471), the final Yorkist victory that restored Edward IV. Many Lancastrians were executed for treason after summary trial by military law.

KEY

Scotland 1314–1560

Early in the War of Independence (1306–14) against England, the Scots had made the "auld alliance" with France – an agreement between the two countries to act together against England. This alliance was renewed at various times during the next three centuries although it is doubtful whether it brought advantages to Scotland.

Conflict with England and the clans

Peace was eventually made some years after 1314, but as Edward III (reigned 1327–77), the young English king, began to assert himself it ceased to be kept [Key]. In 1332 the English king allowed Edward (died 1363) the son of John Balliol (reigned 1292–6), to try to reclaim Scotland from David II (reigned 1329–71), the son of Robert Bruce. Defeat forced David to flee to France and the conflict became absorbed in the Hundred Years War between England and France. At various times in the 14th and 15th centuries Scotland became involved in this conflict.

In spite of frequent wars, which particularly damaged the trade of the principal Scottish towns – those in southern Scotland – the economy developed in this period, although the characteristic features of a primitive structure still adhered to it. From 1349 to 1350 the Black Death struck Scotland as it struck the rest of Europe and this plague returned several times, but because it became mainly an urban pestilence and Scottish towns remained very small, the country did not suffer greatly.

A more serious long-term development in the fourteenth century was the building up of the two branches of the great baronial family of Douglas, descended from Bruce's second-in-command, James Douglas (1286–c. 1330). This family became powerfully esconced in the Border area, where at times it carried on negotiations or wars with English Border families as if it were an independent power. The Lordship of the Isles under the Macdonalds held a similar almost independent position in the Western Highlands and islands. Great independent aristocratic families could often supplant the king in the collection of his revenue and coerce and corrupt the local church, placing members of their own family into the better-paid ecclesiastical positions. Nepotism was not confined to the nobles, many kings also used the Church to provide regular incomes for their bastard offspring.

The power of the Crown

James I (reigned 1406–37) was the first in a series of vigorous, often impetuous, short-lived kings who had a significant effect on the institutions of their country in their turbulent reigns. His reign saw the creation of Scotland's first university, at St Andrews, and the use of Parliament by the king as a means of gaining support from lesser folk in his struggle with the overmighty nobility [3]. The king also began the process by which a professional central court, instead of the King's Council, was developed to hear cases. Under James V (reigned 1513–42), this Court of Session obtained a more regular supply of money for the Crown by increased taxation. This provided funds for the Court – an important development towards professionalism in Scottish law.

James II (reigned 1437–60) reduced the power of the Douglases by the extermination

1 **Scottish troops and their French** allies are shown here attacking Wark Castle in 1385, one of the lesser English Border castles. The "auld alliance" meant that Scottish forces frequently became involved in the Hundred Years War. This illumination is from Froissart's *Chronicles* of the 15th century.

2 **The Black Douglas family's conflict** with a succession of Scottish kings well illustrates the struggle between the nobility and the Crown in medieval Scotland. During the 15th century the power of the Douglas family in the Border area posed a growing threat to the Crown until they were finally suppressed by James II.

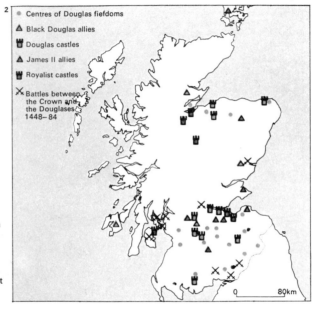

- Centres of Douglas fiefdoms
- Black Douglas allies
- Douglas castles
- James II allies
- Royalist castles
- Battles between the Crown and the Douglases 1448–84

80km

3 **James I** succeeded to the Scottish throne in 1406 at the age of 12, when he was held captive by the English. He remained a prisoner until 1424 when he was released in return for a large ransom. He returned, determined to assert the power of the Crown and to give the Scottish Parliament an importance and authority similar to that of the English Parliament. Under his reign it introduced taxes, passed laws and reforms and supervised trade. A period of vigorous reform began that touched many aspects of daily life, extending the Crown's control. In 1426 a court for civil cases was created that sat three times a year to settle disputes.

4 **James III's reign ended** with an armed rising of the nobility, his defeat at Sauchieburn near Stirling in 1488, and his murder after the battle. This 19th-century print shows the battle with Stirling Castle, where James had in vain sought refuge, in the background. The nobles' rebellion was probably motivated more by James's personality than by his policies: he was suspicious, avaricious and unconcerned with affairs of state. The relatively short reigns of Scottish monarchs, often ending violently amidst intrigue and conspiracy, resulted in a series of long minorities, beginning with James I, that undermined royal authority. For 200 years no Scottish ruler succeeded to the throne as an adult.

of the leaders [2]. James IV (reigned 1488–1513) in 1493 attempted to increase royal authority in the Highlands by destroying the Lordship of the Isles. He was unable to replace this power with effective central rule, and the main result was to leave the Highlands broken into separate and often warring clans. Efforts by successive Scottish kings to have courts appropriate to Renaissance princes led to the cultivation of the arts by James III (reigned 1460–88) [4] – who thereby annoyed his nobility – some splendid poetry in the reign of James IV [5] and great spending by James V on royal palaces.

Protestantism established
James IV's marriage in 1503 to Margaret Tudor (1489–1541) [7], elder daughter of the English King, Henry VII (reigned 1485–1509), was of great long-term significance to both countries, for it led to the union of the crowns in 1603 and, even before that, in the later sixteenth century, to peace between them. But peace was not achieved at first. James IV was drawn into war with Henry VIII (reigned 1509–47) in support of

his renewed alliance with France. James invaded northern England and was killed in an overwhelming Scottish defeat at Flodden Edge in 1513.

In spite of this disaster the Scots clung to the French alliance, partly because of the ruthless attempt of Henry VIII to dominate their country [7]. In particular, Henry hoped to marry his son Edward (1537–53) to James V's daughter and successor, Mary. But James's marriage allied him to the rising family of Guise, who came to represent the Catholic party in France. Meanwhile the weaknesses and corruption of the Catholic Church and the political needs of the government encouraged the promotion of a powerful group of Protestant nobles.

In 1560 the joint issues of external alliance and religion led to a brief war between the Catholic and French regent, Mary of Guise, and the Protestant lords in alliance with the English. The victory went to Protestantism and alliance with England, and this was confirmed in the Reformation Parliament of 1560, when the authority of the pope in Scotland was abolished.

David II (left) was captured by the English at the Battle of Neville's Cross in 1346 which effectively ended his invasion attempt. The English king Edward III (right) held David prisoner for 11 years before freeing him in return for a large ransom. This proved to be a crippling burden for Scotland and taxes were greatly increased to meet the debt. The Scottish economy, already undermined by wars with England, was weakened still further, although over half the ransom money was finally paid. David also debased the coinage by minting more coins to meet the debt, a precedent followed by his successors – the first Stewart kings.

5 One of the more attractive personalities among the early Scottish kings, James IV styled himself in the role of a Renaissance monarch. He built new royal palaces, notably at Falkland and Linlithgow, and encouraged learning and the arts. But he was not so successful in foreign affairs: in support of France, James invaded England in 1513 but his army was defeated at Flodden Edge and he was slain.

6 Margaret Tudor lacked the political drive and skill of her brother, Henry VIII, while sharing similar marriage difficulties. Thus, following the death of her husband, James IV at Flodden, her personal life was a considerable source of instability during the minority of James V. The man shown with her here [left] is probably the Duke of Albany (c. 1484–1536), who acted as regent until 1524.

7 The formidable fortress at Stirling has played a major role in Scottish history. Probably built in the 12th century, it was the birthplace and residence of several monarchs, rivalling the capital of Edinburgh.

8 The Augustinian Border abbey of Jedburgh was one of the richest foundations in Scotland. During the 16th century it was burnt three times by the invading armies of Henry VIII.

45

The Tudors and the new nation state

When Henry Tudor (1457–1509) [1, 2] took the English Crown from the last Plantagenet king on 22 August 1485, he became master of a rich kingdom. Its fertility and its mineral wealth appeared to a Venetian observer of 1500 to be "greater than those of any other country of Europe"; its trade in the northern and western seas was increasing rapidly, and its population was slowly growing. Yet the monarchy itself had minimal prestige, ruined by the mental incapacity of Henry VI (reigned 1422–61; 1470–1) and the confusion of the Wars of the Roses.

The establishment of the Tudor dynasty

In 1485 few estimated that Henry VII's new dynasty would last long; Henry had to earn respect. There were potentially dangerous challengers to his throne: Simnel Lambert (c. 1475–1525), who pretended to be the imprisoned Earl of Warwick (the last male Plantagenet) and who momentarily won over Ireland; and Perkin Warbeck (c. 1474–99) whose claim to be Richard of York, the younger of the princes murdered in the Tower, was taken up by many European rulers. Henry survived partly because of his prudent statecraft, but primarily through the desire of all classes for firm leadership and an end to political uncertainty.

Henry is said to have introduced a "new monarchy", but actually it was no more than the new life breathed into traditional institutions by a strong personality. Although parsimonious, he understood the value of ceremony [2] and pageantry [4] and his court impressed foreigners. Behind this façade lay the increasingly solid support of most of his subjects. The old nobility, weakened but not extinguished by the civil wars, was happier with a subordinate role than before. Henry treated most of these families with respect: he passed the Statute of Livery and Maintenance in 1487 against keeping private armies, but it did not seriously affect their retinues or their local influence.

The king rested his power upon the traditional rulers of the counties, the gentry as justices of the peace; he gave them stronger authority than before and framed his policies with a careful eye on what they would accept. In particular, he emulated Edward IV (reigned 1641–70; 1471–83) in a policy of peace and therefore low expenditure: he avoided straining the loyalty of the gentry with extensive taxation [3]. The main achievement of Henry VII was to nurse the monarchy back to its traditional role of leadership by avoiding serious confrontation with any group of subjects.

The court of Henry VIII

Henry VIII (reigned 1509–47) [Key] was the first Prince of Wales to succeed peacefully since 1422. Far more obviously than his father, the second Tudor king was a typical Renaissance prince: well educated, polyglot, author of a sprightly theological work against Luther, accomplished on lute and harp, a jouster and a bowman, combining magnificence with intellectual power and political will exactly as the age demanded of its rulers. His court was a centre for the new learning: his ministers Richard Fox (c. 1448–1528) and Thomas Wolsey (c. 1475–1530) [6] were great patrons, and his later chancellor, Thomas More (c. 1478–1535), embodied more than any contemporary Englishman the

1 The striking of medals was a characteristic form of propaganda in the 15th and 16th centuries. Henry VII used them together with other projections of the royal image in pageantry and artifice to bolster his weak hereditary claims to the throne. His marriage with Elizabeth of York (1465–1503), shown here with Henry, was thought to give him a much better title to the throne than the right of conquest or the Act of Parliament upholding it, both of which could be reversed. His use of the "Tudor Rose", combining both the red and white roses, symbols of the two factions in the Wars of the Roses, exemplified his desire to appear as unifier of the nation.

2 Henry VII and his queen with their children are depicted with St George and the dragon on this altarpiece, probably made for the royal palace at Sheen. The prominence given to the queen in early Tudor art was new. This painting commemorated Henry's patronage of the Order of the Garter, which honoured equally the old nobility and new soldiers of fortune. Henry did not intend to crush the nobility into submission but rather to forge a new alliance with them. But his unpopular taxation seemed to show that Henry had autocratic intentions. His ministers Richard Empson (d. 1510) and Edmund Dudley (1462–1510) were condemned for treason after the king's death.

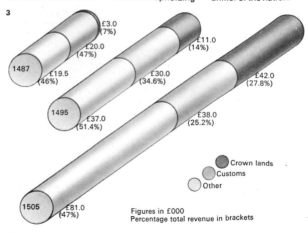

3 Henry VII's revenue grew dramatically in his reign, based on an extremely careful management of Crown estates. Henry aimed to "live of his own" and tried to make even war profitable, by keeping costs low and suing for peace, thus staying independent of both nobility and Parliament. In this way he hoped to establish a strong monarchy, which he regarded as a vital prerequisite for the establishment of English political authority in Western Europe.

4 The baptism of Arthur (1486–1502) Henry's eldest son, was an occasion for a typical royal procession. The name Arthur was chosen to echo that of the semi-mythical British hero whose cult was at its height in the 15th century and to stress the Welsh origins of the Tudors. Similar events were organized at the start of his reign for each main town, to affirm the glory of his rule. Henry also planned a major addition to Westminster Abbey, begun in 1509.

Figures from chart 3:
- 1487: £3.0 (7%), £20.0 (47%), £19.5 (46%)
- 1495: £11.0 (14%), £30.0 (34.6%), £37.0 (51.4%)
- 1505: £42.0 (27.8%), £38.0 (25.2%), £81.0 (47%)

Crown lands / Customs / Other

Figures in £000
Percentage total revenue in brackets

cultivated practical intellect of the Renaissance. Henry's cruelty in the interest of state, dramatically evidenced in the fate of four of his six wives (two of whom were executed and two divorced), only underlines the brilliant, thunderous atmosphere of his court.

Whether wittingly or not, Henry's use of the revived authority of the Crown had, in the form of the Reformation, revolutionary effects on England. He was initially content to work through powerful ministers, the first of whom, Thomas Wolsey, cut a figure as a cardinal hardly less magnificent than his master's. Wolsey established a position of unprecedented dominance in Church and State. Even before the Reformation he planned a wide-ranging reform of the Church, but it was unachieved at his fall from power in 1529, and his legacy was a hierarchy henceforth subservient to the king alone.

Cromwell and the bureaucracy

By 1534 Henry had found in Wolsey's former servant Thomas Cromwell (c. 1485–1540) [7] a minister to carry through all the implications of the break with Rome, and

realize the new potential power of the monarchy. A hard, practical man, Cromwell used the growing authority of Parliament. In his popular reformation of the Church, he was supported by the gentry, whom he manipulated with his system of patronage and an unprecedented network of informers [9]. Yet even Cromwell was only an instrument of government, dismissed and executed by the king in 1540 when his enemies won the ear of Henry.

Henry VIII was by then the master of a terrifying royal power, sustained by an efficient and much reformed bureaucratic machine, and able to impose his own middle way between the proponents of a radical reformation and the adherents of the old, Catholic ways. His achievement, a remarkable display of statecraft, was to have understood and given a lead to the strongest strands in public opinion, from which, as institutionalized in Parliament, he never moved very far. By the time of his death in 1547, the Tudor monarchs had become the natural expression of the growing national confidence of sixteenth-century England.

Henry VIII was an imperious man whose will dominated the political history of his reign. His court was a focus for all kinds of artistic patronage and with John Skelton (1460–1529), the poet, as his tutor he was probably the first English king to know Italian and Spanish. He took advantage of the shrewd diplomacy of his father to make England a respected state, fighting many costly, although rarely glorious, wars. In this policy he claimed to embody the new assertiveness and aggression of Englishmen overseas that also found expression in the steady erosion of the Hanseatic League's monopoly of English trade. The culmination of this nationalism was the Church's break with Rome.

5 The *Henry Grace à Dieu*, a carrack of 1,000 tonnes was built in 1510–14 and became Henry VIII's flagship. By 1510 Henry had won a strong position, holding the balance of power between the Hapsburgs and Valois, but he was never able effectively to assert his authority in Europe although he defeated the French in 1513.

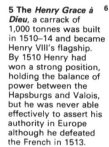

6 Thomas Wolsey, who had ambitions to become pope and to dominate European politics, was the chief architect of Henry VIII's foreign policy before 1529. As papal legate he had great power in the English Church, and seemed almost independent of the king's jurisdiction.

8 Walmer Castle, Kent, was one of the fortresses built by Henry VIII in 1539 as part of a system of coastal defence during a brief alliance of his enemies the Emperor Charles V and Francis I of France. These castles used the most modern style of fortification.

9 The Pilgrimage of Grace was a rebellion of the north in 1536 in opposition to the Oath of Supremacy demanded of all ecclesiastics in 1534. This picture of 1539 shows the judge leaving the execution of Thomas Marshall, abbot of Colchester, who verbally supported the rebellion, uttered treasonable ideas in private and who was determined to resist the suppression of his monastery. It was typical of Cromwell's rule that men could be executed for opinions expressed in private.

7 Thomas Cromwell was the architect of the English Reformation. His ruthless determination, born of soldiering in the Italian wars and in business experience in The Netherlands, served him in good stead in Wolsey's service and later in the king's. A genuine supporter of reform, he believed that the king should be the head of the English Church. He excelled as parliamentary manager, marshalling the broad support that the Tudor monarchy enjoyed, to create a great series of Acts establishing the royal supremacy and suppressing the monasteries. His extraordinary executive ability helped him to enforce them through his system of informers and active control of the JPs. He made many enemies, particularly amongst the nobility, and in 1540 he was executed for treason.

The Reformation

When Martin Luther (1483–1546) posted his *Ninety-Five Theses* on the door of the Castle Church, Wittenberg, Saxony, on 31 October 1517, he was initiating a religious debate in the traditional fashion. But the consequences of his protest were revolutionary and heralded a new historical era: the end of the dominance of a single European Catholic Church in the Middle Ages; the creation of "reformed" or Protestant Churches; a century and a half of "religious" wars that convulsed the emerging nation states of Europe; and a new understanding of the Christian faith that has personally affected millions of men and women throughout the world. All these developments are historically part of "the Reformation".

The original intention

The term Reformation precisely describes Luther's original intentions. His *Ninety-Five Theses* [Key] were an attack on abuses inside the Roman Catholic Church. He denounced the frivolous uses to which the pope put his vast wealth and in particular the way in which he was raising money by the sale of "indulgences" [1], documents that the pardoner Tetzel claimed gave any purchaser automatic remission of his sins.

The history of the Catholic Church had for centuries, however, been a sequence of "re-formations", and for more than a decade before 1517 John Colet (*c.* 1467–1519), Erasmus [3] and Thomas More (*c.* 1478–1535) had been working to cleanse the Church of its follies. What made Luther more than merely a traditional reformer was his deliberate personal conviction coupled with the accidental political situation at that moment in Europe's development.

Luther's complaint against indulgences went beyond distaste of the money involved to a rejection of the whole concept of spiritual book-keeping with God. Luther felt a sense of infinite personal unworthiness that no amount of good works could ever overcome. As an Augustinian monk, a doctor of theology and then professor at the University of Wittenberg he had mortified himself mercilessly but still felt impure, repulsive, sinful – unworthy even to approach God's presence. Only blind faith could save him.

From this conviction was born the doctrine of "justification by faith", which was to inspire the spiritual side of the Reformation. It involved great emphasis on the single gesture of faith – "conversion" – and rejected reliance on the priest as a middleman between the believer and God.

The effect on Germany

Luther's ideas, broadcast by the medium of the printing press, had a dynamic impact throughout Germany and were given immeasurable help in taking root by a fatal four-year delay on the part of the Catholic authorities. Pope Leo X (1475-1521), who hoped to strengthen his personal power by manipulating the imminent election of a new Holy Roman Emperor, adopted the traditional papal tactic of supporting a weak candidate for this position that carried so much influence in Germany. He had already selected as his protégé Frederick the Wise of Saxony (1463–1525), Luther's own ruler and protector. Thus Luther's teachings were not officially condemned until 1521 at the Diet (congress) of Worms.

3 The translation of the New Testament by Erasmus (1466–1536) was an example of Catholic efforts to reform the Church from within. Erasmus satirized the follies and superstitions of the Church, articulating the dissatisfaction that many felt without wishing to divide Christendom against itself. At works such as *In Praise of Folly* (1509) even the pope felt safe to laugh. But Erasmus's intention was more to goad than to reform and he had little hesitation in denouncing the schism that Luther created.

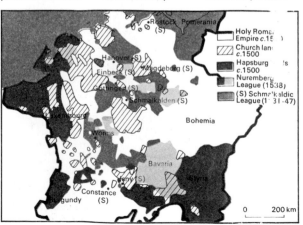

1 The sale of indulgences was to raise money for the rebuilding of St Peter's in Rome. An indulgence was originally a remission from punishment for a sin and was conditional on the sinner's sincere repentance. But in the Middle Ages, indulgences came to be granted to sinners who did good works, such as going on crusades or contributing money to the building of a church. This led to the idea that forgiveness could be purchased as a commodity.

2 The religious orders of monks, nuns and friars provoked hostility. To ordinary people and reformers they seemed idle and excessively wealthy, spending their money on their own enjoyment – not in the service of God. They were envied by rulers for their valuable town properties and country estates.

4 Encouraged by Luther's success and sharing some of his ideals, the peasants of the southwest and central German states rose against their rulers in 1524. But Luther denounced their complaints – mainly political social and economic – and in the face of stern repression the revolts collapsed.

5 The Holy Roman Empire, in theory the political expression of the Catholic Church, was in practice a grouping of rival German states. The Reformation provided the chance many of them had been waiting for to defy the power of the emperor. The Protestant rulers formed themselves into the Schmalkaldic League in 1531 and the emperor replied with the Nuremberg League in 1538. War seemed imminent but a compromise was reached in 1539.

Key map legend:
- Holy Roman Empire *c.*15)
- Church land *c.*1500
- Hapsburg s *c.*1500
- Nuremberg League (1538)
- (S) Schmalkaldic League (1531-47)

Frederick the Wise then sent Luther into hiding for a year and the new emperor, Charles V [6], had neither the time nor the power to control this defiance to his authority. In 1520 Luther had urged princes to throw off the unbiblical authority Rome claimed over the Church in their states and rulers were not slow to profit from this invitation. In 1529 all the Lutheran states and towns in Germany put their names to a "Protestation" against the emperor – the origin of the term Protestant – and after more than 25 years of conflict the Peace of Augsburg in 1555 recognized the right of a ruler to determine his country's religion.

England and Switzerland

The principle of the rights of a ruler had been exercised by Henry VIII (1491–1547) in his Reformation in England, which was confirmed by the Act of Supremacy of 1534. It was essentially a forcible transfer of the supreme power over the Church from the pope in Rome to the English sovereign. As in Sweden in 1527 and Denmark and Norway in 1536-9, there was little pretence that

Thomas Cromwell's dissolution of the monasteries (1536–40) was any more than a confiscation of the Church's wealth.

Only in Switzerland was the "purification" of the old Church's images and decorations a matter of genuine Christian austerity. In Zurich in the 1520s Huldreich Zwingli (1484–1531) had the church organs destroyed because their sound was profane while the citizens as a whole were banded into a new democracy of the faithful.

In Geneva [9] after 1541 Jean Calvin (1509–64) created a holy city that gave shelter to more than 6,000 refugees fleeing from persecution in France, Italy, Spain and, during Mary's reign, from England as well. Calvin's book *Institutes of the Christian Religion* (1536) enshrined the other great Reformation theme of "predestination" – that God chooses His own elect. It was the buoyancy of those who felt the assurance of their own election that inspired the Calvinists in the Netherlands as well as the Huguenots in France, the Presbyterians in Scotland and the Puritans in England and later in the New World.

Martin Luther, an Augustinian monk, was the first great inspirer of the Reformation. On a visit to Rome in 1511 he was appalled by the wealth and spiritual emptiness of the Catholic Church so different from the ideals of primitive Christianity. These ideals became his watchword as he argued against the Church's corruption in his *Ninety-Five Theses* (1517). Luther was not a revolutionary, for he retained vestments and certain Catholic ceremonies, but in his reformed Church the communion cup was given to the congregation, saints were no longer objects of special prayers and Church wealth went to pastoral and educational activities.

6 The Emperor Charles V (1500–58) inherited the lands belonging to the Austrian and Burgundian Hapsburgs and also the kingdoms of Aragon and Castile. This provoked the fear of France, which fought throughout his rule to prevent encirclement, and encouraged German Protestant princes to defy his authority. Defeated in his ambition to reunite Christendom, he gave his possessions to his brother and son.

8 The Bible replaced the priest as the ordinary man's spiritual authority. The scriptures were translated from the Latin and Greek and offered to the people in their own languages – notably German in a translation by Luther, and English in the King James version of 1611.

9 Under John Calvin the Swiss city state of Geneva became the most influential single centre of the Reformation. Its citizens lived under the strict moral rule of the Calvinist Church, which readily burned opponents such as the anti-Trinitarian "heretic" Michael Servetus in 1553.

7 Fountains Abbey was among the finest religious houses destroyed during the dissolution of the monasteries in England (1536–40). The first act (1536) based dissolution on whether a monastery enjoyed an annual income of less than £200. The Act for the Dissolution of the Greater Monasteries (1539) completed the process. Pensions were paid to monks refusing to join the secular clergy and the Crown took the rest. A few lands were kept by the Crown, a few given away, but most were sold to gentleman farmers, thus creating a new class of landowners with the strongest reasons for staying loyal to the new order.

Key	
	Catholic
	Lutheran
	Calvinist
	Anglican
	Greek Orthodox
⚑	Religious centres

Canterbury

Wittenberg

Augsburg

Geneva

Rome

0   500 km

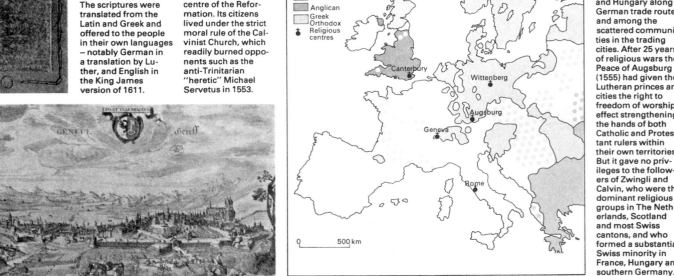

10 By 1560 Lutheranism had spread from north Germany to Scandinavia, Poland and Hungary along German trade routes and among the scattered communities in the trading cities. After 25 years of religious wars the Peace of Augsburg (1555) had given the Lutheran princes and cities the right to freedom of worship, in effect strengthening the hands of both Catholic and Protestant rulers within their own territories. But it gave no privileges to the followers of Zwingli and Calvin, who were the dominant religious groups in The Netherlands, Scotland and most Swiss cantons, and who formed a substantial Swiss minority in France, Hungary and southern Germany.

The English Reformation

The English Reformation had as its particular event Henry VIII's desire for an annulment of his marriage; this the pope was unwilling to grant him. The more general discontent was related to that which brought religious turmoil to the Holy Roman Empire, France and The Netherlands in the early sixteenth century. The Church's taxes drained money from the country to finance the pope's political ambitions; ordained priests could seek exemption from secular penalties; and the pope claimed to appoint higher clergy and bishops. The Church's superstitious practices, too, came under attack. There was a tradition of opposition to the pope that had grown up with John Wycliffe (c. 1328–84) and which had never completely died out, and a mood of questioning old assumptions in the light of Renaissance humanism.

Nationalism and the Reformation

The Reformation evolved from national opposition to external interference. Wycliffe's ideas, although mainly dealing with doctrinal matters, implied a revolt against papal authority. He translated the Bible into English and suggested that the laity should make their own evaluations about religion. Such ideas anticipated those of Martin Luther (1483–1546); but by the early sixteenth century opposition by a nation-state to the universal claims of the papacy was now conceivable. Henry VII (reigned 1485–1509) had built up a monarchy strong enough to win the respect of the powers of Europe. Henry VIII (reigned 1509–47) [Key] was determined to be an ideal Renaissance prince, supreme at home and ostentatiously magnificent abroad.

Henry feared that he would be unable to have a male heir by his first wife Catherine of Aragon (1485–1536). The pope influenced by the Holy Roman Emperor Charles V, Catherine's nephew, was reluctant to annul the marriage. In 1533, Henry's mistress, Anne Boleyn [1], became pregnant, and Thomas Cromwell (c. 1485–1540) said that the problem could be speedily resolved by claiming that the king was not answerable to the pope. The marriage was annulled by Thomas Cranmer (1489–1556) [5], who was made Archbishop of Canterbury to deal with the divorce issue, and in 1533 Catherine was forbidden to appeal to Rome. The Reformation Parliament (1529–36) was directed at every stage of the break with Rome to enact the necessary legislation. In 1534 it passed the crucial Act of Supremacy, declaring Henry to be "Supreme Head" of the English Church, and then sanctioned the dissolution of the monasteries by the Crown.

The introduction of Protestantism

Henry VIII wished to be head of the English Church, but wished to dissociate it from the Lutheran ideas that were spreading through the Holy Roman Empire. Cromwell and Cranmer, however, urged him to adopt a more Protestant attitude, and in 1538 an English translation of the Bible was ordered to be placed in every church.

The reign of Edward VI (1547–53) saw Protestant doctrine more fully accepted [2]. Edward was a minor, and the Protector Somerset (1506–52) relaxed the laws against heretics and welcomed radical foreign preachers to the country. The clergy were allowed to marry and the new prayer books

1 Anne Boleyn (c. 1507–36), was secretly married to Henry in January 1533 to ensure the legitimacy of the child that she was carrying. In the event, however, she gave birth to a daughter, Elizabeth, and not the male heir for which Henry had been hoping. During Anne's later pregnancy, Henry fell in love with Jane Seymour (c. 1509–37), accused Anne of adultery and incest, and had her executed in 1536.

2 Henry on his deathbed is shown giving pious instructions to his young son, Edward VI, to ensure the stability of the Reformation. Also shown are members of Edward's council who carried out many of the most extreme Protestant policies to be adopted in England in the 16th century. Among these was an order against "superstitious" images in churches, which led to much iconoclasm. Chantries – chapels used specifically for the purpose of praying for the souls of those recently dead and thought to be in purgatory – were also abolished in 1547. Their foundations had often included provision for schools, and so many schools were set up under Edward.

3 The prayer book of 1549 introduced a national liturgy in place of the various local "uses" practised previously. A rebellion in the West Country objected to the use of the vernacular in the service, claiming that it was like "a Christmas game". Doctrinally the book was a compromise and was followed by a more Protestant version three years later.

4 Mary I refused to repudiate her mother's faith during Henry's reign, and after her succession she fortified her restoration of Catholicism by marrying Philip II of Spain, leader of the Counter-Reformation. Her ruthless determination to end Protestantism in England earned her the title of "Bloody Mary", but in private affairs she was gentle.

5 Thomas Cranmer ennobled the Reformation with the majestic rhythms of his translations of the Bible and liturgy, but politically he was weak and pliant. On occasion he went against his personal convictions to defer to royal authority. He was the theological inspiration behind the innovations of Edward's reign. Mary made him recant his Protestant faith, but later he renounced the recantation itself, and thrust the hand that signed it into the flames first, when burnt at the stake.

of 1549 [3] and 1552 showed a distinct turn towards Protestant doctrine.

Mary (reigned 1553–8) [4], the daughter of Catherine of Aragon, introduced a severe Catholic reaction; many Protestants were driven into exile, and nearly 300 were burnt at the stake as heretics [6]. But her repression was unpopular: Henry VIII had sold to the gentry many of the lands acquired by the dissolution of the monasteries. As a result, this class had a vested interest in opposing a full restoration of Catholicism, and welcomed the accession of Elizabeth, who, as daughter of Anne Boleyn, seemed certain to restore Protestantism.

The Anglican compromise
Elizabeth I (1533–1603) acceded to the throne in 1558, and sought a middle way between the policies of the previous two reigns. But the return of many of the Marian exiles from Calvinist Geneva and a strongly Protestant Parliament forced her to adopt a more extreme attitude than she intended. She took the title of "Supreme Governor" of the Church, hoping thereby not to offend the

Catholics; the Thirty-nine Articles of belief, to which all priests had to swear in 1563, contained ambiguous assertions acceptable to men of all current persuasions. And she also rejected all suggestions that the episcopacy should be abandoned.

In these ways, Elizabeth hoped to gain loyalty through compromise rather than to satisfy conscience, and despite constant pressure in Parliament and elsewhere from the Puritans (as the politically radical Calvinists came to be known) to modify this settlement, she assisted the Anglican Church to gain a positive identity. Some Puritans tried after the 1570s to be allowed to worship outside the Established Church. Eventually John Whitgift (c. 1530–1604) [7], drove underground all Puritan opposition throughout the country.

Fear of Catholic plots however, continued throughout Elizabeth's reign, allowing the Puritans to pose as good patriots. The Catholic threat remained constant, fuelled from abroad by Jesuit priests and support from Spain, and assisted by a few families in England itself.

Henry VIII, assisted by Cranmer, tramples the pope underfoot while monks wring their hands in despair, in this contemporary cartoon. Henry was determined to make his authority absolute in his kingdom; he claimed that this was the wish of the people.

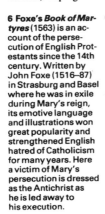

6 Foxe's *Book of Martyres* (1563) is an account of the persecution of English Protestants since the 14th century. Written by John Foxe (1516–87) in Strasburg and Basel where he was in exile during Mary's reign, its emotive language and illustrations won great popularity and strengthened English hatred of Catholicism for many years. Here a victim of Mary's persecution is dressed as the Antichrist as he is led away to his execution.

7 John Whitgift was made Archbishop of Canterbury in 1583, and although Calvinist in his personal views, he strictly enforced the laws against dissenters. His use of the Court of High Commission, the supreme ecclesiastical court of the country, was challenged as unconstitutional, but he ensured that the Puritans were broken as a political force. They reemerged strongly, however, after the accession of James I.

8 A Puritan church, shown here in a 17th-century illustration, was sparsely furnished and austere. The most extreme Puritans, led by Thomas Cartwright (c. 1535–1603) attacked the bishops, hoping to return to the principles of the early Church, accepting only biblical authority. Brownists, led by Robert Browne (c. 1550–1633) were a radical wing hoping to run the Church by a loose federation of ministers elected by their congregation.

9 Fear of "popish plots" and invasions haunted Elizabeth's reign. This illustration of the various insurrections of the Catholics since 1550 forms part of a broadsheet on which a ballad recounting the same events was printed for sale to professional balladeers. In 1570 the pope excommunicated Elizabeth and urged Catholics to depose her. A crisis of conscience ensued for previously unpolitical Catholics, who thereafter were regarded with suspicion if not actually persecuted. There was little danger of a Catholic rebellion since the Revolt of the North of 1569 had proved abortive; but several isolated plots against the queen's life continued throughout her reign, culminating in the infamous Gunpowder Plot of 1605 against James I.

The Counter-Reformation

The Reformation in the early 1500s divided Europe into the Catholic countries of the south and the Protestant countries of the north. Under the protection of the German princes Protestantism became established and the Holy Roman Empire existed in an uneasy state of religious cold war. In the sixteenth century it was believed that two religions could not co-exist in one political community. Heterodoxy, championed by the princes, was an assault upon the secular as well as the spiritual order.

Within the Catholic Church, reformist cardinals such as Gasparo Contarini (1483–1542) advocated a conciliatory policy and reform of abuses. But discussions between Catholics and Protestants at the Diet of Regensburg in 1541 revealed only the impossibility of a compromise and blasted hopes of a revived Christian unity.

Since the Lutheran Reformation a new, formidable Protestantism had assaulted the Catholic Church – the organized Church of John Calvin. As Protestants gained ground in Germany and Switzerland, and missionaries went out from Geneva to France and the Low Countries, the Catholic Church realized the need for action. Between 1536 and 1545 Pope Paul III repeatedly called for a general council, but was forced to postpone it for political reasons. The council finally met in Trent on 15 December 1545. Ostensibly this was a council for all Christendom. But the location in the Italian Alps and Pope Paul's successful coup in determining votes by representative rather than by nation ensured an Italian, papal dominance.

The new orthodoxy
Contarini's followers still hoped for reconciliation with the Protestants. Cardinal Gian Petro Caraffa (1476–1559) and his party were in no such mood. Meeting in three sessions, (1545–7, 1551–2, 1562–3) the council answered the Lutheran challenge for the first time. On all major points of theological controversy, concerning salvation, transubstantiation and the authority of the fathers, the Catholic position was reasserted with a clarity that late medieval theology had lacked. The council made token reforms of the glaring abuses. Most important, the Council of Trent reinforced the authorities of the Church from the bishops to the pope, whose supremacy was not questioned. The defenders of a new orthodoxy were already armed with the Inquisition (established in 1233) and the papal Index of prohibited books. Trent made the Roman Catholic Church one denomination among many – but a denomination that was ready to fight. Even before the council met, Ignatius Loyola (1491–1556) [2], who was appointed general of the Society of Jesus in 1541, a year after the pope's approval, had provided an army of missionaries – the Jesuits.

Beginnings of a religious war
The end of a policy of conciliation meant religious war. Where nobles and princes had emerged as the patrons of the Protestant faiths it meant civil war. In France the rival noble factions of Bourbon and Guise adopting the cause of Calvinism and Tridentine Catholicism (Roman Catholicism as reformed at the Council of Trent) began 30 years of conflict. Political ambition was often the handmaiden of religious zeal.

Catholics 1560
Lutherans 1560
Protestants 1560
Greek Orthodox 1560
Regained by Catholics 1660
Extent of Greek Orthodox by 1660
Holy Roman Empire 1560
Holy Roman Empire 1660
Religious Wars

Augsburg
Trent

0 250km

1 The Counter-Reformation in the century following the Council of Trent won back much of the territory lost to Protestantism. It was most successful in achieving a popular reconversion in Poland, where the enactment of religious toleration in 1573 led to a sudden growth in Jesuit activity in the field of education until the support of Sigismund III (r. 1587–1632) for the Jesuit cause led to the complete suppression of Protestantism. The Counter-Reformation was often marked by the banning of "heretical" books. Catholic control of higher education, supported by royal and noble families, and the denial of Protestant rights. Its success was often achieved by war.

2 Ignatius de Loyola was a Spanish nobleman born in 1491. He underwent a religious experience during a period of convalescence after being wounded in battle. After studying theology at the Sorbonne in Paris in 1534 he formed a group of devout men who swore to serve Christ and his vicar on earth, the pope. His religious order, the Society of Jesus, was strictly organized, its members being subject to rigorous discipline. The theology outlined by Loyola in his *Spiritual Exercises* has been described as a "shock tactic spiritual gymnastic". Originally, membership was confined to 60 Jesuits, but in 1540 the pope authorized the order to increase its membership without limit. By 1556 the order was firmly established in Europe and it grew greatly in size until the mid-17th century, acting as the principal agent of the Counter-Reformation. It conducted widespread missionary work.

3 William of Orange (1533–84), "the Silent", was the largest landowner in The Netherlands. He led the opposition to Philip II's erosion of the aristocratic and constitutional liberties of The Netherlands. During the war William tried to unify the provinces, which were jealous of their rights and promoted religious toleration to prevent a rift between Protestants and Catholics in their defence of common constitutional rights. Dutch independence was recognized in 1648.

4 The Massacre of St Bartholomew's Day – 24 Aug 1572 – was a slaughter of French Protestants (Huguenots). The massacre spread throughout France leading to the outbreak of civil war. Catherine de' Medici (1519–89), the French regent, alarmed at the growing Huguenot political power, plotted against the leaders and instigated the massacre.

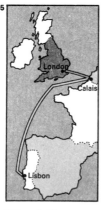

London
Calais
Lisbon

5 The rebellious Netherlands were helped in their struggle against Spain in the 1560s and 1570s by Elizabeth I of England. It became increasingly evident to Philip II that the Low Countries would not be settled while the rebels received foreign aid. In 1580 Philip successfully pressed a claim to the crown of Portugal and the acquisition of a powerful fleet, together with the increasing revenue from the Indies, perhaps persuaded him to launch the Armada. In league with leading French Catholics, Philip hoped to put in at French ports, while his regent for The Netherlands, the Duke of Parma, was to clear towns along the coast to meet the Spanish ships. Philip may have intended the conquest of England (we cannot be sure) or more probably have planned to contain the English while Parma militarily reasserted Spanish control in The Netherlands. The Armada was defeated in 1588.

The popes looked to the Catholic princes of Europe to be the secular arm of Tridentine decrees. In particular they looked to the principal heir of Charles V – Philip II of Spain (1527–98) [Key]. In an attempt to exercise greater control over the prosperous Low Countries Philip introduced the Inquisition. Only during the course of revolt did Calvinism find its champions in the defenders of the Netherlanders' privileges.

In 1555 the Peace of Augsburg had brought a temporary lull to conflict in Germany. For the rest of the century the empire remained in uneasy peace as the Hapsburgs tried to re-establish their authority and the Calvinists (not recognized in the peace) gained ground. The Catholic princes of Germany, acting independently of the emperor, formed their own political league under Maximilian of Bavaria (1573–1651).

Thirty Years War

The signal for conflict was given when the Bohemian subjects resisted the decisions of the Emperor Matthias (1557–1619) to make the staunchly Catholic Ferdinand of Styria

(1578–1637) king of the Bohemians. The Bohemians wanted neither a Hapsburg nor a Catholic. In 1618 they cast two imperial councillors from the window of the council chamber at Prague and called upon the head of the German Protestants, Frederick the Elector Palatine (1596–1632), to defend their cause [8]. Thirty years of war ensued.

The imperial forces, assisted by Maximilian, crushed Frederick and Hapsburg power was restored. By 1629 Ferdinand, now emperor, was strong enough to impose an edict restoring to the Catholic Church all lands secularized since 1552, so undermining the territorial strength of the Protestants. But the strengthening of the Hapsburgs and the identification of Spanish and imperial Hapsburgs with Catholicism brought in turn all their enemies against them. The Swedes [7], then ironically the French, under the Catholic Cardinal Richelieu [9], fought with the Protestant cause against the Hapsburgs. After 30 years of turmoil the weary Emperor Ferdinand III (1608–57) signed the Peace of Westphalia, 1648, in which he recognized the Calvinist faith within Germany.

KEY

Philip II of Spain dominated European politics in the late 16th century. Philip was looked to as the champion of the Counter-Reformation Catholic Church. In practice, as more than one pope complained, he defended first and foremost the interests of the Hapsburgs. His identification of the Hapsburgs with the Catholic interest, using the Inquisition in Spain, complicated the religious and political life of Europe and he was involved constantly in war – against the Turks, the rebellious Dutch, the French Huguenots and the English. Philip made Spain a great power, but in the process he aligned against her almost all the states of Europe.

6 after more than 20 years of civil war in France the political and religious situation was reversed. Now the Catholics feared repression and the Guise feared subjection. Catholics, formerly apologists for divine monarchy, penned tracts justifying rebellion. But Henry of Navarre, who became king in 1589, finally brought peace to France. Renouncing his former Protestantism (saying "Paris is worth a Mass") he thus separated Protestantism from the House of Bourbon. By tolerating the Huguenots in the Edict of Nantes (1598) he appeased his former allies and ended the French civil wars.

6 The Protestant Henry of Navarre (1553–1610) became heir to the French throne in 1584 after the death of the Duke of Anjou. From that date and

7 A

B

Magdeburg 1631 × Breitenfeld 1631
Lützen 1632 × Steinau 1633
× Nuremberg 1632
Nördlingen 1634 × Donauworth 1632

☐ The Empire 1630–34
⊠ Main areas of war
⇨ Sweden enters war
× Imperial-Allied victory
⊠ Protestant-Allied victory

7 Gustavus Adolphus [A] came to the throne of Sweden in 1611 and as a young man defeated Denmark, Poland and also Russia. He built a fleet and a formidable army which transformed Sweden into a great power. The threat to Sweden was the Hapsburg Catholic control of northern Germany [B]. The Polish war persuaded Gustavus to postpone a defensive war against the Hapsburgs in the Baltic, but growing Hapsburg strength after 1629 threatened Swedish security as well as Swedish Protestantism. The Swedes won resounding victories at Breitenfeld in 1631 and Lützen in 1632 but Gustavus Adlophus was killed in the latter battle and without his leadership the Swedes were routed at Nördlingen, 1634.

8 The Defenestration of Prague occurred in 1618 when the Bohemian Protestants hurled two imperial regents from a council window. In 1609 they had obtained from Emperor Rudolph II (1552–1612) a guarantee of religious equality and freedom of worship. Rudolph was succeeded by the old and sick Matthias, who was urged to name as his successor the king of Bohemia. Although they disliked Ferdinand of Styria, the Bohemians consented to his election. The crisis occurred after Matthias had visited Prague securing the election. In his absence the ten regents he appointed denounced the decree of religious freedom and demolished Lutheran churches.

8

9 The policies of Cardinal Richelieu (1585–1642), minister to Louis XIII, reflected the French conflict of interests at home and abroad. The French saw the Catholic Hapsburgs as their greatest threat. If Philip II and III had established strong controls in both Spain and the Low Countries, France would have been sandwiched between two branches of a hostile power. It was the dilemma of the French monarchy that its interests required Catholic orthodoxy at home but support of the Protestant cause abroad. From 1634 Richelieu brought France openly into war with the emperor (until 1648) and with Spain.

9

53

Politics in the age of Elizabeth

Elizabeth I (reigned 1558–1603) of England [Key, 1] believed that as a queen she belonged to a unique species and governed by divine ordinance. She told the House of Commons that matters were revealed to her "princely understanding" that could not be comprehended by "a knot of harebrains", and the head of the body politic was not to be ruled by the foot. But her theory of government was so intuitive and practical that she seldom needed to discuss it. Where James I would philosophize about the respective roles of king and Parliament, she met opposition with curses, demotions and sharp spells of imprisonment.

The organization of government

The heart of the Tudor system was the Privy Council. There, and in its offshoots such as the Star Chamber and High Commission, policy was decided in matters parochial as well as national. Effective government depended on the industry and loyalty of the principal secretary, and in this Elizabeth was scrupulously served by Lord Burghley [5], who was her secretary from 1558 to 1572, and Francis Walsingham (1530–90).

But the decisions of the Council could not be put into effect without the co-operation of the Commons and the unpaid magistracy of the justices of the peace (JPs) who had to enforce a growing corpus of social legislation. Most JPs belonged to the class of rising gentry [4] who were buying land and acquiring seats in Parliament. Thus their enthusiasm for legislation in Parliament reflected their willingness to enforce it.

Elizabeth and Parliament

Elizabeth reserved to the royal prerogative all decisions on national religion, foreign policy, her marriage and, later, the appointment of her successor. Religion was central to all these and the aggressively Protestant Commons wanted to amend the moderate religious settlement of 1559 and demanded a foreign policy hostile to the Catholic powers. Elizabeth would not allow the Commons to debate these issues, but they asserted that they had privileges of freedom of speech and freedom from arrest. Elizabeth, however, declared that the right of free speech meant merely the Commons' right to discuss what was set before them by the royal ministers, not to initiate legislation of their own. Ministers controlled debates through the Speaker, who was at that period a royal nominee and not a servant of the House; dissident members were occasionally imprisoned in the Tower of London.

But it was a losing battle. As inflation devalued the Crown's hereditary revenues from land and feudal dues, Elizabeth remained solvent only by selling lands and offices; and when after 1585 she had to meet the expense of a long war with Spain and rebellion in Ireland she became increasingly dependent on Parliament's support. Refusing assent to taxation was the Commons' ultimate weapon, and although the religious issue was quiescent in the 1590s, Elizabeth had to make concessions over monopolies. Measures for the regulation of trade belonged indisputably to the royal prerogative, and in theory a monopoly for the sale or manufacture of a product was considered a legitimate reward for enterprise. But Elizabeth had been selling monopolies as a

1 **Elizabeth**, seen here in her Armada portrait of 1588, was anxious to build up an image of majesty. But in practical politics she was down-to-earth, and let none of her subjects endanger her power.

2 **Sheep-farming** often replaced tillage as a result of enclosures. The ensuing drop in agricultural employment led Thomas More (c. 1478–1535) to say in his Utopia: "Sheep have become devourers of men".

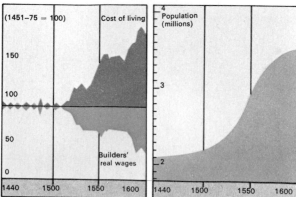

3 **The population of England** rose steadily throughout the 16th century as plague became less virulent. Contemporaries thought that the country was overcrowded and suggested colonization as a means of disposing of the surplus. But the real cause of the unemployment and distress was inflation, a Europe-wide phenomenon of the period, and the failure of wages to keep pace with prices. Even though inflation steadied after the 1560s, when Elizabeth restored the currency after Henry VIII's debasement of the coinage in the 1540s, by 1600 prices were still more than five times greater than a century earlier. Despite the social problems caused by this inflation, it acted as a stimulus to a burst of industrial activity, including coal and iron mining.

4 **Warminster Hall**, on the border of Oxfordshire and Warwickshire was bought in 1572 by Richard Cooper, a successful yeoman. He rebuilt the house using local brown ironstone. The rural middle classes that developed in the 15th century became socially dominant because they bought much of the land available after the dissolution of the monasteries. Many were energetic and eager to succeed, and people complained that they disregarded the traditional obligations of landowners to the peasantry. This was the class that came to challenge the royal authority in Parliament, and in the 17th century was to take over much authority in the countryside from the traditional nobility.

financial expedient, and her surrender on this issue in 1601 was ominous for future attacks on royal authority.

Outside the area of political conflict the Tudor state exercised wide paternal powers. Imports might be prohibited to protect the home producer and exports banned in times of shortage. The Statute of Apprentices of 1563 was an attempt to settle wages and working conditions at a time of economic uncertainty. To assist the fishing industry, Protestant England still prohibited the eating of meat in Lent, and the sumptuary laws upheld the gradations of society by controlling the dress and diet of the lower classes. Despite Puritan opposition to Sunday activity, sports were officially encouraged on Sundays because they contributed to a healthy yeomanry which was considered important to national defence.

Social problems

Economic regulation failed to solve the growing problem of enclosures. The open-field system of strip farming was inefficient, and agriculture benefited from the consolida-tion of more compact fields. But the increasingly common enclosure merely for sheep-farming [2], which employed less labour and might deprive the peasantry of the common land on which they kept their beasts, was a source of hardship for many peasants. By the end of the century Elizabeth's governments had some success in maintaining tillage and checking enclosure to ensure social stability; but the merchants and gentry who bought land were anxious to exploit its full economic value, heedless of traditional rights that villagers might have on it.

The government was more successful in meeting its obligations to the dispossessed. Poverty and unemployment became a serious problem, aggravated by chronic inflation [3], and gangs of masterless men and beggars [6] in the towns caused widespread alarm. A series of measures culminated in the Poor Law of 1601, which distinguished between the sick and incapacitated poor, who were to be assisted from the parish rate; the able-bodied, who were to be provided with materials and work; and the wilfully idle, who were to be branded and whipped.

Elizabeth toured her country in triumphal processions almost every year of her reign. As well as creating a close rapport between the queen and her subjects, on which she prided herself, these progresses enabled her to gauge the dominant mood of the country. The cost of the tours was met by local noblemen whose hospitality she sought; they were thus an important way of reducing the huge expenses of her splendid court. There were many distant parts of England which she rarely visited.

5 **William Cecil, Lord Burghley** (1520–98), acted as adviser to Elizabeth for 40 years, including his times as lord treasurer after 1572. He too was cautious and recognized the limitations on action that were imposed by Elizabeth's unique position as an unmarried queen without obvious heirs. He personally sympathized with the Calvinists, but supported the Anglican settlement publicly, and was careful to maintain strict control over the House of Commons to prevent a decline in royal authority. But he sometimes complained that Elizabeth's policies were vacillating. His son Robert, Earl of Salisbury (1563–1612) inherited his authority in 1598 and served under James I.

6 **Beggars were increasingly numerous** in Elizabeth's reign. Genuine unemployment was aggravated by the ancient system that left each parish responsible for its poor, so that a man travelling in search of work would be moved on quickly before he became a public liability. Despite much protest against heartless landlords, there were also thought to be many professional beggars who had ingenious methods of feigning dereliction and disease. Such beggars roamed the country in hordes. The Poor Law of 1601 tried to distinguish between these and genuinely needy people. It set a fixed rate from parishioners for workhouses. Begging was banned and "sturdy beggars" whipped.

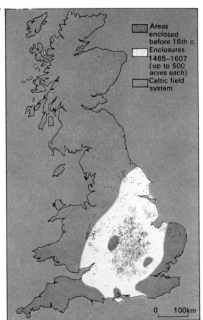

7 **The enclosures of the Tudor period** were mostly confined to the old "champion" (midland) country and even there only 6% of the land was affected. Elsewhere enclosed fields had been used for centuries. Enclosure became less common after 1560.

(map legend) Areas enclosed before 16th c.
Enclosures 1485–1607 (up to 500 acres each)
Celtic field system
0   100km

8 **Education in Tudor England** was reorganized after the monasteries, once the main source of lay education, were destroyed. But many grammar schools, for the children of the middle classes, were set up, as literacy became necessary.

9 **Robert Devereux, Earl of Essex** (1566–1601) was a glamorous nobleman who fascinated Elizabeth in her last years. After falling out of favour, he returned to London from Ireland in 1601 to organize a coup to regain power. On its defeat he was executed.

Elizabeth and the Armada

When Elizabeth I came to the English throne in 1558, France, not Spain was the immediate enemy. Philip II of Spain (reigned 1555–98), at that time a widower, had been married to Mary, Elizabeth's sister, and he proposed marriage to Elizabeth. Although Elizabeth declined the offer, as she was to decline all other offers of marriage, she and Philip had a common fear that the ambition of the Guise rulers of France would threaten their lands.

The threat of Mary, Queen of Scots

The danger to England was from the "auld alliance" of France and Scotland, where Mary of Guise (1515–60) was acting as regent for her daughter, Mary Stewart, Queen of Scots [5], who was married to the French king. Elizabeth connived at and unofficially assisted a Protestant revolution that overthrew French influence in Scotland in 1560, but Mary Stewart's husband died and in 1561 she returned to rule her native country, a beautiful young widow and the most attractive match in Europe. As a Catholic and the great-granddaughter of Henry VII, she was considered to be the rightful queen of England for those of the Catholic faith who regarded Elizabeth as a Protestant bastard.

After a rash and unsuccessful campaign to recover Calais (1562–3), Elizabeth realized the weakness of her position and settled into the waiting game that thereafter characterized all her foreign policy. By procrastination, apparent indecision and calculated twists of policy she weathered crises that brought her advisers to despair. She was evasive on Mary's requests to be acknowledged as her successor; and when in 1568 Mary fled from Scotland, she kept her in protective custody for 19 years. So long as Mary lived, France or Spain would hesitate to make an all-out attack on England: it was not until war with Spain had begun that Elizabeth consented to Mary's execution.

War with Spain

In 1572, the French Huguenots (Protestants) were broken in the Massacre of St Bartholomew, and the revived civil war weakened France's activity as a protagonist in international politics. Since the excommunication of Elizabeth by the pope in 1570, Philip, as secular leader of the Counter-Reformation, had a justification for war against her, and a subdued England would have meant improved routes for him to The Netherlands.

There were provocations on both sides, particularly the English privateers' attack on Spanish shipping and posts in the West Indies, and Catholic plots to murder Elizabeth. Yet the drift to war with Spain was gradual. English commercial ties with Spanish-controlled Flanders were too strong to be easily broken, and Philip gave little support to his envoys when they plotted against Elizabeth's life [2]. Elizabeth likewise was equivocal towards the seamen who captured Spanish treasureships and disrupted the trade routes. She willingly shared the plunder, but she disavowed responsibility. She was equivocal too, at first, towards the Dutch revolt against Spanish rule, because she disapproved in general of rebellious subjects and she had not yet the resources for a head-on conflict with Spain.

The assassination in 1584 of William the Silent, the leader of the Dutch rebels,

1 The fall of Calais, the last English foothold in Europe, in 1558 after 200 years of English control, resulted from a war between France and Spain; England was allied to Spain by the marriage of Mary.

2 Edmund Campion (1540–81) was leader of the Jesuit mission in England that was associated with plots to kill Elizabeth to restore a Catholic monarch. He was betrayed and executed for treason.

3 The English militia of levies organized county by county was the only means of defence on land, since there was no standing army. After 1557 every man between 16 and 60 was liable for training in the use of pike and musket. But to be efficient the militia needed energetic lord-lieutenants; much of its equipment was old and out of date. It was used to defend the Scottish and Welsh borders, and could not be used overseas.

4 Elizabeth sent the Earl of Leicester in command of an official royal army to The Netherlands to stiffen Dutch resistance to the Spaniards after the Catholics had captured Antwerp. He set out in December 1585, but returned a year later in disgrace. The expedition was costly, Leicester had quarrelled with his allies and angered Elizabeth by assuming the title of Governor of the United Provinces. This conflicted with the queen's wish to respect Spanish rights of sovereignty. Leicester returned to The Netherlands in June 1587, but was again recalled in November. He is shown here in command of the troops assembled at Tilbury in 1588. English troops fought in The Netherlands until the peace of 1608.

5 Mary, Queen of Scots (1542–87), the daughter of James V, was sent to France in 1548 to foil plans to marry her to Edward VI of England. She married the future French king Francis II (1544–60) instead. She later married Lord Darnley, her cousin. This was dangerous to Elizabeth because each had a claim to the English throne. Mary was driven from Scotland after the death of Darnley. Elizabeth imprisoned her in Sheffield Castle, to prevent her causing further trouble to England. But Mary was involved in several plots to assassinate the English queen and in 1587 Elizabeth at last consented to Mary's execution. She had been unwilling to do this because they were cousins and because it implied an attack on the royal authority.

prompted Elizabeth to send the Earl of Leicester on an official expedition to help the rebels in 1585 [4], thus provoking the long-feared war with Philip. John Hawkins (1532–95) had by that time reorganized the English navy. To meet the needs of the age he replaced the high-built carracks, fit to operate only in home waters, with fast ocean-going galleons longer in proportion to the beam [Key]. He armed them with long-range cannons, and used smaller crews, which meant less congestion and disease.

Francis Drake (c. 1540–96) employed some of these new ships in raids to harass the Spaniards at little cost. In 1585–6, after a landing in Vigo Bay, he plundered the Cape Verde Islands and attacked San Domingo and Cartagena in the Spanish Main. In 1587 he sailed to Cadiz and destroyed 30 ships of the Armada that Philip was preparing to carry an army to England.

The Spanish Armada
Such tactics delayed and weakened the Spanish invasion plan. Nevertheless it was a formidable force of 130 ships and 30,000

men, commanded by the Duke of Medina Sidonia (1550–1615), that rode into the Channel in July 1588 with the object of joining a Spanish army of 17,000 assembled in the Flemish ports [6]. England's land preparations were so dilatory and inadequate [3] that there could have been little effective resistance if this combined force had landed, or even if Medina Sidonia had interrupted his progress to seize a Channel port.

The English victory over the Armada [8] was a combination of good fortune and skilful tactics, and it was immediately apparent that the Spaniards would never again be able to threaten the existence of a Protestant England. But the war continued until 1604, with few dramatic successes on either side. English involvement in The Netherlands continued, and Elizabeth intervened against Spanish ambitions in France in the 1590s; the Spaniards, on the other hand, tried to intervene in a rebellion against English rule in Ireland [7] in 1596–7. The war became an increasing drain on the resources of both countries and the peace made by James I was well received at home.

The *Ark Raleigh*, later named the *Ark Royal* after being presented to the queen, was one of the finest of the new ships of Elizabeth's reign.

It was a four-masted galleon, the main masts bearing topgallants. Walter Raleigh (c. 1552–1618) built it for his own privateers. During the Armada, it

was the flagship of Lord Howard of Effingham, the English commander. Later it was named the *Anne Royal* after the queen of James I.

6

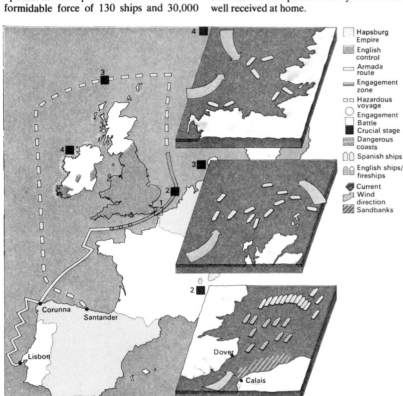

	Hapsburg Empire
	English control
	Armada route
	Engagement zone
	Hazardous voyage
○	Engagement Battle
■	Crucial stage
	Dangerous coasts
	Spanish ships
	English ships/ fireships
	Current
	Wind direction
	Sandbanks

Corunna
Santander
Lisbon
Dover
Calais
Dover
Calais
Dover
Calais

6 The Spanish Armada put out from Lisbon at the end of May 1588, but was immediately beset by storms which forced it into Corunna. It was not until July that it could sail for England. Lord Howard (1536–1624), the English admiral, sailed out of Plymouth when the Armada arrived eventually in the Channel, to secure the windward position, but the Spaniards continued eastwards. There were some serious encounters off Portland and the Isle of Wight, but when the Armada reached Calais, the army it intended to convoy to England was not ready. Fireships sent in by the English caused many Spanish ships to drift out to sea. Medina Sidonia, the Spanish admiral, tried to re-form off Gravelines, but the fleet was destroyed by the superior gunnery of the English at close quarters. As the wind veered south-west, the Spanish had to turn north, and were pursued as far as the Firth of Forth. Bad weather then wrecked the fleet, which limped home with more than half its ships missing. The English did not lose a fighting ship.

7

7 Rebellion in Ireland was dangerous towards the end of Elizabeth's reign. Turlough O'Neill (d. 1595), here seen acknowledging the authority of the English commander Henry Sidney in 1567, kept relative peace, but after his death a countrywide revolt occurred that the Spaniards tried to support in 1596–7. The Irish rebellion was more expensive to Elizabeth than the whole war with Spain.

8 Of the 130 ships of the Armada, only about 50 were designed as fighting craft. The rest carried equipment for the invasion. The galleons themselves were taller and less manoeuvrable than the English ships.

8

Exploration and trade in Tudor England

The sea-captains of the age of Elizabeth (1533–1603) – Drake, Raleigh and Hawkins – provide probably the most enduring myths of Tudor England, but their exploits were built on a history of exploration that went back nearly a century. The motives to explore were various; but the most important were the economic pressure of a rising population, inflation, and declining traditional markets. So too were sheer inquisitiveness and a thirst for adventure, and a national pride that would not permit England's enemies to enjoy the wealth of the New World unmolested.

The changing pattern of trade

Trade in wool and unfinished woollen cloth was England's vital export in the early sixteenth century. But in the 1540s the English currency was devalued by debasement and the exchange rate turned against the English exporter. The ancient "wool-staple", or official distribution centre of English wool in Europe, disappeared with the loss of Calais in 1558, and Antwerp itself declined during The Netherlands' long struggle for independence from Spain. The wool industry therefore was seriously affected and capital was diverted to the enclosure of land for improved agriculture rather than to pasture, and to the development of coal and other mineral deposits. Traders therefore began to look overseas: merchants hoped to sell cloth to the heathen in undiscovered countries. Exploration was therefore central to economic expansion.

The start of English exploration

The first "English" explorer was an Italian by birth, John Cabot (c. 1450–c. 1500) [1], who had settled in Bristol. He set out in 1497, commissioned by Henry VII to discover lands not previously known to Christians, to circumvent the papal bull of 1493 that divided between Spain and Portugal all new territories. All subsequent Tudor voyages only acknowledged territory "effectively occupied" in 1493 as related to this bull. Cabot found Nova Scotia and the important cod fisheries of Newfoundland, and suggested a northwestern route to the Spice Islands and the fabled riches of the East that were to delude many future explorers.

Cabot's son Sebastian (1474–1557) unsuccessfully projected a northeastern passage to India, but the expedition of Hugh Willoughby (died 1554) and Richard Chancellor (died 1556) in 1553 took them to Moscow; the Muscovy Company that they set up traded with Russia and established an overland route to Persia. Earlier, in 1509, Sebastian had crossed the Davis Strait, northwest of Newfoundland, and come to Hudson Bay, which he thought to be the Pacific. In three voyages (1576–8) Martin Frobisher (c. 1535–94) [2] reached the same waters; while John Davis (c. 1550–1605) established that Greenland was separate from the mainland and sailed into Baffin's Bay. The Northwest Passage was never free of ice, and so it could not be, as was hoped, complementary to the Cape Horn and Cape of Good Hope routes. The belief in a great southern continent stretching from the south of Cape Horn to the East Indies was also doomed to disappointment. But in search of these far-ranging and often fictional objectives the Elizabethans sailed the known Earth and sometimes beyond it [4].

1 John Cabot and his son Sebastian discovered Nova Scotia off the North American coast in 1497, but believed that they had found Asia. John died on another voyage a few years later. In 1509 Sebastian sailed past southern Greenland into the Davis Strait, and may have gone as far as Hudson Bay. He later went to Spain and spent many years as pilot-major to the mercantile marine, making explorations of the South American coast. He returned to England in 1547, and helped to form a joint-stock company in 1553 to search for a northeastern passage. This company sponsored the expedition of Willoughby and Chancellor to Moscow.

2 Martin Frobisher claimed to have found the elusive Northwest Passage in 1576, and a Cathay Company was set up to develop trade with China. The following year he thought he had discovered gold, and found backers for a new voyage to Greenland, almost unknown since the Viking voyages of the 10th century. He took some Eskimos, with whom he is shown fighting here, back to London, but the English climate killed them.

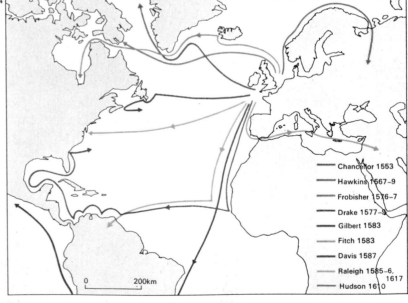

3 Navigational aids were vital for the success of ocean-going voyages and many navigation schools, such as Gresham College, were set up in Elizabeth's reign to teach sailors the new skills. These were as important to fishermen as to explorers. As well as the astrolabe, developed by the Portuguese from Arab designs, but which was much easier to use on land than on a ship pitching at sea, revolutionary innovations included Mercator's world map of 1569. Its projection allowed a compass course to be plotted as a straight line on a map. Another was John Davis's backstaff, which modified the cross-staff.

4 English exploration did not get fully under way until after 1550. Thereafter the main purpose of the voyages was to find a route to the lucrative markets of China and South-East Asia without infringing on the Spanish and Portuguese possessions that had been apportioned by papal bull in 1493. Thus the merchant companies such as the Muscovy Company sought to find new markets for English cloth in exchange for timber and other goods useful for the shipping industry rather than to establish colonies. Few other expeditions proved as profitable to English industry although raw materials brought home included tobacco, potatoes and many minerals. But the hope for the Cathay market was never realized and home industry did not profit from the American colonies until the mid-17th century. It was not until 1583 that Humphrey Gilbert attempted to set up the first permanent colony in the New World, in Newfoundland, but his expedition was destroyed by storms.

Chancellor 1553
Hawkins 1567–9
Frobisher 1576–7
Drake 1577–9
Gilbert 1583
Fitch 1583
Davis 1587
Raleigh 1585–6, 1617
Hudson 1610

0   200km

Voyages to the Caribbean brought the English into contact with the Spanish Empire. In 1562 John Hawkins (1532–95) [5] took Negro slaves at Sierra Leone and sold them to the Spaniards at San Domingo. A second, similar, voyage in 1564 seemed to have established a profitable commerce, but in 1567–8 a Spanish fleet caught him at San Juan d'Ulloa and only two of his ships reached England safely. Hawkins then left the sea to reorganize the navy, but Francis Drake (c. 1540–96), who had been with him at San Juan, returned to the Caribbean and in 1572 sacked Nombre de Dios and captured a treasure-train there.

Later voyages

In 1577 Drake set out in the *Golden Hind* sponsored by the queen, to find a south-western route into the Pacific. Sailing through the Magellan Straits, Drake plundered unguarded coastal towns, claimed possession of California, turned west for the Moluccas, and returned home in 1580 via the Cape of Good Hope [6]. In 1586–8 Thomas Cavendish (1560–92) became the second

Englishman to sail round the world.

Anthony Jenkinson (died 1611) traded in central Asia, Ralph Fitch (*fl.* 1583–1611) traded with Akbar, the great Mogul ruler of India, and James Lancaster (c. 1550–1618) returned with booty from the East Indies. From such individual enterprises companies were formed to exploit the commercial gains, notably the East India Company (1600). But colonization to establish permanent settlements, rather than trading posts, grew more slowly. Its motives were commercial, to obtain markets and raw materials; political, to weaken Spain; religious, to spread God's word; and social, to re-settle the unemployed. Humphrey Gilbert (c. 1539–83) died on a voyage to colonize Newfoundland, and his half-brother Walter Raleigh (c. 1552–1618) was imprisoned in the Tower of London before his settlement of Virginia took root [9]. Seduced by legends of fantastic wealth, Raleigh sailed to the Spanish Main (northern South America) in 1595, and the failure of a second expedition in 1617–18 to find Eldorado, the mythical golden city of the Incas, resulted in his execution.

KEY

Francis Drake captured a Spanish treasure ship in March 1579 in the Pacific Ocean, in the course of his voyage round the world, and thereby ensured the financial success of his trip. Sixteenth-century Spain depended on large shipments of gold and silver from the New World and their capture could be seen as a contribution to the defence of England and the Protestant faith. The expeditions also took home raw materials.

5 John Hawkins was the pioneer of the slave triangle that became the basis of English prosperity in the 18th century. He later became treasurer of the navy and introduced many innovations in the design and manning of the ships.

6 During his circum-navigation of the globe Drake crossed the Pacific from California to the Spice Islands. There he received a great welcome from the natives of the Moluccas, and took aboard three tonnes of cloves. He also made an agreement with the Sultan of Ternate for future supplies of spices which were so highly valued that Drake preferred them to jewels.

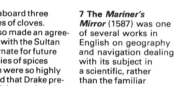

7 The *Mariner's Mirror* (1587) was one of several works in English on geography and navigation dealing with its subject in a scientific, rather than the familiar fanciful, way.

7

8

THE PRINCIPALL NAVIGATIONS, VOIA-GES AND DISCOVERIES OF THE Englishnation, made by Sea or over Land, *to the moft remote and fartheft diftant quarters of the earth at any time within the compaffe of thefe 1500 yeeres: Deuided into three feuerall parts, according to the po-fitions of the Regions wherunto they were directed.*

The firft, conteining the perfonall trauels of the Englifh vnto Iudea, Syria, A-rabia, the riuer Euphrates, Babylon, Balfara, the Perfian Gulfe, Ormuz, Chaul, Goa, India, and many Iflands adioyning to the South parts of Afia: toge-ther with the like vnto Egypt, the chiefeft ports and places of Africa with-in and without the Streight of Gibraltar, and about the famous Promon-torie of Buena Efperança, &c.

The fecond, comprehending the worthy difcoueries of the Englifh towards the North and Northeaft by Sea, as of Lapland, Scrikfinia, Corelia, the Baie of S. Nicholas, the Ifles of Colgoieue, Vaigats, and Noua Zembla toward the great riuer Ob, with the mightie Empire of Ruffia, the Cafpian Sea, Georgia, Armenia, Media, Perfia, Boghar in Baktria, & diuers kingdoms of Tartaria.

The third, and laft, including the Englifh valiant attempts in fearching al-moft all the corners of the vafte and new world of America, from 73 de-grees of Northerly latitude Southward, to Meta Incognita, Newfoundland, the maine of Virginia, the point of Florida, the Baie of Mexico, all the In-land of Noua Hifpania, the coaft of Terra firma, Brafill, the riuer of Plate, to the Streight of Magellan: and through it, and from it in the South Sea to Chili, Peru, Xalifco, the Gulfe of California, Noua Albion vpon the backfide of Canada, further then euer any Chriftian hitherto hath pierced.

Whereunto is added the laft moft renowned Englifh Nauigation, round about the whole Globe of the earth.

By Richard Hakluyt Mafter of artes, and fometime Student fometime of Chrift-church in Oxford.

Imprinted at London by GEORGE BISHOP *and* RALPH NEWBERIE, *Deputies to* CHRISTOPHER BARKER, *Printer to the Queenes moft excellent Maieftie.* 1589.

8 Richard Hakluyt the younger (c. 1552–1616) was a clergyman who, taunted in France that the English had achieved little in exploration, wrote *Principall Navigations* (1589–1600) to vindicate his countrymen by writing a detailed record of their voyages. Earlier he had written pamphlets to encourage settlers to go to Virginia. But it was hard to persuade investors to become involved in the new colonies, in which profits took far longer to accrue than in privateering expeditions. The joint-stock companies that were the usual form of investment meant that traders sought profits from single trips, not long-term advantages. But by 1600 permanent control of the East Indian trade seemed desirable.

9

9 The first settlements of Virginia were failures. Conceived of as a means to tap the vast resources of North America for England and to provide a safe market for English cloth, they were organized by Walter Raleigh (who never went to Virginia himself) and were commanded by Richard Grenville (c. 1542–91). Two expeditions – in 1585 and 1587 – were sent and established on Roanoke Island, but, as a result of the climatic extremes and Indian hostility, the first returned home with Drake after one winter and the second disappeared without trace. Each comprised more than 100 men and women, but Francis Bacon called them "the scum of people and wicked condemned men".

The Stuarts and Parliament 1603–42

In 1603 the peaceful transfer of the English crown to James VI of Scotland (1566–1625), who thereby became James I of England [1], was greeted with joy and relief. The collapse of the new Stuart dynasty was not inevitable. There were, however, severe stresses in seventeenth-century England.

Deep-rooted problems

Royal service and its ensuing favours were important to the landed classes and they formed a staple issue in politics. Elizabeth I had played off the resulting factions against one another to preserve her freedom of action. The rebellion (1601) of the Earl of Essex (1566–1601) destroyed this system and left Robert Cecil (1563–1612), Burghley's son, as the Crown's dominant adviser. James's predilection for favourites eventually brought this monopoly to the Duke of Buckingham [4]. This monopoly encouraged corruption in the search for and exploitation of patronage and office.

The amount of administration required of government in defence and foreign policy and in management of the economy, social problems and reform in the Church had been steadily growing during the Tudor period. By 1600 the available machinery and money were inadequate. Central government was wasteful, and in the country the Crown depended on voluntary work by the gentry, who were deeply suspicious of central authority, hard to discipline and capable of wilful inertia. In Parliament the representatives of that same gentry were unwilling to vote the Crown an adequate share in the increasing national wealth. In 1610 an attempt at basic reform of royal finances (the Great Contract) proposed to exchange the Crown's profit from the wardship of minors and other feudal impositions for a regular peacetime tax. Its failure led the king to exploit for cash his rights of monopolies, customs, wardships and grants of honour.

Parliament's unwillingness to pay for what was needed meant that it had no effective control over the actions of the government. The king could defeat attempts to put pressure on him by dissolving Parliament, and there were real fears about its permanent survival. Before the 1640s it had little

thought of any constitutional limitation of the king's power; agitation about parliamentary privileges arose directly from concern about the king's policies [5]. To have any influence, Lords and Commons had to work together, and in the 1620s much parliamentary protest was engineered by nobles who wished to oust Buckingham.

James's revenue and foreign policy

James I was not the man to make the necessary major reforms and in two areas he made matters worse. First, the royal finances had been affected by inflation, and Elizabeth left a debt of £100,000 net, 30 per cent of her annual peacetime revenue. By 1608, however, James's wanton extravagance had increased the royal debt to some £500,000. Second, in the field of foreign and religious policy, James ended Elizabeth's Spanish War in 1604 in favour of a sensible policy of avoiding European conflicts. As pressure grew against Protestants in Europe with the start of the Thirty Years War in 1618, the king's determined policy of peace and his attempts to negotiate with Madrid

2 CONCILVM SEPTEM NOBILIVM ANGLORVM CONIVRANTIVM IN NECEM IACOBI J. MAGNÆ BRITANNIÆ REGIS TOTIVSQ ANGLICI CONVOCATI PARLEMENTI

1 **James I told Parliament** in 1610 "The state of the monarchy is the supremest thing on earth". On several occasions James, a genuine scholar, spelled out the implications of the theory of the divine right of kings. Both he and his audience took it for granted that the monarch, as the earthly representative of God, was the basis of all political authority. But as the Stuarts persisted in policies that seemed evidently wrong, the assumption eventually came into question. In its stead, Parliament began to assert the traditional authority of the Common Law, which was propounded in an extreme form by Edward Coke (1552–1634), who helped to draft the Petition of Right (1628).

2 **The Gunpowder Plot** (1605), was an attempt on the king's life by a few religious fanatics desperate at their failure to secure a relaxation of the laws against Catholicism on James's succession. Its discovery raised fear of Catholicism to fever pitch, and this hysteria was repeated during the crisis of 1640–42.

3 **Charles and Buckingham went to Madrid** in 1623, hoping to secure Charles's marriage to a Spanish princess. The plan was the culmination of James's policy of peace with Spain. But the policy was unpopular at home; Charles's return unmarried (shown here) was greeted with great celebrations. He and Buckingham then allied with the critics of James's foreign policy and helped first to bring down Lionel Cranfield, the lord treasurer, and his regime of strict economy, and then forced James into a war with Spain that he could not afford. Enthusiasm for the war soon declined.

4 **George Villiers, Duke of Buckingham** (1592–1628), was a younger son of a minor Leicestershire squire. In 1615 he captivated James by his physical charm and athletic prowess and he "jumped higher than ever Englishman did in so short a time, from private gentleman to a dukedom". The interest of Villiers and his family in corruption prevented any possibility of reform, and his moderate abilities did not justify the military and diplomatic authority he was given. He gave James and Charles uniformly bad advice and encouraged them in short-term decisions that always led to honour and profit for Buckingham. He was assassinated in 1628 after he had involved England in war with France as well as Spain, and inspired disastrous and much criticized expeditions against Cadiz (1625) and to La Rochelle three years later.

looked like appeasement of Catholicism [6] Although James was personally a convinced Calvinist, he flirted with the growing High-Church or Arminian faction in the Church, which stressed ceremony, tradition and episcopal authority. To most Englishmen, Arminians seemed little better than Catholics, and the king's toleration of them looked extremely dangerous [Key, 8].

Charles and the rise of opposition

Charles I (reigned 1625–49) [7], unlike his father, asserted his authority without regard for his dependence upon the co-operation of its subjects. In the Book of Orders, 1631, he attacked the local autonomy of the JPs, insisting on a uniform performance of their duties. Autocratic rule by the Earl of Strafford [9] in Yorkshire and Ireland seemed ominous for the country at large. Charles's archbishop, William Laud (1573–1645), imposed Arminianism on the Church in many areas, including Scotland in 1637. Immoderate opposition in the House of Commons in 1629 impelled Charles to rule without Parliament. Ship Money, an occasional local rate,

became a nationwide annual tax in the 1630s, extending taxation to yeomen and freeholders, hitherto largely exempt.

Although Charles increased his income to a million pounds a year, this was insufficient to oppose a rebellion against Laud in Scotland in 1639. Appeals for money were turned down, JPs refused to act, and the forces raised by Charles mutinied. The Scots occupied northern England, and to pay their wages off Charles was forced to call Parliament for the first time in 11 years.

The Long Parliament (1640–60), called after the Short Parliament (1640) failed to support Charles, was at first overwhelmingly traditionalist and quickly destroyed the alleged novelties of Charles I's "personal rule". A rebellion in Ulster in October 1641 forced Parliament to choose between trusting Charles with an army or insisting on revolutionary constitutional limitations before finding the money to quell the revolt. Polarization on the need for guarantees or the dangers of constitutional change, which would imply social change, split the political nation and led to the outbreak of war.

KEY

Preaching was the principal means of influencing public opinion or spreading information in the 17th century. Charles I said "People are governed by the pulpit more than the sword in times of peace". The regulation of sermons and religious lectures was an area of dispute between the Puritans and the Church authorities, especially the Arminians. St Paul's Cross, seen here, was the main preaching place in London and was carefully controlled by the government. Social and political implications, as much as theological ones, made religion a sensitive issue. James was reluctant to impose any aggressive religious policies, and often engaged in theological disputes.

5

6

7

7 Charles wore this elaborate costume in January 1640 in the masque *Salmacida Spolia* at a time when Scotland was in rebellion. It was light blue cloth embroidered with silver, white stockings, a silver cap and white feathers. The isolated culture of the court, symbolized by these Inigo Jones masques and Charles's patronage of such artists as Rubens and Van Dyck, presented the image of Charles, the embodiment of virtue, ruling an idyllic, contented and peaceful nation. But in this, his last masque performance, he played the Platonic king responding to adverse times with endurance and patience, a new image of himself that he retained until his death in 1649.

5 John Eliot (1592–1632), once a protégé of Buckingham, led the outspoken opposition to Charles's policies in the Commons in 1629. He criticized government negatively and believed in the divine right of kings.

6 Henrietta Maria (1609–69), a French princess, married Charles in 1625. The match was unpopular, especially because he tolerated her Catholicism. She led a court faction against Laud and Wentworth.

8
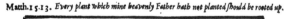
Matth. 15.13. *Every plant which mine heavenly Father hath not planted should be rooted up.*

9

8 This religious cartoon sets the orthodox Anglican cleric holding the humanly inspired Book of Common Prayer alongside the papist priest with his Devil-inspired superstitions and against the Puritan minister with the divinely inspired Bible. Thanks to Charles's intransigent support for Arminianism, the minority opinion that "root and branch" reform of the Church was necessary grew in strength in the 1630s. So, as well as questioning the king's right in law to command an army for Ireland and Long Parliament also challenged the validity of episcopal authority in general.

9 Thomas Wentworth, Earl of Strafford (1593–1641), was a critic of Buckingham in the 1620s, but entered Charles's service in 1628 fearing that the Commons might undermine royal authority. He was made the scapegoat for the "11 Years Tyranny". He was attainted by Act of Parliament (1641) and Charles could not protect him, under pressure from the London mob, which, as an organized pressure group increasingly threatened the king. Wentworth's execution, shown here, was a vital victory over Charles.

The English revolution

The English revolution (1640–60) was the first of the modern revolutions and it compares closely in many ways with the later French and Russian revolutions. Each political revolution follows its individual and complex pattern of development, but some common stages can be identified.

The revolutionary pattern

These stages include an initial period of political and intellectual excitement, with the collapse of the old regime; the emergence of a radical leadership as the political crisis becomes protracted; an eventual halt to the leftwards movement of the revolution; the consolidation of power by a strong-arm and often military-based party and a return towards political stability; and sometimes a formal restoration and a collapse of the revolutionary movement. These stages can be seen in the English, French and Russian revolutions, with the manifest exception that in Russia there has been no restoration of the Romanov dynasty.

The first stage of the English revolution [2] was the constitutional or "bloodless" revolution of 1640–41, which weakened the old absolutist regime. It began in November 1640, when Charles I (1600–49) summoned the Long Parliament to help him out of a financial crisis. Charles, isolated and deeply unpopular, was forced to agree to a wide-ranging set of constitutional reforms that gave Parliament a much more prominent place in the constitution. These changes were accompanied by much political excitement and debate, especially after the ending of press censorship [4] in July 1641.

The escalation of the crisis

The second stage saw the revolution move leftwards, as the political crisis escalated into civil war. The Long Parliament split into rival parties in the autumn of 1641, the Royalists (Cavaliers) forming a King's party in opposition to the Parliamentarians (Roundheads), who were prepared for further political and religious reforms. Charles attempted unsuccessfully to arrest his main opponents in January 1642 and then fled from London. He thus entered the first civil war (August 1642–April 1646) from a weakened position,

because the Parliamentarians held London and the machinery of central government. The Parliamentarians were not, however, able to clinch their dominance until the reorganization of their forces into the disciplined and zealous New Model Army in January 1645. This successfully harnessed militant Puritanism to the Parliamentarian cause. The army, ably directed by Sir Thomas Fairfax (1612–71), won a decisive victory over the Royalists at Naseby in June 1645.

The third stage marked the apogee of the leftwards movement of the revolution. The victorious Parliamentarians themselves split at the time of their success in 1646 and 1647. The more conservative group were the Presbyterians, who, together with the Scots, then allied themselves with Charles. The more radical party, the Independents, backed by Oliver Cromwell (1599–1658) [8] and the army, attempted a settlement, failed and remained hostile to Charles. The second civil war (February–August 1648) was a brief but bitterly fought contest, which ended with Cromwell's overwhelming defeat of the Scottish army at Preston in August 1648.

1 **Parliament** was a well-established institution before 1640 with its own traditions, procedures and privileges. In the House of Commons' chamber there were a Speaker (centre), two committee clerks, the serjeant-at-arms (carrying the mace) and MPs.

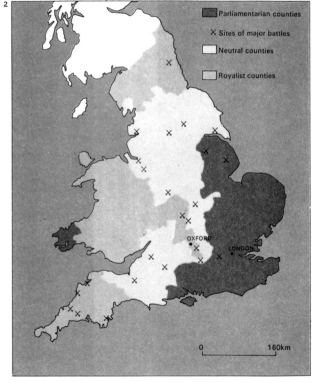

Parliamentarian counties
X Sites of major battles
Neutral counties
Royalist counties

2 **In the first civil war** the Royalists were strongest in areas remote from London in the north and west, while the Parliamentarians kept the capital and the populous southeast. Fighting followed for control of divided areas.

OXFORD

LONDON

0   160km

3 **The elegant portrait of Charles I** by Anthony van Dyck concealed the king's small stature but emphasized his regal dignity and a certain melancholic determination. Van Dyck was appointed official court painter in 1632 by Charles, who was a famous art patron.

4 **The end of press censorship** in 1641 brought a flood of pamphleteering and debate. All tradi-tional ideas were opened to discussion and argument. Before long, moderates on the Parliamentary side called for caution in reform, stressing the Aristotelian "golden mean". They warned of the "new extreme" among radical political and religious groups as much as the "old extreme" of the enemy.

It was followed by the purge of Parliament (Pride's Purge) in December 1648, the trial and execution of Charles on 30 January 1649, and the abolition of the monarchy and House of Lords in February of that year – a sequence of events that was unprecedented in European history.

At the same time Cromwell and the army leadership broke with the lower-class radical political party, known as the Levellers [6]. They pressed for fundamental constitutional changes, implicitly challenging the political and social power of landowning society. In the autumn of 1647, the Levellers briefly challenged Cromwell for control of the army itself. But Cromwell decided to crush the movement. A Leveller army mutiny was defeated at Burford (Oxfordshire) in May 1649. Deprived of its army base, support for the Levellers rapidly waned. But the difficulty of Cromwell's position – sandwiched between left and right – was accentuated: he was a regicide, as well as the man who had broken the Levellers.

The fourth stage represented the gradual return to political stability. The New Model

Army was, in the 1650s, a force of more than 60,000 men. The importance of its power was shown in the brutal suppression of the Irish rebellion (1649–50) and the routing of a further Royalist uprising (1650–51).

Cromwell and collapse of army rule

Cromwell proved the most successful ruler (1653–8) because he was both a skilled politician and a brilliant general. His regime had some foreign policy successes, such as peace with the Dutch in 1654 and victory over Spain (1656–8), but this system did not last long after his death in 1658.

The fifth stage in the revolution therefore saw an initial period of political confusion with the collapse of army rule, followed in due course by the restoration of Charles II (1630–85) in May 1660 at the invitation of the Convention Parliament. The restored monarchy [9] was much weaker than it had been previously, and it was the landowning gentry as represented in Parliament who were the ultimate victors of the English revolution, ensuring the permanent end to absolutist monarchy.

The civil wars marked a breakdown in ordered political and social life and animosities heightened during the course of the fighting. There were not only political and religious divisions between the Royalists and Parliamentarians in 1642, but

also social ones. The Royalists were satirized as courtiers and rakes; the Parliamentarians as low-born moralists. The Royalists drew support from some of the gentry and most of the peerage, who often wore lavish costume and long hair, denoting them as men of

social standing and wealth. The Parliamentarians also had considerable backing among landowners, but they derived additional support from urban merchants, tradesmen and artisans, who were often motivated by Puritan zeal and wore shorter hair and sober clothing.

5
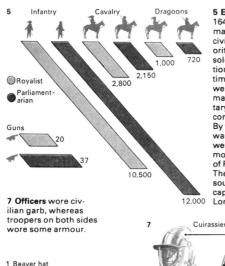

Infantry   Cavalry   Dragoons

720
1,000
2,150
2,800
10,500
12,000

● Royalist
● Parliamentarian

Guns
20
37

7 Officers wore civilian garb, whereas troopers on both sides wore some armour.

1 Beaver hat
2 Gorget
3 Partisan
4 Burgonet with face bar
5 Wheel-lock pistol
6 Pistol holster

7   Cuirassier

Captain of infantry

5 Edgehill (23 Oct 1642) was the first major battle of the civil war and the majority of officers and soldiers were in action for the first time. The two armies were fairly evenly matched and in military terms the outcome was indecisive. By the end of the war, the king's forces were only a little more than half those of Parliament. The king marched south to set up his capital in Oxford, as London eluded him.

6 A key development in the 1640s was the growth of the first organized, mainly lower-class political party in English history. This group, known as the Levellers, played an important political role in the years 1647–9 before eventually being defeated by Cromwell. The Levellers did not have one party leader, but a dominant part was played by "Freeborn John" – the spirited propagandist, John Lilburne (1614–57), shown here. The Levellers called for a considerable extension of the franchise and were suppressed by both king and Parliament.

6

8

8 Oliver Cromwell was a military genius and a pragmatic politician. He ruled as Protector and tried to reconcile discordant factions, staunchly upholding the principle of religious tolerance.

9 The restored monarchy in 1660 was much weakened and power was shared with Parliament. The "Cavalier Parliament" was opened amid much state pageantry on 22 April 1661 with Charles

II riding in procession from the Tower of London. The landowning gentry had learned to fear a powerful monarchy and standing armies, and they soon became critical of Charles and his ministers.

9

The Commonwealth and Protectorate

The execution of Charles I on 30 January 1649 [1] inaugurated an era of constitutional experiment for England. Without a monarchy or a House of Lords, a republican government was established by the House of Commons – now reduced to a "Rump" composed chiefly of the most radical "Independent" members who had survived "Pride's Purge", the exclusion of members opposed to the king's execution. The Scottish Presbyterians, who refused to recognize the Commonwealth, were defeated at Dunbar in 1650, and the young Charles Stuart at Worcester in 1651; Oliver Cromwell [Key] also subdued Ireland in a brutally efficient campaign (1649–52). The Rump passed the Navigation Act (1651) providing for sea trade to be carried in British ships, and enforced it by a successful war at sea against the Dutch (1652–4) [3].

The Cromwellian Protectorate
Despite these military successes, Cromwell became impatient at the Rump's slowness to promote domestic reforms, and forcibly dismissed Parliament in April 1653 [4]. There

followed a brief and ineffectual experiment (June-December 1653) with the Nominated, or "Barebones", Parliament, which was made up of religious zealots and was intended to lead the country towards truth.

Cromwell thus became the foremost political as well as military leader of the English Revolution. In December 1653, he was appointed Lord Protector, an office he held until his death. Having come to power by unorthodox means, Cromwell was faced with many difficulties, but he was powerful and successful, although not popular.

In the 1650s the "army of the saints", although politically radical, developed into a highly disciplined force, whose support Cromwell was always careful to retain. The survival of his regime was thus ultimately dependent upon the existence of a loyal standing army of 60,000 men. Cromwell was not, however, simply a ruthless seeker after power for its own sake. He was undoubtedly ambitious, but he was also motivated by a deep commitment to the principle of religious toleration. His domestic policies were not as revolutionary as his career in the

1640s had suggested; he opposed monarchial absolutism and believed in parliamentary rule. He was a pragmatist concerned with ensuring the survival of his experiment, and (as he himself said) not "wedded and glued to forms of government."

Foreign and domestic policies
One solution to a legacy of domestic problems after a period of revolutionary turmoil is to turn attention outwards with an aggressive foreign policy. Cromwell, like Napoleon, did this. He made peace with the Protestant Dutch in 1654 but then waged war against the Catholic power of imperial Spain (1655–8). This policy pleased some English commercial interests; but primarily it allowed Cromwell to invoke glorified memories of earlier wars against Spain under Elizabeth I. Cromwell achieved legal, administrative and educational reforms despite continuing financial problems posed by the war and standing army [7]. No dramatic social changes were attempted. In religious matters, Cromwell extended freedom of worship to all Puritan groups,

1 The execution of Charles I in 1649, after a trial, as a tyrant and traitor shocked many people at home and abroad. But it established the principle that a ruler was accountable to Parliament.

2 *Areopagitica* (1644) by the poet John Milton (1608–74) was a passionate plea for freedom of speech and liberty of conscience. Milton later acted as an apologist for the Commonwealth and Protectorate.

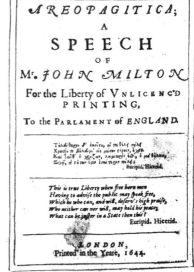

	Trade value	
	Dutch	English
1648	£254,191	£203,054
1650	£214,853	£276,066
1652	£138,561	£266,070
1654	£106,431	£364,486
1656	£176,838	£338,486
1658	£151,389	£352,704
1660	£186,205	£285,000

Shetlands
SCOTLAND
Newcastle
Scarborough
ENGLAND
Texel
The Gabbard
Amsterdam
NETHERLANDS
Rotterdam
London
Kentish Knock
Portland
Plymouth
Folkestone
Dungeness

3 The first Anglo-Dutch War (1652–4), between the two main Protestant republics, sprang from longstanding commercial and colonial rivalries that had been exacerbated by the mercantilist-inspired Navigation Act of 1651, which permitted only English ships to serve English or colonial ports. The war resulted in disruption of the Dutch carrying trade and consequent English gains. The English navy under Robert Blake (1599–1657) defeated the Dutch at Portland (1652) and Texel (1653). These successes marked England's emergence as a major maritime power, and henceforth English foreign policy was marked by much greater concern for the significance of commercial and colonial interests.

4 The dismissal of the Rump Parliament in 1653 arose from Cromwell's impatience for domestic reform. But the act left him politically isolated; a satisfactory constitutional settlement with other Parliaments eluded him.

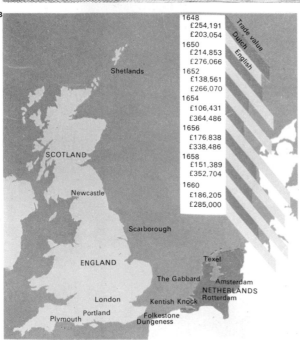

AREOPAGITICA;
A
SPEECH
OF
Mr. JOHN MILTON
For the Liberty of VNLICENC'D PRINTING,
To the PARLIAMENT of ENGLAND.

LONDON,
Printed in the Yeare, 1644.

including the most radical ones. Members of the now-eclipsed Church of England [5] had to worship secretly, but actual persecution was directed only against Catholics, whose creed was thought to be too intolerant to be allowed to continue unchecked.

The return of conservatism
Although in the 1650s Cromwell had many critics, pressure for abolition of social distinctions and redistribution of wealth, which had appeared in the later 1640s among lower-classes and in the army, the Levellers and Diggers, had largely disappeared – partly as a result of a run of good harvests (1653–6) that reduced food prices and allayed economic discontents. Gentry landowners, finding their authority largely intact, were quiescent. An attempted Royalist uprising in March 1655, led by John Penruddock, attracted little support, but the government panicked and introduced the rule of the major-generals in June 1655. An experiment in direct military control in local affairs, this brought Cromwell's popularity with the gentry to its lowest point.

Cromwell, however, sought constantly to achieve a constitutional agreement with landowner representatives in Parliament [6] that would give his rule a solid basis. He called two parliaments (1654–5, 1656–8) and wrangled with both. But eventually he realized the extent of parliamentary opposition to the major-generals, and dismissed John Lambert, the army "strong man", in July 1658, after accepting a new constitutional settlement, the Humble Petition and Advice, in May 1657. It strengthened Parliament, restored the Upper House, which had been abolished in 1649, and sought to consolidate Cromwell's authority by making him king – an offer he refused under pressure from the army.

When death toppled Cromwell from power, his regime, in the hands of his son Richard, "Tumbledown Dick" (1626–1712) and the now-divided army leaders, did not long survive him. Stuart monarchy was eventually restored in May 1660 [9] and the Church of England was revived. This ended an important era of upheaval and experiment in English history.

Oliver Cromwell (1599–1658) came from a minor landed family and entered Parliament in 1628. His military skill as a commander in the civil wars of the 1640s made him a natural leader of the parliamentary side. Determined to achieve constitutional reform, he supplied the strength of purpose needed to unify the nation without a king.

5 Puritans destroyed religious images in many churches and tried to curb Sunday recreations for all the people.

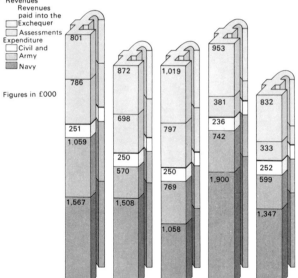

6 Public reporting of Parliament was stimulated by some expansion of press freedom in the period 1640–60. Cromwell's search for a political consensus on which to base the Commonwealth, and his difficulties with his two parliaments, were widely reported. The members of Cromwell's parliaments were drawn from the ranks of the respectable landed gentry society, but political discussion was common among all classes.

A PERFECT DIVRNALL OF THE PASSAGES In Parliament:

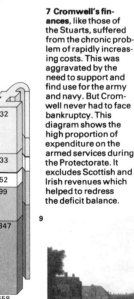

7 Cromwell's finances, like those of the Stuarts, suffered from the chronic problem of rapidly increasing costs. This was aggravated by the need to support and find use for the army and navy. But Cromwell never had to face bankruptcy. This diagram shows the high proportion of expenditure on the armed services during the Protectorate. It excludes Scottish and Irish revenues which helped to redress the deficit balance.

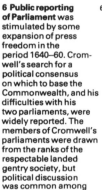

7 Revenues				
Revenues paid into the Exchequer				
☐ Assessments				
Expenditure				
☐ Civil and				
☐ Army				
☐ Navy				

Figures in £000

1654	1655	1656	1657	1658
801	872	1,019	953	832
786	698	797	381	333
251	250	250	236	252
1,059	570	769	742	599
1,567	1,508	1,058	1,900	1,347

8 The *Eikon Basilike*, first published in 1649, created the legend of Charles the Martyr. Written probably by John Gauden (1605–62) but supposed to be by Charles himself, it emphasized his dignity in adversity. Charles's posthumous reputation greatly assisted the cause of monarchy during the Commonwealth, but it is unlikely that he would have approved of the form of monarchy that his son accepted.

9 Events leading to the Restoration in May 1660 were complex. Richard Cromwell succeeded his father peacefully but faced difficulties from Parliament in 1659 and from the army, and resigned in May 1659. Power reverted to the divided army leadership which argued with the Rump, recalled for lack of any other source of authority, in the summer of 1659. An attempted Royalist rising in September 1659 received little support for fear of renewed civil war. Eventually General Monck (1608–70), army commander in Scotland, marched on London and summoned the Convention Parliament, which recalled Charles. The king's return was greeted with popular enthusiasm, but this followed rather than caused his restoration.

The Restoration of the Stuarts

The powers and position of the English monarchy, restored in 1660, were defined by the Convention Parliament (1660) and in the early sessions of the Cavalier Parliament (1661–79). Both these assemblies, like Charles II (1630–85) himself, wished to avoid the extremes of recent years. Parliament insisted on maintaining the limitations imposed on the Crown by the "constitutional revolution" of 1640–41. The king was not granted too large a revenue, so that he would be forced to call Parliament frequently to ask for more. Thus Charles had to summon Parliament almost every year until the very end of his reign. The gentry who sat in Charles II's parliaments were quite prepared to uphold the royal authority, provided the king used it in ways they approved.

The religious settlement

Charles's success as king therefore depended on his ability to keep the trust and goodwill of the House of Commons, above all by respecting the religious prejudices of the country. In the 1640s the old Church of England had been dismantled. In the resulting vacuum of religious authority new movements such as the Baptists and Quakers had grown and multiplied. The House of Commons of 1661, however, re-established the Church of England with severe laws against Protestant Nonconformists. Charles was not happy with this extremism. Apart from his personal Catholic tendencies, he was tolerant by nature. In 1660, before returning to England, he issued a declaration at Breda promising liberty to tender consciences, subject to the approval of Parliament. Parliament would not let him keep his promise, but Charles tried in 1662 and 1672 to procure greater liberty for Nonconformists.

More explosive was the problem of Catholicism, which became linked in the 1670s with questions of foreign policy. In 1670 Charles allied himself with Louis XIV (reigned 1643–1715) of France [Key]. In 1672 together they attacked the Protestant Dutch Republic, which was almost overrun by Louis's army. Louis was already feared as the archetype of absolutism and militant Catholicism, and Charles's alliance with him seemed doubly sinister when it became clear in the 1670s that Charles's brother James, Duke of York (1633–1701) [7], later James II, had become a Catholic. As Charles had no legitimate children, James was the heir apparent, and the prospect of the first Catholic monarch in England since Mary (reigned 1553–8) overshadowed the politics of the last half of Charles's reign.

Opposition to Catholicism

English Protestants had long identified Catholic rulers with both absolutism and cruel persecution [4]. In 1678 Titus Oates (1649–1705) [5], a disreputable adventurer, came forward with allegations of a "Popish Plot" to assassinate Charles and make James king. Three times between 1679 and 1681 the Commons passed bills to exclude the Duke of York from the succession, but neither the king nor the Lords would agree to them. Led by Anthony Ashley Cooper, Earl of Shaftesbury (1621–83) [6] the "Exclusionists" (who formed the nucleus of the embryonic Whig Party) mounted a strident campaign of petitions, propaganda and demonstrations. Echoes of the Civil War

1 **The Treaty of Breda** (1667) ended the 2nd Anglo-Dutch War. England thus renounced claims to the Dutch East Indies, but in return gained control of New York and New Jersey. Earlier, in 1660, Charles issued a declaration at Breda, in The Netherlands, promising a general pardon for activities during the revolution, as well as religious toleration, should he be invited back to the throne. He thus removed any obstacles to his restoration.

2 **Charles II**, unlike his father and brother, was a charming and popular man, although reluctant to devote himself to the details of government. Temperamentally suited to absolute government, he was determined not to be exiled again; and his cynical view of human nature made him try to control his ministers by playing one off against another. Much of the politics of his reign was therefore confused. This bust was made by Honoré Pellé.

3 **The Royal Society** was incorporated by Charles II in 1662. At that time interest in science was fashionable. The Society's early proceedings ranged from demography to botany, reflecting the polymathic interests of the members. The early Fellows included courtiers and dilettantes as well as men of outstanding talent such as Wren, Boyle and Newton. Above all, perhaps, the Society spread an understanding of "natural philosophy" to the ruling élite of England and thus contributed to the acceptance of the social thought of the Enlightenment and indirectly inspired the Industrial Revolution.

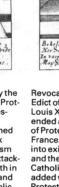

Romes Scarlet whore doth here in Triumph Ride;
And Spurns off Soveraign Crowns in Height of Pride
Poor Christians and brave Cities too shee Burns
And Stabbs and Poisons daily serve her Turns.

Behold our Church (like Esther here doth tender
Her Supplication to the Faiths Defender
In vain Rome Plots, whilst Charles & Scepter Sways
May Sled and Gibbet end all Traitors Days.

4 **Fear of Catholicism** during the Restoration was based on the Protestant feeling that not only was it erroneous and idolatrous theologically, but that it was a malign political force as well. It was thought that Catholic rulers, however gentle by nature, would be forced by the pope to persecute Protestants. The aggressive rule of Louis XIV in France seemed to show a clear link between Catholicism and absolutism, attacking Protestants both in his own kingdom and in the Dutch Republic. In particular the Revocation of the Edict of Nantes by Louis XIV in 1685 ended all toleration of Protestants in France. Many went into exile in England and their reports of Catholic intolerance added weight to the Protestants' fears of James II. Thus when James imprisoned for sedition seven bishops who refused to read his Declaration of Indulgence in May 1688 that promised toleration to the Catholics, as well as Dissenters, his attack on the Anglican Church, was seen as an attack on the rule of law.

CAROLVS II
SOCIETATI
REGALIS
AVTHOR
& PATRON...

agitations worried the more conservative opponents of Exclusion (who became known as Tories). They rallied to the king and helped Charles survive the exclusion crisis, permitting the peaceful accession of James II in 1685.

At first all went smoothly. James easily crushed a rebellion by James, Duke of Monmouth (1649–85) [8], an illegitimate son of Charles II and James's Protestant rival for the throne in the Exclusion crisis. But the Tories' co-operation with James soon ended. James hoped to give the Catholics religious liberty and political equality by repealing all the laws that prohibited Catholic worship and excluded Catholics from public office. The Tory Parliament of 1685 was strongly royalist but also strongly anti-Catholic. Annoyed by the Tories' hostility, James tried to persuade the Protestant dissenters to support a general toleration that would include Catholics. In 1686, despite opposition from Archbishop Sancroft (1617–93), he set up an ecclesiastic commission that was seen as an attempt to subject the Church to his religious policies. Meanwhile he stretched his powers

as Charles I had done in order to admit Catholics to places in the army, the administration and the universities.

The "Glorious Revolution"

James's nephew, William III of Orange (1650–1702), was closely interested in developments in England. Already the dominant political figure in the Dutch Republic, William had a claim to the English throne through his wife Mary, James's elder daughter, and he was eager to use England's fleet and wealth in his lifelong struggle against France. By 1688 William feared that he might be cheated of the succession, because late in 1687 it was announced that James's queen was pregnant. By the time James's son was born, in June 1688, William had decided to invade England in response to an invitation from leading political figures. He landed with his army on 5 November [9]. James fled to France and in February 1689 Parliament offered the crown jointly to William and Mary, and the rule of law, enshrining the supremacy of the landed interest over the monarch, was assured.

KEY

Charles II usually followed Louis XIV, not vice versa as in this cartoon. Except for the period 1678–81, Charles was allied with Louis (whose power he envied) or was benevolently neutral. Louis gave him several subsidies to help him to stay independent at home, and to resist Parliament's demands for a war against Louis, whom most Englishmen saw as the main enemy. Initially Charles sought the French alliance to avenge England's failure to win the 2nd Anglo-Dutch War of 1665–7.

5 Titus Oates, the main witness in the Popish Plot, had spent a year as a Jesuit novice and the stories that he told were based on the information he collected at various seminaries. Despite inconsistencies, he spoke so compellingly that many believed him. The murder of the magistrate to whom Oates first recounted the plot appeared to confirm all that he said. In 1685, however, he was convicted of perjury and flogged. The crisis allowed Shaftesbury, a former supporter of Charles who now feared his conversion to Roman Catholicism, to drum up anti-Catholic agitation and turn it against James, the Catholic heir to the throne. He died in voluntary exile in Holland.

6 The Earl of Shaftesbury had been a royal minister in the 1660s and early 1670s. His organization of the Exclusionists into a coherent parliamentary group was important for the development of political parties.

7 James II served as an able commander of the fleet during the 2nd Anglo-Dutch War, but as a Catholic he lacked Charles's popularity, and quickly alienated all the support that he had at his accession.

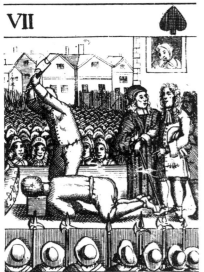

VII

The late D of M beheaded on Tower Hill 15 July 1685

8 The Duke of Monmouth landed in Dorset in 1685 to assert his claim to the throne. He won little gentry support and was easily beaten at Sedgemoor. His followers were treated with severity by Judge Jeffreys (c. 1648–89) in the so-called Bloody Assizes, at which 200 were hanged and 800 transported. Monmouth himself was executed.

9 William of Orange landed at Brixham late in 1688 with an army of 15,000 men. But his invasion succeeded without bloodshed (hence its name, the "Glorious Revolution"), as James's army commander John Churchill (1650–1722), later Duke of Marlborough, went over to William's side at the last moment, removing James's last source of support in the country.

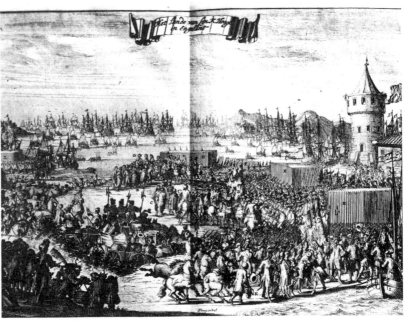

Pepys's London

The London of Samuel Pepys (1633–1703) [Key] was small (Marylebone and Mile End were in the country) and consisted of two cities: London, the commercial and financial centre; and Westminster, centre of government, politics and aristocratic society. The two were so different, culturally and politically, that there was often tension between them. Pepys, however, straddled both worlds. A Londoner by birth and a civil servant by profession, he moved easily between his office and lodgings near the Tower and the court at Whitehall. A man of quick intelligence, who paid careful attention to detail, he rose from a comparatively menial post to become James II's chief naval administrator.

Diary of a somebody

There was nothing very unusual about Pepys's rise to wealth and prominence. The Tudor and Stuart civil service offered a career open to talents. What was unusual about Pepys was his diary, which gives an unequalled panorama of life in London between 1660 and 1669: the politics of court and Parliament; meetings with naval contractors and mistresses; music and the theatre; food and drink; and tensions at the office and quarrels with the neighbours.

Insatiably curious and endlessly sociable, Pepys wanted to know everything that was going on and jotted it down, in shorthand, when he got home. On 25 March 1661 he told how, returning home, he "took up a boy that had a lanthorn, that was picking up rags, and got him to light me home, and had great discourse with him, how he could get sometimes three or four bushells of rags in a day, and got 3d a bushell for them, and many other discourses, what and how many ways there are for poor children to get their livings honestly":. Gossip about Charles II's sexual cavortings is juxtaposed with details of admiralty business or the latest experiment performed before the Royal Society. National humiliations such as the Medway disaster [6] appear alongside details of a meal.

Congestion, crime and natural disasters

At the Restoration, London [1] was the largest city in England. Its population – not far short of 500,000 – was more than ten times that of Bristol, its nearest rival. Little more than a century earlier, its population had been only 50,000 and it now displayed all the symptoms of unplanned urban growth. Within the old medieval walls rising population and property values encouraged landlords to build upwards and to overcrowd their property [3] despite municipal attempts to control them.

The fastest growth was to the east and north – Stepney, Whitechapel, Shoreditch, Clerkenwell – and south of the river in Southwark. There the speculative builder and slum landlord operated almost unchecked. Jerrybuilt tenements and insanitary courts housed artisans and porters, watermen and sailors, Huguenots and Irish.

As the population had far outgrown the flimsy machinery of law and order, crime flourished. Violence was never far below the surface in Restoration London. Drunken quarrels ended in murder. Courtiers and soldiers showed a casual disregard for human life. On public holidays law students from the Inns of Court and gangs of apprentices roamed the streets looking for trouble.

1 **London before the Great Fire** was a chaotic jumble of houses. Old St Paul's dominated the skyline and London Bridge, lined with homes and shops, was the only bridge across the Thames. The city's streets, filthy with rubbish, were dangerous at night because of criminals. The River Thames served as the main highway. It was quicker and cleaner than the narrow and congested cobblestoned streets.

2 **Charles II and his mistress Nell Gwynn** converse in the presence of diarist John Evelyn (1620–1706). Such a scene, wrote Evelyn, made him "heartily sorry". He was shocked by the king's promiscuity.

3 **Houses huddled against each other** in London. Most dwellings were built of wood, (despite regulations against its use) and they had narrow frontages, steep roofs and projecting upper floors.

4 **The plague of 1665–6** was carried by the rats that infested London's teeming tenements, and deaths exceeded 15 per cent of the population. By far the worst year was 1665. Carts trundled through the streets at night to collect corpses for communal burial. The court moved out of London as did many people. Houses touched by pestilence were vacated and the door marked with a red cross and with the words "Lord have mercy upon us".

Such a crowded, ill-housed population was vulnerable to the ravages of disease and fire, both of which struck terribly in the 1660s. The last great outbreak of bubonic plague (1665–6) [4] claimed more than 70,000 victims in London. Pepys wrote on 30 July 1665: "It was a sad noise to hear our bell to toll and ring so often to-day, either for deaths or burials; I think five or six times." The Great Fire of 1666 [5] destroyed most of the City of London. On 2 September Pepys watched the progress of the fire, "a most horrid malicious bloody flame".

Rebuilding and expansion

Out of this catastrophe came a chance to rebuild according to a single coherent plan [7] a great swathe of central London from the river up to London Wall and from Fenchurch Street to Fleet Street. From the ashes emerged a new city with broader, cleaner streets, brick-built houses, a much purer water supply and a whole series of churches [8] designed by the brilliant young architect Christopher Wren (1632–1723).

London had long been the greatest port in the kingdom, and under Charles II new trading companies were established, notably the Royal African and Hudson's Bay companies. But the main source of the impressive commercial growth of the 1670s and 1680s lay elsewhere. First, by protective legislation and naval power England began to challenge the Dutch dominance of the international carrying trade. This would at length enable London to replace Amsterdam as "the world's entrepôt". Second, these years saw a massive increase in imports and re-exports of sugar and tobacco from England's Caribbean and North American colonies. In addition, London was the hub of the growing internal trade within England.

Farther west, between the City of London and the City of Westminster, lay an area that had largely escaped the fire. Here were the palaces of the nobility, situated within convenient distance of Parliament and the royal palaces of Whitehall and St James's. The Strand had been developed much earlier and the main growth areas in Pepys's day were in Pall Mall, Piccadilly and St Giles's Fields – around the West End of the future.

KEY

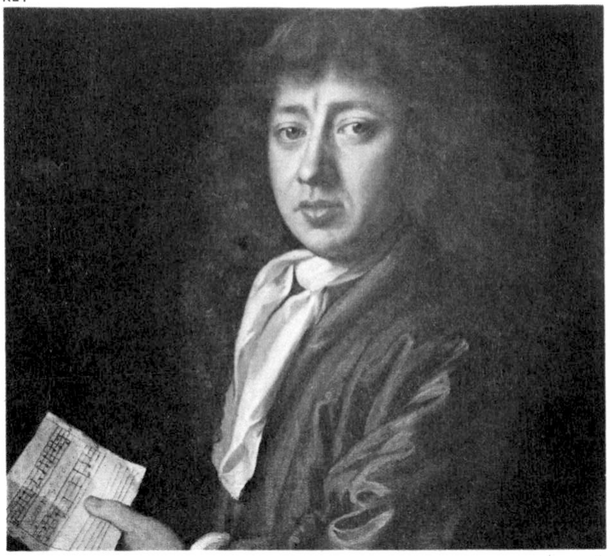

Samuel Pepys held an important post in the Navy Office, and was an MP and president of the Royal Society. His diary shows him to have been cultivated, fastidious, ambitious and lecherous.

5

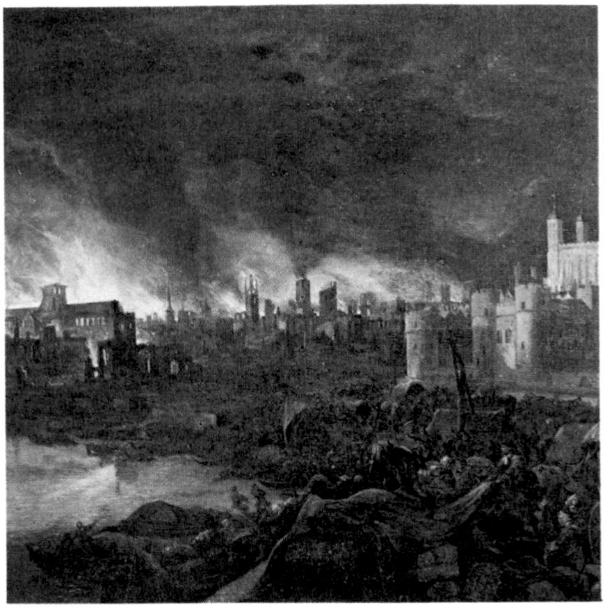

5 The Great Fire (1666) began in a baker's house in Pudding Lane and raged for three days. It destroyed 13,000 houses, St Paul's, 87 parish churches and many public buildings. Deaths were few but half the population was rendered homeless.

6

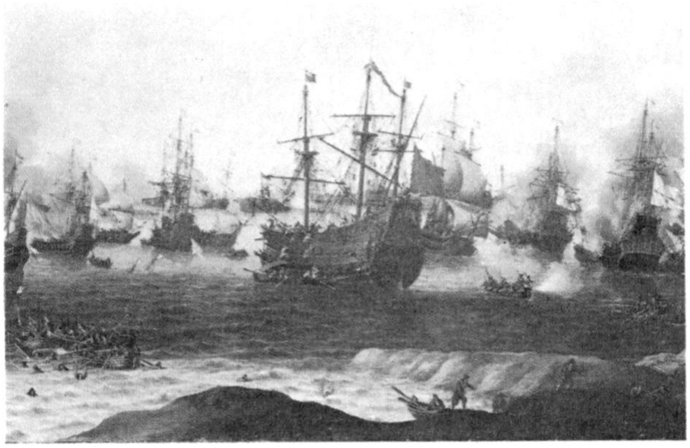

6 A Dutch fleet sailed up the Medway in June 1667, found defences almost nonexistent, and burned, sank or captured several of the king's greatest ships. The flagship *Royal Charles* was among those captured. Meanwhile, wrote Pepys bitterly, the king was chasing a moth with his mistress. The Dutch Wars flared intermittently from 1652 to 1674.

7

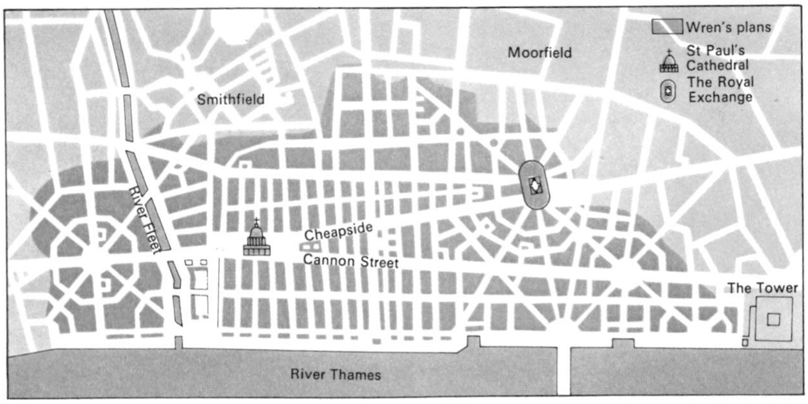
Wren's plans
St Paul's Cathedral
The Royal Exchange
Moorfield
Smithfield
River Fleet
Cheapside
Cannon Street
The Tower
River Thames

7 Several plans for rebuilding London were advanced after the Great Fire. Christopher Wren proposed that broad, straight streets should be laid down in a geometric pattern. A new St Paul's and Royal Exchange were the main focal points of his scheme, which featured several piazzas. But a shortage of money and conflicting interests meant that no scheme was adopted in full. Instead, the shape of the city was decided by a special committee.

8

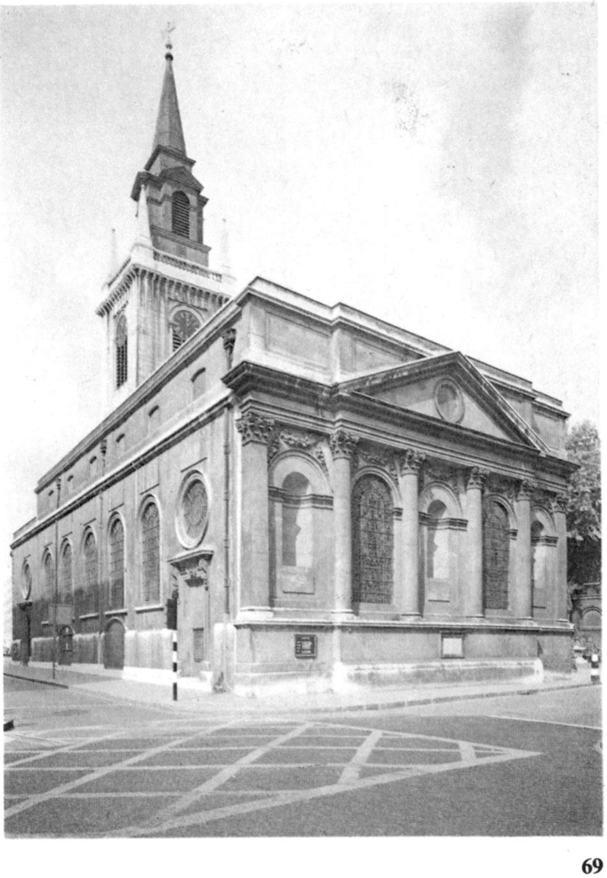

8 St Lawrence, Jewry, was one of the 53 churches that Christopher Wren built in London following the Great Fire. He was appointed Surveyor-General in 1669 with the task of rebuilding the city. These churches have distinctive spires but Wren lavished most attention on their interiors in which he made an interplay of rhythms and light spaces. No authority was able to buy enough land to organize the rebuilding in a centralized manner; but stringent regulations limited private builders.

Scotland from 1560 to the Act of Union

The religious upheavals in Scotland during the first half of the sixteenth century, initiated by the Reformation, found wide support for political as well as spiritual reasons. The new religious ideas were welcomed by those wishing to loosen the alliance with Catholic France in favour of England, and the nobles, who hoped to gain much from a weakening of the Church's power.

The Reformation and the Crown

With the abolition of papal authority in 1560, Calvinism quickly became the official belief in Scotland, but the ruler, Mary, Queen of Scots (reigned 1542–67), was a Catholic and a member of the French royal family [1]. On the death of her husband Francis II of France (reigned 1559–60), Mary returned to Scotland to try to establish her authority as queen.

She proved to be a clever politician but her power and public appeal were always limited by the tremendous influence of John Knox (1505–72), the leading preacher of the new church [3]. Eventually, in 1567, she was forced to abdicate by the nobility, who were angered at her turbulent marriages [2]. In

1568 she had to take refuge in England, and the nobles put her infant son James VI (reigned 1567–1625) on the Scottish throne with the expectation that a king so created would be their puppet.

On this point the nobles failed. James grew up to become the most effective ruler of any of the Stewarts. He did this without funds or force, but purely by negotiation and hard work, particularly helped by the fact that he was expected to inherit the English throne. He and his cousin, Elizabeth I of England (reigned 1558–1603), both wanted peace on the Border. In 1603, Elizabeth on her death-bed acknowledged James as her heir. James, known thereafter as James I, moved to England but continued to control Scotland as he said "by my pen" [Key].

James's son Charles I (reigned 1625–49) could not do this because he did not have the intimate knowledge of the country. His policy of personal rule made the Scottish nobility uneasy for their rights and powers while his religious policy was seen, rightly or wrongly, as contrary to Presbyterian principles. When Charles produced a prayer book

for Scotland in 1637 [4] it provoked the Scots to formulate a claim for their traditional liberties – the National Covenant. Charles's attempts to bring an English army to suppress the Covenanters led to the Long Parliament, and thus contributed to the start of the English Civil War in 1642.

The English Parliament persuaded the Scots to join in the first Civil War (1642–6) by accepting the terms laid down by the Scots in the Solemn League and Covenant, of 1643. But after the war, power lay in the hands of the Parliamentarians' army, which wanted an independent church system with liberty for the individual congregation. Efforts by the Scots to insist on Presbyterianism led to the second Civil War (1648), the execution of Charles (1649) and occupation of Scotland by Oliver Cromwell (1599–1658) [6].

Stuart restoration and dethronement

When the English Parliament called Charles II (reigned 1660–85) back to the throne [7], it was taken for granted that he would rule in Scotland too. However, some of the extreme

2 Mary's execution (shown here) took place in England in 1587, on the reluctant orders of her cousin Elizabeth. Mary had been driven out of Scotland in 1568 after the death of her cousin and husband Darnley, who had ordered the murder of Mary's Italian favourite, David Rizzio, in 1566. Elizabeth imprisoned Mary, who was also the heir to the English throne, for many years to prevent her from endangering Elizabeth's foreign and religious policies.

1 After the death of Henry II of France in 1559 (shown here), the French crown passed to Francis, the husband of Mary, Queen of Scots. This association of the Scottish queen with Catholic France weakened her popularity in Scotland; she adhered to her foreign tastes even after she returned to her home country in 1560. Her marriage to Darnley, also a Catholic, in 1565, was an attempt to overawe the Protestant opposition of Knox and Murray.

The Arch-Prelate of St Andrewes in Scotland reading the new Service-booke in his pontificalibus assaulted by men & women, with Crickets stooles Stickes and Stones.

3 John Knox compiled, with other Calvinist ministers, *The First Booke of Discipline* (1560) which was the blueprint for the creed and constitution of the Protestant Church in Scotland. It decreed a hierarchy of Church courts, substantial stipends for ministers of the new Church, and proposed a generous programme of public education. This last had only limited success because the nobility refused to surrender enough of the old Church's wealth to finance it.

4 The revised prayer book was introduced by Charles I in 1637 and caused widespread disturbances. Much of this was against its imposition on Scottish congregations, but many Scots also regarded the book as a source of dangerous innovations. Popular unrest led to the Covenant of 1638 – a signed agreement to defend the reformed religion. The rebellion of the Covenanters culminated in the First Bishops' War in 1639 which was peacefully settled in the same year. However, the Scottish assembly, organized to resolve the conflict, and the Scottish Parliament openly defied the king. Charles was refused funds for his army by the Short Parliament, and his forces were defeated in the Second Bishops' War in 1640.

Presbyterian Whiggamore Party refused to accept any government not chosen by them; this and Charles's policy of re-establishing episcopacy led to disturbances. In this period the Scottish economy became dependent on trade with England. Scotland had to take part in English wars, even when the opponents were The Netherlands (1665–7, 1672–4), its main trading partner, and economic nationalism in France and Sweden further deprived Scotland of overseas markets.

The Revolution of 1688–9 against the Catholicizing policy of James II (VII) (reigned 1685–8) was, like the Restoration, made in England and accepted in Scotland. But there was a larger and more effective resistance group this time, particularly in the Highlands, where many preferred James to the new King William III (reigned 1689–1702) because of William's reliance in Scotland on the unpopular house of Argyll. These Highland Jacobites, or supporters of the Stuart (as the Stewarts became known after 1603) line, defeated William's army in 1689 at the Battle of Killiecrankie in the southern Highlands, but were prevented by a regiment of Covenanters defending Dunkeld from breaking through into the Lowlands. Later, the remaining Jacobite clans were brought to temporary submission by the Glencoe massacre in February 1692 [8].

Events leading to the Union

With the failure of William III and the next ruler, Anne (reigned 1702–14), to produce an heir, there was a possibility that the Scottish Parliament might bring back James rather than accept the Hanoverian successor chosen by England. This reasoning seems to have persuaded the English to accept the idea of uniting the parliaments of the two countries. The increasing dependence on trade with England meant that economic sanctions could be used to compel the Scots to accept a union. There was a period of increased interest in the Jacobite cause, and hostility to England in the early 1700s, but in 1707 economic generosity by England and political generosity by Scotland brought about the union of the parliaments in Westminster [9], although leaving the laws and church systems of the countries distinct.

KEY

The English and Scottish Crowns were united in 1603 when James VI was crowned James I of England. But James was not able to effect a parliamentary union of the two kingdoms.

5 James Graham, Earl of Montrose (1612–50), was a leader of the Covenanters in the Bishops' Wars, although later, in the Civil War, he campaigned brilliantly for the king in Scotland.

6 General Monck (1608–70) commanded the English army in Scotland under the Protectorate. He took his army to London and made possible the restoration of the monarchy in 1660, with Charles II as king.

7 Charles II was crowned by the Marquess of Argyll (1606–61) [centre, right] in 1651, after compromising with the extreme Presbyterian Party. This ended in defeat by Cromwell in 1651.

8 The Massacre of Glencoe in 1692 took place after the Jacobite rising at Killiecrankie, three years earlier. William III demanded an oath of allegiance from the Highland clans, and the Macdonalds of Glencoe did not take it. As an example to other clans, 38 of the clan were slaughtered by government troops.

9 The Act of Union, in 1707, was made by commissioners from both countries and then passed into law by the separate parliaments. This process was relatively easy in England, but the Scottish Parliament needed a great deal of persuading by the Duke of Queensberry (1662–1711), shown attending Queen Anne's signing of the treaty.

Europe 1500–1700

In the first half of the sixteenth century the economy of Europe was dominated by a steady price rise; in the second, by unprecedented inflation. Price increases were felt first in Spain and resulted from the greatly increased imports of gold and silver from new mines in Mexico and Peru. The effects of this massive importation of bullion [5] were later offset by its export to other parts of Europe to liquidate Spain's unfavourable trade balances, to supply the needs of her armies in The Netherlands and by way of smuggling across the French frontier. Until these movements of bullion took effect general prices in the rest of Europe had risen more slowly than in the Iberian Peninsula.

Stimulus to international trade

This different rate of inflation in the European countries imparted a further stimulus to the expansion of international trade which had followed the discovery of the New World. The Baltic trade in corn with southern Europe, soon to be controlled and financed by the Dutch, was also promoted by the tendency of food prices to exceed those of manufactured goods. This was because an impressive growth in population in Europe [1, 2] – from 50–60 million in 1450 to nearly 100 million in 1600 – increased the demand for foodstuffs when supply was restricted by poor yields in corn-producing areas of eastern Europe.

Although industry still catered mainly for the provision of luxuries to the wealthy, commercial expansion led to a greater use of credit facilities and an extension in public banking, especially in Italy where Genoese financiers arranged the transfer of Spanish remittances to The Netherlands.

The Dutch "economic miracle"

In the seventeenth century many of these trends were reversed. Inflation was checked in the second decade by decreasing imports of bullion from the New World. International trade, buttressed by the defence requirements of the Thirty Years War (1618–48), later experienced a downturn and stagnated. Competition between the powers for a preponderant share of world trade led to the adoption by most governments, except the Dutch, of mercantilism, a system of protectionist trade policies.

The shift of the centre of commercial activity from the Mediterranean to the Atlantic seaboard, however, continued. The chief beneficiary, apart from England, was the Dutch Republic, which won virtual great-power status by its pre-eminence in the carrying trade, exploration and finance [8]. This "economic miracle", occurring in a period of general contraction, rested on Dutch control of the North Sea herring and the Newfoundland cod fisheries; on technical expertise in shipbuilding and insurance; on the elimination of the Portuguese from the Far Eastern spice trade and the Spanish from their monopoly of commerce with South America; on the international, exchange and credit facilities provided by the Bank of Amsterdam (founded in 1609) [11]; and on the policy of toleration which induced the prosperous victims of religious persecution in Spain and France – the Sephardic Jews and Huguenots – to settle in Amsterdam [Key].

Economic and naval warfare between the Dutch Republic (the United Provinces of the

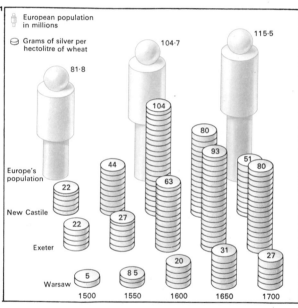

1 **The rapid rate of inflation** during this period (in which all food prices rose steeply) has no conclusive explanation. But population growth seems to have been a major factor.

2 **The growth of population** during the sixteenth century was considerable. The increase seems to have begun around 1450 and become more rapid after 1500. The recurrence of plague and the long duration of European wars had, by the mid-seventeenth century, reduced the rate of growth once more. The diagram illustrates the changing population figures of the major European nations between 1500 and 1700.

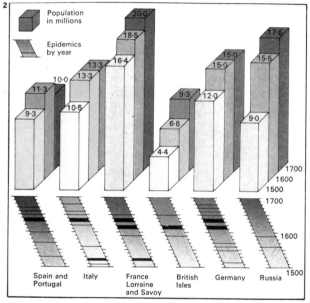

3 **Death by plague** had been common in Europe for almost two centuries. Periodic epidemics were a major check on population growth, but it is difficult to assess accurately the effects of plague in an age when routine diseases and accidents also made a significant contribution to the high mortality rate. Between a sixth and a third of the population died in each epidemic, although this figure could rise to as much as two-thirds, as happened in Germany in the 1630s. Plague also had some long-term effects; unstable social and economic conditions pushed up the age of marriage and thus lowered the birth-rate. Worst hit by the plague were the crowded, badly housed urban poor.

4 **In early modern Europe** life was hard for the ordinary man, as depicted by Bruegel the Younger. Beggars were a common sight and for the labourer the holy days of the Church were the only respite from the burdens of his day-to-day existence. But the Church also ordained that periods of abstention from any work or indulgence must be strictly observed. Such decrees were often not followed; in Charles I's reign, Archbishop Laud (1573–1645) encouraged sports on the sabbath.

5 **Silver mined in the New World** and imported by Spain had a considerable influence on political and economic life in Europe. How Spain distributed this bullion between 1580 and 1626 is shown here. Spending in Spain and The Netherlands reflects the huge sums used for defence. The rest of Europe, learning from Spain, looked to trade to provide the wealth necessary for military power.

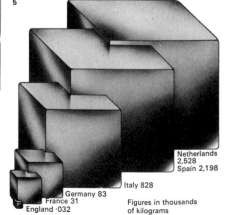

Netherlands 2,528
Spain 2,198
Italy 828
Germany 83
France 31
England ·032

Figures in thousands of kilograms

northern Netherlands) and their main rivals, England and France, impaired Dutch commercial supremacy [6] in the late 1600s; it was finally undermined during the War of the Spanish Succession (1701-14).

European society, 1500–1700

The society of early modern Europe was principally agrarian with 90 per cent of the population deriving a living from the land. Farming was carried out under the jurisdiction of the manorial lord, although the farmer was also governed by various local customs. Inflation, however, was a social solvent that loosened the characteristic rigidity of sixteenth-century society where status was determined by law and not by wealth. The medieval concepts of a "just price" and a controlled economy also ceased to be valid. Until the end of the sixteenth century the pressure of population on the means of subsistence involved a fall in living standards and a decline in real wages.

The more volatile situation in the seventeenth century enabled the emergent middle classes to consolidate their wealth and to improve their social status. Generally the people who profited most were those who could charge higher prices without in turn having to pay them. These were the farmers whose tenure was secure and those noblemen who could evict their tenants and exploit the land. For those who were landless or whose title to their land was insecure, the real effect of the price rises was eviction, vagrancy and perhaps death by starvation. Because a smaller work force was needed for pasture farming many were condemned to a life of wandering as beggars [4]. From the landowners' point of view labour was relatively cheap and this helped to stimulate improvements in agricultural and manufacturing processes.

The seventeenth century saw the growth of mining, finishing industries (such as dyeing), tobacco-growing and even market gardening. But the place of "manufacture" in this period was the cottage and not the factory; cloth was distributed piecemeal to be spun, dressed or dyed by rural labourers or farmers, whose living standards improved as prices tended to fall.

KEY

Amsterdam, more than any other city, illustrates the revolution in the economic life of early modern Europe. During the 17th century the axis of economic activity shifted north – from a concentration on trade in the Mediterranean to a prevailing emphasis on Atlantic trade. As the centre of the Dutch carrying trade, Amsterdam became a mart, a world bank and a centre of insurance for traders.

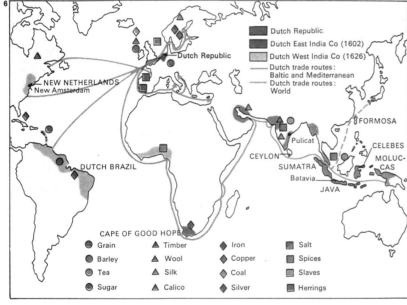

6 The Dutch held economic sway in Europe principally by carrying the products of other countries. The central areas of the carrying trade were the Mediterranean, the English Channel and the Baltic. The East Indies were the source of spices and luxury goods for resale in Europe. The West India Company had the more political aim of reducing Spanish trade by privateering.

7 Wealth and culture went hand in hand during the golden age of Dutch trading. Dutch art of the 17th century reflects the alliance, as in Rembrandt's celebrated portraits of wealthy Dutch merchants.

8 Rich Amsterdam merchants provided most of the backing for the Dutch East India and West India Companies. Both were joint-stock companies in which there were many shareholders, thus dividing the risks as well as the profits involved in colonial trade. The diagram illustrates the sources of the capital invested in the two companies when they were originally formed.

9 Cloth was one of the most important 17th-century manufactures. Italian silk damask-weaving techniques of the 15th century (shown here) were taken to England from Flanders in the 16th century.

10 Venice was one of Europe's most important trade centres at the start of the sixteenth century. However, the wars in the early part of the century and the colonization of the New World shifted the focus of trade to Atlantic ports such as Amsterdam and Bristol.

11 The growth of joint-stock trade over long distances gave rise to the need for more flexible instruments of credit and exchange. Significantly, the Dutch first broke from the tradition of raising money from private families such as the Fuggers, and the Bank of Amsterdam (shown here) was set up in 1609. The Bank of England, opened in 1694, was modelled on it.

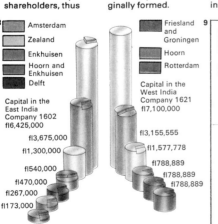

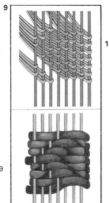

Amsterdam	Friesland and Groningen
Zealand	Hoorn
Enkhuisen	Rotterdam
Hoorn and Enkhuisen	
Delft	

Capital in the East India Company 1602
fl6,425,000
fl3,675,000
fl1,300,000
fl540,000
fl470,000
fl267,000
fl173,000

Capital in the West India Company 1621
fl7,100,000
fl3,155,555
fl1,577,778
fl788,889
fl788,889
fl788,889

Science and technology 1500–1700

By the dawn of the sixteenth century the European Renaissance was well under way, and during the following two centuries the broad basis of modern science was laid. Knowledge of Greek science was widespread and an inquiring spirit that led to a critical examination of ancient ideas prevailed. As a result, the ancient practices of astrology and alchemy were being discarded; some scientists and philosophers realized that nature had to be investigated rationally.

The revolution in astronomy

The first fruits of this new approach came in astronomy. In 1543 the theory that the Sun, not the Earth, was the centre of the universe appeared in *De Revolutionibus* by Nicolas Copernicus (1473–1543). This theory profoundly affected man's view of himself and his place in nature. In astronomy the Copernican theory stimulated a spate of precise observations – notably by Tycho Brahe (1546–1601) – laying the basis for seventeenth-century discoveries with the telescope. Johannes Kepler (1571–1630) used Brahe's observations in his reinterpretation of the planets' motions in terms of ellipses instead of the complex Copernican system of circles. In England, Francis Bacon (1561–1626) advocated the empirical method but denigrated the use of mathematics for the interpretation of results, unlike René Descartes (1596–1650), whose work contains many of the philosophical ideas that were at the root of the new spirit of enquiry. Descartes wanted to lay a rational foundation for religion and science to give them a mathematical validity, proof against scepticism and superstition. He formulated an entire philosophical system that postulated a wholly mechanical universe in space completely filled with fluid matter [1].

The Italian astronomer, mathematician and physicist Galileo Galilei (1564–1642) became the first person to use the telescope to study the heavens. Galileo's conclusions about mechanics laid the foundations for later work, particularly Newton's [6]. But his belief in a universe governed by mathematically regular laws led to great hostility, not least from the Church. The genius of this period was Isaac Newton (1642–1727), whose *Philosophiae Naturalis Principia Mathemetica* is one of the most important works of modern science. In it he defined his laws of motion [Key], developing Kepler's and Galileo's work, and he first formulated the law of universal gravitation. Newton also made important contributions to mathematics, including the invention of calculus, although it had been formulated quite independently by Gottfried Leibniz (1646–1716), the German mathematician.

Discoveries in optics

Science gained new impetus in the seventeenth century from the invention of the telescope and the microscope. Galileo, using the telescope, was able to observe mountains on the Moon, spots on the Sun, the phases of Venus and the four larger satellites of Jupiter. Improved instruments followed, Newton perfecting the first reflecting telescope in about 1668. This led to further discoveries, as well as the use of the telescope as a celestial measuring instrument of great precision, and the establishment of national observatories in Paris and at Greenwich [2].

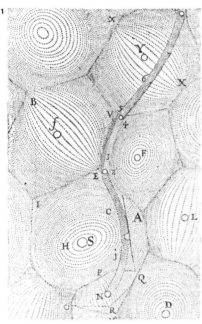

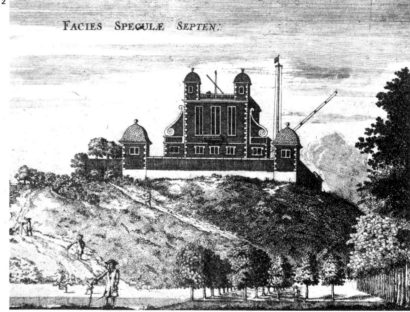

1 Descartes' idea of the universe rejected the theory of the existence of a vacuum and held that matter filling the universe was perpetually moving in vortices with stars at their centres. Some stars became planets with orbits in the vortex of another star. Comets wound their way between and across vortices, as in this engraving.

2 The Royal Observatory at Greenwich was founded in 1675 to compile a new star catalogue for navigational use. Designed by Christopher Wren, it became an important centre for accurate astronomical observations. The meridian of zero longitude still runs through Greenwich, but actual observation is now done in Sussex.

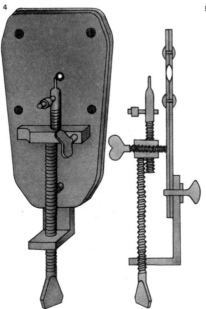

3 Vesalius, the great 16th-century anatomist, is shown holding a partly dissected human arm. The portrait is taken from his book *De Humani Corporis Fabrica*.

4 The powerful, single-lens microscope was designed in the 17th century by van Leeuwenhoek.

5 The discovery of the circulation of the blood was published by Harvey in his book *De Motu Cordis,* in 1628. Harvey is shown in Hannah's painting demonstrating the principle to Charles I.

The seventeenth century saw much fundamental work on optics. Willibrord Snell (1591–1626) determined the law of refraction of light. Christiaan Huygens (1629–95) used this knowledge to improve telescopes, also working with information from Kepler's study of lenses. Above all, Newton showed that white light could be split by a prism into components of every colour.

Developments in medicine

In 1538 Andreas Vesalius (1514–64) [3] produced his vast study of the human body – the first to go against the teachings of Galen (AD c. 130– c. 200). Vesalius' successor at Padua University, Bartolommeo Eustachio (1520–74), discovered the Eustachian tubes of the ears. In the next century Hieronymus Fabricius (1537–1619) laid the foundations of embryology and discovered valves in the veins, a finding that was used by William Harvey (1578–1657) [5] who, in 1628, announced his discovery of the circulation of the blood. Marcello Malpighi (1628–94) discovered the capillaries connecting veins and arteries and, like Jan Swammerdam

(1637–80) after him, used it also in embryological studies. The microscope greatly helped to advance medical and biological knowledge during a period when they became increasingly based on physiological experiment. In Holland, Anton van Leeuwenhoek (1632–1723) devised his own microscopes to study blood and spermatozoa as well as microscopic life forms [4].

In the sixteenth century botanical encyclopedias became common. In the next century Nehemiah Grew (1641–1712) used the microscope to study the sex organs of plants, and Robert Hooke (1635–1703), John Ray (1627–1705) and others began to reclassify the plant and animal kingdoms. In chemistry, Robert Boyle (1627–91) experimented on the physical properties of air and formulated his law on the relationship between the pressure and volume of a gas.

Rationalism and observation now replaced superstition and dogma as scientific guidelines. With this new spirit scientific societies could flourish; the Royal Society was founded in 1660 in London and the Académie des Sciences in Paris in 1699.

The third of Isaac Newton's three laws of motion states that to every action there is an equal and opposite reaction. An experiment designed to prove the validity of the theory is shown in this early 18th century book on Newton's laws. A metal globe emits a jet of steam in one direction and causes the "engine" to react by moving in the opposite direction.

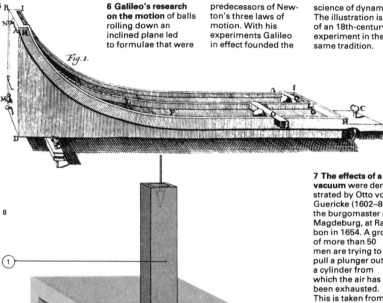

6 Galileo's research on the motion of balls rolling down an inclined plane led to formulae that were predecessors of Newton's three laws of motion. With his experiments Galileo in effect founded the science of dynamics. The illustration is of an 18th-century experiment in the same tradition.

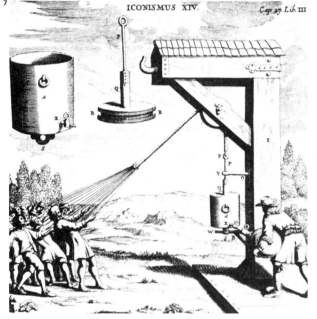

ICONISMUS XIV.   Cap 29 Lib. III

7 The effects of a vacuum were demonstrated by Otto von Guericke (1602–86), the burgomaster of Magdeburg, at Ratisbon in 1654. A group of more than 50 men are trying to pull a plunger out of a cylinder from which the air has been exhausted. This is taken from von Guericke's book *Experimenta Nova*.

8 A 16th-century ventilator for a mine worked as follows. A water wheel [6] drove a fan through step-up wooden gearing. The blades [3] of the fan were tipped with feathers [4] and ran inside a drum [2]. Air was sucked down the ventilation shaft [1] by the fan and distributed by a duct [5] to the mine workers.

9 Printing from movable type radically improved the dissemination of knowledge about scientific discoveries in Europe by the 16th century. This woodcut of 1568 by Jost Amman shows a printing works with compositors setting up type in the background, while in the foreground the press is being operated.

The age of Marlborough

In January 1689 William III controlled the government and armed forces of England. He alone could maintain order and prevent confusion and was therefore in a strong enough position to prevent Parliament from imposing new restrictions on his power. The Declaration of Rights, read to William and Mary before they were offered the Crown, condemned James II's abuses of power and otherwise was so vague as to be unenforceable. William's position seemed as strong as that of Charles II in 1660, but with one crucial difference – Charles was granted a revenue for life; William was not, and as a result was to rely on Parliament for money.

England at war

From 1689 to 1697 and again from 1702 to 1713 England was involved in European wars of unprecedented scale. England declared war on France in 1689 because James II had fled there and hoped to recover his throne with the help of Louis XIV. But once involved, the English found themselves caught in the meshes of European power-politics. The English navy was already

formidable but William III also turned the English army into the great fighting force that John Churchill, Duke of Marlborough (1650–1722) [3] was to use so brilliantly in a series of battles [4, 8]. Under Charles II England had been neither a major European power nor a military power, but by 1713 it was both. The War of the Spanish Succession concerned the future of the ailing Spanish Empire, and the treaty of Utrecht that ended the war in 1713 established Britain as the major colonial power.

The huge sums needed to sustain the war intensified the Crown's dependence on Parliament. Never before had the Commons voted so many taxes. The Triennial Act (1694) meant that new parliaments were called every three years, and were thus less easily managed by the government. Members of Parliament naturally wanted to know how their taxes had been spent, and demanded more and more detailed accounts. The Commons began to take a much more constructive attitude towards finance, voting taxes, not to spend on the war, but to pay interest on long-term loans from the public.

Parliamentary taxes constituted excellent security and, as a result, the government's credit was good. It could therefore borrow vast sums much more cheaply than could the other European monarchies. But the king's credit now depended so much on Parliament that its management became more important than ever. Those politicians who could control the Commons were in a position to make the king heed their advice.

The war also led to a great expansion of both the armed forces and the revenue administration. Ministers thus had many more rewards at their disposal than in the past; they used offices and pensions to buy support in and control of the Commons.

Whigs and Tories

Because the government had to borrow more money, those institutions that could lend on a large scale became increasingly powerful. These included the great trading companies and the Bank of England, established in 1694 [5]. The rise of this "moneyed interest" broke the landowners' traditional monopoly of political power. Country gentlemen saw

1 **William III** (r. 1689–1702) and Mary (r. 1689–94) were invited jointly to the throne in order to save the country from James II's Catholicism; William, who had been fighting Louis XIV for many years in The Netherlands, saw English naval strength as vital for him to defeat France permanently. This print shows him holding a globe on which Belgium, England and Scotland are marked as "free", and France and Spain are "to be freed".

2 **The Quakers**, whose Synod is shown in session, were one of several Protestant sects that had sprung up in England by 1660 and asked only for toleration. Before 1640, although there had been disputes about the form of the Church of England, only the most extreme questioned the need for a single national Church. Anglican magistrates and clergy regarded the new sects as socially and politically subversive – Quakers refused to doff their hats to their social superiors – and so Dissenters were persecuted sporadically under Charles II. The persecution ended with the 1689 Toleration Act, although Dissenters were still excluded from public office.

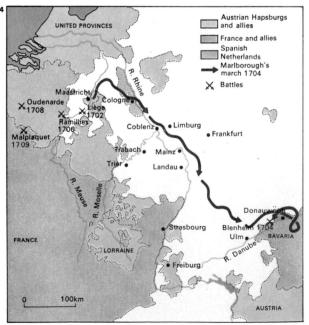

3 **John Churchill, Duke of Marlborough,** owed his rise first to the favour of James II and then to the great influence of his own wife Sarah Jennings (1660–1744) over her close friend Anne, James's younger daughter; Anne became queen when

William died (1702). It was Marlborough's great credit with Anne, more than his as yet unproven military genius, which led William to groom Marlborough from 1700 to 1702 to succeed him as leader of the great coalition against France.

4 **The War of the Spanish Succession** (1702–13) saw England, Holland and Austria joined against France. At Blenheim (1704) after a quick march across Germany, Marlborough eliminated Bavaria, and prevented Louis from knocking out the

Austrians by attacking Vienna. From 1705 Louis' efforts were concentrated in the southern Netherlands where, after some striking allied successes, at Ramillies (1706) and Oudenarde (1708) he was bogged down in a war of attrition until 1713.

Austrian Hapsburgs and allies
France and allies
Spanish Netherlands
Marlborough's march 1704
Battles

the wars as a conspiracy to divert their hard-earned money into the pockets of bankers, contractors and civil servants. As the landowners were mostly Tories and the moneyed men mostly Whigs, this feeling added to the new bitterness of party politics. High taxation eventually made the wars unpopular and Marlborough himself was removed from his command and retired to Blenheim Palace [Key] as the result of a political vendetta, soon after a sweeping Tory election victory in 1710.

The other great political issue of the period 1689–1714 was religion. The Toleration Act of 1689 allowed most Protestant Dissenters [2] to worship freely but not to hold public office. The Church of England lost its monopoly of religious worship and of education. In 1695 the clergy also lost the last vestiges of their control over the press. Even so, the universities were still closed to Dissenters. The rigid Anglicans, concentrated in the Tory Party, bitterly resented this erosion of the Church's authority. They attacked Dissenting schools and occasional conformity (whereby a Dissenter took the sacrament in

an Anglican church in order to qualify for office). The Tories' views might be reactionary but they had a great deal of popular support. In 1710 Dr Henry Sacheverell was impeached by the Commons after an intemperate sermon. The sermon sold a hundred thousand copies, Sacheverell became a popular hero and his Whig prosecutors were routed in the general election of 1710 [6].

The whirl of party politics
That particular period experienced the most vigorous electoral politics seen in England before 1832. The electorate was volatile and independent – and predominantly Tory. Other than the support of the moneyed interest the Whigs had one great electoral asset, fear of Jacobitism – of a return of Catholic rule if James II's son could seize power. The Whigs exploited this fear after the failure of the Jacobite rising of 1715. They had already won over the new king, the Hanoverian George I (1660–1727) [7]. But after the political excitement of Anne's reign came the relative political stagnation of the age of Walpole and the Whig supremacy.

Blenheim Palace, which stands in a beautiful park in Oxfordshire, was designed for Marlborough by John Vanbrugh (1664–1726). It testified to the gratitude of Parliament to a great general and to the profitability of high office.

5 An early bank-note issued by the Bank of England in 1699 is illustrative of the bank's steadily growing capital. The Bank of England was one of the first commercial banking companies to be established in England. It was originally incorporated to lend the government £1,200,000, and empowered to issue paper money. It established the National Debt as a means of financing the war, leaving the debt for later generations to pay.

The Mytre in one hand and league in t'othu Shew that the Tubster is a fickle Brother.

6 Henry Sacheverell (c. 1674–1724) became famous in 1709 for his sermon "The perils of false brethren", in which he stated that subjects should offer no resistance to their governments, and he criticized the Glorious Revolution of 1688–9 as an act of resistance to the divinely sanctioned monarch. In particular he violently opposed the toleration of Dissenters, arguing for a strong episcopacy, and by implication supported the agreement ("league") by which Louis promised to help James II to regain his throne. The Whigs impeached Sacheverell for sedition but the London mob rioted on his behalf and sympathy for him contributed to the Tory electoral victory in 1710.

7 The ceiling of the Painted Hall now in the Royal Naval College at Greenwich depicts the two foreign rulers who symbolized England's deliverance from Catholic rule: William III and George I (r. 1714–27). The latter was named heir to the throne after it became clear that Anne would leave no heir. The ceiling was painted by James Thornhill (1675–1734) and the dining hall is one of the most magnificent frescoed rooms in Britain.

8 The allied victory at Blenheim was made possible by two principal factors. The first of these was Marlborough's bold tactics. The French centre was weak and relied on marshy ground between the rival armies to impede the progress of the English and Austrian forces. But Marlborough's cavalry picked and floundered its way across with the aid of planks and brushwood and then routed the French infantry. The second factor was guile – even deceit – which Marlborough used to hoodwink the English and Dutch governments into allowing their troops to give battle so far from home.

The age of Louis XIV

In 1660 France was internally divided, rent by faction. The rebellion of the "officers" and nobles in the Fronde – years of chronic civil unrest from 1648 to 1653 – had presented a threat of civil war and driven Cardinal Mazarin (1602–61), the first minister during Louis XIV's minority, from Paris. The work of Richelieu in re-establishing the authority of the monarchy had collapsed. France needed a strong adult king. In March 1661 Mazarin died and the young Louis, then 23 years old, decided to dispense with a first minister and to rule as well as reign. By that decision he restored to the crown the charisma surrounding it and the obedience owed to a divinely appointed king. He was determined to restore authority and majesty to the Bourbon dynasty in France and in Europe and, further, to end the disorder that affronted a dynasty ordained by God.

The theme of order is important in understanding Louis XIV's policies at home and abroad. Louis' obsession with order is depicted best at Versailles [3]: the architecture of the palace and the plan of the gardens and fountains follow the rules of symmetry;

elaborate ceremonial accompanied the king's actions throughout the day. Louis reduced the powers of nobles, *parlements* and the various provincial and national interest groups which he felt had swelled beyond their true station. Centralization extended court authority into the provinces. Agents of the central government (*intendants*) supervised regional affairs while the nobles were kept busy with entertainment at Versailles. Order demanded too the eradication of heresy. The French Protestants (Huguenots) lost the right to practise their faith and were forced to conform or go into exile by the revocation of the Edict of Nantes in 1685.

Foreign policy
The same belief in order and justice lay behind Louis' foreign policy. He aimed to restore to France all territories to which it once had a claim and to extend the nation to its "natural frontiers". What Louis saw as rights, the rest of Europe regarded as naked aggression. War characterized the reign of Louis XIV and campaigns were almost continuous from 1667 onwards. The War of

Devolution, concerned with Louis' claim to the Spanish Netherlands, was fought during 1667 and 1668; the war against Holland from 1672 to 1678; the War of the League of Augsburg from 1688 to 1697; and the War of the Spanish Succession from 1702 to 1713. The needs of war directed all departments of government to require new taxes and increases in the traditional *taille* (land tax) and *gabelle* (salt tax) to further administrative and technological developments.

Economic policy
The economic policies of Jean Baptiste Colbert were a response to the needs of war. France needed to be self-sufficient if she was not to depend on her enemies, especially the Dutch. Colbert attempted to stimulate the growth of native French industries [5] – iron and textiles – and especially the production of luxury goods, such as silk and lace. When these fashionable goods were acquired from the Mediterranean and the East Indies they were often brought to France by the Dutch and had to be purchased with bullion. As contemporary economic attitudes associated

1 A majestic image was a central facet of the absolutism of Louis XIV. The pre-eminence of the king was seen as part of divine and natural order, the establishment of his power a duty to God. Louis described that pre-eminence in his memoirs: "All eyes are fixed on him [the King] alone; it is to him that all wishes are addressed; he alone receives all respect; he alone is the object of all hopes . . . no one can raise himself but by gradually coming close to the royal person or estimation . . . one can even say that the splendour emanating from him in his own territories spreads as by communication into foreign provinces."

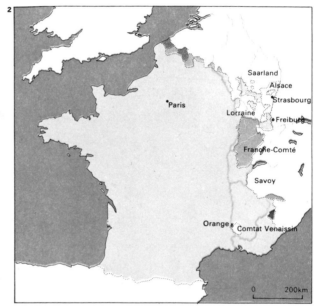

France in 1661

Acquired in Treaty of Aix-la-Chapelle 1668

Acquired in Treaties of Nijmegen 1678–9

Ceded to Savoy in 1696

Acquired in Treaty of Ryswick 1697

Acquired in Treaty of Utrecht 1713

2 France's northern and southern defences were strengthened by the acquisition of various frontier towns by treaties. Louis XIV's foreign policy was directed to annexing to France areas that would consolidate the frontiers. The map shows the territories gained over the course of 50 years.

3 The palace of Versailles, commenced before 1671, was the microcosm of the ideal order which Louis wanted for the kingdom. Situated 19km (12 miles) west of Paris, which had been the scene of the disorder of the Fronde, Versailles was built and the gardens laid out with geometric proportions. When the full court was established there in the 1680s, seven or eight thousand dependants were lodged to pass their time in admiration of the royal splendour or in the attractions of elaborate court games. But detachment from Paris made the monarchy remote. It symbolized an ideal and an administration that had been superimposed on the reality of political life.

power with the possession of bullion these imports could not be tolerated. More trade and industry meant more power and wealth. Mercantilist economic theory meant economic war and because of this Colbert embarked upon a tariff policy [6] to hamper the Dutch. The French East India Company was formed in an attempt to wrest trade from the Dutch in the colonies which remained an important source of bullion.

For much of his reign Louis appeared to have fulfilled his desires. Order was established at home, territories were conquered and recognized as French possessions by treaty, military victories were won. Colbert's new industries enjoyed some success and France emerged as a rival to the legendary commercial supremacy of the Dutch and the English. The glory of the Bourbon dynasty was recognized: Versailles and French absolutism became the model for other monarchs to emulate.

But the achievements were won at the cost of great strain at home and the enmity of almost every power in Europe. As the cost of war reached unprecedented levels royal finances began to fail. Louis never felt strong enough to tax the nobility and there was no developed system of credit in France. When in 1688 William of Orange, the Stadholder of Holland, became King of England the might of two naval powers was joined and the financial resources of the two most advanced commercial nations in the world were placed at the disposal of Louis' bitterest enemy.

Reaction and rebellion
As war continued and defeats piled up there was mounting reaction in France. The peasants, who bore the brunt of taxation but who were the least able to pay it, rebelled. Towards the end of the reign, shortages of grain became acute. Serious crises in 1693–4 and 1709–10 forced up grain prices and led to many deaths in country areas. The nobility reacted against Bourbon ambition and ostentation. Many trumpeted the virtues of the humbler life of pastoral simplicity and rural retreat. Louis' absolutism, centred on Versailles, became more and more remote from the nation, a symbol of the strength and the limitations of autocratic rule.

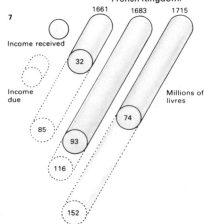

The glory of Louis XIV (1638–1715), the Sun King, is symbolized in his emblem.

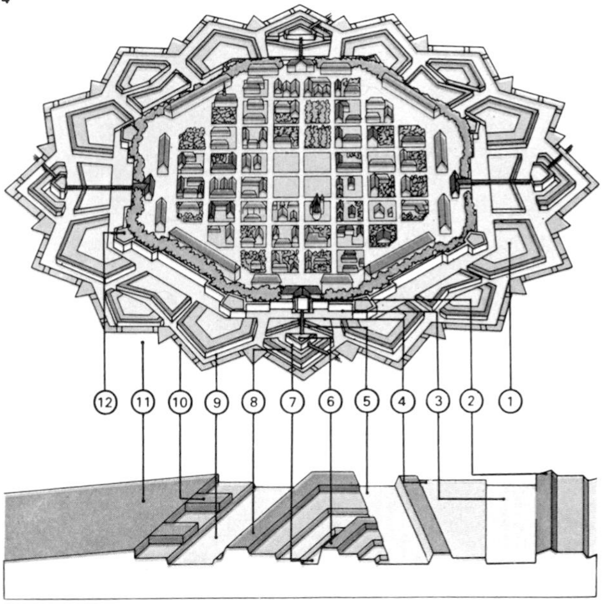

4 Methods of fortification were greatly improved by Sebastian de Vauban (1633–1707), as demonstrated by Neuf Brisach fortress at Alsace. Situated vulnerably on flat ground, its defences extended in depth round the whole circuit by detaching bastions [1] from the inner line, filling the gaps with *demilunes*, surrounding *ravelins*. First came the curtain [2], then a moat [3], *tenaille* [4] and second moat [5]. Next a *ravelin* [6], moat [7], *demilune* [8], outer moat [9], covered way [10] and lastly the *glacis* [11], sloping to outer ground level. The inner rampart was commanded by angled "bastion towers" [12].

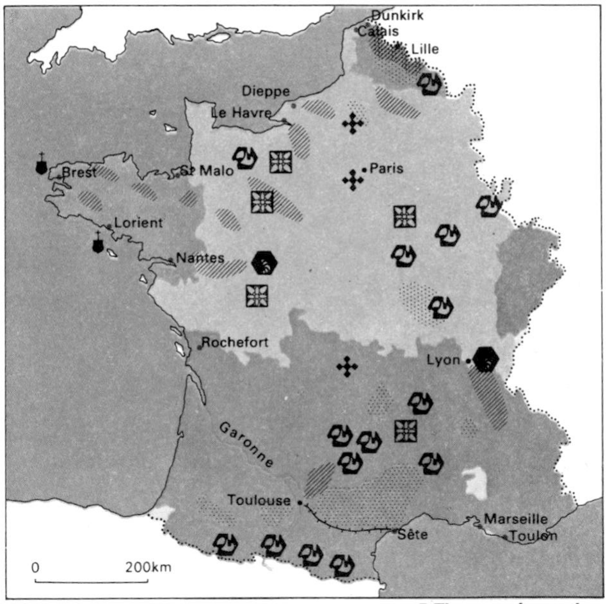

5 The map shows the industries fostered by Colbert (1619–83) as part of his mercantilist policy. It shows too the internal customs areas that had resulted from the gradual growth of the French Kingdom.

Key:
- The five major "tax farms"
- "Foreign" provinces
- Provinces not under French control
- Ports
- Canal du Midi
- Linen
- Cloth
- Tapestries
- Lace
- Shipbuilding
- Iron works
- Silk

Map labels: Dunkirk, Calais, Lille, Dieppe, Le Havre, Brest, St Malo, Paris, Lorient, Nantes, Rochefort, Lyon, Garonne, Toulouse, Marseille, Sète, Toulon
0 200km

6 Colbert sought to bring order to the multiplicity of internal and external tariffs which impeded French trade. He also intended to employ a protective tariff to defend newly developed French industries and to hit at Dutch and English competition. The first tariff (1664) was primarily a product of the first aim of consolidation. The second, of 1667, strongly protected the French textile industry. The tariff brought retaliatory duties against French wine, and economic rivalry brought war with the Dutch in 1672. At the Peace of Nijmegen (1678), economic questions were settled in favour of the Dutch and the customs tariffs of 1664 and 1667 were lifted.

6 A Fine English and Dutch woollens, piece of 25 ells
B Fine Spanish woollens, piece of 30 ells
C Flemish tapestries per hundredweight
D Lace and embroidered linen per pound
E Tanned ox leather per dozen hides
F Tin plate per barrel

○ 1667 tariff in livres
○ 1664 tariff in livres

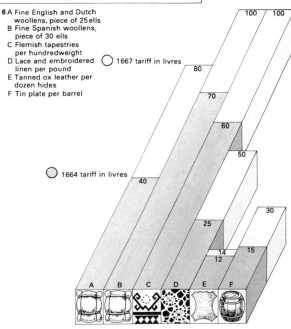

7 One of the major financial problems of the monarchy stemmed from the difficulty of collecting taxes and ensuring the moneys due actually arrived at the Treasury. Under Colbert the process of tax collection was improved, although taxes increased. Following Colbert's death in 1683 and with growing reaction against the costly wars of Louis, the situation deteriorated. By 1715 more than half the income due failed to arrive.

7
Income received
Income due
1661 1683 1715
32
85
93
74
116
152
Millions of livres

Medieval Russia 900-1600

The first Russian state emerged out of the Slavic settlements northeast of European Byzantium between the sixth and ninth centuries AD. The Russian Slavs occupied a large belt of territory bounded by the Carpathian Mountains, the Baltic Sea and the headwaters of the Volga, Don, Dnieper and Dniester rivers. In the 800s, fierce Viking merchant-warriors, called Varangians, conquered the area and established a federation of city states whose centre was Kiev and which was ruled by the grand prince of Kiev. The existing Slav ruling class assimilated the Varangian princes and established a lucrative trade with Constantinople [1]. In contrast to the barter economy of the medieval West, money and credit systems were used and a prosperous commercial civilization grew up.

Byzantine influence in Kievan Russia

By 1100, bolstered by commercial wealth and contact with the Byzantine Empire, Kievan Russia had become a powerful state and the centre of a flowering culture. From her chief trading partner Russia accepted the cultural heritage of Byzantine Orthodox Christianity. Missionaries introduced Orthodox liturgy by means of a language that, using the Cyrillic alphabet, became the basis of modern Russian. Grand Prince Vladimir I (c. 956–1015) adopted Orthodoxy as the official religion and a metropolitan bishop arrived from Constantinople and set up an ecclesiastical organization. Byzantine styles of building [2] and icon painting flourished [3].

The Russian political and social structures contrasted sharply with their Western counterparts. Three governmental elements managed to co-exist – the ruling Riurik dynasty had to share power state-wide with a council of noblemen (*duma*) and with the town meetings (*veche*) at local level. The princes and their relations stood at the top of the social order, followed by the merchant-soldier-landowner class of boyars [9], then landowning peasants, tenant farmers and slaves. Kievan peasants were as a rule free to buy, sell and inherit land in their own right and owed no vassal-like allegiance to the great landholders. Kievan law recognized few class differences and most non-slave citizens were equal in the eyes of the law.

During the twelfth and thirteenth centuries Russia was profoundly affected by events beyond her frontiers. The growth of competing Venetian trade routes, raids by Asiatic tribes, the decline of Byzantium, and the rise of Poland-Lithuania and the Mongol Empire all contributed to Kiev's disintegration; there was also internal political and dynastic strife. Russian links with Constantinople loosened and the economic strength of the Kievan state began to decline. The great city of Novgorod with its mercantile democracy and rich hinterland was able to establish its independence [8], but western Russia fell under Polish-Lithuanian (and hence Roman Catholic) control and eastern Russia was overrun by the Mongol Empire, which was expanding rapidly under Genghis Khan (1167–1227) and his successors.

The emergence of Moscow

It was under Mongol rule that the principality of Moscow (Muscovy) first became important and then asserted political control over most of what is now European Russia. The

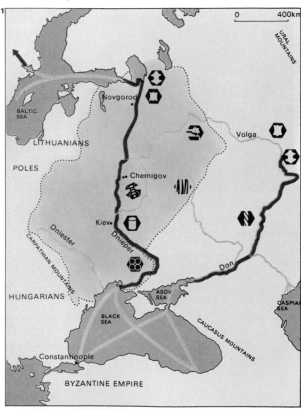

	Kievan state
	Furs
	Honey
	Wax
	Wood
	Slaves
	Flax
	Hemp
	Hides
	Sea routes
	River routes

1 Trade was essential to the Kievan economy. Kiev owed its importance to its location on the international trade route that connected the Baltic Sea with the Mediterranean – the water road from the Varangians to Byzantium. Great annual trading convoys floated down the River Dnieper and, via the Black Sea, to Constantinople. At the Byzantine capital the products of the Russian forests – chiefly furs, honey and beeswax – were exchanged for spices, wines, perfumes and weapons. The river route was protected against nomads by soldiers.

Eastern end

2 Construction of Sophia Cathedral, Kiev, began in 1037, during the reign of Grand Prince Yaroslav ("the Wise", c. 1036–54). One of the first major Byzantine-inspired churches in Russia, it set an example for innumerable Orthodox churches built during the next nine centuries. A brick, cross-domed basilica, its square plan was based on that of the Hagia Sophia in Constantinople. A Russian innovation was the arrangement of 13 cupolas – 12 smaller domes surrounding a large central dome, while the eastern end of the church ended in five semi-circular apses.

3 Christianity penetrated the Russian land long before it became the official state religion (c. AD 988). Kievan Russia remained largely a cultural province of Byzantium and the icon was one of the most permanent gifts from Constantinople. It was an important vehicle for conveying religious truths to the masses. At first, icon painting, represented here by the 12th-century "Virgin of Tenderness" from Byelozersk, relied heavily on the Byzantine style.

4 Native architectural styles emerged in the Russian villages, where local circumstances such as a ready availability of timber had more influence on church-building than far-away Byzantine examples. The Church of Our Lady of Vladimir in Belaya Sluda is typical.

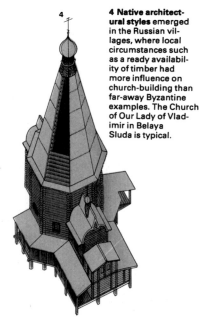

5 Muscovite icon painting reached its peak in the 14th and 15th centuries. The most famous masterpiece of this period, the "Old Testament Trinity", was painted in about 1411 by Andrei Rublev (c. 1370–1430), Russia's greatest iconographer.

grand dukes of Moscow, descended from a branch of the Riurik family, were originally the tax collectors of Sarai (the Mongols' western headquarters on the lower Volga). By treaty, conquest, purchase and the strategic marriage of their offspring, the grand dukes emerged with the largest territory [6] and as the head of a coalition that eventually drove out the Mongols. The grand dukes' nicknames reveal the variety of their methods – Iuri ("Long Arm", reigned *c.* 1149–57), Vsevolod ("Big Nest", referring to his fertility, reigned *c.* 1176–1212), Ivan I ("Money Bags", reigned *c.* 1328–40).

Development of national monarchy

Between 1460 and 1600 Moscow vastly increased in size and strength and its rulers took on the trappings of a national monarchy. Ivan III ("the Great", 1440–1505), with a series of brilliant diplomatic and military campaigns, dealt the final blow to the disintegrating Mongol Empire in 1481 by forming an alliance with various Mongol confederations. He began to see his newly independent realm as a successor to the

recently vanquished Byzantine Empire. He married Sophia, niece of the last emperor, and adopted the Byzantine double-headed eagle as a royal symbol. Ivan IV ("the Terrible", 1530–84) conquered fresh Lithuanian and Mongol territory and crowned himself "Tsar (Caesar) of all the Russias" [7].

The fall of Constantinople to the Ottoman Turks in 1453 aided the establishment of a separate Russian Orthodox Church. The seat of the Church had moved from Kiev to Moscow in the fourteenth century and a distinct Russian style in architecture [4] and painting [5] had emerged there by 1589, when the first Russian Orthodox patriarch was sworn in.

Modern Russia owes its political and social character to Moscow rather than to Kiev. The Russian state, consolidated as a mercantile economy, gave way to an agrarian one and while feudalism was on the wane in the West the roots of serfdom were being sunk in Muscovy. To compound the problem, no class of townsmen or independent farmers emerged that was capable of setting limits on the power of the crown.

The crown of Vladimir Monomach (1053–1125) was a gift from the Byzantine emperor. The notion that it symbolicly bestowed imperial succession rights on the Russian dynasty gained credence during the national awakening of the 15th century. This bolstered Moscow's claim to be the secular and spiritual successor to fallen Constantinople. Vladimir was one Kievan ruler whose folk-hero status extended into Muscovite times. He married Gyda, the daughter of Harold of England, who had fled soon after the Battle of Hastings (1066).

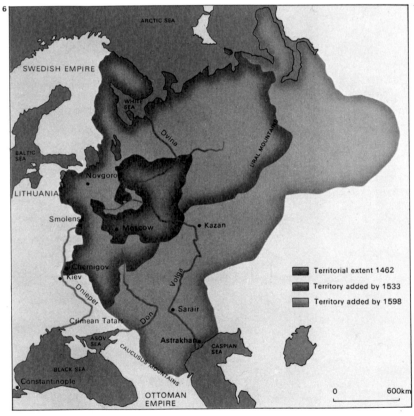

6 The expansion of the Muscovite principality (founded mid-12th century) was helped by the absence of mountain barriers within European Russia. By 1452 Muscovy controlled headwaters of the major rivers leading to the White, Black, Azov and Caspian seas. Ivan III and Vassily III conquered Novgorod (1478) and Smolensk (1514). Ivan IV established control over areas on the Don and Volga and extended Russian territory eastwards across the Urals.

Map legend:
Territorial extent 1462
Territory added by 1533
Territory added by 1598

0   600km

7 Ivan "the Terrible" earned his name. His childhood coincided with a period of court intrigue and open conflict among boyars. The young Ivan's exposure to these confrontations – often culminating in stranglings and dramatic chases through the palace – stunted his moral growth. At 13 years of age, four years before taking the throne, he ordered the murder of the high-ranking boyar Andrei Shuisky. Near the end of his reign he killed his own son in a quarrel. Whether because of childhood experience, madness, spinal disease or calculated attempts to destroy the power of the boyars, Ivan ruled in an arbitrary fashion. He was subject to alternating bouts of sadism and religious melancholia and his tactics against internal "enemies" included executions, property confiscations and mass deportations. This portrait is by V. Vasnetsov.

8 The city of Novgorod and its province became an independent republic early in the 12th century. Novgorod's economic strength was based on a flourishing handicrafts industry and trade in forest products. Its ruling institution, as in other Russian towns, was the *veche*, made up of all free citizens, which was responsible for foreign policy and the election of civil and military authorities. Novgorod held off the Lithuanians and Mongols for over three centuries, but finally succumbed to the superior force of Muscovy in 1478.

9 The Russian boyar class developed in Kievan times out of the intermarriages between the Varangians and the native Slavic aristocracy. Under Moscow they were given large tracts of land as rewards for military service. Leading boyar families had hereditary access to privileged positions in the state administration. This woodcut by Michael Peterle (1576) shows a procession of boyars and merchants at the Austrian court of Maximilian II.

Early modern Russia

The seventeenth and eighteenth centuries saw the transformation of Russia from a medieval kingdom into a powerful, modern state. Her population more than doubled, from 15 million to 35 million; she acquired territory from Sweden, Poland, Lithuania and Turkey until, by 1700, Russia was the largest European state [8]. She also developed a modern army and navy and a centralized civil service. The two rulers chiefly responsible for this metamorphosis were Peter the Great (1672–1725) [Key] and Catherine the Great (1729–96) [6].

Military and economic expansion
Russia's territorial expansion was achieved with a new army and navy based on compulsory service, equipped with new weapons and led by trained officers. By the 1670s Russia had the largest army in Europe. Military growth and the increasing cost of administering and equipping the armed forces – particularly with artillery – strained both the economy and the administrative structure inherited from the Riurik dynasty. New sources of revenue had to be tapped and repeated attempts were made to improve the tax-collecting system [2].

To increase taxable wealth and satisfy military and naval needs, Russia's rulers actively encouraged the growth of trade and industry. A nationwide market was formed as local and regional trade barriers were eliminated [7]. Foreign trade – especially with Britain and Holland – increased during Catherine II's reign from 21 million roubles to 71.3 million, thanks to the acquisition of ice-free ports on the Baltic and Black seas. Russian iron and hemp found large British markets, and hemp was also sought after by the fledgling United States. High import tariffs and borrowed French mercantilist doctrines helped Russia's balance of trade and fewer goods were imported. With European money and technical knowledge, Russia became more self-sufficient.

The new aristocracy
The increasing volume and complexity of state affairs demanded the creation of a modern civil service. Theodore III (1656–82) abolished the Muscovite system of choosing military officers and civil officials according to the positions occupied by their fathers. Peter I ("the Great") accelerated the decline of the upper nobility (boyars) by creating a civil service staffed by career officials recruited from the lesser gentry. Promotion through the military and administrative ranks was achieved according to merit. Anyone advancing halfway up a scale of 14 ranks automatically became a nobleman. Thus, in theory, nobility became a mark of impersonal service to the state.

Peter I set up separate administrative "colleges", based on the Swedish system. The most powerful of these dealt with the army, the navy, foreign affairs and finance, and reflected his priorities. Alexander I (1777–1825) brought this arrangement into line by introducing ministries. By the beginning of the 1800s there were more than 18,000 civil servants, whose upkeep absorbed 10 per cent of the state budget.

The new service nobility soon grew into an increasingly privileged class (the *dvorianstvo*) whose sons found it easier than those who were not nobles to reach the top rungs of

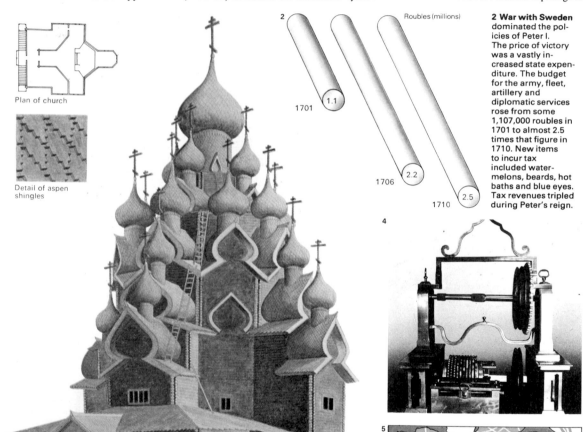

Plan of church

Detail of aspen shingles

Roubles (millions)

1701 — 1.1
1706 — 2.2
1710 — 2.5

2 War with Sweden dominated the policies of Peter I. The price of victory was a vastly increased state expenditure. The budget for the army, fleet, artillery and diplomatic services rose from some 1,107,000 roubles in 1701 to almost 2.5 times that figure in 1710. New items to incur tax included watermelons, beards, hot baths and blue eyes. Tax revenues tripled during Peter's reign.

3 Peter, portrayed as a cat in this derisive cartoon, inspired much hostility by breaking with tradition and shaving his beard.

4 Peter's lathe was one of his many Western acquisitions – his interest in European craftsmanship is legendary. A restless, vigorous person, with great manual dexterity, he became master of dozens of crafts, including shipbuilding, and was as much at home working on the wharves as he was conducting affairs of state. While travelling incognito in Europe he disguised himself as a carpenter.

— Central radial avenues
— Canals
▱ Gardens

1 Peter and Paul Fortress
2 Winter Palace
3 Admiralty
4 Nevsky Prospect

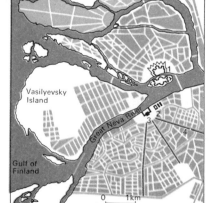

Vasilyevsky Island

Great Neva River

Gulf of Finland

0   1km

5 St Petersburg was founded in 1703 on Baltic marshlands. Peter mercilessly requisitioned over 100,000 labourers each year to build the city. With its canal system and Western architecture, St Petersburg became known as the "Venice of the North".

1 The cultural gap between the educated élite and the masses is a theme that has pervaded the history of modern Russia. No more striking contrast could be offered than that between the baroque and rococo buildings of St Petersburg and local, wooden church architecture. The latter could be quite splendid, as in the case of the Church of the Transfiguration on Kizhy Island in north Russia (1714), with its 22 aspen domes and its sculptural unity of composition. Village life could go on for decades and remain largely unaffected by the artistic and literary currents that reached St Petersburg from the West. While Catherine II and her court spoke French and lived in Italianate palaces, the villager spoke Russian and lived in a hut. While culture among the ruling classes became increasingly secular, the Church provided the only example of civilized culture experienced by the masses.

the bureaucratic ladder. Catherine II ("the Great") confirmed their right to own serf-populated estates and their exemption from taxation, corporal punishment and even the obligation of service. It was left to the peasants, who formed 90 per cent of the population, to bear the brunt of the tax burden. The institution of serfdom, which made them chattels of the landowners, was formerly recognized by the law code of 1649. Throughout the eighteenth century landowners gained increasing powers, including the right to punish serfs by military conscription or exile to Siberia. Laws against runaway serfs were tightened and the state's role in enforcing them became paramount.

There was nothing in the tradition or self-interest of the *dvorianstvo* to prompt them to seek limitations on the power of the crown. Indeed, they depended on its strength to guarantee their position as officers and administrators and their wealth as serf-owners. Nor was any other social class able to challenge the tsar. The power of the old aristocracy had lessened, the urban middle class remained small and dependent on royal

favour, and the clergy became further reduced in power as Russia became more Westernized and secular.

The Church's declining power

The Russian Orthodox patriarchate enjoyed a brief revival during the reign of Michael (1596–1645) when Patriarch Philaret, Michael's father, ruled Russia as the "second lord" at the side of his weak son. But when Patriarch Nikon tried to assert a measure of independence from Tsar Alexis (1629–76), he was demoted by the Church Council of 1666. Peter I abolished the patriarchate in 1721 because it was largely opposed to his reforms and replaced it with a Holy Synod of bishops under a state-appointed layman.

The political humiliation of the Church did not eliminate its cultural influence, particularly in rural areas, but the nobility became more receptive to secular, European artistic and literary styles. The eighteenth century saw the emergence of a Westernized élite who spoke better French than Russian and designed new buildings in the contemporary styles of France and Italy [9, 10].

Peter I, more than any other person, was responsible for the conversion of the medieval tsardom into the modern Russian state. He, with Catherine II, stood out from the rest of the Romanov dynasty because of keen intelligence and determination. Peter's contributions to Russia's modernization were many: he rebuilt the army on a permanent basis, created a navy, reformed the tax system, expanded mining and manufacturing and remodelled the civil service. His statue, commissioned by Catherine II and erected in St Petersburg's Senate Square, symbolizes Peter's enormous strength and, significantly, faces due west.

6 Catherine II was the philosopher and educator of modern Russia. A student of the works of Montesquieu and Blackstone and a friend of Voltaire, she considered herself an "enlightened despot", much like Austria's Joseph II and Prussia's Frederick II. Most of Catherine's good intentions were corrupted by the realities of power, but she did lay the groundwork for the Russian state school system. By the end of her reign (1796) there were 22,210 pupils and 760 teachers in 288 primary and secondary schools. One result of her work was the development of an intellectual class in the 19th century.

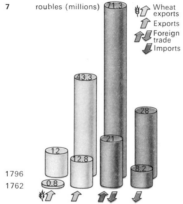

roubles (millions)

Wheat exports
Exports
Foreign trade
Imports

71.3
43.3
28
12
12.8
21
8.2
0.8

1796
1762

7 Catherine's economic policies furthered the expansion of Russian trade and investment. During her reign most internal trade barriers were abolished and she entered into trade agreements with Britain, Poland, Denmark, Turkey, Austria, Naples, Portugal and France. In the same period foreign trade grew enormously: the percentage growth in exports was 230, in imports 250.

Territorial extent by 1689
Territory added by 1725
Territory added by 1796

SIBERIA
St Petersburg
Moscow
Kiev
OTTOMAN EMPIRE
AFGHANISTAN
MONGOLIA
CHINA
0   1,500km

8 The Romanovs' urge to acquire large new territories was part and parcel of an insatiable desire for new maritime outlets. By 1700 Russia was the largest of the European states. Peter won a length of the Baltic coast after two decades of war with Sweden. Catherine II annexed areas of Poland and Lithuania, giving Russia Austrian and Prussian borders for the first time. War with Turkey yielded a Black Sea coast and rights of commercial passage into the Mediterranean.

9 An ornate rococo style was favoured for domestic architecture by aristocrats of 18th-century Russia. Illustrated here is the lavish Knight's Dining Room, now restored to its original design, in the Great Palace at Pushkin.

10 The stateliness of Renaissance and baroque public buildings complemented the domestic architecture of St Petersburg (now Leningrad). The city's Western feel is the result of its canals as much as of its unity of style.

Enlightened despotism

The wave of new ideas that swept Europe in the eighteenth century, and has come to be known as the Age of Enlightenment, had its origins in the scientific and rationalistic movements of the seventeenth century. The spirit of rational enquiry that typified the writers and thinkers of the eighteenth century also had important political repercussions. Radical criticism of existing institutions, values and practice were the characteristic features. In Europe these ideas were more or less accepted by powerful monarchs, creating "enlightened despotism".

The influence of writers
The most common feature of the ideas of the *philosophes*, as this group of thinkers was called, was their faith in reason and the critical spotlight they cast upon the accepted institutions and practices of the age. Among the most influential writers and thinkers were Voltaire [Key], Charles-Louis Montesquieu (1689–1755), Denis Diderot (1713–84) and Jean Jacques Rousseau (1712–78), whose ideas on politics and society attracted a large following among the educated classes of

Europe. Although the political theories of such thinkers would in ideal circumstances have led many of them to favour constitutional government [4] and consultative institutions, they were often prepared to act as advisers to powerful absolute rulers such as Frederick the Great of Prussia (1712–86) and Catherine the Great of Russia (1729–96). In this capacity and in their general writings they advocated a number of specific reforms, such as the introduction of equality before the law, the abolition of serfdom, religious toleration and the reduction of noble and clerical privilege.

The "enlightened despots", however, did not form a consistent and coherent group. Many European rulers adopted the ideals of the *philosophes* because they were useful in their own domestic political arrangements. Thus the application of enlightened legislation was varied and conditioned by individual circumstance. For many monarchs the need to increase revenues was central to their aims, which made them favour intellectual attacks upon noble and clerical privileges such as exemption from taxation. Similarly,

European rulers had a vested interest in the efficient economic exploitation of the lands under their control. Hence many of the policies of the "enlightened despots" can be explained in terms of the traditional doctrine of *raison d'état* (for the good of the country).

Implementation of Enlightenment ideas
Many European monarchs practised to some degree the policies advocated by the *philosophes*. Among the most sincere was Joseph II (1741–90), Holy Roman Emperor, in whose 10-year reign as sole ruler a large number of reforms were initiated [8].

Frederick the Great of Prussia, who succeeded to the throne in 1740, was keenly interested in the ideas of the *philosophes* and presented himself as an exponent of their ideals. In practice he was a firm and authoritarian ruler who placed the interests of the Prussian state and of his own power before the ideals of the Enlightenment. He emancipated the serfs on his own estates, although for military rather than humanitarian reasons, but he failed to eliminate serfdom elsewhere in Prussia because it

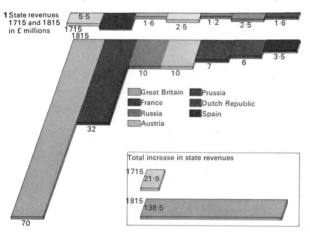

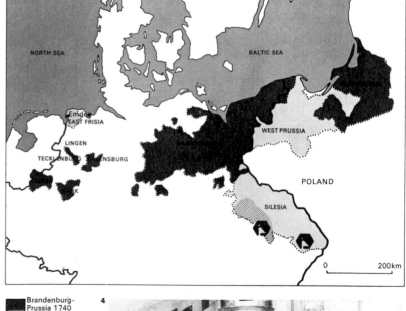

1 The rapid growth of agriculture and industry in 18th-century Europe helped state revenues to rise rapidly. Greater power wielded by the European states also helped them to secure greater taxation from their subjects. Because Great Britain's economic growth outstripped that of other countries, she was able to expand government revenue faster and to higher levels than many larger countries.

Brandenburg-Prussia 1740

Territories gained 1740–86

Coalfields

Textiles

Boundary of Holy Roman Empire

2 Frederick the Great's acquisition of Silesia in 1740 gave him an economically valuable area, to which he added East Frisia in 1744 and West Prussia in 1772, to expand Prussia's borders.

3 Monarchs still played an important part in leading their nations in war. George II (1683–1760), shown here, was the last British monarch to lead his troops in person, during the Battle of Dettingen in Germany in 1743.

4 The "Tobacco Parliament" was an informal gathering of political advisers with Frederick I of Prussia. The idea of such assemblies sprang from the Physiocratic concept of "legal" despotism in which elected landowners would guide the monarch in his deliberations. In spite of support from writers and intellectuals, the tendency towards strong government militated against such elected bodies. The centralizing reforms of Frederick and Joseph II, for example, led to the extinction of provincial administration and institutions. Even where constitutional bodies existed, however, they tended to represent the interest of the propertied classes (especially landowners and merchants) only.

would alienate the nobility. He did, however, reform the legal system and establish more humane punishments. His economic policies were strictly mercantilist [2] and drew little from the progressive economic ideas of the Physiocrats (a school of political economists). He used state monopolies and protectionist tariffs to raise extra revenue and to foster established industries.

Similarly, Catherine the Great of Russia was an admirer of the ideas of the Enlightenment, maintaining correspondence with Voltaire and entertaining Diderot at court. Her most idealistic proposal was a reform of the Russian law code, issued as the "Instruction" of 1767; to discuss it she called together a Legislative Commission representing the whole nation. The reform, however, broke down because of differences of opinion among the delegates and the outbreak of war with Turkey. In spite of her superficial desire to adopt enlightened policies such as the emancipation of the serfs, she was forced to compromise with existing vested interests. Her "Charter of the Nobility" in 1785 placed the serfs even more firmly under the control of

the landowners and established the nobility in their status, forging an alliance between them and her dynasty that was to last almost to the Russian Revolution.

Other influences in Europe

Elsewhere in Europe the ideals of the Enlightenment were adopted rather unevenly [6]. In Portugal, Sebastião Pombal (1699–1782), as chief minister from 1751–77, applied himself to strengthening the state and its economy by expelling the Jesuits and attacking noble privilege. He standardized administration, adopted free trade policies and granted civil rights to the Jews. On the other hand he also maintained a rigorous police system and threw hundreds of people into prison.

"Enlightened despotism" took many forms and therefore is not a precise description of the great variety of motives and policies adopted by European rulers in the eighteenth century. However, its legacy of humane and rational legislation, in theory if not in practice, laid foundations for liberal governments of the post-revolutionary era.

Voltaire [left] was the pen-name of François Marie Arouet (1694–1778). One of the great French *philosophes*, he was on occasion a guest at the "enlightened" courts of Europe. The degree of respect that he was accorded by Frederick the Great of Prussia is clear in this painting of the two. Voltaire was the greatest playwright of his time, writing more than 50 plays. He was exiled to England in 1726 after an argument with a powerful nobleman. From 1734 to 1749 he lived with Mme du Châtelet, one of the most educated women of the day. After her death he lived in Berlin and Switzerland, returning to France just before his death.

5 Maria Theresa's long reign over Austria (1740–80) laid the foundations for the rule of her son Joseph II. She helped to transform the diverse Hapsburg dominions into a centralized nation state and initiated many progressive reforms in the spheres of education, law and the Church. Her son completed her work by emancipating the serfs in 1781, imposing administrative uniformity upon the state and stimulating rapid economic development.

6 Enlightened principles also influenced lesser monarchs such as Charles III, seen here (centre) entering Madrid, king of the Two Sicilies (1735–59) and of Spain (1759–88). In Naples he sought to bring solvency and order to a poverty-stricken state, while in Spain he provided an enlightened government with the aid of able ministers. Poverty was tackled through workhouses while schools, roads and canals were constructed and education secularized.

Kingdom of Poland
Land acquired by Russia
Land acquired by Brandenburg-Prussia
Land acquired by Austria
= 1 million people

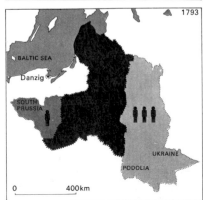

7 Poland was repeatedly dismembered and partitioned in the 18th century. Her elective monarchy proved a considerable weakness and led to the involvement of her powerful foreign neighbours in her internal struggles. With a backward economy, a small army and little revenue she was in no position to defend her frontiers. All her monarchs in the 18th century were the nominees of foreign powers. The first partition occurred in 1772, when Prussia, Russia and Austria took a total of a third of her former land area and half her population. In 1793 more was seized and in 1795 the remainder was divided between the three neighbouring powers.

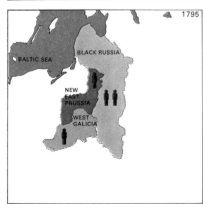

Proposed tax reforms, 1789

8 Joseph II planned to commute the feudal labour obligations of the peasants to their landlords, the state and the Church into a new tax based on a fixed percentage of their gross yearly income. This would form a new land tax which was to apply equally to all subjects in the empire. This diagram shows the percentage distribution of a peasant's income before and after the proposed scheme. However, the reform was abolished in 1790, on Joseph's death, before it became effective.

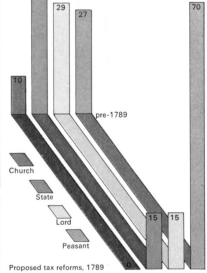

Europe: economy and society, 1700–1800

The most important economic developments of the eighteenth century [2] took place in Britain, France, the Low Countries and parts of Germany; eastern and southern Europe made much less progress. At one extreme Britain was, by the end of the century, well on the way to becoming the first industrial nation, a development given theoretical backing by the work of economists such as Adam Smith (1723–90). At the other extreme countries such as Russia and Italy retained economic systems little different from those of the medieval period. Socially, too, the most striking developments occurred in the countries on the Atlantic seaboard.

Population growth and better harvests

One development common to Europe as a whole in this period was population growth, caused chiefly by a declining mortality rate [5]. In advanced countries, economic expansion also increased the demand for labour, permitted more children to be supported and encouraged earlier marriage.

Population growth was encouraged by, and stimulated, agricultural improvement [4]. Large tracts of land were brought into cultivation and new techniques and crops were harnessed to meet the demand for foodstuffs for a growing population. Yields and animal weights rose during the century, especially in northwestern Europe. Elsewhere, agriculture often remained backward and near to subsistence. Famine continued to afflict many communities in southern and eastern Europe until the nineteenth century, although the adoption of the potato as a subsistence crop helped to increase supplies.

Agricultural practice varied enormously along with different systems of tenure and landholding throughout Europe. In Russia and much of central and eastern Europe, serfdom was still in force. In other areas a landowning peasantry had emerged, ranging from the relatively prosperous peasants of the Low Countries to the poorer ones of Brittany. In the British Isles the poor tenants of southern Ireland, the landless agricultural labourers of the "enclosed" counties of southern England and the semi-feudal "crofters" of Scotland, contrasted with the prosperous tenant farmers and great landowners.

International trade played a vital part in the economy of many states. Trade expanded in the eighteenth century, especially for the Atlantic countries with their easy access to West Indian, American, African and Asiatic markets. Britain and France both made large strides in trade, founding the prosperity of a merchant middle class in cities such as Bristol, Liverpool, Bordeaux and Nantes.

Domestic trade and manufacturing

Internal trade also flourished, aided by improvements in river and road transport [Key]. In many countries agricultural produce, in particular grain, was the major commodity traded, but timber, coal, mineral ores, stone and other products were carried in ever-increasing quantities.

Growing population and increasing wealth in Britain and other European countries stimulated the demand for a wide range of manufactured goods, but this increased output was still achieved by pre-industrial methods [3]. The domestic system and hand-working remained the principal means of producing textiles, iron, pottery and a wide

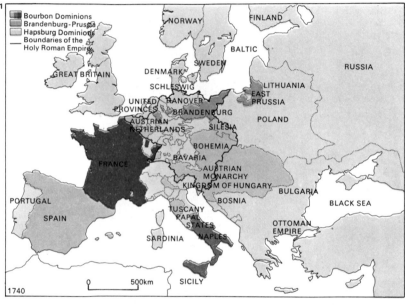

1740

1 Political stability was a characteristic of 18th-century Europe until the French Revolution in 1789. The previous century witnessed the consolidation of a number of powerful nation states, ruled by well-established monarchies (in Britain, France, Prussia, Austria and Russia). Despite changing dynasties and disputed successions, political authority had been established in these countries for a long period. Much of Germany and Italy, however, remained a jumble of petty states and kingdoms separated until the middle of the next century. Poland was another unstable monarchy, subject to encroachment and partition by other powers. Europe's political boundary in the southeast was the Ottoman Empire – in decline but still dominant in the Balkans.

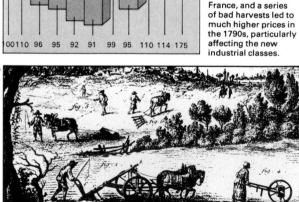

2 Price indices for a range of goods in 18th century British suggest that the cost of living decreased until the latter part of the century. Favourable economic conditions and an expansive social environment were the key to political stability. Good harvests made for cheaper food while early industrial enterprises began to reduce the cost of many everyday items such as clothing, furniture and domestic utensils which, together with widely available foodstuffs, comprise the bulk of this index. One result of the overall price stability was a higher birth-rate, reduced infant mortality and a longer life expectancy because of better diet. The consequent strain on food supplies, exacerbated by the effect of war with France, and a series of bad harvests led to much higher prices in the 1790s, particularly affecting the new industrial classes.

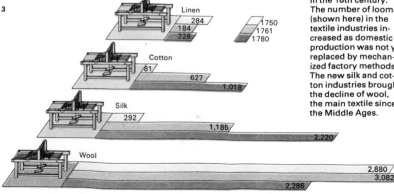

Linen
284
184
228

Cotton
81
627
1,018

Silk
292
1,185
2,220

Wool
2,880
3,082
2,286

1750
1761
1780

3 The textile industry in Berlin grew in the 18th century. The number of looms (shown here) in the textile industries increased as domestic production was not yet replaced by mechanized factory methods. The new silk and cotton industries brought the decline of wool, the main textile since the Middle Ages.

4 Rising demand for food stimulated the adoption of improved techniques, new crops, better farming implements and machinery. By the 1750s increased production had all but eliminated serious famine in western Europe, but periods of scarcity persisted, especially as population grew towards the end of the century. Improvements were propagated by enthusiasts such as Arthur Young (1741–1820) and the French economists.

range of other goods. In Britain, water power was the most widely used source of energy for manufacturing, as steam power was obtaining a foothold only by the end of the century. The units of production were generally small, domestic organization being by far the most widespread, although the expanding coal mines and textile towns of Britain, France and Belgium were beginning to concentrate production. Overall, outside Britain, the picture was one of gradual expansion affecting most European countries.

Minuets and misery

European society remained essentially traditional in the eighteenth century. Most of the population still lived in a hierarchic, rural society based upon agriculture. The village and small market town continued to dominate social environment and culture for most people. In these areas, religion still played an important role in everyday life and helped to cement social bonds. Parishes, manors and guilds remained the typical forms of social organization and in most of Europe social structure was little affected by economic changes. Although serfdom was attacked in some "enlightened states" and was abolished in the Hapsburg dominions by Joseph II (1741–90), in Russia it was increasing. Peasant revolts and periodic riots over various causes did little to shake social structure before the French Revolution.

In contrast, the capital cities such as London, Paris, Vienna and St Petersburg continued to grow in size, adding many magnificent buildings and becoming centres of government and major markets. Merchant cities, such as Liverpool and Bordeaux, also grew rapidly, bringing new standards of comfort to the upper and middle classes [7]. For these classes education and prosperity led to the development of a sophisticated urban culture, shown in the demand for literature and art and in the access to wider means of communication such as newspapers and journals. For the poorer urban populations, living conditions were much harsher, with bad housing, health and low incomes [6]. Crime was rife in most towns and cities and was usually met by savage punishment, including torture and death for trivial offences.

Improved travel was one of the most important features of 18th-century Europe. Much easier movement by road, river and canal greatly stimulated trade and the first industrial developments. For the wealthy, better communications created the basis for a common European culture.

5 Total (millions)

European population 18th century

Year	Total (millions)
1700	115
1750	140
1800	187

☐ = 1 million

Population 1750 and 1800

	1750	1800
Russia	19	29
Hapsburg Empire	20	27
France	22	26
Italy	15·5	18
Great Britain	10·5	15·5
Prussia	3·5	6

5 The major factor in population growth was a fall in the death-rate. Better diet, an improved climate, the decline of some major diseases and an increase in personal hygiene (aided by increasing availability of cheap soap and washable cotton clothing) contributed to lower mortality. Smallpox inoculation and improved midwifery perhaps also played a part. Increased life expectancy in Western Europe thus led to a population increase, which had previously been checked by epidemics and famine. Even in Eastern Europe and Russia, where the improvements had less impact, the population increase was marked.

7 Improved living standards among the upper and middle classes led to the building of elegant town houses in many European cities. New squares, like those in London's West End and Edinburgh's New Town, evinced Britain's commercial wealth. The merchant cities of the Continent, such as Amsterdam and Bordeaux, and the great governmental centres such as Versailles provided the basis for an affluent urban society. Spas and fashionable resorts such as Bath (shown here) and Dresden provided recreation for the rich, who generated a demand for luxury goods and cultural amusements. The rich also enjoyed improvements such as street lighting, parks and water supply.

6 Harshness and squalor were still the lot of the poor, even in the age of enlightenment. Cheap spirits became readily available through large-scale distilling and caused chronic drunkenness. Food and drink adulteration by crooked traders was common, promoting death and disease in the larger urban slums. Moral tracts condemned the "Gin Lane" conditions of the urban poor.

British Grenadier
Austrian Infantryman
Soldier of the Spanish Imperial Army

8 Armies in the 18th century consisted of long-service volunteers or conscripts. Harsh discipline, low pay and bad conditions attracted only the poor and criminals into the ranks, while officers, from the nobility, used influence to gain commissions. Distinctive uniforms were chosen by commanders – warfare was formalized and long-range weapons were inaccurate.

England under the Hanoverians

England of the Hanoverian period, which began on 18 September 1714, with the arrival of Georg Ludwig (1660–1727), Elector of Hanover, at Greenwich to become George I of England [1], was a country generally free from the turbulence of the seventeenth century and the social and intellectual ferment of the nineteenth. Its apparent stability and prosperous complacency were revealed in politics, in religion, in commerce and in letters; the reigns of both George I and George II (reigned 1727–60) exhibited an external, though superficial, calmness that rested on the settlement of old quarrels at home and expanding power, naval and trading, overseas. Samuel Johnson (1709–84) [Key] represented the age, in his rational thought, political conservatism, and dry religious orthodoxy.

The Hanoverian succession

George I knew no English when he came to the throne. Both he and his son were more interested in Hanover than in England. George II was the last English monarch to lead his army into battle in Europe, at Dettingen in 1743. They both spent much of their time out of England, so that the House of Hanover did not become fully naturalized until the reign of George III (reigned 1760–1820).

Yet the royal court remained the centre of social life and of politics, the source of the patronage that was the cement of the political structure. The strife of the Civil Wars and the party rancour of the age of Queen Anne (reigned 1702–14) gave way to the politics of consensus, presided over by the Whig oligarchy established between 1721 and 1742 when Robert Walpole (1676–1745) [3] served as first minister.

The Whig politicians who had backed the Hanoverian succession undertook a long period of effectively one-party rule. The Jacobite uprisings of 1715 and 1745, attempting to restore the Stuarts to the throne, were dismal failures and tainted Toryism with disaffection and rebellion. The Whig landed gentry fused its interests with the court and the great merchant-financiers [2,6] and gained a stranglehold on the House of Commons and government service. Elec-

tions [5] remained unruly affairs, but the tiny electorate, the heavy cost of fighting elections (more or less direct bribery of the voters was common practice), and the large number of rotten and "pocket" boroughs kept the House of Commons under the control of the Whig government managers. The most famous and untiring of these was the Duke of Newcastle (1693–1768), who was Secretary of State (1724–48) and first minister (1754–62).

The growth of the empire and the expansion of trade and industry meant that the civil service became more elaborate. The Treasury, the Customs and Excise, the Admiralty and the War Office all expanded, and the dispensers of royal patronage often rewarded the place-hunting "friends" of the government with jobs in these departments.

The growth of the cabinet system

The cabinet began to develop as the main organ of government under the Hanoverians. Walpole, often considered to be the first prime minister (the term is still an unofficial one), bypassed the old Cabinet Councils

1 George I, aged 54 on his accession to the English throne, became king by virtue of the Act of Settlement of 1701, which had made his mother, Sophia, Electress of Hanover, heir to Anne's throne. This was done to prevent a return of the Stuart line. George, who had ruled as a despot in Hanover, had little liking for the English people or their liberal constitution and left the day-to-day running of affairs to his ministers.

2 Marine insurance companies, such as Sun-Fire, whose sign is shown here, were important to the development and the protection of 18th-century commerce. Most of these companies were financed as joint-stock enterprises. *Lloyd's List*, with news about merchant shipping, first published in 1734, is the oldest daily paper still published in London. Hanoverian prosperity rested on the profits of Britain's expanding trade empire.

3 Robert Walpole, here talking to Arthur Onslow (1691–1768), Speaker of the Commons, was defeated on his 1733 Excise Bill. He found that patronage alone could not guarantee a majority in the Commons as the substantial minority of "country gentle-men" was not bound to ministers by patronage. The development of the cabinet system was widely feared at this time and did not become fully established until the second half of the century. Walpole was criticized as a secretive, power-seeking man.

4 The War of Jenkins' Ear (1739–41) interrupted a long spell of peace for England. It was declared in response to the merchants' demand for protection at sea against the Spaniards. The ear, here being shown to Walpole by Capt. Jenkins, was allegedly torn off by Spanish coastguards. The war was fought mainly at sea near to the Spanish colonies, and although Britain won no important territorial advantages, the disruption hastened the decline of the Spanish Empire.

of privy councillors and relied on an inner cabinet of four or five of the Crown's principal ministers. They were not yet united by party – the resignation of the first minister rarely entailed that of any other – but the process had begun by which the cabinet and party were to oust the Crown and patronage from the centre of the political stage. The eighteenth century was the golden age of the mixed constitution, with a much-praised balance of King, Lords and Commons in the constitution or limited monarchy established by the "Whig revolution" of 1688–9.

The rise of Methodism

The Church of England was dormant following the bitter sectarian disputes of the previous two centuries. Protestant dissenters and Catholics were excluded from the universities as well as many public offices, unless they paid nominal allegiance to the established Church. Secure in its monopoly, the Church upheld a bland, unquestioning view of the truth of Christianity. Political obeisance to a powerful Whig patron was the way to a bishopric [8].

In such circumstances, it is not surprising that the most important religious movement of the century was the evangelical revival led by John Wesley (1703–91) [9]. His highly organized preaching tours, combined with the founding of "cells" in towns and villages, made Methodism by 1760 the most dynamic body of opinion in the country, and by 1800 there were more than 100,000 Methodists. The Anglican Church was implacably opposed to Wesley and no bishop would ordain for him or his assistants. In 1784 he therefore broke with the Church and began to ordain his ministers himself.

Wesley appealed principally to the poor of a society marked by great inequalities. The Duke of Newcastle had an annual income of more than £50,000 from his estates in 12 counties, whereas a handloom weaver worked for less than a shilling (5p) a day. Nevertheless, although the mass of the people possessed neither the vote nor property, they had basic political rights – freedom from arbitrary arrest, trial by jury, the right to political demonstration – which were denied to most of their European contemporaries.

Samuel Johnson, essayist, poet, critic and lexicographer, gave the English language its first systematic and formal, if idiosyncratic, setting in his *Dictionary* of 1755. He was gregarious and noc- turnal, and drank water and tea rather than wine. He lived com- fortably but was never rich. In 1760 George III rewarded him with a civil-list pension of £300 a year. A resolute Tory, John- son condemned the American rebels and defended the wealth and doctrines of the Church of England. He was renowned for his acerbic wit, re- corded by James Boswell (1740–95), in the first great English biography.

5 Electoral violence, seen in this painting by William Hogarth (1697–1764), resulted from bribery of the voters, but it became less common as the century progressed. The Septennial Act (1716) greatly reduced the frequency of elec- tions, and in 1761 only four elections were contested for county seats.

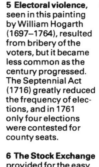

6 The Stock Exchange provided for the easy reinvestment of funds in new trading ven- tures or in industry. Since there was little social distinction drawn between wealth acquired in trade and that derived from land, the aristocracy happily contributed to the financial expan- sion that won for Bri- tain the title "A nation of shopkeepers".

7 Cricket was widely played and was first organized on a county basis in the 18th cen- tury, thanks to the patronage of the great landowners. It epitomized the rela- tive social harmony of rural areas, in con- trast to the often vio- lent towns, where riots such as the Gordon Riots of 1780 might occur. Lord's cricket ground was opened in 1787 by Thomas Lord for the White Con- duit Club, later the Marylebone Cricket Club (MCC).

8 The bishops carried out few pastoral duties, dispensed much pat- ronage and often lived richly while the over-worked lower clergy suffered. This cartoon suggests that the episcopal life- style had become quite unsuitable; 1,200 bene- fices in the 18th cen- tury had annual in- comes of less than £20.

9 John Wesley offered the poor a promise of individual salvation, an idea that seemed to be genuinely egalitarian. His appeal to the per- sonal worth of each individual quickened a response, especially in the new industrial towns of Wales and the north, where the Church of England was inactive.

The agricultural revolution

Historians have often described the changes that occurred in British farming during the course of the eighteenth and nineteenth centuries as an agricultural "revolution". The phrase was coined in the nineteenth century by those who saw comparable changes in the mode of production and social relationships on the land to what was happening in industry. More recent research has tended to emphasize the long drawn-out evolution of agricultural change and the varied pattern that it presents over the country as a whole. The earliest books on farming techniques had appeared in the early sixteenth century and enclosure had started in the thirteenth century, accelerating in the sixteenth century.

The results of new techniques

Whether or not the phrase "agricultural revolution" is an exaggeration, changes in British agriculture between, say, 1700 and 1870, were real and substantial. Greatly improved output, new crops, and improved techniques were matched by a number of important social developments.

Many of the changes in agricultural practice made wider use of established ideas. The use of rotation of crops, for example, particularly the utilization of root crops such as the turnip as a part of the rotation and a source of winter feed for animals, was known in the seventeenth century. Selective breeding of livestock was familiar to earlier generations but was impracticable under the open field system of agriculture where animals were herded together in the common field.

Agricultural historians have identified the hundred years before 1750 as one of slack demand for farm products because of an upward trend in harvests and a largely static population. From 1750 onward, however, a discernible rise in population and generally poorer harvests provided a stimulus to investment in agriculture and the application of fresh techniques in order to increase production. A number of pioneers, such as Jethro Tull (1674–1741), Charles "Turnip" Townshend (1674–1738), and Robert Bakewell (1725–95) popularized the new techniques. Probably the most important of these were the use of crop rotation, scientific breeding of animals, and the use of crops such

as turnips and lucerne as animal fodder. These improved yields led to heavier and healthier animals – within the century the average weight of sheep sold in London nearly trebled and permitted the wintering of livestock on stored feed. New implements such as improved ploughs [7] and harrows, as well as Tull's revolutionary seed drill, contributed to the improvement of yields [2].

The effects of enclosure

Many of these techniques could not have been applied without reorganization of landholding. Enclosure of land [Key, 4] into self-contained units had been going on for centuries; more than one-third of England was enclosed by 1600, usually by agreement among local landowners. From the mid-eighteenth century, much land was enclosed through private Acts of Parliament. Enclosure involved creating separate holdings out of the medieval common and "open" fields. Generally it eliminated the inefficiency of farming strips in each field and the wasteful system of leaving one field fallow each year, and it also permitted farmers to experiment

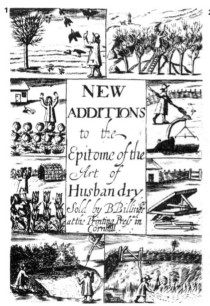

1 Agricultural manuals and tracts helped to spread the use of new techniques among farmers from as early as the 16th century. During the late 18th century agricultural improvement became a fashionable concern: King George III (r. 1760–1820) himself ran a model farm at Windsor.

2 Jethro Tull's famous horse-drawn seed drill, first used in 1701, is regarded as having initiated the mechanization of agriculture. Before this invention, seed was laboriously broadcast by hand, which was a wasteful and uncertain procedure.

3 Richard Weston's (1591–1652) *A Discours of the Husbandrie used in Brabant and Flanders* (1645) spread Flemish agricultural ideas among English farmers. It described methods of crop rotation and several techniques by which poor soils were improved.

A
DISCOURS
OF
HUSBANDRIE
USED IN
Brabant and Flanders:
SHEWING
The wonderful improvement of Land there; and serving as a pattern for our practice in this
COMMON-WEALTH.

The Second Edition, Corrected and Inlarged.

LONDON,
Printed by *William Du-Gard,* dwelling in *Suffolk-lane,* near London-stone, *Anno Dom.* 1652.

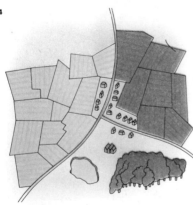

4 The effects of enclosure upon landholding can be seen from the plans of a typical parish. Before enclosure, many villages preserved the medieval layout of large open fields in which each inhabitant held by custom a few strips. The intention was to give everybody a share of good and bad land. But this meant that the land between each strip was wasted and involved unnecessary journeys between different fields. It was impossible to experiment with new techniques, and most

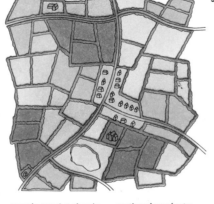

people used a simple system of rotation that left one field fallow for a year. Enclosure consolidated holdings and permitted improved agriculture. The progressive farmers supported it, and those with large holdings often provided incentives in order to obtain better tenants at greater rents. After enclosure, all the land was divided up, and hedges were usually planted to mark the new field boundaries, in this way creating what is now the familiar English landscape.

5 The Game Laws restricted the taking of game to men of property. In 1671 freeholders with less than £100 worth of property and leaseholders with less than £150 were prohibited from taking deer, hares, rabbits, pheasants or partridges. As enclosure progressed, the areas in which labourers and smallholders could legitimately take game were still further reduced. Harsher game laws were introduced, including imprisonment, transportation and even death in the case of resistance to gamekeepers. Mantraps (such as the one shown) and spring-guns were used to deter poachers, and gamekeepers were given wide powers. But the 19th century saw a relaxation of these laws.

90

with new techniques on a consolidated holding. Nearly 3,000 enclosure acts were passed between 1751 and 1810, the largest number being passed during the Napoleonic Wars (1803–15) when, due to trade dislocation, food prices were at their highest [10].

Poverty and prosperity

The enclosures of this period were once believed to have contributed to the pauperization of the agricultural labourer by depriving him of his rights of grazing on the common and rendering his smallholding uneconomic. This view has now changed. Many smallholders remained and the number of families working on the land actually rose between 1750 and 1831. Migration did take place from the land, and many smallholders were pushed into the ranks of wage-labourers, but this was more the effect of population growth than of enclosure. Pauperization of the agricultural labourer arose from chronic rural unemployment and concomitantly depressed wage levels.

On the other hand, owners of large farms tended to prosper. The landed classes of the eighteenth century had ample wealth for housebuilding, the creation of rich collections, and foreign travel. The wealthier of their tenants and professional farmers were also able to build substantial farmhouses. That tireless observer of rural life, William Cobbett (1762–1835), among others, noticed that the social status of farmers had greatly improved by the 1820s, but that it had the effect of making them more distant from their employees. Much contemporary comment satirized the social pretensions of farmers and their families in the early nineteenth century. But it took several decades for the typical pattern of Victorian rural society – which was that of large landowners, tenant farmers, and landless labourers – to emerge.

Expansion of the cultivatable acreage and improved yields provided the food for a growing urban population. Precise production figures are not available, but Britain's ability to feed itself despite the virtual trebling of its population between 1750 and 1850 was not the least remarkable feature of the development of its economy.

Enclosure was generally completed with little serious disagreement. To obtain an Act of Parliament took time and required the agreement of many of the local landowners. The land also had to be accurately surveyed and the appropriate legal titles established. The allocation of land was usually fair. Each enclosure act appointed commissioners to distribute the land.

6 The "Pangborn Hog" was a gigantic prize pig reared on Tidmarsh Farm in Berkshire as a result of systematically controlled and scientific breeding. There were also new strains of other animals by selective breeding. Among the farmers who popularized new breeds of sheep was Robert Bakewell of Dishley, Leicestershire. He was so successful that he managed to double the amount of meat obtainable from each of his sheep.

7 Agricultural improvements owed little to new machinery, apart from Tull's seed drill. But many small improvements were carried out on existing implements. An improved plough with a metal blade, for example, was produced in 1703, and wooden ploughs were gradually superseded. The Rotherham plough, shown here, included a metal blade and appeared in 1730.

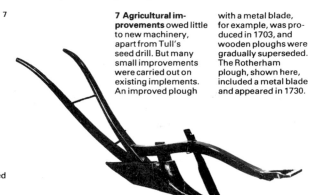

8 Arthur Young (1741–1820) was a famous propagandist for the techniques of agricultural improvement in Britain. In his books and articles he argued that large-scale farming, using enclosure, the latest techniques and plentiful capital would greatly increase production. His writings provide historians with a rich source of information about the social, political and economic life of the 18th century.

9 Holkham Gatherings was the name given to a series of agricultural shows organized by Thomas Coke (1752–1842) of Holkham in Norfolk. Coke was a pioneer of agricultural improvement and, like many others, he was a propagandist for the new methods. He experimented with root crops, especially the swede, helped to improve breeds of cattle, sheep and pigs, and was the first to grow wheat instead of rye in western Norfolk.

10 Agricultural output increased during the 18th century as new methods of farming were introduced. Rapid population growth stimulated demand at home; exports also increased. Here the average annual export of corn is shown for each ten-year period. Domestic prices reached a peak at the time of the Napoleonic Wars but fell slightly after 1815. The protective Corn Laws kept prices up, but even when these were repealed, in 1846, farming remained prosperous.

Period	Export (quarters)
1697–1706	74,100
1707–1716	118,700
1717–1726	133,700
1727–1736	168,200
1737–1746	280,000
1747–1756	448,700

10,000 quarters (56lbs)

The English in Ireland

At the end of the Middle Ages, Ireland remained a partially conquered country in which opposed cultures coexisted uneasily. English influence was confined to the colonized counties around Dublin. Beyond that "Pale" were some 90 independent lordships, two-thirds of them ruled by Gaelic dynasts, the rest by gaelicized Anglo-Norman lords. The only significant governmental function was defence, and this was entrusted to the FitzGeralds of Kildare.

The Reformation and anglicization

The weakness of the state was of merely local importance until the Reformation, by altering England's relations with Europe, gave Ireland a new strategic significance. After 1534, an attempt was made to improve international security by extending English control in Ireland. Direct rule was introduced on the basis of imported governors, civil servants [1] and armies, but experience soon revealed that control could not rest on military conquest alone and there followed an associated programme of anglicization.

Both Gaelic and Anglo-Norman lords resisted encroachments on their autonomy, and the situation was complicated by the tenacity with which both natives and settlers adhered to their Catholicism.

The conquest was poorly financed, piecemeal and protracted. It was brought to completion only when the outbreak of war between England and Catholic Spain made Ireland a strategic liability. In the Nine Years War (1595–1603), an Ulster-based confederacy of Gaelic lords led by Hugh O'Neill (c. 1540–1616) was defeated, and the incoming James I (reigned 1603–25) became the first English king to rule all Ireland. Thereafter, anglicization proceeded quickly.

The self-exile of the defeated northern leaders made possible the systematic "plantation" of Ulster with English and Scots settlers [4, 7]. The discriminatory enforcement of English property law allowed a widespread public and private expropriation of the Irish to take place elsewhere. A sizeable group of immigrant Protestant landowners gradually developed. Their influence was contested by the older Catholic colonists,

who vowed loyalty to the Crown and sought guarantees of their property rights but were rebuffed in the 1630s when Lord Deputy Wentworth (1593–1641), later the Earl of Strafford [5], confiscated a proportion of their land to further a colonizing scheme he was promoting in Connaught.

Protestant conquest

When the Ulster Irish rose in rebellion in 1641, the Catholic colonists joined them. Both were united in fearing that the growing influence of the English Parliament and the Scots would overturn the practical toleration of Catholicism in Ireland. There was little unity of purpose, because the colonists, who possessed one-third of Ireland, had much to lose, while the Irish, joined by returning exiles from Europe, had much to gain. The English Civil Wars created disabling divisions on the English side, but after Charles I (reigned 1625–49) had been executed, Oliver Cromwell (1599–1658) conquered Ireland easily and ruthlessly [6]. A vast expropriation followed, in which no distinction was made between the Gaelic Irish and the

1 Edmund Spenser (1552-99) served as a minor official in Ireland and acquired plantation lands in County Cork where he wrote much of *The Faerie Queene*. His grandson was designated an "Irish papist" by the Cromwellians, deprived of his estate and transplanted to Connaught with many other Catholics.

2 Thomas Lee (d. 1601), here fancifully portrayed as an Irish knight dressed for bogland terrain, was one of the many English adventurers who sought their fortunes in 16th-century Ireland. Others included Richard Grenville (c. 1542-91), Humphrey Gilbert (c. 1539-83) and Walter Raleigh (c. 1552-1618).

3 Crannogs, artificial islands of brushwood, peat, logs and stones sometimes surrounded by a timber palisade, mostly date from the early Bronze Age, although Neolithic remains have been found in some. They provided a secure home for the more important families in low-lying and marshy areas. Some were still inhabited in Ulster during the 16th century.

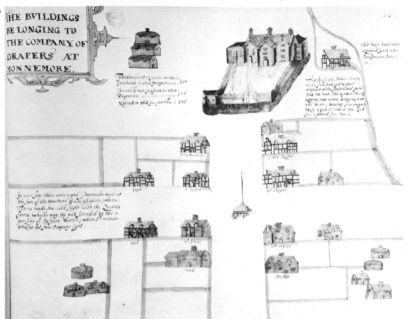

4 The village, in plantation areas, was not only a unit of defence, but a symbol of civilization. In Ulster, as this contemporary map detail shows, they were composed of neat timber-framed houses and cottages that contrasted sharply with the native Irish settlements in which wattle and turf houses clustered together.

5 The independence of the Lord Lieutenant of Ireland, the Earl of Strafford, posed a threat to the power of the English and Scottish parliaments when they joined forces against the Crown in 1640. He was charged with treason, the Irish Parliament readily attested to his misgovernment and the discontents of three kingdoms converged to lead to his execution.

Catholic colonial community. This was not accompanied by systematic settlement however, and existing Protestant settlers benefitted largely.

When Charles II (reigned 1660–85) was restored in 1660, his dependence upon Protestant support ensured that only token modifications of this arrangement were possible. But the fact that his brother and heir, James II (reigned 1685–8), was a Catholic gave hope of redress, and Catholics in Ireland rallied to James's support when he was deposed in 1688, while Protestants transferred their allegiance to William of Orange (reigned 1689–1702) [Key].

The Protestants were confirmed in their ownership of Irish land, and the government confirmed in its power to rule Ireland without reference to the interests of its Catholic population. Protestant supremacy was secured by a system of laws designed to depress Catholics, and particularly the remaining Catholic landholders, rather than to suppress Catholicism. Important changes within the Catholic community followed. As the population increased steadily, and land-

lords responded to demand by letting their land in ever smaller units, settlers and natives gradually merged into a depressed peasantry. In the towns, by contrast, where economic activity was less affected by penal constraints, a Catholic middle class desirous of its full rights slowly developed.

Union with England
The privileged society of Irish Protestants quickly acquired local interest and ambitions. No longer needing English support to uphold their position, they came to resent English control. Their claims for recognition of Ireland's legislative independence were conceded in 1782.

Circumstances soon challenged the basis of Protestant ascendancy. Indeed, the growth of republican separatism produced an abortive rising in 1798 so that when the government proposed the political union of England and Ireland as the most secure arrangement, Irish Protestants recognized the scheme as the best means of protecting their position in the future [10]. In 1800, the Irish Parliament voted itself out of existence.

The Battle of the Boyne between James II and William of Orange in 1690 was fought for control of the English throne. The battle was part of a wider European conflict and the armies were international, but it incidentally decided the future of Ireland. William's victory established a Protestant domination that excluded the Catholic descendants of English settlers from the colonial community and led them to assimilate with the Irish.

6 When Cromwell landed in Ireland in 1649 his purpose was not only conquest but also revenge for the reputed massacre of Protestants in 1641. This vengeance was exacted on the town of Drogheda (shown here) although its commander was English, its garrison was Royalist and the townspeople had played no part in the rebellion of 1641. The inhumanity of Cromwell's campaign remains impressed upon Irish folk memory.

7 The character of settlement varied widely. In all planted areas, settlers were interspersed among natives, but in Ulster, particularly in the unofficial, Scottish-based northeastern settlements, they were a fair reflection of society; elsewhere the lower classes were greatly under-represented. In unplanted areas, land ownership changed radically: in 1641 Catholics held 59 per cent of Irish land; by 1703 their share had fallen to 14 per cent.

English Pale by early 17th c.

Plantations established under
James I
Elizabeth I
Mary I
Unplanted areas

ULSTER

MONAGHAN

CONNAUGHT

LEINSTER

MUNSTER

0   50km

8 The impressive classical façade of the Custom House in Dublin symbolizes the prosperity of the privileged in the late 18th century and suggests the extravagance of their life-style.

9 Edmund Burke (1729–97), the statesman and philosopher, left Ireland as a young man, although his parliamentary championship of the interests of the American colonists was informed by an Irishman's understanding of their situation.

10 By the Act of Union, the centuries-old Irish Parliament exchanged its recently won legislative independence for Irish representation at Westminster. Its passage was widely believed to have been procured by bribery. In fact Irish Protestants chose to surrender their power to a protective England of their own accord. Despite Protestant identification with England, the English persistently regarded them as Irish, as this contemporary cartoon suggests.

Scotland in the 18th century

With the passing of the Act of Union in 1707, Scotland ceased to be an independent country and became part of Great Britain. Sixteen Scottish peers were elected to join the House of Lords (English membership 190) and 45 MPs sat in the House of Commons (English membership 513) at Westminster. Scottish MPs were notoriously pliable to the government's will at Westminster. The effective management of Scottish affairs in Parliament passed to government "managers" – the Dukes of Argyll for much of the century and thereafter usually the lord advocates, of whom Henry Dundas (1742–1811) William Pitt the Younger's confidant, was the most famous and effective.

The Jacobite rebellions

Enemies of the Union were few and far between, except for the Jacobites who supported the exiled House of Stewart's claim to the throne. In 1715, the Earl of Mar (1675–1732), a former supporter of the Union whose political ambitions had been blocked, attempted to raise the country for James Edward, the Old Pretender (1688–1766), James II's son. The rising won most support in the Highlands, but petered out after the inconclusive Battle of Sheriffmuir in November 1715 [1].

In 1714, the Young Pretender, Prince Charles Edward Stewart (1720–88), made a second attempt on the throne. In August he landed in Inverness-shire from a French ship and proclaimed his father King of Scotland and England. Even among the Highland clans only a minority followed him, and despite initial successes in which he took Edinburgh and defeated a Hanoverian army at Prestonpans, Charles was relying upon English Jacobite and French support when he marched on London in November [3]. The Jacobite army reached Derby and after some hesitation, in the face of mounting opposition forces under the Duke of Cumberland (1721–65), turned back northwards.

In April 1746, Cumberland caught up with Charles at Culloden [4] where the Jacobite army, outnumbered and poorly organized, was heavily defeated. The rebellion was finally crushed and Charles forced to flee back to France. The Union remained intact. Even the Jacobites had primarily wanted to regain the British throne for the Stewarts rather than to re-establish Scottish independence. With their defeat there was no further challenge to Westminster government for nearly half a century, and in the aftermath of Culloden the power of the Highlanders was broken for ever.

Economic consequences of the Union

The satisfaction that most Scots felt for the Union in the eighteenth century rested largely on an economic base and the new markets opened up by the Union with England. Although there was little dramatic change in the condition of the country until after 1760, even in the first half of the century food became more plentiful, the cattle trade with England expanded and linen emerged as the first major Scottish industry.

The tobacco trade, too, became an important source of prosperity to Glasgow and the west of Scotland when in the 1740s Scottish merchants secured bulk contracts to supply tobacco to France. The link forged with Virginia remained important until after

1 After the Battle of Sheriffmuir the cause of the Old Pretender was doomed. The rebel prisoners were taken south to be tried by courts in Carlisle and London because it was feared that they would not be punished severely enough under Scottish law. Here one of the two executions of the rebels, that of Lord Derwentwater (1689–1716), is shown.

2 Rioting broke out in Glasgow in 1725 following the decision by Westminster to extend the tax on malt to include Scotland as well as England. An angry mob attacked the house of Campbell of Shawfield who had supported the measure in Parliament. It was essentially an anti-government riot and not pro-Jacobite.

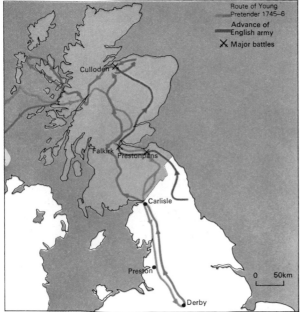

Route of Young Pretender 1745–6
Advance of English army
X Major battles

Culloden
Falkirk
Prestonpans
Carlisle
Preston
Derby

0   50km

3 Prince Charles's march through Scotland and into England was almost unopposed. His army took Edinburgh without a shot, routed a Hanoverian army at Prestonpans, captured Carlisle and marched on London. But after reaching Derby, the Prince retreated northwards on 6 December 1745.

4 The bloody battle at Culloden, near Inverness, on 16 April 1746 was an overwhelming victory for the Hanoverian forces and effectively broke the Jacobite cause forever. In its aftermath many of the defeated clansmen were butchered by the victorious army under the Duke of Cumberland.

the American Revolution (1775–83).

Towards the end of the century economic change became more rapid and far-reaching. In the Lowlands landowners and their tenants began enclosures, turnip husbandry and more intensive forms of farming both for animals and grain. By 1790 this had transformed the Lothians and was beginning to have an impact elsewhere. In the Highlands the "crofting system" was introduced whereby tenants had smallholdings along the shore and spent part of their time fishing or gathering seaweed ('kelp') from which an industrial alkali was manufactured. Everywhere in the countryside population increased rapidly, many migrated to gain employment in the towns or settled round the new industries such as Carron Iron Works (founded 1759) or the cotton mills at New Lanark (founded 1785) [9].

The Scottish Enlightenment
During this period of economic prosperity, Edinburgh flourished exceedingly. Its enterprising town council planned a New Town focused on Princes Street and George

Street; by 1800 this was attracting fashionable and middle-class families to its splendid homes in large numbers [Key]. The Scottish universities, especially Edinburgh and Glasgow, gained a worldwide reputation. Thinkers such as the philosopher David Hume (1711–76), economist Adam Smith (1723–90), the poet Robert Burns (1759–96), painters and architects such as Henry Raeburn (1756–1823) and Robert Adam (1728–92) and inventors such as James Watt (1736–1819), created "Scottish Enlightenment" of learning and ingenuity without parallel in the past [6, 8].

Not everyone, however, was convinced that the system was incapable of improvement. In the last decade of the century Scottish radical sympathizers with the French Revolution, especially the Friends of the People and the United Scotsmen began to make demands for a more democratic form of government [7]. Dundas and Pitt suppressed them as they had also suppressed English radical clubs, but in the nineteenth century the radicals' challenge proved more enduring than that of the Jacobites.

Charlotte Square in Edinburgh was the most splendid of the squares built in the New Town in the 18th century. The planning and construction of the New Town reflects the growing wealth and prosperity of the professional classes in 18th-century Edinburgh. Robert Adam was the main architect of this square and the elegant, classical style for which he is famous dominates the New Town.

5 The Royal Bank of Scotland was founded in 1727 largely because the Bank of Scotland's directors were suspected of Jacobitism. Even today the rival banks issue different notes.

6 The *Encyclopaedia Britannica*, compiled by a "society of gentlemen", first began to come off the Edinburgh presses in weekly numbers in December 1768. The editor was William Smellie (1740–95), a local printer, and the work aimed to provide "a dictionary of the arts and sciences". The three volumes of the first edition were completed in 1771 and an expanded second edition was begun in 1776.

Encyclopædia Britannica;
OR, A
DICTIONARY
OF
ARTS and SCIENCES,
COMPILED UPON A NEW PLAN.
IN WHICH
The different SCIENCES and ARTS are digested into distinct Treatises or Systems;
AND
The various TECHNICAL TERMS, &c. are explained as they occur in the order of the Alphabet.

ILLUSTRATED WITH ONE HUNDRED AND SIXTY COPPERPLATES.

By a SOCIETY of GENTLEMEN in SCOTLAND.

IN THREE VOLUMES.

VOL. I.

EDINBURGH:
Printed for A. BELL and C. MACFARQUHAR;
And sold by COLIN MACFARQUHAR, at his Printing-office, Nicolfon-ftreet.
M.DCC.LXXI.

7 Thomas Muir (1765–98), an Edinburgh lawyer and leader of the Friends of the People, was tried for sedition before Lord Braxfield in 1793. This was one of a series of trials held in the wake of the French Revolution that were aimed at Jacobin radical societies. After a hearing notorious for the violent bias of Braxfield, Muir was sentenced to transportation to Botany Bay for 14 years.

8 The school system in Scotland was the cornerstone of the great flowering of intellectual life in the late 18th century that was the Scottish Enlightenment. The ability to read and write was much more widespread than in England, and in many areas the rural parish school (supported by a tax levied on local landowners) educated both rich and poor. In the Highlands and towns, however, the parish system was inadequate and would often be supplemented by the wealthy with private tuition. The universities in the 18th century, in particular Edinburgh, flourished and established an eminent tradition in law, medicine and philosophy.

9 The new technology of Richard Arkwright (1732–92), made it possible to spin cotton fibres by water power. Arkwright introduced his new technique into Scotland at New Lanark (shown here) because he wished to undercut English labour costs. In 1799 the mills were sold to Robert Owen (1771–1858). Owen made the community at New Lanark world-famous for his pioneering social reforms: in working conditions, housing and education.

Exploration and science 1750–1850

The advances in exploration and science made in the eighteenth century were based upon the scientific movement and overseas expansion of Europe in the years before 1700. Scientists and explorers were assimilating and extending the pioneer exploits of seventeenth-century giants such as René Descartes (1596–1650) and Isaac Newton (1642–1727). Greater knowledge of the non-European world excited interest in its huge range of exotic flora and fauna and its geography, and questioned many accepted notions about the universe and its origins.

Growth of technical knowledge
In part the growth of knowledge depended upon technical innovations: improvements in navigational instruments, such as the sextant and the marine chronometer [1], facilitated scientific exploration. Captain James Cook (1728–79) commanded three voyages of exploration between 1768 and 1776 and the precision of his navigation depended on these new techniques. On his expeditions Cook charted large areas of the Pacific, including New Zealand, and added the islands of Tahiti

and Samoa to existing maps. He also contributed greatly to knowledge of the variety of cultures and natural history.

Scientific discovery also depended upon improvements in instrumentation. The use of a greatly improved telescope by William Herschel (1738–1822) led to the discovery of the planet Uranus in 1781. More sensitive balances contributed to chemical discoveries that displaced the phlogiston theory of combustion. In mathematics trigonometry and calculus were greatly advanced by men such as Johann Bernouilli (1667–1748) and Joseph Lagrange (1736–1813). In physics the properties of heat were investigated by Joseph Black (1728–99) in Glasgow where he met James Watt, inventor of the first efficient steam engine.

Impact of electricity and chemistry
Electricity was one of the principal fields of the physical sciences to be developed. Luigi Galvani [7] discovered "galvanic" (current) electricity, and Alessandro Volta obtained it from his "voltaic pile" or battery, which quickly made electrolysis possible.

In chemistry many natural elements were isolated for the first time. Joseph Priestley (1733–1804) is usually credited with the discovery of oxygen, while Antoine Lavoisier (1743–94) laid the basis for the modern treatment of chemical reactions. In botany the standard classification of plants was devised by the Swedish botanist Carolus Linnaeus (1707–78) [3], while the French naturalist Georges Buffon (1707–88) in his *Histoire Naturelle* suggested that the earth had evolved through a far longer time than the six thousand years of biblical history. Other pioneers included Charles Lyell (1797–1875), whose *Principles of Geology* [5] emphasized the theory that the processes of geological change were long, slow and uniform, and this was as true of the remote past as of the present. Many more speculative but competent naturalists such as Erasmus Darwin (1731–1802) and Jean Baptiste Lamarck (1744–1829) were already propounding the idea of organic evolution, that is, the descent of the present races of animals and plants from antecedent, dissimilar forms.

Many advances in the physical sciences

1 **The marine chronometer**, developed by John Harrison (1693–1776), revolutionized maritime navigation in the 18th century. Latitude had been easy to fix for centuries, but the chronometer made it possible for the first time to establish longitude to within half a degree. Harrison's invention won him a government prize of £20,000.

2 **The paintings of animals** by George Stubbs (1724–1806) revealed a deep interest in and knowledge of anatomy. A friend of eminent natural scientists, he published a series of anatomical studies. Among them were reconstructions of animals from material brought by Joseph Banks from the Pacific. Stubbs painted this study for William Hamilton.

3 **Carolus Linnaeus**, the Swedish botanist, founded modern biological classification with his *Systema Naturae* published in 1735.

4 **Alexander von Humboldt** (1769–1859) made his name as a traveller to many parts of the world and as a geographer, natural historian, ethnographer and oceanographer. His main work was the multi-disciplinary *Kosmos* (1845–62), which attempted to synthesize all knowledge of the universe. He is shown here with his close companion, the Frenchman Aimé Bonpland (1773–1858) (right). He examined wildlife on Mount Chimborazo in the Andes and ascended to a record height in these mountains. At this time vast areas of the world were still unknown. Although the existence of all the continents was known by 1800, there remained large tracts of unexplored land beyond the coastlines of many of them. Settlement was steadily filling the gaps in the Americas but great areas of the Pacific and elsewhere remained untouched. Original accounts of Africa, South America and Arabia were also published during the 19th century.

were directly related to and stimulated by economic activity, trade and industrial processes. Physics played an important part in the rise of the new technologies upon which the Industrial Revolution was based, especially the harnessing of steam power.

The scientific investigations of the Enlightenment very quickly spilled over into other spheres that touched more directly upon politics. The rationalists of the eighteenth century who discovered laws underpinning the physical world were soon joined by writers and thinkers who saw similar laws in politics; thus the scientific movement also gave rise to the "laws of political economy". *Essay on Population* (1798) by Thomas Malthus (1766–1834) produced a mechanical and inevitable theory of demography, similar to that accepted by the classical economists, Adam Smith (1723–90) and David Ricardo (1772–1823). The concept of immutable laws governing political behaviour was adopted by the utilitarian thinkers, such as Jeremy Bentham (1748–1832) and James Mill (1773–1836). Similarly the scientific movement extended to the study of man and by the early nineteenth century produced the first works of sociology and comparative law.

Science and religion

Undoubtedly the most important effect of the scientific movement was its impact upon conventional religious beliefs. Clearly the account of the Creation contained in the Old Testament was not literally true and the world was older than the Bible suggested. Fossil evidence was clear proof of the existence of life on earth at hitherto unthinkably remote periods. Moreover, to some the evidence of geology and of fossils disproved the Old Testament idea of simultaneous creation of all living things. Although these ideas encountered intense hostility and were at first rejected, they provoked profound questioning about the place of revealed religion in the scientific age. *On the Origin of Species by Means of Natural Selection* (1859) by Charles Darwin (1809–82) [Key] detonated an explosion of ideas that had been gradually accumulating during the late eighteenth and early nineteenth centuries.

Lampooned as an ape, Charles Darwin attracted, with other scientists of his time, the wrath of society when his discoveries and arguments undermined the traditional and biblical accounts of man's creation. The investigation of foreign cultures, and the new scientific approach to the world of nature, threw European institutions and conventional thought into sharper focus and led to questions about their assumptions and legitimacy. As a result, Darwin and others who supported his theory were treated for some time with hostility by their contemporaries who held more orthodox opinions.

5 The foundations of modern geology were laid down in the 18th century with the study of rock strata and with attempts at geological dating. The frontispiece of Lyell's *Principles of Geology*, (1830–33) is shown here. The work formulated an evolutionary theory of the earth rejecting earlier writers who had tried, for theological reasons, to reconcile geological and fossil evidence with literal interpretations of the Old Testament.

6 Accurate observations of flora and fauna provided one of the most important vehicles of early scientific enquiry. Natural history attracted professional and amateur collectors and precisely illustrated studies proliferated. This illustration of *Phyllanthus niruriodes* [A] is from a collection called *Hindustan Plants*. The fish [B] formed part of a collection that appeared in a German publication by Schinz (1836).

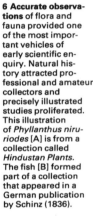

7 In the physical sciences one of the most important fields of development in the 18th century was electricity. Luigi Galvani (1737–98) of Bologna is seen here demonstrating in 1786 the effect of electrical impulses on a frog's nerves. Benjamin Franklin (1706–90), Volta (1745–1827), Ampère (1775–1836) and Ohm (1787–1854) also experimented with electricity.

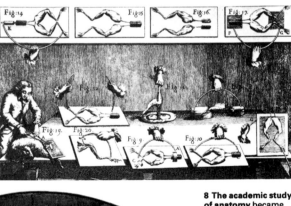

8 The academic study of anatomy became accepted by the 18th century. Its teaching was much advanced by the work of Hermann Boerhaave (1668–1738), and John Hunter (1728–93) and his brother William (1718–83), seen here giving a lecture to the Royal Academy in London. It was not until the advances in chemistry and bacteriology of the 19th century that the causes of diseases were diagnosed accurately and aseptic and antiseptic procedures made surgery less risky.

9 The old wives' tale that dairy maids never caught smallpox led to an effective counter to the disease – Jenner's vaccination. Epidemics of the disease were rife and regularly killed or scarred great numbers of people, especially children and young persons. In many countries it had replaced the plague as a major check on population growth. Inoculation using human virus was used among the poor in the 18th century but it was expensive and dangerous with a high risk of serious infection. Edward Jenner (1749–1823) examined the traditional view, saw that people who had caught the relatively harmless cowpox were immune from smallpox and was able to develop a vaccine that carried a minimum risk of ill effects and could be made widely available. Inoculation remained in use in many European countries even after the development of vaccination, but it was finally made illegal in Britain in 1840.

International economy 1700–1800

During the eighteenth century trading links between Europe and the rest of the world strengthened into commercial bonds that were vital to the prosperity of several European states and to many of their merchants and workmen. The rise of Great Britain to a dominant position in trade, overtaking the Dutch, Spanish, and French, showed itself in extensive contacts and trading arrangements with the Americas and Asia [5]. There was a general expansion of trade at the same time, particularly in the Atlantic, in which other countries, especially France, shared. Expansion of trade brought with it specialization in shipping and financial business and provided a stimulus to the increased production of manufactured goods in Europe.

Incentives for trade expansion

The expansion of European influence in the years before 1700 had introduced a wide range of precious and tropical products which were the staples of extra-European trade. Gold and silver bullion had provided one major component of the trade of the declining Spanish Empire, but this trade had

also included spices, tobacco, coffee, sugar and cocoa. A growing taste in Europe for tropical products gave merchants the incentive to incur the risks of long overseas voyages. Merchants from countries such as Britain and France, which were relative latecomers to colonial trade, made greater efforts in the 1700s to capture part of the trade controlled by the older empires.

Several commercial wars were fought by the other European nations to open up the colonial trade of the declining Spanish Empire to their merchants. In 1715 British merchants obtained permission in the Asiento Treaty to deliver 4,800 slaves annually to the Spanish colonies and for one ship a year to trade with Panama. In all other respects, Spain tried to keep her colonial trade closed. But because Spain was unable to supply all the needs of her colonists, there was much illicit traffic, especially in slaves and in manufactured goods. After the Seven Years War (1756–63) this rigid control was relaxed and Britain and France seized a greater part of the Spanish American trade.

Similarly, British and Dutch ships cap-

tured an increasing share of Portuguese trade. In the East, the Dutch had taken over much of the old Portuguese Empire. With stations in Ceylon, Bengal, Malabar and Batavia their influence extended as far as Japan. Organized through the Dutch East India Company based on Batavia in Java, they carried on a lucrative trade in spices, coffee, and silks. By the end of the century, however, they began to feel the effects of competition from the British and French.

French and British power

France had colonies in North America, including Quebec and Louisiana, and in the West Indies, including Guadeloupe and Martinique; she held Senegal in Africa and colonized Madagascar and Mauritius in the Indian Ocean. In India, France maintained important trading positions at Pondicherry and Chandernagore. From these colonies and contacts French trade grew rapidly in the late eighteenth century, especially with the West Indies. After the Seven Years War, however, France lost Quebec and much of her influence in India. Nonetheless her

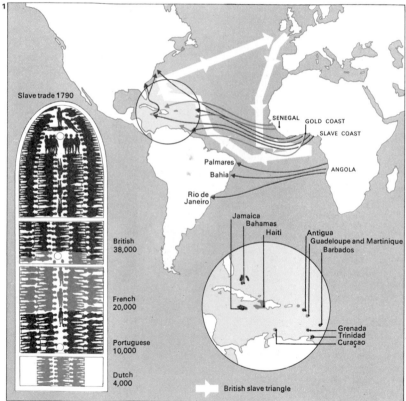

Slave trade 1790

British 38,000

French 20,000

Portuguese 10,000

Dutch 4,000

SENEGAL
GOLD COAST
SLAVE COAST
Palmares
Bahia
ANGOLA
Rio de Janeiro
Jamaica
Bahamas
Haiti
Antigua
Guadeloupe and Martinique
Barbados
Grenada
Trinidad
Curaçao

British slave triangle

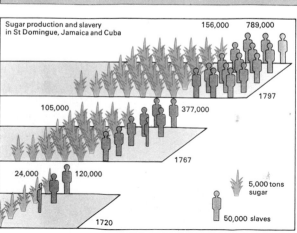

1 The triangular route taken by slave ships from European ports such as Liverpool, Bristol and Bordeaux took them to Africa to collect slaves, across the Atlantic to sell them and back again with cargoes bartered in exchange. The major share of the slave traffic was carried on by Great Britain by the end of the 18th century, supplying plantations in the West Indies and in the Americas.

2 Brest, on the Atlantic coast of France, and other Atlantic ports such as Bristol, Bordeaux and Liverpool grew enormously rich on the profits of the slave trade and colonial traffic.

Sugar production and slavery in St Domingue, Jamaica and Cuba

156,000   789,000
1797
105,000   377,000
1767
24,000   120,000
1720

5,000 tons sugar
50,000 slaves

3 Economic development in the West Indies depended on a steady supply of slave labour from Africa. The slave population and sugar production grew to satisfy the European demand for sugar.

4 Smuggling in the 18th century was a common way of avoiding heavy duties on commodities such as spirits, wines and tobacco. Revenue men waged an intermittent war with smugglers in many parts of Europe, especially in remoter areas.

busy trade with the remainder of her colonies led to the expansion of ports such as Bordeaux, Nantes, and Brest [2]; Marseilles prospered with the Levant trade.

The major rising power was Great Britain, which exerted its superiority over the older empires by the middle of the century and conducted all the trade of its colonies in British-registered ships. In spite of the loss of the North American colonies, trade continued to expand with the Americas both through chartered companies, such as the Hudson's Bay Company [8], and through more open commerce. The vastly profitable but inhuman slave traffic was primarily in British hands by the end of the century, the "Triangular Route" [1] between Britain, Africa, and the Americas providing great profits upon which mercantile cities such as London, Liverpool and Bristol flourished. Second only to the slave traffic in importance was the sugar trade [3], which provided, with other tropical produce, a valuable re-export trade to continental Europe. In the Indian Ocean the British East India Company triumphed over the French and controlled Bombay, Bengal, Madras and most of southern India; but by the end of the century the trade was opened up and the company's monopoly broken.

Stimulus for industrialization

Expansion of trade led to increases in merchant shipping and the development of more versatile credit and financial institutions. In London, firms of shipping insurers, such as Lloyd's, began to supplant the Dutch. Growing trade led to relaxation of the old mercantile ideas of monopolistic companies and favoured the adoption of *laissez-faire* ideas of free trade and open competition.

In many countries industries grew up that refined tropical products and re-exported them either to other European countries or back to the colonies as manufactured goods. Thus sugar-refining, tanning, distilling and many other processes became early examples of industrial activity. The most striking development by the late eighteenth century was the rapid rise in raw cotton exports from the southern states of America to the growing British textile industry.

Worldwide expansion of Europe's trade in the 18th century was carried in ships such as this heavily armed East Indiaman.

5 Trading horizons widened in the 18th century as European contact with hitherto exotic countries became more regular. Tea plantations in China were developed to meet a taste for tea in Britain and an extensive trade also grew up in silk, porcelain and spices. Although China limited European influence to specified trading centres, these provided a foothold that was extended in the next century.

6 Speculation, greed and dishonesty were caricatured by the satirist William Hogarth (1697–1764) in 1720 when the South Sea Company, upon which heavy speculation had centred, collapsed and led to a change of government. Financial and credit institutions in the 18th century were often unstable, partly because governments were apt to draw on them for credit and also because investors panicked easily.

7 Spanish financial institutions, established in the 16th century, shared in the great expansion of European trade in the 18th century. This deposit certificate, dated 1759, is from the Real Compañía de Comercio of Barcelona.

8 The Hudson's Bay Company, whose Fort Garry, Manitoba, trading post is shown here, was founded by the British in 1670 to open up a lucrative trade in Canada, supplying Europe with furs, timber and salted fish. Simultaneously, the colonists at Albany and New York were extending trade with Indians. France was also active in the Canadian trade but lost its share in 1763 when it was defeated in the Seven Years War and thereafter surrendered control of Canada to Britain.

British colonial policy in the 18th century

British exploration overseas began in earnest in the sixteenth century and the foundations of the Thirteen Colonies in America were laid in the reign of Charles II (1660–85) [1]. Nevertheless the modern British Empire is usually dated from the Treaty of Utrecht (1713). The treaty gave Britain some minor gains in the Caribbean; France yielded its claims to Newfoundland and Nova Scotia; Spain ceded Gibraltar and Minorca to Britain and, most important, transferred to it the *asiento*, giving Britain the right to furnish slaves to the Spanish colonies and to send one ship a year to trade in those colonies.

Anglo-French rivalry

For a century the power of Spain had been on the wane. After 1713 France and Britain were the great rivals and during the next century a series of wars between the two nations, ending in Wellington's victory at Waterloo (1815), raised Britain to the rank of the world's dominant colonial power. In the eighteenth century it was understood that trade was power. The Anglo-French wars were fought to win control of the world's trade, especially the highly profitable trade in slaves and sugar.

The eighteenth-century empire was based on the "triangular trade". British ships carried manufactured goods to Africa, exchanged them for slaves [9], sold those in the West Indies and the southern American colonies, and returned home with cargoes of sugar, tobacco and raw cotton. By 1750 hardly a trading or manufacturing town in England was not connected with the trade. Between 1670 and 1786 more than two million slaves were transported from Africa to British colonies.

The imperial economy was run on the principle that the colonies provided raw materials and accepted in return manufactured goods from the home country. This system was strictly maintained by the Navigation Act, passed in 1660, which required that trade between Britain and the colonies be carried by British-built ships manned by British crews. Produce going from the colonies to foreign parts had first to pass through a British port. This trade with the protected market of the American colonies was impor-

tant, too, to British industry, which had to seek new outlets after the colonies won independence. It also hindered the growth of colonial industry and thus encouraged the American demand for independence.

Defeat of the French

Before the American Revolution began, Britain, led by William Pitt (1708–78) later Earl of Chatham, won a great victory over France in the Seven Years War (1756–63). The war was fought to gain two aims: supremacy at sea and the capture of French trading posts, and it spread over Europe, India, the West Indies and Canada. Wolfe's victory at Quebec (1759) secured Canada's fish, fur and timber for Britain [2]; Eyre Coote (1726–83) and Robert Clive (1725–74) won victories in India which brought Bengal under the rule of the East India Company.

At the Peace of Paris (1763) the French sugar islands – Guadeloupe and Martinique – were returned to France, and Cuba to Spain, in order to satisfy the West Indian planters who feared lower prices from an increased sugar supply. But the war achieved one great

1 **The presentation of the first pineapple** grown in England to Charles II is an exotic example of the change in British eating habits that followed the colonization of the New World. Maize, which has a yield ten times higher than wheat; the potato, which thrives in poor soil and made possible Ireland's population explosion; the kidney bean and pumpkin were all introduced into Britain in the late 16th century, but it was not until the 18th century that their widespread cultivation brought about any significant improvement in the diet of the peasantry. In this period, the colonies were intended to benefit the mother country rather than become independent economic entities.

2 **British interests in Canada** in the 18th century were mostly in the hands of chartered companies. The largest of these was the Hudson's Bay Company, whose founders were given a royal charter by Charles II in 1670. Canada provided furs, fish and, most important, timber to build warships for the navy. But from a commercial point of view the country was insignificant compared, for example, with the Sugar Islands. From 1762 to 1776, the value of British imports from Grenada alone was eight times that from Canada, whereas exports from Britain to Grenada were double the value of those to Canada.

3 **An English fleet attacked Portobelo,** a Spanish port on the Colón peninsula of Panama, in 1739. Spain was declining as a colonial power by the mid-17th century and Britain was anxious to ensure that France, the chief rival for control of the Spanish dominions, did not gain control of the most important Spanish colonies. The import of bullion from the New World had mostly stopped by this time; sugar was the valuable crop for which the European nations were struggling in the Caribbean.

4 **New Yorkers** pulled down the statue of George III, symbolizing their revolt against Britain. But the loss of the American colonies meant merely a reorientation of the empire towards India; and British trade with the USA itself soon grew.

result: it deprived France of huge markets in Canada and India and, by making those places British, provided scope for the industrial expansion of Britain. Without India, the cotton industry of Lancashire would not have had the market to sustain its spectacular growth between 1780 and 1820.

Britain and India

In 1776, the very year that the American nation was born, British control over India was tightened. At the beginning of the century there were no more than 1,500 English in all of India – traders and their families, concentrated in the ports of Madras, Calcutta, Surat and Bombay. They were concerned only with making money and were not interested in penetrating inland nor in the destiny of Britain to rule over a native population. But conflict with the French, who had established themselves at the ports of Pondicherry and Chandernagore, was endemic throughout the first half of the century. In 1754 royal troops were for the first time sent out to assist the private armed forces of the East India Company.

At the end of the Seven Years War Britain had won supremacy in India. But the area was still under the management of the East India Company, which steadily tightened its grip on Bengal, collecting taxes and administering justice. The wealth that it extracted from the Indian peasantry [5], and the severity of its judicial administration, aroused criticism at home and led to the great political scandal of the century, the impeachment of Warren Hastings (1732–1818) [6]. It also produced the India Act of 1784. By that date control of Bengal had, under the governorship of Charles Cornwallis (1738–1805) and Richard Wellesley (1760–1842), been extended over most of the subcontinent. It was in these circumstances that the power of the East India Company was curtailed by making it responsible for the administration of the whole of India jointly with the Crown department, the Board of Control.

France made one last, heroic attempt under Napoleon to regain its position as the world's leading power. This ended with Wellington's victory at Waterloo in 1815.

The port of Bristol prospered from having almost a monopoly of the lucrative West Indian slave trade during Walpole's administration. With a population of about 50,000, it was, after London, the second largest town in 18th-century Britain.

5 Some Britons made huge fortunes out of their service with the East India Company. These "nabobs" lived ostentatiously in India, and at home bought seats in Parliament to influence policy.

6 The impeachment of Warren Hastings, for corruption and mistreatment of natives when he was governor of Bengal (1772–85), began in 1788. The trial dragged on for seven years and ended in Hastings' acquittal.

7 Gibraltar, first occupied in 1704, became a British possession by the Treaty of Utrecht (1713). Spain joined France and the USA in the war against England in 1779 and besieged the colony for four years. George III tried to barter Gibraltar for Spanish colonies in America, but by the Peace of Paris (1783) Britain gave up East and West Florida to Spain and retained Gibraltar.

8 Penal settlements were set up in the new colonies of Australia in the late 18th century. The first convicts were sent to New South Wales in 1788, and to Van Diemen's Land (Tasmania), shown here, in 1803. Transportation was generally for life, but it could often allow the convict to establish himself in the colony; at the time there were more than 100 offences in England that could bring the death penalty.

9 Commemorative medallions, such as this one by Josiah Wedgwood (1730–95), were struck to encourage the abolition of the slave trade in the British Empire. This took place in 1807 and resulted partly from an evangelical campaign by William Wilberforce (1759–1833), and partly because British sugar-planters wished to stop the flow of slaves to their French rivals when their own plantations were at their maximum production and could survive without the import of more slaves.

101

India from the Moguls to 1800

In 1192 Muhammad of Ghur destroyed the Rajput princes at Tarain. In the next ten years the Muslims overran the Ganges plains and founded the Sultanate of Delhi (1206). This marked the beginning of Islam's long dominance over Hindustan (northern India) which survived into the 1700s and created an entity that was distinct in the Islamic world.

The three centuries that followed saw the rise and fall of dynasties – the Turco-Afghans, Khaljis, Tughluks, Sayyids and Lodis – under which the Delhi Empire sometimes expanded as far as the Deccan and the south (as it did under the megalomaniac Alaudin Kalji, or under Muhammad-bin-Tughluk the greatest of the sultans) and sometimes contracted into the narrow regions around Delhi and Agra (as it did under the Lodis) [2].

The regions continued to challenge the centre; invasions from the north (of which Timur's sack of Delhi in 1398 was the most ferocious example) still threatened the empires, and Delhi remained unable to dominate the Deccan.

Two new forces, however, were to alter the old patterns: Mogul rule and European expansion. In 1526 Babur (1483–1530), driven from his mountain stronghold in Firghana, crushed the Lodis at Panipat and established the Moguls in Delhi. In 1498 the Portuguese explorer Vasco da Gama sailed into Calicut, the precursor of other seaborne powers from Europe who in time were to be the heirs of the Mogul.

Mogul Empire

The great Mogul rulers – Babur, Humayun, Sher Shah and, above all, Akbar [3] and Aurungzebe [4] – brought more of India under one empire than any ruler since the time of Ashoka in the third century BC and gave it a more sophisticated administration than it had ever possessed. But the Great Mogor (Mogul), sitting on his peacock throne, surrounded by his great entourage of courtiers, concubines and slaves, his vast numbers of elephants and camels, and backed by his 200,000 cavalry, had built an empire on a fragile base. Mogul rule was the rule of foreigners and it was expensive. Built by conquest, it could not be sustained by force alone. Despite all the trappings of imperial power, the army and the centrally controlled military bureaucrats (the *mansabhadars*), the Moguls were forced to come to terms with their Indian subjects. This meant they had to give reasonable freedom to the magnates who actually controlled the land. They had to tolerate Hinduism and above all they had to avoid meddling too much in local affairs. All this qualified the notion of Mogul power – more overrule than real empire – and helps to explain the decline of the Mogul Empire [6].

The problem of revenue

Like all land empires in pre-modern times, the fundamental difficulty the Mogul rulers faced was how to raise revenues from limited sources, while retaining the co-operation of local notables, the *zomindars*. One obvious device was to extend the empire but, as Aurungzebe discovered, more conquest meant more expense. Another was to try to extract more land revenue from their subjects, but in the end the Moguls lost the co-operation of the local notables, who were squeezed from above and resisted by the

1 The ruins of the fortress and city of Tughlukabad, near Delhi, are an example of the feckless manner in which Indian cities were made and unmade by rulers who sought to commemorate themselves by building new capitals. Constructed between 1321 and 1323, Tughlukabad was soon abandoned by Muhammad Tughluk Shah in favour of Deogir, ostensibly because of bad water.

2 The Sultanate of Delhi at the death of Iltumish (1236) and, 100 years later, under Muhammad-bin-Tughluk (*c.* 1325–51), when it reached its greatest extent, are shown on the map. It indicates that Muslim dynasties had dominated northern India for centuries before the Moguls and had made attempts apparently, only temporarily successful, to dominate the Deccan and the south of India.

Sultanate of Delhi 1236

Expansion of Sultanate of Delhi by 1335

0 — 800 km

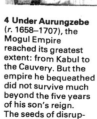

3 Akbar (*r.* 1556–1605), the most celebrated Mogul emperor, was the almost exact contemporary of Queen Elizabeth I. He vastly expanded the Mogul's territories, gave them an efficient system of government and tried to encourage new sources of work. In his effort to conciliate his Hindu subjects and to stamp out Muslim bigotry, the emperor tried, but without lasting success, to create for India a new religion reconciling the different beliefs.

4 Under Aurungzebe (*r.* 1658–1707), the Mogul Empire reached its greatest extent: from Kabul to the Cauvery. But the empire he bequeathed did not survive much beyond the five years of his son's reign. The seeds of disruption, always present, were germinated by his religious intolerance; he alienated the Rajputs, the military prop of the empire; at great cost he conquered, but failed to integrate, the Deccan; he neglected Hindustan and fought the Marathas in the south.

5 The Red Fort at Delhi, built by Shah Jehan (1592–1666), was surrounded by massive red sandstone walls 22.8m (75ft) high and enclosed a complex of palaces, gardens, military barracks and other buildings. The fort, like many other masterpieces of this reign, including the Taj Mahal, illustrates the splendour of Mogul rule in India.

peasantry below. These inherent difficulties were made worse by Aurungzebe's religious intolerance, which alienated the Rajput allies and confirmed the Marathas in their hostility. A sequence of ineffectual successors after Aurungzebe reduced the throne at Delhi to the plaything of factions; more invasions from the north culminated in Nader Shah's sack of Delhi in 1739.

Rise of the East India Company
With the collapse of Mogul rule, India was parcelled out among a set of virtually independent "country" powers – Bengal and Oudh under the Nawabs, Mysore under the Muslim dynasty of an adventurer, Hyderabad under the Nizam and the Maratha confederacy marauding throughout India from its western base.

This was the background to the territorial rise of the British-owned East India Company. The company had gone to India to trade not conquer. Throughout the eighteenth century its directors protested that commerce, not dominion, was their aim. But by the mid-eighteenth century the British,

long established in their factories at Calcutta, Madras and Bombay [8], had a trade (mainly in Indian cotton goods) that was worth protecting both against the smaller French company and against Indian disruption [7].

When Britain and France fought in Europe, the companies in India could not stay neutral. Faced by a more powerful English company, Joseph François Dupleix (1697–1763) of the French East India Council decided, during the Austrian War of Succession, to improve the odds by using Indian allies against his rival.

The English soon adopted the French tactic. Robert Clive (1725–74) used it to win the Battle of Plassey (1757) and thereby gain Bengal. Dupleix's idea of using Indian resources to pay for European expansion gave Britain the richest province of India and set her firmly on the road to dominion [9].

By the time William Pitt (1759–1806) and Henry Dundas (1742–1811) began to think of an Indian Empire as part of the swing eastwards of British expansion, the East India Company had already become the heir of the Moguls.

After the Afghan defeat of the Marathas at Panipat (1761) Mahadaji Sindhia (1727–94), a bluff but literate soldier of fortune, built a large empire in Hindustan. Acting nominally as the soldier of the *peshwa* (sovereign), he became the master of the Mogul ruler, Shah Alam, and the "actual sovereign of Hindustan from the Sutlej to Agra, the conqueror of the princes of Rajputana, the commander of an army". But although he modernized the Maratha armies, giving them artillery and recruiting Muslim and Jat soldiers and European officers in his service (one of whom he is entertaining here), his power was fragile because his domains lacked the resources to support his armies.

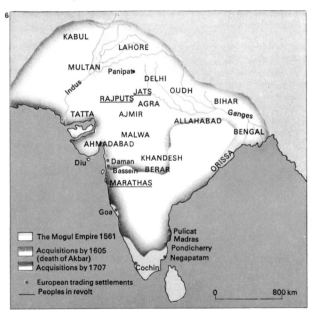

6 The rise of the Mogul Empire and the early signs of its decline are indicated on the map. By 1561 Akbar had created a unified Mogul Empire in the north of India; by 1707 when Aurungzebe died, the Mogul Empire had reached its utmost limits. But the Rajputs, Jats and Marathas were already in revolt and the European seaborne powers, who were to be the heirs of the Moguls, occupied the coast.

The Mogul Empire 1561
Acquisitions by 1605 (death of Akbar)
Acquisitions by 1707
• European trading settlements
— Peoples in revolt

0   800 km

7 The English settlement at Fort St George in Madras was one of the earliest in India, set up in 1639. The struggle with the French for mastery centred upon the south and the fort was crucial.

8 Bombay was ceded by Portugal to the English in 1661 and granted to the East India Company in 1668. Its fort helped to defend English commercial interests located on the west coast of India.

9 In 1765 Shah Alam made his grant of the *diwani* – the right to collect land revenue – to Clive, by then the real master of Bengal. The fact that the Mogul, although politically impotent by this time, was still seen as the source of legitimacy in ratifying the company's authority in Bengal, shows the conservatism of Indian politics; it is also indicative of British reluctance to move from trade to dominion that Clive did not demand more power.

10 The East India Company's fortunes in the late 17th and 18th centuries were built upon the export of hand loom cottons whose thread was spun in villages throughout India, sometimes with the aid of the *gharkha*, or spinning wheel, illustrated here. The 19th century saw the decline of village spinning and weaving, and India became the largest market for Lancashire's cotton goods. In the 20th century Gandhi revived the hand loom.

China from 1368 to *c.* 1800

The Ming or "Brilliant" dynasty (1368–1644) was founded by a Buddhist peasant who became leader of the rebel bands that overthrew the Mongol rule. He made his capital at Nanking and gave himself the title Hung Wu (reigned 1368–98). Under the new emperor the government reverted to the T'ang system of Confucianism, taxes were reduced and peasants were encouraged to work harder by being allowed to keep the land they reclaimed. The empire expanded, taking in vassal states which included Annam and Siam. Maritime expansion also occurred and under the able command of Admiral Cheng Ho fleets of exceptionally large Chinese vessels made seven expeditions between 1405 and 1433 to places as far away as Sri Lanka, the Persian Gulf and parts of Africa. The ships carried merchandise and Cheng Ho was able to establish trading relations with about 30 ports.

Protection of the homeland
At home the government was determined to defeat further invasions from the north. The Great Wall was repaired, many towns were fortified and Nanking was surrounded by a wall 32km (20 miles) long and 18m (60ft) high. This "closed door" policy of the Ming was similar to that of the early Sung period, which had also established Chinese rule over the Middle Kingdom after a period that had witnessed foreign intervention.

In spite of this attitude the Ming were to see the arrival of Europeans from the south. The Portuguese established a settlement in Macao and were followed by missionaries.

The Ming built numerous palaces and splendid tombs, the most famous being the Imperial Palace in Peking [1] and the tombs of the emperors north of the city [3, 4]. In 1958 that of the Wan-li emperor was opened to reveal three lacquer coffins containing the bodies of the emperor and two of his wives.

The end of the Ming dynasty
In spite of all the elaborate precautions for security, the Brilliant dynasty reached its end when northern barbarians, in this case the Manchus, entered north China. They came at the request of the Ming commander who sought their help to unseat a rebel, Li Tzu-ch'eng, who had made himself master of Peking. Rather than submit to humiliation the last Ming emperor hanged himself and the rebel emperor in his turn was overthrown by the Manchus whose leader, Fu-lin (1638–61), proclaimed himself emperor and set up the Ch'ing or "Pure" dynasty.

For a century and a half the Manchus governed wisely; they provided the country with domestic prosperity and extended its boundaries beyond all previous limits. The emperors ruled as conquerors and skilfully protected themselves against rebellion by instituting a system of banners. These were military and administrative divisions in which the people were systematically registered, taxed and conscripted.

The Manchus were unable either to read or write and accepted the Ming examination procedure for the selection of civil service officials. They were careful, however, to forbid the Chinese to hold office in their native provinces and they also divided responsibility in such a way that the officials were obliged to keep a check on one another. The Manchus were more sophisticated than

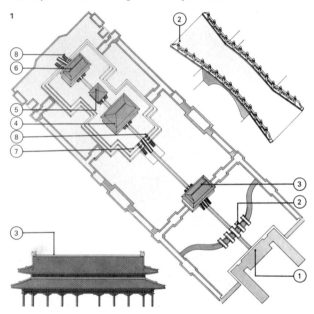

1 **The Imperial Palace** in Peking was the seat of 22 Ming, and Ch'ing emperors after Peking became the capital in 1421. Begun in 1406, the palace now covers 720,000m² (7,750,000 sq ft). The palace is an assemblage of imperial buildings, the most important [shown here] containing the ceremonial halls. The principal entrance is through the Meridian gatehouse [1] leading to the Golden Water River with its five marble bridges [2]. After the second gatehouse [3] lies the first great hall [4], which holds the imperial throne. The halls [5, 6] stand on the marble, three-tiered Dragon Pavement [7] with triple staircases [8].

2 **Chinese astronomers** were the most persistent and accurate observers of celestial bodies anywhere before the Renaissance. The importance of the calendar for a primarily agrarian society and the state interest in astrology meant that astronomy was of central importance in their lives. In contrast with Europe, scientific work was not a private concern and astronomers often worked from the Imperial Observatory in Peking. Their observations, like the work of scientists in many other fields, were included in large encyclopedias that were compiled and published at the instigation and sole expense of the state.

3 **The tomb** of the Ming Wan-li emperor (1573–1620) is situated at the foot of rugged mountains to the northwest of Peking. The complex is approached by an avenue lined with impressive stone sculptures of guardian animals, soldiers and officials. Work on the tombs began in 1584 and took four years.

4 **The throne of the Ming Wan-li emperor** was placed in his tomb. Ming emperors generally enjoyed an unprecedented, although often abused, degree of power. Ultimately the Ming dynasty fell to the invading Manchus who seized Peking in 1644, but already during Wan-li's reign internal dissent and foreign attacks threatened Ming power.

the Mongols and proved to be neither barbarous nor destructive, but in fact grew to admire Chinese culture. One of their first acts was to request a group of scholars to write a history of the Ming dynasty which was followed by a vast encyclopedia, the *Ssu-k'u ch'uan-shu*, comprising 36,000 volumes, begun in 1772 and completed in 1781.

The influence of the Manchu

Abroad Manchu authority spread to Manchuria, Mongolia, Tibet and Turkestan. During the Ch'ien Lung era their armies entered Burma, Nepal and Annam [6]. As the empire grew in size and wealth foreigners increased their pressure to trade with this huge untapped territory. The Jesuits, who had been accepted during the Ming dynasty, were now followed by other Catholic orders from Europe and before the end of the seventeenth century Franciscans, Dominicans, Augustinians and members of the Society of Foreign Missions in Paris had established themselves in several cities in the interior.

European merchants did not penetrate China as readily as the missionaries, but they persisted in their efforts and eventually limited trading facilities became available for the French, British, Dutch and Portuguese. In 1784 the first of many ships from the United States arrived. By the middle of the eighteenth century British trade, the monopoly of the British East India Company, had outpaced all others [8].

Chinese silk, tea, cotton and porcelain were in endless demand in Europe. However, business could be carried out only through selected groups of Chinese merchants, the Co-Hung. There were no fixed tariffs, a policy that increased corruption amongst officials. The Chinese were forbidden to teach the foreigners their language and foreigners had to submit to Chinese law in Chinese courts, where the Chinese with their belief in group responsibility held the foreign communities liable for the misdemeanour of any of their members.

Such conditions soon became impossible. The Western trading countries therefore sent missions to Peking [5], which began the lengthy process of bringing China out of her diplomatic, cultural and economic isolation.

This Ming imperial crown, decorated with a phoenix, is indicative of Ming wealth and their patronage of the arts.

5 The first official British mission to China was made in 1792 by Lord Macartney (1737–1806) and came at a time of demands for increased trading rights as the British and other foreign powers pressed for a foothold. Already the British East India Company had a monopoly over the trade in tea. However, the mission was treated by the Ch'ienlung emperor as purely diplomatic.

6 The Manchu Empire in 1800 covered a large area of central and South-East Asia. But already European and Russian expansion in search of trade threatened this shaky conglomerate.

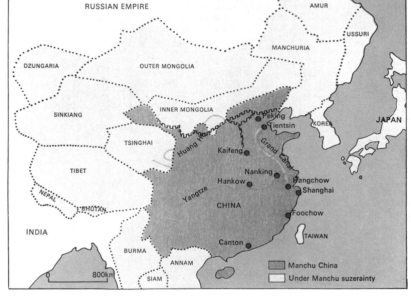

RUSSIAN EMPIRE
AMUR
DZUNGARIA
OUTER MONGOLIA
MANCHURIA
USSURI
SINKIANG
INNER MONGOLIA
JAPAN
TSINGHAI
Peking
Tientsin
KOREA
Huang Ho
Kaifeng
Grand Canal
TIBET
Nanking
Hankow
Hangchow
Shanghai
Yangtze
CHINA
NEPAL
BHUTAN
Foochow
INDIA
TAIWAN
Canton
BURMA
ANNAM
0   800km
SIAM
☐ Manchu China
☐ Under Manchu suzerainty

7 This Sinocentric map (*c.* 1800) shows China at the centre of the world, both culturally and geographically, as a "middle kingdom" surrounded by barbarians. China was generally self-sufficient and pursued a policy of aggressive isolationism, believing that little was to be gained by contact with other peoples.

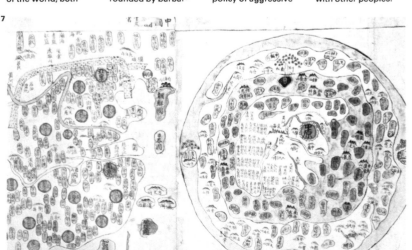

8 European ships moored in the port of Canton in the 18th century reflected the West's desire to trade with China. Western merchants regarded the China trade as an immensely rich prospect, but China refused to allow trading. From 1557 the Portuguese had had a monopoly of trade with China from Macao until the Dutch began to trade but attempts by the British East India Company in the early 17th century failed to gain official approval. The Europeans pressed for greater trading concessions, but from the 1750s all foreign trade had to go through Canton and was strictly supervised by the state. British trade in tea grew during the 18th century and in the 1780s they began to smuggle in opium profitably from India.

Japan 1185–1868

In 1185, following five years of civil war, Minamoto Yoritomo ruled much of Japan from his headquarters at Kamakura. In Kyōto the emperor reigned, but effective power lay in the hands of the Minamoto house which had defeated the previous ruling family, the Fujiwara.

The new Japanese rulers

In 1192 the emperor recognized this new reality. Yoritomo was made shōgun (general), as head of the military class, and his followers were rewarded with further rights in land at the expense of their defeated enemies. Some became military governors of distant provinces, others supervised tax collection on the estates of imperial courtiers. On these foundations Yoritomo created a practical and efficient administration which gradually but inevitably eroded the basis of imperial power.

This new power produced a new spirit and a new culture. Warriors (samurai) rejected the ceremonial of established Buddhist sects and turned to simpler, more austere, forms of religion. Zen temples were built in Kam-akura. A new Buddhism was preached and the scriptures were translated into Japanese.

In 1221 this dynamic government defeated an imperial revolt against its authority. Fifty years later it overcame a greater challenge from Asia. In 1274 and 1281 the vast Mongol armies of Kublai Khan [1] invaded Japan but effective defences and the power of the "divine wind" (kamikaze) repulsed these expeditions.

In time jealousy and hatred of the Hōjō grew and in 1333 Ashikaga Takauji joined Emperor Daigo II in destroying their power [3]. The emperor then tried to re-establish his authority but the Ashikaga resented their poor rewards and in 1336 Takauji drove Daigo II from Kyōto, replacing him with a puppet. Two years later he became shōgun.

The long civil war

By 1467 the rising economic and military strength of the great provincial houses was uncontrollable. As the shōguns grew weaker civil war broke out and continued for a hundred years. In this unrest, Europeans first reached Japan and began to influence its domestic politics. In 1543 the Portuguese arrived and soon Jesuits began to spread their missionary activities.

When Oda Nobunaga (1534–82) began the task of unification, religious and secular forces obstructed his advance. In 1571 he destroyed the temples of monastic armies and two years later extinguished the power of the Ashikaga line. In 1582 he was assassinated in Kyōto but his chief commander Toyotomi Hideyoshi (1537–98) continued his campaign. Soon Hideyoshi dominated Japan and threw his armies against Korea. His death ended these adventures and left Tokugawa Ieyasu supreme at home. Ieyasu officially became shōgun in 1603 and sought to establish peace throughout Japan [2].

Like his predecessors Ieyasu re-measured lands and regulated taxes. He relegated his enemies to outer provinces and concentrated his allies in central Japan. Fortifications were controlled and spies recruited. Lords or their families were compelled to reside at his new capital of Edo (later Tokyo). Confucianism became the official ideology to create a comprehensive social philosophy from the

1 **In 1274 Kublai Khan** launched a force of almost 30,000 troops against western Japan, but violent storms drove his ships back to their bases. Seven years later a second expedition (shown here) landed in Kyushu. Well-organized resistance, stone defences and gales combined to repel the invaders. There were fears of a further onslaught, but in 1294 Kublai Khan died and his preparations were abandoned.

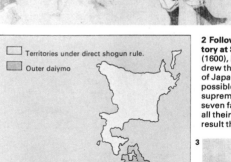

2 **Following his victory at Sekigahara** (1600), Ieyasu redrew the political map of Japan to reduce possible threats to his supremacy. Eighty-seven families lost all their lands. As a result the territory of Ieyasu and his allies was increased and concentrated in central Japan. Traditional enemies were relegated to outer provinces. With minor adjustments, these boundaries survived until 1868.

Territories under direct shogun rule.
Outer daiymo

Tsugaru
Nambu
Satake
Date
Sea of Japan
Uesugi
Kanawaga
Edo
Maeda
Yokohama
Uraga
Sumpu
Ikeda
Todo
Asano
Mori
Hachisuka
Yamanouchi
Kuroda
Arima
Nabeshima
Pacific Ocean
Hosokawa
Nagasaki
Kagoshima
Shimazu
0   300 km

3 **Ashikaga Takauji** (1305–58) supported the Emperor Daigo II in destroying the Kamakura military government. Later he drove the emperor from his capital and made himself shōgun in 1338.

4 **Tokugawa Ieyasu** (1543–1616) was the son of a middle-rank lord who rose to become political master of Japan. After serving as a successful general under Nobunaga and Hideyoshi, he destroyed his rivals at the battle of Sekigahara. In 1603 he became shōgun and proved to be an astute and determined politician. He limited the power of the emperor and his regime continued until 1868.

samurai code of conduct (bushido) and society was modelled on an agrarian ideal. Warriors were a privileged élite, farmers next in importance; craftsmen and merchants of lowest esteem. Ieyasu's successors developed his policies [5, 7]. They also suppressed Christianity and restricted foreign trade in the interest of political stability. A few Dutch [5] and Chinese merchants resided at Nagasaki but no Japanese could go abroad.

The nineteenth century

One result of the Tokugawa peace was commercial growth, undermining samurai power. On several occasions after 1700 the shōgun's government tried to solve this problem by returning to the principles of Ieyasu. Austerity was encouraged and officials dismissed. More land was cultivated and townsmen were urged to return to their villages. Merchants made forced loans to warriors and censorship increased. None of these measures was successful for very long.

Parallel with this growing domestic crisis, Japan faced increasing threats from the Western powers. At first foreign ships were driven off and seclusion maintained, but this could provide no lasting solution. In 1853 Commodore Matthew Perry (1794–1858) led a US naval squadron to the Japanese coastline [6] and demanded stores and an opening up of diplomatic relations. After a year's delay his requests were granted and agreements were made with other powers.

From 1859 the Western powers traded at Yokohama, Hakodate and Nagasaki and diplomatic contacts increased. The Tokugawa made more agreements with foreign powers but many Japanese feared colonization. Foreigners were murdered and warships brought destructive retribution. A sense of national crisis covered Japan. The Tokugawa built warships and cannons and began modernization [8]. Yet their measures seemed insufficient for national survival. For centuries the emperors had reigned, mainly as figureheads, from their court at Kyōto; now many turned to the emperor for inspiration and in January 1868 warriors from the western provinces restored his power [Key]. The Tokugawa era was at an end; a modern imperial age had begun.

The Emperor Mutsuhito (1852–1912), aged only 16 at the time of the Meiji restoration (1868), played an important role in symbolizing its legality. In later years he was a focus for national unity and supported policies of modernization. He moved his court to Edo, which he renamed Tokyo.

5 After 1641 under the Tokugawa regime all Dutchmen trading with Japan were confined to the island of Deshima, Nagasaki (shown here), and their wives and children were forced to leave the country. Throughout the centuries, this small, secluded group of Dutch merchants provided Japan's only link with the West and supplied much vital information. Japanese scholars studied science from Dutch publications.

6 In July 1853 Perry's naval squadron arrived off Japan to demand the ending of isolation. These talks were unsuccessful but in 1854 Perry returned to sign Japan's first modern treaty.

7 The Tokugawa period (1600–1868) saw a growth in education and literacy. Village schools, such as this one at Okayama, gave a simple education to children from backgrounds other than the samurai.

8 Following the forced opening up of Japan in 1854, the Tokugawa government feared a Western invasion and ordered the construction of this furnace at Nirayama to produce European-style artillery, an example of military modernization.

Subsaharan Africa 1500–1800

The appearance of a Portuguese fleet off the west coast of Africa in the mid-fifteenth century marked a new and decisive stage in the history of the continent: the beginning of a long and tumultuous relationship between Africans and Europeans. The Portuguese were followed by the Dutch in the sixteenth century and then by British, French and other Europeans a century later.

Complementary systems of trade

The many trading posts which these Europeans established on the coast, and linked to the Europe-based worldwide system of trade, complemented an existing trans-Saharan commercial network. This had been operating for at least 500 years and was forged between Arabic-speaking people from North Africa and black Africans living south of the Sahara. However, the European and trans-Saharan commercial systems were separated by the vast distances of the West African hinterland and never clashed.

A surprising feature of this period in view of these twin commercial presences is the relatively little influence which these foreign cultures had on Africa as a whole. Many Africans in the Sudanic belt had become Muslims in the 500 years of Arab trading in North Africa – a process that set up stresses in African societies and eventually provoked the Holy Wars of the nineteenth century. These states continued to look north to the Muslim world for their external contacts. Equally, some of the savanna and forest peoples began to turn to the Christian newcomers in the south for their contacts with the outside world. However, many peoples in western Africa, and nearly all of those of central and eastern Africa, were entirely outside the direct influence of either Arabs or Europeans until 1800.

The purely passing effect of foreigners is well illustrated by the history of the East African coast. Here Arabs had established trading settlements at favourable harbours on the coast and nearby islands – for example, Mombasa and Zanzibar [3]. These settlements were part of a large and prosperous Muslim trading system in the Indian Ocean, which at the end of the fifteenth century was taken over by the Portuguese. By the end of the seventeenth century the East African settlements had reverted to Muslim control. Neither the Arabs nor Portuguese in all this time had any contact or influence with any but the peoples actually living on the coast, except in the Rhodesia/Zambesia area where gold spurred inland expeditions.

Human beings – "a most profitable trade"

When the Portuguese first arrived in West Africa, like European adventurers in the New World, they were interested in gold and luxury tropical products. But they and the Dutch, British, French and others who followed them quickly came to realize that there was only one profitable commodity in Africa – human beings [1]. The lands of South and Central America, the Caribbean islands and the southern parts of North America required large labour forces to exploit the silver mines and, more important, the tropical crops – sugar, coffee and cotton – growing there. Within a few decades the transatlantic slave trade came to dominate relations between blacks and whites in western and central Africa.

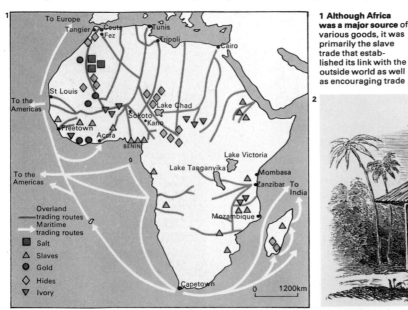

1 **Although Africa was a major source** of various goods, it was primarily the slave trade that established its link with the outside world as well as encouraging trade routes from within it. There was a steady flow of slaves to Muslim lands but most were shipped from west and west-central Africa for labour in the New World.

Overland trading routes
Maritime trading routes
■ Salt
△ Slaves
● Gold
◇ Hides
▽ Ivory

0   1200km

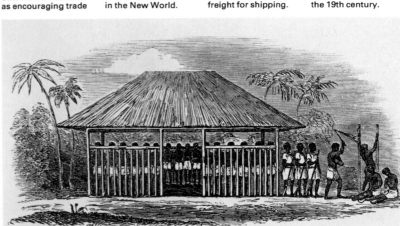

2 **Before they were shipped** to the New World slaves were assembled in barracks or "barracoon", where they were treated much as any other freight for shipping.

The slave trade was so lucrative that European traders made little effort to develop large-scale trade in other commodities until the 19th century.

3 **The great slave market at Zanzibar** became the centre of Arab trading on the east coast after the Portuguese evacuation at the end of the 17th century. Here the Arabs traded with the native rulers who raided and enslaved their weaker neighbours to exchange them for guns and cloth.

4 **The inhuman disposition** of a human cargo is shown on this plan of the *Brookes*, a vessel of the late 18th century. The Atlantic crossing, the notorious Middle Passage, took a terrible toll of lives and was not as profitable as the sugar, cotton and tobacco carried back to Europe.

From 1451, when the first cargo in this barbaric trade was shipped across the Atlantic, until the early 1870s, when the slave trade finally came to an end, it has been estimated that almost ten million Africans arrived in the Americas – one of the largest migrations of peoples in history. The peak of the trade was the 50 years from 1760 to 1810, by which time most of the European nations had abolished the slave trade; during these years, over four million Africans were taken away from their homelands.

Most of the African slaves came from the inland regions – from Senegal right round the bulge of West Africa to the Angola region of west-central Africa. The African middlemen, who sold the slaves to the European "factories" on the coast [5], prospered from the trade, as did powerful raiding states such as Asante and Dahomey [6].

In the area of the Congo estuary and Angola, the Portuguese and their agents were more active in venturing inland in search of slaves. In the nineteenth century the East African slave-trading network, which up to then had been in Muslim hands, was tapped to supply slaves to Brazil and Cuba, where slavery persisted longest.

There is no doubt that the slave trade much increased the level of violence among many African peoples. This is especially true of the Niger delta region, neighbouring areas of southern Nigeria, in the interior of Angola and, later in the period, in east-central Africa where Arabs controlled the trade. In a number of instances the resulting breakdown of social order led, ironically, to increased interference by the Europeans who were responsible for the violence in the first place.

Purely African cultures
During the 300 years from 1500 to 1800, in the areas of Africa unaffected by the trans-atlantic slave trade, societies were developing under their own momentum. New and powerful states emerged, such as Ruanda and Buganda (in the fertile lands between the great lakes of East Africa) and the states farther south, on the plateaus of central Africa. The kingdom of Monomatapa faced the Portuguese in the Zambezi valley and the Rozvi state dominated the plateau.

KEY

Foreign influence – Muslim from the northern interior and European from over the sea – was a striking feature of African history between 1500 and 1800. African societies proved to be flexible but discriminating about these influences, a capacity reflected in their art. The kingdom of Benin, founded about 1400, was a rich source of art, mainly producing bronze sculptures similar to the figure shown here. Benin sculpture was based on a tradition that was more than a thousand years older than the kingdom itself, but the artists managed to assimilate influences from Western culture without departing from this venerable tradition.

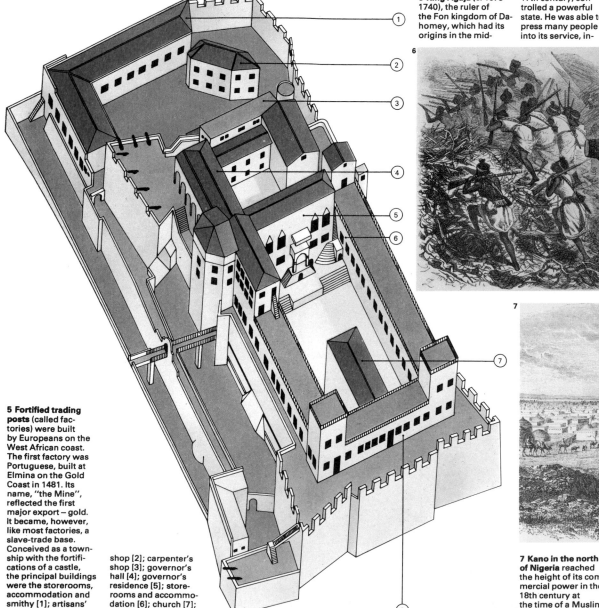

5

5 Fortified trading posts (called factories) were built by Europeans on the West African coast. The first factory was Portuguese, built at Elmina on the Gold Coast in 1481. Its name, "the Mine", reflected the first major export – gold. It became, however, like most factories, a slave-trade base. Conceived as a township with the fortifications of a castle, the principal buildings were the storerooms, accommodation and smithy [1]; artisans' quarters and workshop [2]; carpenter's shop [3]; governor's hall [4]; governor's residence [5]; storerooms and accommodation [6]; church [7]; and hospital [8].

6 King Agaja (c. 1673–1740), the ruler of the Fon kingdom of Dahomey, which had its origins in the mid-17th century, controlled a powerful state. He was able to press many people into its service, including these famous units of women soldiers, in the drive to establish the state against its rivals.

7 Kano in the north of Nigeria reached the height of its commercial power in the 18th century at the time of a Muslim revival. Usuman dan Fodio, leader of one of the principal Nigerian tribes, the Fulani, founded the Caliphate of Sokoto in 1807 and two years later took Kano.

Settlement of North America

The growth of the English economy in the late Middle Ages was achieved through increasing mastery of the seas. Between 1400 and 1600 English seamen ranged ever farther into the Atlantic, to Iceland, Greenland, Labrador and the northern seaboard of what is now the United States of America. Their search was primarily for fish. Discovery was a long and often discontinuous process; at times the English led the way, at others they trailed behind the Spaniards, Portuguese and French. Eventually the greater part of North America was to fall to the English, while Spain held the stronger empire in Central and South America, but the process of resolution was understandably slow.

The first emigrants from Europe

The settlement of the southern United States began in the sixteenth century: the first permanent city in North America – St Augustine, Florida – was founded by the Spaniards in 1565. They had explored and conquered the densely populated empires of Mexico and Peru (the population of Aztec Mexico when they arrived is said to have been as great as that of Western Europe). The English and French in the following century went to the West Indies and North America where they found vast, sparsely populated lands inhabited by semi-nomadic peoples living at subsistence levels. After 1700 free migration, as distinct from the importation of black slaves, was nearly all into the English colonies of the eastern seaboard, although most of these many new migrants were Scots, Irish, Germans or Swiss.

The first serious attempt to found a permanent English settlement on North American soil was made by Sir Walter Raleigh (1552–1618) at Roanoke Island off the coast of Virginia in 1584. Not all of the experience gained in voyages to and from this colony during the next six years was happy; some of it was indeed tragic, for the first settlers mysteriously vanished without trace. Raleigh's venture was partly a strategic move in the long sea war between England and Spain and, when his colony perished, the shoreline north of Spanish Florida was left open to other European powers.

The next attempt to establish an English colony in the area, the Jamestown settlement – established by the Virginia Company in 1607 [3] – was basically a commercial venture, although the aims of the company included helping to build a strong merchant fleet, training mariners for England's protection, spreading the gospel and planting a Protestant colony in a land still threatened by Catholic Spain.

Principal reasons for settlement

Trade and religion were the two principal motives for the founding of North American settlements [7]. Religious enthusiasts, hampered at home by the Inquisition in Spain and the Court of High Commission in England, were sometimes willing to venture into the unknown, but without the prospect of trade with Europe they could survive only in subsistence conditions. During the 50 years following the foundation of Jamestown, further colonies were established, mostly by the English. Plymouth was established in 1620 by the Pilgrim Fathers, who sought religious and civil autonomy from the English government, and Maryland by Lord Balti-

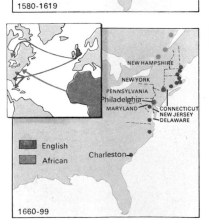

1580-1619

English
African
French

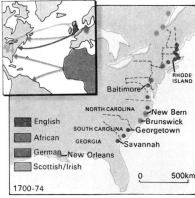

1620-59

English
African
Dutch
Finnish/Swedish

Montreal
Portsmouth
Salem
MASSACHUSETTS
Boston
Providence
New Amsterdam
Fort Christina
Plymouth
Newport
New Haven

Tadoussac
Quebec
BERMUDA
GUYANA
VIRGINIA
Jamestown
Roanoke
FLORIDA

1660-99

English
African

NEW HAMPSHIRE
NEW YORK
PENNSYLVANIA
Philadelphia
MARYLAND
CONNECTICUT
NEW JERSEY
DELAWARE
Charleston

1700-74

English
African
German
Scottish/Irish

RHODE ISLAND
Baltimore
NORTH CAROLINA
New Bern
Brunswick
SOUTH CAROLINA
Georgetown
GEORGIA
Savannah
New Orleans

0   500km

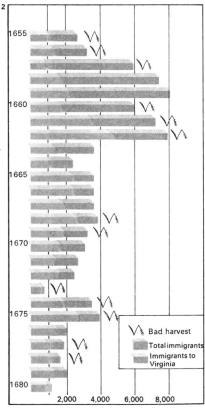

1 The pattern of migration changed over the years. From 1580 to 1619 England settled the eastern seaboard while France established settlements in Canada and down the Mississippi. The next 30 years saw the increase of African slave migration as well as the establishment of New England and the Scandinavian and Dutch colonies. Then England consolidated her hold and the Irish, Scots and Germans led the march westwards.

2 The numbers of migrants to the colonies depended upon high prices and food scarcity at home set against labour shortages in the colonies and the large profits to be made there. Emigration increased noticeably after three successive years of bad harvests in the west of England in the late 1650s. As the century wore on tobacco prices dropped, the amount of land available dwindled and fewer made the journey.

1655
1660
1665
1670
1675
1680

Bad harvest
Total immigrants
Immigrants to Virginia

2,000   4,000   6,000   8,000

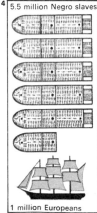

5.5 million Negro slaves

1 million Europeans

4 Six and a half million people had crossed the Atlantic to the New World by the 1770s. One million whites came from Europe – mostly from England, France, Germany and Spain; the other five and a half million were Negro slaves from West Africa, who were transported in appallingly cramped conditions in the slave ships. Chained flat to the decks they could cause little trouble and needed less food, thereby maximizing the profits of the traders.

3 James I (1566–1625) granted charters to some merchants to colonize the eastern seaboard of North America. The London Virginia Company was allocated what is now Virginia and Maryland and the Plymouth Company the coast of New England as far as Maine. This company's charter was revoked and a royal colony, whose council's seal is shown, established in 1624.

BEST VIRGINIA

5 Tobacco introduced to Virginia in 1612 became the main export by 1619 and with cotton was to remain the staple product of the Southern states, despite the repeated efforts of successive English governments during the colonial period to diversify their economies. The Northern states, at first a major source of furs and timber, developed their mineral resources, notably coal and iron, from the 18th century onwards, thus laying the basis for their early industrial development.

more, for Roman Catholics, in 1632. In 1625 the Dutch founded New Amsterdam, later renamed New York, as a trading post, to be followed by the Swedes and Finns.

French beginnings in North America stemmed from the trading activities of fishermen and fur trappers who established trading posts along the St Lawrence waterway. Then Samuel de Champlain (1567–1635) founded Quebec in 1608 and in less than 30 years the French had established posts as far west as Wisconsin. By 1660 a portage route from Lake Superior to Saskatchewan had been located and by 1720 New Orleans had been founded to guard the mouth of the Mississippi. Thus by the mid-eighteenth century the French had occupied, albeit sparsely, the whole of middle America, threatening the expansion of the English.

Influence of European events
Meanwhile, the Spanish North American empire, which included the whole coastline of the Gulf of Mexico as well as Florida, blocked English expansion to the south. But it was mainly events in Europe in the shape of the Seven Years War (1756–63) [11] that were to weaken France and Spain and to allow the English to fill the vacuum these two nations left in America. When George III (1738–1820) came to the throne of England in 1760, the French were confined to eastern Canada and the Great Lakes, while Spanish territory, vast in area although virtually unoccupied, stretched from Panama almost to the Canadian border west of the Mississippi. With the Treaty of Paris (1763) France lost all her North American possessions to Britain with the exception of the small island group of St Pierre et Miquelon, while Spain ceded Florida. Fearing a resurgence of French and Spanish power, however, the English set up a buffer zone west of the Alleghenies and east of the Mississippi.

Having consolidated their position, the British determined to exploit their possessions in North America. But it was the unwillingness of these colonies, now 13 in number, to submit to taxation without representation in Parliament that led to the American Revolution and Declaration of Independence in 1776.

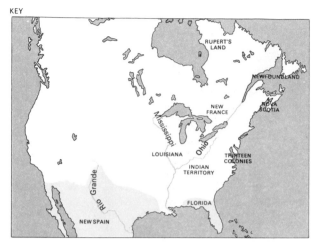
KEY

☐ Under British control 1756
☐ Under French control 1756
☐ Under Spanish control 1756

Conflicting claims to the North American continent were the subject of intense and bitter rivalries between France, Spain and England throughout the 18th century. By the Treaty of Paris England gained all France's important North American possessions; Spain was too much weakened to assert her claims.

---

6 Indentured servants made up a large part of the total number of early emigrants. Orphans, petty offenders, political and religious prisoners, younger sons of impoverished landowners and young men and women who possessed a taste for adventure and a better life, bound themselves, or were bound for a term of years, to work for a planter in Virginia or the West Indies. In theory they were taught to become planters themselves and at the end of their term, usually four or five years, they were allowed to go free and were given 20 hectares (50 acres) of land and other essentials to start up on their own. The indentures shown were recorded at Bristol, July 1660. The first reads: "William Wilkes of Chipenham Yoman bound to John Bridges Merchant for eight years in Virginia the usual conditions on the Ship Goodwill".

6
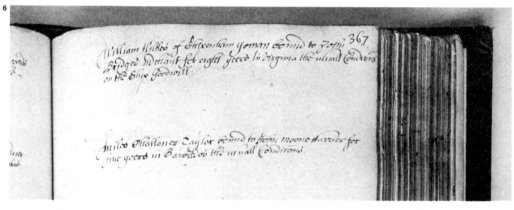

7 Many Quakers left England in the late 17th century when they conflicted with laws passed at the restoration of Charles II on questions of worship, freedom from oaths and military service.

8 John Harvard (1607–38), an English clergyman and graduate of Cambridge University, founded Harvard College at Cambridge, Massachusetts, in 1636 within six years of the establishment of that colony.

9 Pocahontas (1595–1617), the daughter of Powhatan, an Indian chief in Virginia at the time the white man came, became a Christian and married John Rolfe, a prominent settler. This provided a period of peace.

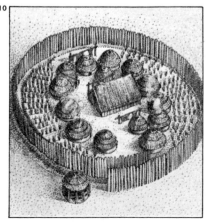

10 Indian villages, the homes of semi-nomadic hunters, bordered the rivers that flow into Chesapeake Bay and the creeks and inlets of New England. The early settlers bartered beads and trinkets for large tracts of land, much of it already cleared for cultivation, thus beginning the relentless process of Indian dispossession. Ports such as Baltimore and Fredericksburg were established around Chesapeake Bay by the 18th century.

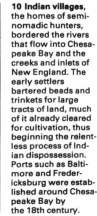
British dragoon

French infantryman

11 The British and French clashed on numerous occasions in the Seven Years War (1756–63). Regiments on both sides adopted uniforms designed more for splendour than efficiency or camouflage. Shown here are a trooper of the 10th British dragoons and an officer of the Regiment de Saint Germain. A significant part of the war was fought in North America, ending in defeat for the French. The 1763 Treaty of Paris that ended the war vastly increased Britain's territory in America.

The American Revolution

The American Revolution was both a rebellion and an act of nation-building. It was a political upheaval in which Britain's 13 Atlantic coast colonies in America gained their independence and formed the embryonic United States. The revolution was also the first national struggle in modern times for the rights of the individual and the establishment of democratic government.

The British colonies

The Treaty of Paris of 1763, which ended 70 years of colonial wars between Britain and France, gave the British complete victory in North America and control over vast new territories in Canada and as far west as the Mississippi. It caused fundamental changes in attitude both in Britain and in the 13 colonies. The colonists were now rid of the great external threat that had made them rely on Britain for defence. Since Britain was spending large sums to defend the new territories, it was felt that the terms of trade with the colonies should be revised so as to improve their profitability and to increase the local contribution to defence.

To achieve this a Sugar Act was passed in 1764 and a Stamp Act in the following year; and wider use was made of Admiralty courts in their enforcement [1]. The colonies reacted strongly, demonstrations and rioting broke out, and a congress was called in New York which defined the major objections: first that the acts had been imposed by the British Parliament in which the colonists had no representation, and secondly that the colonists, like all British subjects, should have the right to trial by jury, not by arbitrary courts. Such was the opposition that the Stamp Act was repealed in 1766. But in the same year, a Declaratory Act was passed which asserted that Britain had the right to legislate for the colonies if it so wished.

A year later, this right was put into force with a series of acts taxing glass, lead, paper and tea. Widespread unrest followed, climaxing with the "Boston Massacre" [4] in 1770. Most of the acts were repealed, but in 1773 another Tea Act was passed giving favourable trading terms to the East India Company. The colonists again objected and at the "Boston Tea Party" a cargo of tea was dumped into the harbour [3]. In Britain, acts were passed putting the government of Boston under direct British control.

First Continental Congress

When this became known, representatives of the colonies (except Georgia) met in 1774 at the First Continental Congress in Philadelphia [2], where a petition was drafted insisting that there should be no taxation without representation. The Congress also prepared an association between the colonies which would regulate their own trade. The British government, led by Lord North (1732–92), replied that a state of insurrection now existed in the colonies. Both sides prepared for war.

The first fighting took place on 19 April 1775 when Massachusetts militiamen fired on British troops at Lexington and Concord. An attempt by the militia to prevent the British improving their defences around Boston led to the Battle of Bunker Hill [7] on 17 June. A Second Continental Congress met and established an army with George Washington (1732–99) as its commander. As

A Total British revenue from the 13 colonies 1763-4 £2,000 pa
B Cost to Britain of maintaining army in the colonies 1764 £350,000
C Expected yield of Sugar Tax £25,000 pa
D Expected yield of Stamp Tax £100,000 pa
E Total actual British revenue from the colonies 1764-8 £30,000 pa

1 During the 17th century, the British colonies in North America had had the right to tax themselves embodied in their charters and had thwarted attempts by the British to obtain any more revenue from them. But in 1763, faced with heavy debts and the need to support a standing army in North America, Britain tried to relieve some of the burden by imposing a series of taxes on the colonies without consultation. The taxes fell far short of Britain's revenue expectations but they aroused the colonists in defence of their traditional rights and "Taxation without representation is tyranny!" became a rallying cry of the revolutionaries.

3 On 16 December 1773 about 50 colonists disguised as Indians boarded three British ships in Boston harbour and dumped their cargoes of tea overboard to discourage enforcement of a tea tax. British reprisals, including a commercial blockade of Boston, led to the calling of the Continental Congress.

Jefferson   John Adams   Sam Adams   Franklin   Hancock   Washington

2 The Continental Congress, which met in Philadelphia on 5 September 1774, was a gathering of delegates from 12 colonies (Georgia did not attend until the following year) called to prepare a declaration condemning British actions. There was little talk of independence, but the government in Britain reacted strongly, treating the actions of the Congress as rebellion. When the Second Congress met a year later, fighting had broken out and it was rapidly accepted as the effective governing body of the rebels. Although it had no statutory powers, it managed to maintain its position of leadership. It was the Congress that took the vital steps to issue the Declaration of Independence and to move towards a federal constitution.

4 The "Boston Massacre" was the first violent clash between colonists and British troops. Three men were killed and two seriously wounded when troops who had been jeered at and attacked by a Boston crowd, opened fire without orders.

royal government collapsed, the Congress took over as the governing body.

On 4 July 1776, the Congress institutionalized the break with Britain by passing the Declaration of Independence, which gave a valuable boost to American morale, but had little immediate effect on the precarious position of the ex-colonies with their coasts and trade blockaded by British sea power and with their small, ill-trained forces faced by professionals [5]. However, the British commanders made only fumbling attempts to seize the initiative and a force under General Burgoyne (1723–92) was forced to surrender at Saratoga [6].

Victory for the colonists
This victory was crucial in persuading France to send a fleet to help the Americans in April 1778 and to declare war on Britain in July. With their naval communications now threatened, the British fell back from Philadelphia, and Washington was able to contain them around New York. The British then attempted to switch the centre of the war to the southern states of Georgia and

South Carolina. Meanwhile, Washington was working steadily to build up the strength of his army, and when an expedition led by General Cornwallis (1738–1805) attempted to link up with British forces in the north, it was cut off and forced to surrender at Yorktown on 19 October 1781.

This defeat convinced the British that the war must be ended. Negotiations were begun in Paris with an American delegation led by Benjamin Franklin (1706–90) and John Adams (1735–1826) and peace was formally ratified in September 1783.

Immediately after hostilities ended, steps were taken to forge a sense of American nationalism from the shaky wartime unity of the now independent states. A federal constitution, drawn up in 1787, became effective in 1789. A Bill of Rights was added in 1791 to protect the rights of individuals.

The success of the revolution encouraged and inspired democratic and libertarian movements elsewhere in the world during the following decades, particularly in Europe and notably in France, where revolution took place a few years later.

KEY

1 New Hampshire
2 New York
3 Massachusetts Bay
4 Connecticut
5 Rhode Island
6 Pennsylvania
7 New Jersey
8 Maryland
9 Delaware
10 Virginia
11 North Carolina
12 South Carolina
13 Georgia

0 200km

The 13 colonies in America were the seeds from which the United States grew. Resentful of British taxes and repressive measures, stirred by the attractions of liberty and independence, they joined together in 1776 to declare themselves an independent nation.

5 American   British

5 British "redcoats" were well-trained, professional soldiers who were generally superior in conventional battles to the imperfectly trained American volunteers. It was George Washington who kept the armies in existence despite repeated disappointments and who used the American skill in guerrilla tactics to wear down the British until they could be outmanoeuvred.

6 John Burgoyne surrendered a British army trapped at Saratoga to Horatio Gates in October 1777 after a forlorn attempt to invade the 13 colonies from Canada. The news of American victory encouraged the French to ally with the rebels.

7 At the Battle of Bunker Hill, outside Boston on 17 June 1775, the Americans twice drove back British assaults before retreating. The first major battle of the revolution, it was an expensive British victory, in which the Americans proved that they could fight.

3 Scottish-born John Paul Jones (1747–92) took the revolution to sea by raiding British shipping. Called upon to surrender when his vessel *Bonhomme Richard* was battered by HMS *Serapis*, Jones replied, "I have not yet begun to fight" and went on to capture *Serapis*.

9 A primary objective of the Constitution was to establish a balance of power between the executive (the president), the legislature (Congress) and the judiciary (Supreme Court) to prevent the emergence of tyranny. Much political power was reserved for the states, represented in Congress by senators.

9
⟹ Electoral power
⟹ Executive power
⟹ State power

⟹ Legislative power
⟹ Judicial power

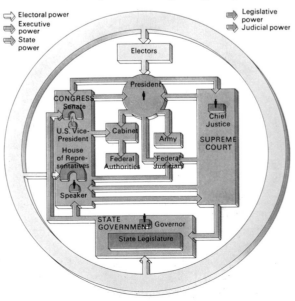

Electors
President
CONGRESS
Senate
U.S. Vice-President
House of Representatives
Speaker
Cabinet
Chief Justice
Army
SUPREME COURT
Federal Authorities
Federal Judiciary
STATE GOVERNMENT   Governor
State Legislature

10 Thomas Paine (1737–1809) emigrated to Philadelphia from England in 1774 and soon became one of America's most influential revolutionaries. His pamphlet *Common Sense* and his *Crisis* papers profoundly stirred popular sentiment in the country with their impassioned pleas for liberty, condemnation of tyranny and powerful arguments favouring American independence. His tracts were often read to American soldiers to bolster morale during the war.

The early Industrial Revolution

Britain was the first industrial nation in the world. From the middle of the eighteenth century, a number of factors launched Britain into a period of self-sustaining economic growth by the first decade of the nineteenth century. However, the origins of the Industrial Revolution in Britain lay in the pre-industrial period; by the middle of the eighteenth century there was already a thriving commercial economy, with a growing population, developing agriculture, and expanding trade both at home and abroad.

Population growth

The growth of Britain's population from the mid-eighteenth century was not directly caused by industrialization although a large workforce was an essential factor in the development of industry. A run of good harvests in the first half of the century, low food prices, favourable climatic conditions, the decline of plague and a number of minor improvements in health all contributed to lower death rates and a consequent rise in population [2]. By the end of the eighteenth century, birth-rates began to rise, too, as

people in the industrial towns were able to marry earlier and to have, and keep, more children. Unlike Ireland, where population growth led to impoverishment and, ultimately, to famine, Britain's commercial and agricultural prosperity meant that a growing population contributed to increasing demand for products of every kind. Increased consumption was a stimulus to industrial innovation and methods of production.

In the past, periods of agricultural expansion had been checked by harvest failure, population level and economic downturn. By the middle of the eighteenth century, the profits of thriving overseas trade enabled landowners to borrow capital to increase agricultural production [5]. With increasing demand and prices for foodstuffs, agricultural expansion followed. The enclosure movement grouped the old open fields and common lands into individual, more efficient units, on which more productive techniques could be applied, such as improved animal husbandry, new root crops and the first agricultural machines. Enclosure, secured through Parliamentary Acts, had affected about 20

per cent of the area of England by 1845. Capital was required to make the most of enclosure and it led to many smaller farms being amalgamated into larger holdings. Contrary to common myth, enclosure did not depopulate the countryside, but often increased the demand for agricultural labour.

Increased demand

The continued profitability of foreign trade [1], particularly as the colonies grew, provided the capital for increases in production to meet demand at home and abroad. One of the first industries to feel this increased demand was mining, with the need for more domestic and industrial fuel. Output was increased 400 per cent in the course of the eighteenth century through the use of steam pumping engines to keep mines from flooding. Coal was an important raw material for many industrial processes as well as the fuel for steam power. Coal and iron together laid the foundations for the development of industry [4]. The iron industry of the early eighteenth century depended on charcoal for smelting and had a relatively small output.

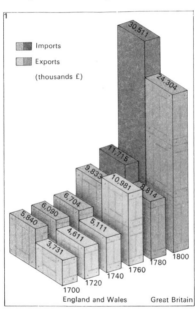

1 **Industry was stimulated** by growing demand, both at home and abroad. Britain's overseas trade experienced a rapid expansion from the 1680s, providing new market opportunities and the capital for investment in new techniques. New colonial markets acquired after the Seven Years War proved lucrative, as Britain engaged in the "Triangular Trade" carrying factory goods to Africa and the West Indies, transporting slaves across the Atlantic and bringing back colonial produce to Europe. Britain's largest export commodity in the first half of the 18th century was woollen textiles, but this was later overtaken by cotton.

Imports
Exports
(thousands £)

30,511
24,304
11,715
9,833 10,981 8,614
6,704
6,090 5,111
5,840 4,611
3,731

1700 1720 1740 1760 1780 1800
England and Wales   Great Britain

2 **Europe's population** increased from the 1750s, and despite some appalling conditions in towns (here shown at one extreme in one of William Hogarth's Gin Lane pictures), mortality rates declined. The cause of this is not fully understood but may have been related to the end of plague epidemics after 1700 and improvements in hygiene after 1800, such as the availability of cheap soap, easily washable cotton clothing and improved water supply. Increased population because of earlier marriage and larger families provided a growing market for cheap industrial products and also the necessary ready supply of labour.

3 Water mill

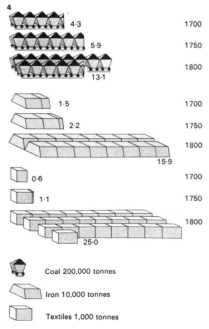

4

4·3   1700
5·9   1750
13·1   1800

1·5   1700
2·2   1750
15·9   1800

0·6   1700
1·1   1750
25·0   1800

Coal 200,000 tonnes
Iron 10,000 tonnes
Textiles 1,000 tonnes

3 **Mills driven by water** provided the motive force for many processes before the Industrial Revolution, including grinding corn and spinning yarn. A flourishing woollen industry already existed in areas where water power was readily available, such as the Cotswolds, East Anglia and the West Riding of Yorkshire. Many early machines could be driven by water power and the first phase of industrialization was based almost entirely upon the use of water-driven machinery.

Both the cotton and woollen industries developed on the slopes of the Pennines with abundant water power. It was only with the development of efficient steam power after 1776 that industry began to concentrate upon the

coalfields and no longer had to depend on the hilly regions. The use of coal and invention of coke-smelting enabled industry to expand and escape the problems of a critical shortage of wood for fuel. However, the change to steam was gradual.

4 **The most striking developments** in 18th-century industry were shown in coal, textiles and iron production. Coal mining expanded with the rise of steam power, a growing population and improvements in communications. Wool output increased to meet domestic and foreign demand, but mainly using traditional processes. Cotton production grew dramatically with the use of machinery and steam power until it became Britain's principal export commodity. Iron production also increased rapidly with the introduction of coke-smelting. These developments were evidence of a broad expansion of techniques to meet opportunities presented by rapidly growing markets.

The discovery by Abraham Darby of coke-smelting at his Coalbrookdale works in the 1730s revolutionized the production of cheap iron and enabled it to be used in the first machines and iron structures.

Allied to these developments, there was a major advance in technological power following the patenting of the improved Boulton and Watt steam engines after 1774. They used much less fuel than earlier models. Beside pumping, Watt's steam engine of 1769 was harnessed to drive machinery.

Labour-saving machinery
After steam power, the most important innovations were associated with the growth of labour-saving machinery. They occurred most dramatically in the cotton industry, which witnessed technical breakthroughs in weaving (Kay's flying shuttle, 1733) then in spinning [Key] and gradually in other processes. The harnessing of steam power to machinery in the cotton industry led to the first factories in which the production processes were concentrated under one roof [7]. Although many factories still relied on water

power [3], the development of the factory system in cotton foreshadowed the growth of the factory and the use of steam in other industries. Woollen production, for example, expanded mainly by using traditional methods such as water power. Gradually, however, the introduction of machinery and the use of steam power drew it towards the coalfields of the West Riding of Yorkshire.

Concentration of production needed both capital and cheap transport. Capital was provided out of the profits of agricultural improvement and overseas trade. Country banks, although subject to panics and bankruptcies, did provide a basic network of credit for industrial and agricultural development. By 1800 there were about 70 London banks and about 400 country banks, usually issuing their own notes. The Stock Exchange was founded in 1773.

Land transport remained slow and expensive for bulky products, in spite of the development of turnpikes. River transport was cheaper, but it was only with the development of the canal network that bulky products could be moved cheaply [6].

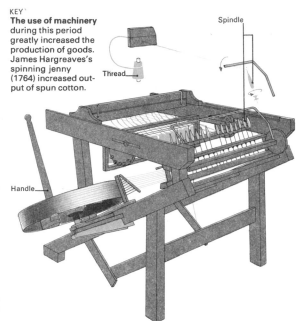

KEY
The use of machinery during this period greatly increased the production of goods. James Hargreaves's spinning jenny (1764) increased output of spun cotton.

Spindle

Thread

Handle

5 Agriculture could be highly profitable in the later 18th century thanks to a growing population and new techniques, as witness this substantial farmhouse in Gloucestershire. Enclosures grouped fields into more efficient units, permitting the use of four-crop and other rotations while selective breeding and inventions such as Jethro Tull's seed drill contributed to increased agricultural prosperity.

6 Transport developments played a vital part in the Industrial Revolution by widening markets and allowing production to be concentrated where goods could be brought by cheap bulk transport.

8 Josiah Wedgwood (1730–95) pioneered the large-scale production of pottery at his Etruria works near Stoke-on-Trent. He was a self-educated man and typical of those who made the Industrial Revolution.

Turnpikes and improved road surfaces increased passenger traffic by road, but the most important advance for industry came with the development of canals. The Bridgewater Canal between Worsley and

Manchester was built for the Duke of Bridgewater by James Brindley (1716–72), an engineer who remained illiterate until his death. The canal, opened in 1761, halved the cost of coal in Manchester by

reducing transport costs. In the "canal mania" that followed, an extensive canal network was built up and many early industries were based on it, giving them access to raw materials and markets.

7 A pioneer of the factory system, Sir Richard Arkwright (1732–92) built this cotton mill at Cromford, Derbyshire, which Joseph Wright of Derby painted in the 1780s. The first factories were built for the textile industry, where mechanization

and the use first of water power, then of steam, made concentration of production essential. Factories increased in size as steam became the principal source of power. The words "factory" and "mill" were synonymous for a long while.

9 Labour conditions were often poor in the early stages of the Industrial Revolution. Child labour was common, especially in the textile industry, with long hours of work, low pay and frequent accidents. Women also worked in the textile

factories, where they made up half the workforce. Though women and children had worked on the land, these new industrial conditions provoked a series of Parliamentary enquiries in Britain and by the mid-19th century Factory Acts were

passed, restricting hours of work and prohibiting women and children from certain areas of employment, such as work underground. By 1900 most other industrialized nations had also introduced some form of factory legislation.

Pitt, Fox and the call for reform

The age of the younger William Pitt (1759–1806) and Charles Fox (1749–1806) saw the beginning of the transformation that turned Britain from an agricultural society governed by a narrow oligarchy of the landed classes into an urban, industrial society with democratic rights for most of its inhabitants. During the 60-year reign of George III (reigned 1760–1820), economic and social change greatly enlivened political debate.

Party lines tended to harden during the latter part of the century, replacing the more fluid groupings of the time of Robert Walpole (1676–1745), and reflecting the rise of more divisive issues in politics, such as the American crisis, the power of the Crown, and the Wilkes affair. Out of these were born the demand for parliamentary reform and the emergence, for the first time since 1715, of something approaching a two-party division under the leadership of Pitt and Fox.

The power of the Crown

The accession of George III provoked a period of instability in British politics. The king's dismissal of the existing administration under the elder William Pitt (1708–78) and the Duke of Newcastle (1693–1768) was followed in 1762 by the elevation of the king's favourite, the Earl of Bute (1713–92), to lead the administration. These actions, as well as the pronouncements of the new king, reawakened fears that the Crown would attempt to dominate politics and that the mixed constitution of Crown, Lords and Commons, embodied in the Glorious Revolution of 1689 would be undermined.

In fact, George III was not aiming at the royalist reaction that his opponents feared. An inexperienced and obstinate young king, he wished to free the Crown from the domination of the group of politicians that had held power under George II (reigned 1727–60), especially the elder Pitt. The allegations that the king tyrannized his ministers and controlled a vast web of patronage were much exaggerated.

Nevertheless the resentments of the ousted Whig leaders were articulated in Edmund Burke's *Thoughts on the Cause of the Present Discontents*, published in 1770 [3]. Burke argued that the manipulation of patronage by the Crown permitted the monarch to dominate Parliament and rest his government upon a small group of "King's Friends", thus destroying the independence of the House of Commons.

At the beginning of George III's reign the attempts to exclude the MP John Wilkes (1727–97) [Key] seemed to suggest that the Commons was no longer an independent body or even representative of those who already had the vote.

Demands for reform

Hence the early years of George III's reign saw the rise of demands for reform. These were intended to reduce the influence of the Crown by removing the "rotten" boroughs and giving more seats to the large county electorates and some of the new manufacturing towns. The agitation for reform by the Yorkshire Association under Christopher Wyvill (1740–1822) and by John Wilkes's supporters in Middlesex and the City of London reflected feeling among small landowners and merchants. The war with America aroused still more dissatisfaction.

1 William Pitt, 1st Earl of Chatham, was secretary of state from 1756 to 1761 and the foremost politician of his age, known as the "Great Commoner". During his period in power he was absorbed in the Seven Years War (1756–63) and left the management of Parliament and elections to the Duke of Newcastle. Pitt kept free of party ties and showed no interest in parliamentary reform, despite his close friendship with Wilkes. His last political act was to plead for a policy of self-government under the Crown for the American colonies. He formed a second administration in 1766, but ill health forced him to retire from politics in 1768.

2 Charles James Fox was the effective leader of the Whigs during the last decades of the 18th century. Independent minded, a brilliant orator and a spendthrift who amassed huge gambling debts, Fox is remembered for his vigorous opposition to the Crown and his support for parliamentary reform and the anti-slavery movement. As a party leader he was not very successful, holding office only twice, in 1783 and 1806. His bitter opposition to George III deprived him of royal favour and kept him from power. In addition, his support for the French Revolution split the Whigs and lost him support, as did his opposition to Pitt's repressive acts in the 1790s.

3 Edmund Burke (1729–97) was one of the leading politicians and political philosophers of the 18th century. A Whig, he articulated the theory of "loyal" opposition to the government of the day, blaming the corruption and alleged oligarchic tendencies of George III's reign for political instability and the disorders of the Wilkes affair. He sympathized with the American colonists' struggle for independence from England, but was opposed to the French Revolution for destroying the historically established, traditional institutions of the country. He broke with Fox and the Whigs over this in 1791 and campaigned for war against France until his death in 1797.

4 The Gordon Riots in June 1780 were caused by opposition to the removal of legal penalties from Roman Catholics. In 1779, an extreme Protestant Association was formed by Lord Gordon (1751–93) to prevent what was believed to be growing Catholic power. Petitions and demonstrations were followed by a week of rioting and looting in central London after the Commons refused to debate their cause. Newgate prison was stormed and burned (shown here), property looted and the Bank of England attacked. More than 400 people were killed in the rioting and looting.

Its incompetent handling, leading to defeat, contributed in 1782 to the fall of Lord North's (1732–92) administration, which had held power since 1770.

The re-emergence of two parties

After a confused period with three ministries in under two years, William Pitt formed a government in 1784. Although he never used the word "Tory" himself, Pitt proved, over his long administration, to be the re-founder of the Tory Party. Fox then emerged as the leader of the Whigs and the effective opposition. The early struggles with George III had helped to sharpen party lines and legitimize opposition. Although the Whig and Tory parties were still more fluid than they were to become, Pitt and Fox provided leadership to a more coherent grouping of supporters than had been the case earlier in the century.

The passing of the "economical reform" acts in 1782 – reducing the number of officers in the pay of the Crown eligible to sit in Parliament – contributed to the waning of royal influence. The professionalization of the civil service under Pitt and his drive for

greater economy further reduced offices and sinecures. George III's recurrent breakdowns into insanity contributed to the decline of monarchical power, culminating in his permanent incapacity in the last ten years of his life. Even so, the king retained sufficient personal influence to exclude Fox from office for much of the period and to support Pitt's administration. It was the king's obstinacy over Catholic emancipation that forced Pitt's resignation in 1801.

The last years of Pitt and Fox were dominated by the impact of the French Revolution and the wars with France. Pitt was forced to act against the threat of subversion in England with a series of repressive measures, culminating in the treason trials of 1794 – aimed at the radical Corresponding Societies – and the Two Acts of 1795. During those years, Fox alienated many of his parliamentary supporters by his support of the French Revolution at a time when its excesses shocked the majority of propertied opinion. Nonetheless, his opposition to the policies of Pitt and his brilliant oratory preserved the Whig's image as the party of reform.

John Wilkes achieved notoriety as one of the early champions of reform after he was arrested for criticizing George III in his *North Briton* newspaper, in 1763. Wilkes claimed immunity as an MP, but he was expelled from the House of Commons. In 1768 Wilkes was elected MP for Middlesex. He became a focus for popular discontent with the Government and was able to manipulate this to cause riots in London in 1768. Imprisoned, Wilkes was re-elected three times, each time being expelled by the Commons. In 1774 he was finally allowed to take his seat in the House, but his assertion of popular opinion and freedom in politics was not forgotten.

5 Poor harvests and high prices caused several waves of food riots in the late 18th and early 19th centuries. In particular, the wars with France from 1793 led to great hardship and many popular disturbances. In 1800, the price of corn was more than treble the price in 1790.

6 William Pitt, the Younger who led the Tory Party from 1784, is shown here dominating the House of Commons. He held office with only a short break, from 1801–04, until his death. His inexperience led to early defeats of his attempts to reform Parliament and create a police force for London, but he soon established a stable and efficient administration. Pitt reduced patronage and reorganized the civil service, while settling colonial affairs in India with his India Act of 1784. As a war minister after 1793, he was not totally successful. Taxation and defeats abroad made his Government unpopular, but he weathered the crisis, introducing repressive measures against the radical societies at home. In 1801, he resigned over the king's opposition to Catholic emancipation, but returned as prime minister in 1804 for two troubled years before his death.

7 The movement for parliamentary reform gathered momentum in the last 25 years of the 18th century. This cartoon shows reformers attacking the "rotten" boroughs, the virtually uninhabited towns that still elected members to Parliament. Old Sarum was a notorious example of this – there a handful of voters returned two MPs. In addition, many seats were at the disposal of landed patrons, the so-called "pocket" boroughs. The larger manufacturing towns such as Manchester, Sheffield, Birmingham and Leeds were unrepresented, and the voting qualifications varied from town to town. The younger Pitt introduced a bill in 1785 to remove some of the rotten boroughs, but it was defeated in the Commons.

8 Agitation for reform culminated in the Reform Bill struggle of 1830–32. The Whig Government was returned in 1830 pledged to carry a reform bill. But rejection of the bill by the Lords in 1831 precipitated severe rioting in many parts of the country. At Bristol there were four days of riots and in Nottingham the castle was burnt (shown here) by supporters of the bill. The bill was finally passed in 1832.

The French Revolution

The prestige and apparent power of the absolute monarchy that Louis XIV (1638–1715) had built up disguised fundamental weaknesses that were to become serious under his successors. French society was increasingly divided into a small aristocracy jealously defending its privileges of wealth and partial exemption from taxation [2]; a growing middle class frustrated by its lack of political power and the incompetence of royal government; and the peasantry which did not own enough land for security from bad harvests and which hated the feudal dues it had to pay the aristocracy.

Calling of the Estates-General

During the reign of Louis XV (1710–74), royal prestige was damaged by a series of disastrous wars with Britain, and the government went deep into debt despite a general increase in trade and industry. Even success in helping the American colonists [1] at the beginning of the reign of Louis XVI in 1774 only highlighted the contrast between American ideals of liberty and democracy, and repression and privilege in France. An economic slump began in the 1780s and the state of royal finances became so bad that an attempt was made to tax the privileged classes. They refused to pay and the king was forced, for the first time since 1614, to call the Estates-General. When this met in 1789, the Third Estate – the bourgeoisie, or middle classes – swiftly tired of the actions of the aristocracy and clergy and on 17 June proclaimed itself a National Assembly [4A] with the intention of preparing a new constitution.

While this political crisis had been growing, a disastrous harvest in 1788 had brought many peasants and industrial workers close to starvation [3], and riots had broken out in many parts of France. When, on 11 July 1789, Louis (1754–93) dismissed his popular minister Jacques Necker (1732–1804), there was widespread protest.

Anti-royal feeling grows

The people of Paris stormed the Bastille [Key] on 14 July and there was a general breakdown of social order throughout France with aristocratic property being looted or seized. The National Assembly stripped away the privileges of aristocracy and clergy and the king had to leave Versailles for the Tuileries palace in Paris.

The political turmoil continued over the next two years with attempts to establish a new constitution and with anti-royal feeling growing. Confiscation of aristocratic and Church land and wealth gave the new government welcome financial help, but an issue of paper currency – the *assignats* – soon led to renewed inflation. In June 1791 the king attempted to flee abroad but was recaptured at Varennes. Popular hostility to him increased when the Emperor of Austria and the King of Prussia issued a declaration saying that the ancient rights of Louis would soon be restored. In September a new constitution [4B] was introduced setting up a legislative assembly and giving the king a strictly limited role. But tension rapidly grew between moderate constitutionalists and extreme anti-monarchists.

In April 1792, war was declared on Austria. As royalist armies backed by Austria and Prussia gathered on France's borders [6] the mob demanded that the

1 The Marquis de Lafayette became a popular hero when he led the French volunteers who helped the American colonists break free from Britain. With other aristocrats he joined the National Assembly in 1789, presenting a declaration of rights and organizing the National Guard. A moderate reformer, he became trapped between Jacobin extremists and the court and fled in 1792.

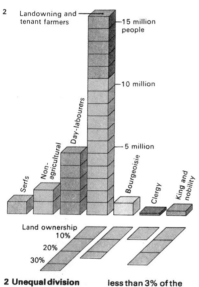

2 Unequal division of land with more than 40% owned by less than 3% of the population was a major grievance and fundamental problem of French society. As most of the nobility and clergy were largely exempt from taxation, the principal share of the burden fell on the bourgeoisie and the more prosperous of the peasantry.

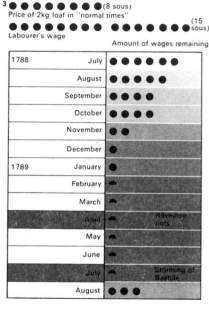

3 Prices rose steadily during the 18th century as a result of increases in population (more than 50%) and money supplies and relatively slow expansion of industrial and agricultural production. This had the effect of making the upper classes even more determined to hold on to their privileges, while the lives of the peasants and industrial workers became even more precarious. In "normal" times a loaf of bread cost a labourer about half a day's wage, but bad harvests in 1788 and 1789 lifted bread prices to the point where they almost matched wages. This precipitated political tension and rioting.

4 The meeting of the Third Estate as the National Assembly [A] on 17 June 1789, pledged to end feudal privileges, was the political start of the revolution. The constitution it produced [B] was a limited monarchy with power residing in a Legislative Assembly elected by citizens who paid direct taxation at least equivalent to three days' wages of a labourer per year. The 1791 Constitution also divided France into the local government *départements* that are still in use.

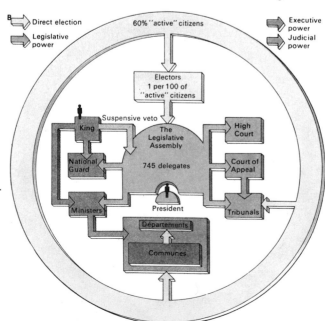

Assembly act against the king. In September Prussian armies invaded France, precipitating a massacre of captured aristocrats. An unexpected victory over the invaders at Valmy on 22 September relieved the pressure. On the same day France became a republic ruled by a Constituent Assembly which was elected by the extremist Jacobins, the most radical group to hold power during the revolution.

The king was put on trial and executed [5] in January 1793. In the following months, defeats by the *émigré* armies, pro-royalist risings in La Vendée and the south, and continuing economic problems prompted the Assembly to appoint a Committee of Public Safety to exercise emergency powers and to order total mobilization. A reign of terror began during which more than 40,000 "enemies of the revolution" were sent to the guillotine. All organized religion was officially abolished and replaced by worship of the Supreme Being.

By spring 1794 the republican armies had rallied; in June 1794 the counter-revolutionary armies were decisively

defeated at Fleurus, and in July the Jacobin leader, Maximilien Robespierre (1758–94), who had been virtual dictator for a year, was overthrown and executed. A reaction set in with moderates seizing power. In 1795 a basically conservative constitution was set up headed by a five-man Executive Directorate.

Emergence of Napoleon

The Directorate made peace with Prussia and The Netherlands, but launched a major offensive against Austria by sending a young general, Napoleon Bonaparte (1769–1821), to campaign in Italy [7]. He was brilliantly successful during 1796, forcing Austria out of the war. He then led an expedition to Egypt to cut Britain's communications with her Indian Empire, but it was finally forced to abandon the campaign when Horatio Nelson (1758–1805) destroyed his fleet at the Battle of the Nile in 1798. Meanwhile the Directorate had become profoundly unpopular with all sections of the population and when Napoleon returned in October 1799 he was able to engineer a *coup* that gave power to three consuls [8], of which he was the senior.

The storming of the Bastille on 14 July 1789 was seen by contemporaries and later generations as the true beginning of the revolution. Although the political crisis began more than a year earlier, the rising of the Paris mob against this ancient prison and symbol of absolutism was of fundamental importance. It forced the basically middle-class National Assembly to ally with the people to prevent a royalist counter-attack and it led to uprisings in the provinces in which aristocrats' estates were seized, land deeds destroyed and officials murdered. It paved the way for feudalism's downfall, transferring political power from the king to the legislature.

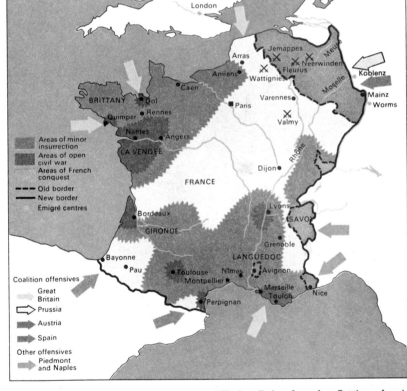

5 The execution of Louis XVI on 21 January 1793 followed the threat of an invasion of royalist *émigrés*. Popular opinion turned wholly against the king and the Jacobins were able to seize power and declare France a republic on 22 September 1792. Victory over royalist forces at Valmy gave them the self-confidence to try the king and his execution symbolized the break with the past system.

6 France's neighbours were antagonized by the gathering forces of the revolution. Aristocratic *émigrés* formed a nucleus of resistance and had support from Austria and Prussia. Their first invasion was halted at Valmy and the republic then counter-attacked, occupying Nice, Savoy and Belgium after a victory at Jemappes (November 1792), invading the Rhineland states and threatening Holland. After the

king's execution, war was declared on Spain, Holland and Britain but military reverses followed, with a major revolt in La Vendée and enemy offensives in southern France, Belgium, Alsace and Britanny. Unprecedented emergency measures put down internal revolts, the invasions were repelled and Belgium and Holland were reconquered. By the end of 1795, France had made peace with all its enemies except Austria and Great Britain.

Areas of minor insurrection
Areas of open civil war
Areas of French conquest
Old border
New border
Emigré centres

Coalition offensives
Great Britain
Prussia
Austria
Spain
Other offensives
Piedmont and Naples

7 Napoleon Bonaparte led the French armies in Italy in 1796–7. Although the Directorate intended the campaign as a diversionary effort, Bonaparte won an extraordinary series of victories, inspiring his conscript troops and using a mobile strategy to defeat the conventional Austrian armies. Once again, in 1800, he led French troops into Italy, crossing the Alps (a route romantically pictured here) to defeat the Austrians at the battle of Marengo.

8 The installation of the Conseil d'Etat on 24 December 1799 made Bonaparte First Consul. With the prestige of his victory in Italy and the Egyptian campaign behind him, Napoleon was the most powerful man in the turbulent political scene at the turn of the century. The failure of the Directorate to solve internal problems had lost it all support and Napoleon hoped to use his widespread popularity to persuade the assemblies to vote him into power without any

fuss. But they refused to do so and he had to use troops to drive them out and allow a small rump of supporters to vote through a constitution. This gave power to a first consul who was assisted by two colleagues and a senate nominated by the consuls. Napoleon then made use of a new device – the plebiscite – to obtain popular support. He announced that three million votes had been cast in favour of the new constitution and only 1,562 votes against it.

Napoleonic Europe

In 1800, Napoleon Bonaparte (1769–1821) [Key] became First Consul of France, then still menaced by hostile states. His new constitution confirmed the conservative policies of the Directorate and concentrated internal authority in his own hands. Once in power, he acted swiftly to achieve peace in Europe. After a surprise crossing of the Alps, he shattered Austrian power in Italy at the Battle of Marengo on 14 June 1800 and made peace with her at the Treaty of Lunéville. Russia, under the pro-French Tsar Paul (1754–1801), also ceased hostilities against Napoleon and in December joined Prussia, Denmark and Sweden in a French-inspired League of Armed Neutrality designed to weaken Napoleon's chief remaining foe, Britain, by blocking her trade with continental Europe.

War and peace

Although Paul was soon assassinated and succeeded by the pro-English Alexander (1777–1825), Britain made peace with France at the Treaty of Amiens in March 1802, agreeing to return all her overseas conquests except Ceylon and Trinidad, while Napoleon agreed to evacuate Holland and Naples. However, Napoleon soon aroused British suspicions by looking for new colonies, by refusing to evacuate Holland, and by extending French power in Germany. When the British realized that French markets would still be closed to their goods, and that Napoleon was building up Antwerp as a commercial rival, they refused to evacuate Malta and war broke out again in May 1803.

During the years of comparative peace between 1800 and 1803. Napoleon began the internal reconstruction of France which was to be his most lasting achievement. The Bank of France was established in 1800 and tax collecting centralized; the law was remodelled and codified, and a centralized secondary school system was set up. Napoleon's concordat with the Papacy extended his power – the Catholic Church gave up its claims to nationalized Church property in return for state support. In 1802 Bonaparte became First Consul for life with the power to nominate his successor.

The renewal of war identified Britain as

Napoleon's most stubborn and dangerous enemy and at first he tried to defeat her by invasion. However the Royal Navy blockaded the coasts of France and Spain for more than two years and then under Vice-Admiral Horatio Nelson utterly destroyed the French and Spanish fleets at the Battle of Trafalgar on 21 October 1805 [2].

Military and economic strategy

Even before this interim defeat of his invasion plan, Napoleon, who had declared himself emperor [3] in 1804, had had to redeploy the Grande Armée to meet a renewed threat from Austria and Russia, who were now joined in a Third Coalition with Britain. In a swift campaign he smashed an Austrian army at Ulm on 20 October 1805, occupied Vienna and defeated the Russians at Austerlitz [5] on 26 December. At the Treaty of Pressburg with Austria, Napoleon gained complete control of Italy and unified much of Germany outside Prussia in the Confederation of the Rhine. Prussia felt obliged to intervene, but was defeated at Jena and Auerstadt in October

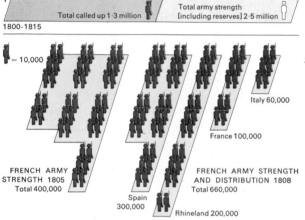

1 **Total called up 1·3 million**   **Total army strength (including reserves) 2·5 million**
1800-1815

☦ = 10,000

Italy 60,000

France 100,000

FRENCH ARMY STRENGTH 1805 Total 400,000

FRENCH ARMY STRENGTH AND DISTRIBUTION 1808 Total 660,000

Spain 300,000

Rhineland 200,000

1 Conscription on an unprecedented scale laid the foundation for the armies that enabled Napoleon to dominate Europe. From 1800 to 1812, an average of 85,000 men were called up from France each year. The demand for military manpower grew increasingly onerous, especially in 1812 with the costly invasion of Russia. Total deaths during the Napoleonic wars were about one million, of which 400,000 were French.

2 Nelson's annihilation of the combined French and Spanish fleets at Trafalgar was the decisive event in the long naval war and convinced Napoleon that direct assault on Britain was impossible. Saved from invasion, Britain used her superb navy to blockade the coasts of Europe and her wealth to organize resistance to France. Napoleon was forced to extend his control of neighbouring states to stifle British trade and the hostility this caused finally brought down his empire.

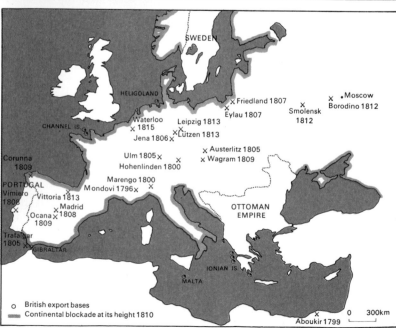

3 As Emperor of the French, Napoleon used the trappings of imperial glory to consolidate his new dynasty. Most Frenchmen responded but some felt he had betrayed the egalitarian ideals of the Revolution.

4 Brilliant victories in an almost continuous series of campaigns enabled Napoleon to establish France temporarily as the main power in Europe. In controlling the "traditional" powers of Austria, Prussia and Russia by a mixture of war and diplomacy, he enjoyed almost total success. But the need to extend and consolidate the Continental System led him to become trapped in a guerrilla war in Spain and then to launch the disastrous invasion of Russia.

SWEDEN

HELIGOLAND

Friedland 1807   Moscow
Eylau 1807   Borodino 1812
Waterloo   Leipzig 1813   Smolensk 1812
1815   Lützen 1813
Jena 1806   CHANNEL IS

Corunna 1809   Ulm 1805   Austerlitz 1805
Hohenlinden 1800   Wagram 1809
PORTUGAL   Marengo 1800
Vimiero 1808   Mondovi 1796
Vittoria 1813   OTTOMAN EMPIRE
Madrid 1808
Ocana 1809
Trafalgar 1805   IONIAN IS
GIBRALTAR   MALTA

○ British export bases
▬ Continental blockade at its height 1810

Aboukir 1799   0   300km

1806. Napoleon occupied Berlin and defeated the Russians at Friedland in June 1807. Meeting the tzar at Tilsit, he persuaded him to enter an alliance with France against Britain, which once again remained Napoleon's sole effective opponent.

Napoleon now sought to defeat Britain economically by using force to prevent her trade with any part of Europe. Despite the power which his victories had given him, the British continually found ways of smuggling in their goods, and Napoleon had to try to extend his "Continental System" ever farther afield. The military presence [1] and resulting economic hardships made Napoleon's rule increasingly unpopular with his subject nations.

In 1808 Napoleon forced Charles IV (1784–1819) of Spain and his son Ferdinand to abdicate in favour of Napoleon's brother Joseph. The Spanish revolted and the British sent an army to support them. The Spanish campaign cost Napoleon more than 50,000 men and led to his first defeat on land. In 1810, Napoleon tightened up the Continental System by annexing Holland and the

German coast. Europe was thrown into a commercial crisis that persuaded the tsar to end his alliance in December 1810.

Retreat from Moscow
In June 1812 Napoleon launched a massive invasion of Russia with 611,000 men. His troops reached Moscow, but lack of supplies and military reverses forced them into an undisciplined winter retreat, which left only some 10,000 men fit for combat [7]. In February 1813 Prussia declared war on France and Austria, and many subject states followed. Napoleon was defeated at Leipzig in October and the Allies pushed into northern France while the British invaded across the Pyrenees. Paris was occupied on 30 March 1814; Napoleon abdicated on 11 April and was exiled to the island of Elba.

On 1 March 1815, Napoleon took advantage of quarrelling among the Allies and the unpopularity of the restored Bourbons in France to re-establish his power. But defeat by the Duke of Wellington (1769–1852) at Waterloo [8] on 18 June 1815 led to his exile on St Helena where he died in 1821.

Napoleon Bonaparte, the Corsican-born general who made himself Emperor of the French, had the military genius to win France a short-lived supremacy over most of Europe. But it was his reforms of French society in codifying the law and rationalizing education and administration that were his greatest achievements. Some of them endure to this day.

5 Napoleon's victory at Austerlitz and the campaign that preceded it showed all the qualities of speed and decisiveness that made him one of the greatest generals the world has seen. Having force-marched the Grande Armée from the Channel to the Danube, he destroyed an Austrian army at Ulm and then pushed a Russian force back until it rejoined the main Russian army at Austerlitz. In the ensuing battle he used a combination of devastating artillery barrages and massive infantry assaults to sweep the Russians off the vital heights commanding the field of battle and into a precipitate retreat.

French Empire 1812
Dependent states 1812
French Allies 1812

6 Almost all Europe in 1812 was either ruled directly by Napoleon or members of his family, or allied with him. At the outset Napoleon had been able to draw on widespread support in Europe for the revolutionary ideals of overthrowing the old order. He furthered his own power by using the desire of neighbouring states for freedom, organizing many small states of Italy and Germany into dependent republics and setting up the Confederation of the Rhine that effectively ended the Austrian-dominated Holy Roman Empire.

7 The invasion of Russia was Napoleon's decisive error, celebrated by a Cruikshank cartoon. The Russians refused to make peace when Moscow was occupied and used scorched earth and guerrilla tactics to destroy the invasion armies and encourage subject states to rise.

8 Napoleon was finally defeated at Waterloo, near Brussels, by British and Prussian troops led by the Duke of Wellington and Marshal Blücher. An alliance of major European powers and conquered states had previously forced Napoleon to abdicate, but he had viewed exile on Elba only as an interlude. When the restored Bourbons had earned the dislike of most Frenchmen and the Allies were bickering among themselves at Vienna, he returned and marched to Paris with popular support. But the shock tactics of the Grande Armée met their match at Waterloo where the British infantry held firm against cavalry and infantry assaults until relieved by the Prussians.

Nelson and Wellington

For many centuries Britain opposed any European power that threatened to dominate continental Europe and from 1793 to 1814, with a short break in 1801–2, it fought to defeat the spreading power of revolutionary France. Lacking a large army, Britain had to rely on the traditional strategy of organizing alliances of other continental powers while using its naval supremacy to weaken France by blockade. Whenever possible, troops were sent to help anti-French forces, but Britain's major contributions to the ultimate defeat of France were a willingness to continue fighting, alone if necessary until new allies were found, and the use of a long-established prowess at sea.

Britain's weapons

The Royal Navy had long been recognized as the bulwark of British security but conditions of service were grim. The numbers of recruits needed to man the wartime fleet could only be maintained by forcible impressment [1] and the recruitment of convicts. Once enlisted, men were rarely allowed to leave.

In contrast to the conscript armies of Europe, the British army at that time was a small volunteer force numbered in tens, rather than hundreds, of thousands. Officers were able to buy their commissions, received no professional training and usually paid scant attention to the welfare of their men. By the end of the eighteenth century, however, efforts were being made to organize supply and medical services [2].

Nelson's great triumphs

Throughout the Napoleonic Wars Britain was fortunate to be served by a number of exceptional naval officers who proved to be both fine seamen and outstanding leaders. The greatest of these was Horatio Nelson (1758–1805).

At the outbreak of war Nelson commanded a ship-of-the-line in the Mediterranean and acquired a reputation as an active, able officer. During the Battle of St Vincent on 14 February 1797 his initiative in breaking the line of battle led to the capture of four enemy ships. For his part in the victory Nelson was knighted and promoted to rear-admiral. Wounded in several engage-

ments, he lost an eye and an arm but his mental powers remained undiminished. In 1798, when Napoleon attempted to cut Britain off from India and its other eastern possessions by invading Egypt, Nelson annihilated the French fleet in the Battle of the Nile, fought in Aboukir Bay. Of the 17 French ships, 13 were captured or destroyed.

The victor of the Nile, now created Baron Nelson of the Nile, took command of the Mediterranean fleet in 1803. For the next two years, in a remarkable display of seamanship, Nelson off Toulon and Admiral William Cornwallis (1744–1819) off Brest kept the French fleet immobile. In 1805 the Toulon force managed to slip out and head for the West Indies meaning to return, link up with other forces and establish temporary command of the Channel so that Napoleon could invade Britain. But the French were forced into Cadiz while the British gathered outside under Nelson's command off the Cape of Trafalgar. When the combined French and Spanish fleet emerged it was utterly destroyed in battle [5] on 21 October 1805. Although Nelson was killed on the quarter-

1 The hated press-gangs, armed with cudgels, terrorized towns as they went ashore and roamed the streets in search of able-bodied men for the navy. Victims were forcibly seized and dragged aboard for medical examination. Volunteers were few, for life at sea meant separation from their wives and families for long periods, bad food, wretched conditions and brutal discipline; yet morale under Nelson was high.

2 Women were considered to be more a hindrance than a help in the army of Wellington's day, as implied in this drawing by Thomas Rowlandson. Some wives, but not many, were allowed to accompany their husbands on a campaign: the number was limited to between 2 and 6 per company of 100. Those women who did go received half-rations free. Some even took children as well. The women cooked meals, did soldiers' washing and acted as nurses. They had an eye for booty, too. Wellington once observed that "The women are at least as bad, if not worse, than the men as plunderers".

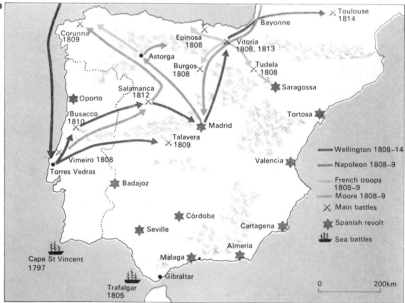

3 The French took Spain swiftly and compelled the British to leave. After Oporto fell (1807) Portugal appealed to Britain for aid and Wellington sailed with a force of 17,000. Napoleon ordered his commanders to drive the British into the sea, but the French themselves were expelled from the Peninsula and sent scurrying across their own border, with Wellington in pursuit. Napoleon later said that the "Spanish ulcer", with constant guerrilla activity and rioting, undermined his empire.

Map labels: Toulouse 1814, Bayonne, Corunna 1809, Epinosa 1808, Vitoria 1808, 1813, Astorga, Burgos 1808, Tudela 1808, Saragossa, Salamanca 1812, Oporto, Busacco 1810, Madrid, Tortosa, Talavera 1809, Vimeiro 1808, Torres Vedras, Valencia, Badajoz, Córdoba, Cartagena, Seville, Almeria, Cape St Vincent 1797, Malaga, Gibraltar, Trafalgar 1805

Legend:
— Wellington 1808–14
— Napoleon 1808–9
— French troops 1808–9
— Moore 1808–9
× Main battles
★ Spanish revolt
⚓ Sea battles

0   200km

4 HMS *Victory*, Nelson's flagship at Trafalgar, was typical of the ships-of-the-line that formed the main battle fleet. Floating batteries with 60 to 120 guns firing in broadsides and a complement of 700, these slow, unwieldy vessels could remain at sea for years on end. Built at Chatham, and launched in 1765, *Victory* was 69.5m (227ft) long with a beam of 15.5m (52ft). She had more than 100 guns, the largest of which were two 68-pounders, 30 32-pounders and 28 24-pounders.

deck of HMS *Victory* [4] at the height of the engagement [6], he died knowing he had won a decisive victory.

The road to Waterloo
Nelson's success ended any hopes Napoleon had of invading Britain. The French emperor was therefore forced to try to destroy Britain by closing Europe to British trade. When Portugal and Spain refused to join the blockade, the French invaded. Britain was thus given the opportunity to intervene militarily. An expedition to Spain under John Moore (1761–1809) was compelled to retire but in August 1808 a second force under Sir Arthur Wellesley (1769–1852) [Key], later Duke of Wellington, landed in Portugal.

An Anglo-Irish aristocrat, Wellington learnt his soldiering skills in India from 1796 to 1805. After taking part in unsuccessful expeditions in north-western Europe in 1806 and 1807 he was given command in the Peninsula. There for the next three years he showed great skill in tying down vastly superior French forces [3]. He was always prepared to withdraw behind defences when

necessary, but emerged to inflict a succession of defeats on the French. Finally in 1811 he launched a major offensive that cleared the Peninsula, winning major victories at Salamanca and Vittoria before invading south-west France in 1814 [7].

Napoleon abdicated and left for exile in Elba, but almost a year later he returned to France in an attempt to regain the throne. To meet this renewed threat Britain and the allies – Austria, Prussia and Russia – appointed Wellington to command a combined army gathered in Belgium. Despite being surprised by the speed of Napoleon's opening manoeuvres, Wellington held his ground against superior forces near the village of Waterloo [8] until the arrival of a Prussian army under Marshal Gebhard von Blücher completed a crushing victory.

For the second time Napoleon abdicated and went into exile – this time to St Helena, until his death in 1821. The victories of Nelson and Wellington, coupled with the nation's industrial and commercial supremacy, now made Britain the most powerful nation in the world.

"A Wellington Boot, or the Head of the Army": this 1827 cartoon shows the Iron Duke's distinctive profile and characteristic footwear. Taciturn and aloof, he affected to despise the troops he commanded as the "scum of the earth" but he based his tactics on their steadiness under fire. He chose defensive positions and relied on the discipline of his men to break the massive infantry and cavalry assaults of the French which had shattered most other adversaries. He hid an emotional nature under an icy manner and he cared for the welfare of his men. They repaid him with their respect and by beating the finest troops of Napoleon's *Grande Armée*.

5 At Trafalgar the British fleet went into action in two columns. Realizing that he was outnumbered 27 to 33, Nelson eschewed traditional tactics of the single line of battle, and succeeded brilliantly, capturing 19 enemy vessels.

6 Nelson's death overshadowed the triumph of Trafalgar. Hit on the shoulder by a musket-ball from a sniper, he was taken below decks where he died four hours later. A stern disciplinarian and a born leader, he displayed in battle great bravery and daring, tactical genius and shrewd judgment. His devotion to duty was absolute and the men he led revered him.

7 Wellington had a great welcome when he rode into Toulouse on 12 April 1814. The battle, he said, had been "very severe": combined deaths were 7,700. Victory, however, seemed complete when he learnt later that day that Napoleon had abdicated.

8 The Battle of Waterloo (1815) made Wellington a national hero. Napoleon had crossed into Belgium on 15 June and thrust back the Prussian army at Ligny but failed to rout them. Then on the morning of Sunday 18 June he attacked Wellington at Waterloo. Wellington had 67,000 men with 150 guns, Napoleon had 72,000 with 250 guns. The battle soon became a pounding match with few manoeuvres, but the arrival of the Prussians in the early evening brought swift and total victory.

The Congress of Vienna

Even before Napoleon Boneparte's first defeat, in 1814, the idea of an international diplomatic assembly to restore order in Europe was proposed by Prince Metternich of Austria (1773–1859). Intended to ratify decisions made at the first Treaty of Paris, the congress was announced and from September 1814 delegates from throughout Europe arrived in Vienna [Key]. From the start the congress was dominated by four great powers, Austria, Britain, Prussia and Russia, although Prince Talleyrand (1754–1838) soon skilfully gained an equal voice for France.

The distribution of rewards

It was hoped to prevent any one power from gaining more than its fair share of rewards, and to establish a balance of territorial interests. In fact Russia took the major share and established a dangerous foothold in Europe. From this time until the Crimean War (1854–6), fear of Russia was a dominant theme in European diplomacy.

At the Congress of Vienna, however, the immediate fear was that France might cause another European war. Three buffer states were created to hinder her expansion eastwards [1]. The Kingdom of Piedmont was strengthened; Belgium (previously the Austrian Netherlands) was joined with Holland in the Kingdom of the Netherlands; and the Holy Roman Empire (consolidated by Napoleon into the Confederation of the Rhine) became the German Confederation – 39 states joined in a weak *Bund* and dominated by an Austrian president.

Yet in the treaties of Paris of 1814 and 1815, France was generously treated. The frontiers of 1790 were restored and an army of occupation was installed only until France had paid an indemnity of 700 million francs to the Allies – a condition met by 1818. Although the monarchy was restored in the shape of Louis XVIII (1755–1824), he was obliged to reign under the Charter of 1814.

A new political settlement

In addition to the territorial changes, political settlement was considered essential for future peace. The French Revolution was largely blamed for the upheavals and wars of the previous generation. The best hope for stability seemed to lie in the restoration of the legitimate monarchs who had been overthrown. To try to prevent future disturbance in central Europe, the heads of state of the German Confederation were advised to offer constitutions to their subjects – advice which, for the most part, they subsequently ignored.

Finally, the Vienna settlement itself had to be maintained; to this end the four great military powers – Austria, Russia, Prussia and Britain – renewed their Quadruple Alliance and pledged to uphold the settlement, by force if necessary, for 20 years. Viscount Castlereagh [5], the British foreign secretary, in particular saw the alliance as fundamental to the maintenance of the balance of power in Europe, and the four powers agreed to hold periodic peacetime conferences to settle disputes and problems that might arise.

But the relative co-operation and harmony of views shown at Vienna did not continue in the four later congresses held between 1818 and 1822. Austria, Prussia and Russia had formed the Holy Alliance in September 1815. They rapidly adopted the view

1 **The map of Europe had to be redrawn** after the 1815 Vienna settlement. The Hapsburg Empire received the Illyrian provinces and the two Italian provinces (Lombardy and Venetia) in return for the former Austrian Netherlands (Belgium). Sweden won Norway, which had been Danish; Russia kept her conquest, Finland, and dominated the new "puppet" kingdom of Poland. Prussia kept Polish Posen, received almost half the Kingdom of Saxony and an area of the Rhineland that included the iron and coal resources of the Ruhr. Britain consolidated her overseas empire and naval routes with the Cape of Good Hope, Malta, the Ionian Islands, Ceylon, Mauritius, Tobago, St Lucia and Heligoland. Partly through these overseas acquisitions, Britain grew relatively remote from 19th-century European politics.

2 **The diplomats at Vienna** reached compromises over their territorial ambitions but there was to be no compromise with the new forces of liberalism and nationalism. Within 15 years unrest in Spain, Portugal, Italy, Germany and France showed the growing desire for constitutional restraints on the monarchies that had been restored. Nationalists were crushed in the Polish revolt of 1830.

but they won independence for Belgium (1830) and Greece (where war with the Turks began in 1821). These threats to the Vienna settlement were the main topics discussed at the four subsequent congresses: Aix-la-Chapelle (1818), Troppau (1820), Laibach (1821) and Verona (1822). Greek independence was a blow, weakening Turkish resistance to the nationalist claims of her other Balkan states.

that the powers should intervene in the internal affairs of European countries where stability was threatened, a doctrine repudiated by Britain.

Britain therefore ceased to send official representatives to congresses after Aix-la-Chapelle. Finally Britain dealt the death blow to the congress system by forcing acceptance of Greek independence against the interests of Russia and the protests of both Austria and Prussia.

Consequences for Europe
The settlement reached by the Congress of Vienna shaped the following generation in Europe. The Continental powers were committed to upholding the status quo they had created, and they interpreted their obligations with a rigidity that turned the settlement into a straitjacket. Liberal revolts attempting to introduce constitutional limits to the powers of the restored monarchs were crushed almost without exception, although they were successful in France, Switzerland and Belgium in 1830 because it was neither convenient nor in the interests of all the

powers to intervene [2]. The settlement had ignored nationalist feelings in the distribution of rewards and creation of buffer states, and there were revolts in Belgium and Poland and growing unrest in Italy and Germany. Furthermore, the old multi-national empires had been confirmed – the Hapsburg and the Ottoman (Turkish) in Europe.

The Greek revolt of 1821 proved disastrous for Turkey. Its success encouraged other Balkan states to push for independence and weakened the ability of Turkey, the "Sick Man of Europe", to resist. The Hapsburgs had added Croats and Italians to their multiplicity of nationalities. Nationalism anywhere was to be treated as an epidemic that could spread and destroy their empire. Metternich [3] used his skill at the Congress of Vienna, his influence in the congress system and his authority in the German Confederation and the whole of Italy to wipe out any symptom of nationalism. The Metternich system of repressive measures spread from the Baltic to Sicily. But the Congress of Vienna did succeed, in a formal sense in securing European peace.

In 1815 Napoleon was safely on St Helena and the waltz took fashionable society by storm. The monarchs of Europe danced to celebrate the restoration of their political power and the promise of armed backing by all powers. Five monarchs and the heads of 216 princely families arrived in Vienna for the peace negotiations and the festivities. Their fear of revolution and desire to restore the political situation of the 18th century meant that France was left intact.

3 Prince Clemens von Metternich was foreign minister of the Hapsburg Empire from 1809 until the revolution of 1848. To many he seemed the champion of autocracy, reaction and the police state.

4 A grand sleigh ride was included in one of the weekly programmes issued by the Festivals Committee responsible for entertaining the visitors. The expenses were paid by the emperor.

6 Viscount Castlereagh (1769–1822) was Britain's foreign secretary from 1812. Regarded as reactionary at home he proved too liberal for the congress system, which he had hoped would provide a diplomatic arena for peaceful change.

6 Frequent liberal and nationalist revolts threatened the settlement but were usually suppressed. Eugène Delacroix (1798–1863) won the *Légion d'honneur* for his painting "Liberty leading the People", after the successful French revolt of 1830.

European empires in the 19th century

The Austro-Hungarian, Russian and Ottoman empires were all deeply involved in the Balkan countries through most of the nineteenth century. The diplomatic and military conflicts between the three powers were a result partly of their own political ambitions and partly of aggressive national independence movements in the disputed areas.

The Serbian struggle for independence
It was in Serbia, one of the Ottoman provinces in the Balkans, that a subject nationality first challenged the political power of the Ottoman Empire. Turkish rule in Serbia, which had been conquered in 1389, had become particularly tyrannical at the end of the eighteenth century. The local military commanders (*dahis*) exercised a largely independent authority. In 1801 they executed the pasha of Belgrade, the sultan's own representative, and in 1804 they ordered the execution of 72 Serbian village elders. The Serbian uprising of 1804 under Karadjordje [3], a capable military leader, started off as a protest movement against the excesses of Turkish rule, but after striking military suc-

cesses it developed into a movement aimed at winning full independence.

Russia offered some military and diplomatic support tò the Serbs, to whom it was tied through the Orthodox religion and the Slav race, but it was chiefly a combination of Turkish weakness and Serbian resistance that enabled the rebels to remain independent for eight years. The Turks finally crushed the Serbian revolt in 1813 but within 18 months the Serbs revolted again, this time under the leadership of Milos Obrenović (1780–1860), a greater diplomat than Karadjordje.

Obrenović worked out an agreement with the Turks under which Serbia remained formally a Turkish province garrisoned by Turkish troops, but was allowed to share in the administration of justice, to maintain a militia and to summon a national assembly in the capital, Belgrade.

Serbia's struggle for independence was not fully consummated until 1878 when the Congress of Berlin [8] recognized it as an independent state. However, the example of the successful Serbian struggle had a powerful effect on the other Balkan nationalities,

inspiring the growing nationalistic movements, especially among the other southern Slavs living under both the Ottoman and Hapsburg empires.

The unification of the Slavs
The effect was greatest in the Hapsburg Empire where many Serbs had fled from the Turks in the seventeenth century. The Orthodox Church was a powerful link between the Serbs in Serbia and the others outside. Fear of being crushed by the twin pressures of forcible germanization from Vienna and magyarization from Budapest brought the Croats and other Slavs, notably the Slovenes, closer together [7].

In the 1848–9 anti-Hapsburg revolution, the Croat general Josip Jelačić (1801–59) fought against the Hungarian revolutionaries with Serbian and Slovene support. But Vienna, after the successful crushing of the 1848–9 revolution, introduced a centralist, strongly germanizing rule. The existence of a semi-independent Serbia fired the imagination not only of the Serbs but of the Croats and Slovenes as well. Linguistic similarities

1 Napoleon's victory over Austria at Marengo in June 1800 began the process of the Hapsburgs' expulsion from northwestern and western Europe. Francis I was forced in 1806 to give up the title of Holy Roman Emperor which the Hapsburgs had held for many centuries. From then on Austria looked to the southeast.

2 Lord Byron, who raised an army in the cause of Greek independence, died of fever at Missolonghi in 1824. On 20 October 1827 the Turkish fleet was destroyed at the Battle of Navarino by Britain and France. In 1829 the Treaty of Adrianople recognized Greece's autonomy, and independence came in 1832.

3 Two of the most important figures in the Serbo-Croat independence movement were Ljudevit Gaj (1809–72) [A] and Karadjordje (Georgije Petrović (1768–1817) [B]. Gaj founded the movement for the political and cultural emancipation of Croatia from Austria. Karadjordje led the uprising against the Turks in 1804. After the suppression of an uprising in 1813 he fled first to Austria and later to Russia.

4 Montenegro was conquered by the Turks in 1499, but a large area of its forbidding mountain territory remained outside their grip. From there Montenegrins like these raided the towns that the Turks held. Following the successful wars against the Turks in 1876–8, Montenegro was recognized as an independent state by the 1878 Congress of Berlin. As a result Montenegrin territory was increased by 70% and the population of the country almost doubled.

fostered the idea that all Serbs, Croats and Slovenes were one nation of Jugoslavs or southern Slavs. This idea was developed further in Pan Slavism, a nationalistic movement that agitated for the cultural and political unity of all the Slavonic peoples.

The effect of Russia's foreign policy

Russia saw these movements as instruments of its own drive towards Constantinople and access for its navy all year to ice-free waters. Meanwhile, with Prussia squeezing Austria-Hungary out of Germany since 1815, Austria developed a renewed commitment to its Balkan role. Because of its mistrust of the new nationalism of the Balkan Slavs, Austria in the first half of the nineteenth century also became a protector of Turkey. In response, Russia stepped up its support for Turkey's and Austria's enemies.

Turkey enjoyed the support of Britain, Russia's chief adversary; Britain was joined in the early 1850s by France. After a quarrel over the holy places of Palestine on 21 July 1853, Russia occupied the principalities of Wallachia and Moldavia, which were still

under Turkish suzerainty, as a "material guarantee" for the concessions to her "just demands" in Palestine.

On 4 October 1853, Turkey declared war on Russia, as later did Britain and France, believing the integrity of the Turkish Empire to be at stake. Austria stayed neutral but in so doing harmed Russia and greatly increased the hostility between the two powers. The Russian forces were worn down in the Crimea [5] until Tsar Nicholas I died in February 1855. His successor Alexander II sued for peace.

The result of the Crimean War checked Russian ambitions in the Balkans, opened the Danube to international navigation and neutralized the Black Sea. The Turkish Empire's territorial integrity and independence were guaranteed and so were Serbia's liberties. In 1859 the election of Alexander John Cuza (1820–73) as Prince of Moldavia and Wallachia prepared the official union of the two principalities as Romania, which became formally independent in 1878. However, the Ottoman Empire continued to decline up to 1914.

Suleiman's Mosque still stands as a symbol of the once mighty empire of the Ottomans. In decline from the 17th century, the empire was still strong enough in the early 19th to resist Russian expansionism and maintain some power in Europe.

5

6

5 The Battle of the Alma on 20 September 1854 was the first big engagement of the Crimean War between Russia and Turkey, Britain and France. Following the Treaty of Paris in 1856, Russia's dominance in southeast Europe ended and Turkey gained a new lease of life under the joint protection of the European powers.

6 Railways linked the two main centres of the Hapsburg Empire – Vienna and Budapest (whose station is pictured here) – with the outlying provinces. Vienna's railway to the port of Trieste was built in 1854; her imports in 1869–73 increased by 83% compared with the preceding five years. Budapest was linked to Rijeka (Fiume) in 1873.

7

7 The coronation of Francis Joseph took place in Budapest on 8 June 1867. A dualist empire emerged as a result of a compromise (*Ausgleich*) between Vienna and Budapest in 1867: Francis Joseph was separately crowned in Vienna as emperor of the Austrian half of the dual monarchy and as king of its Hungarian half in Budapest. The Hungarians reached an agreement with Croatia in 1868, guaranteeing it special status and some autonomy within the Hungarian half of the monarchy. But the new Magyar nationalism was resisted by the Romanians, Croats, Serbs and Ukranians. In the Austrian half of the empire the Czechs led the autonomy struggle against pan-Germanism.

8 The Congress of Berlin produced an uneasy compromise that carried the seeds of future conflict. It gave Austria-Hungary control over the strategic province of Bosnia-Hercegovina but not the title to permanent occupancy. Serbia developed large-scale propaganda among its fellow Serbs and other southern Slavs in Bosnia-Hercegovina and other southern Slav-inhabited provinces of the Hapsburg Empire. In 1908 Austria-Hungary carried out the annexation of Serbia. Bulgaria, cheated of access to the Aegean and of Macedonia, nursed a grievance against Britain and other powers except Russia and Serbia. Romania gave up southern Bessarabia to Russia, which lost control of Constantinople.

8

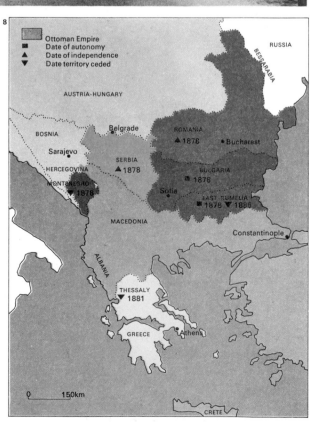

Ottoman Empire
■ Date of autonomy
▲ Date of independence
▼ Date territory ceded

RUSSIA

AUSTRIA-HUNGARY

BESSARABIA

BOSNIA

Belgrade

Sarajevo

HERCEGOVINA

MONTENEGRO
▲ 1878

SERBIA
▲ 1878

ROMANIA
▲ 1878

Bucharest

BULGARIA
■ 1878

Sofia

EAST RUMELIA
■ 1878 ▼ 1886

MACEDONIA

ALBANIA

Constantinople

THESSALY
▼ 1881

GREECE

Athens

0   150km

CRETE

Latin American independence

Most of the 20 republics that comprise present-day Latin America became independent between 1810 and 1824 – the period that began after juntas set up in major cities of the Spanish American Empire had refused to accept Napoleon's brother Joseph as their ruler and ended with the last significant battle for freedom, at Ayacucho in Peru.

Haiti had seized independence from France some years earlier, in 1804. The Haitians subsequently imposed their rule upon neighbouring Santo Domingo, which did not achieve freedom as the Dominican Republic until 1844. Brazil, the Portuguese Empire in America, became independent with very little bloodshed in 1822 and, the prince regent, Dom Pedro I, was crowned its emperor. Uruguay emerged as a separate state in 1828 after Argentina and Brazil had fought to claim it. Cuba remained a Spanish possession until the end of the nineteenth century, when the Spanish-American War (1898) led to its becoming independent although bound by close ties with the United States. Panama was a province of Colombia until 1903, when its inhabitants successfully revolted. Its new government leased in perpetuity to the United States (which had assisted the revolt) the strip of land 16km (10 miles) wide through which the Panama Canal, completed in 1914, was to be cut.

The consequences of independence

The independence of Latin America meant essentially that men of European stock who were born there replaced men from the Iberian Peninsula in positions of power and privilege. The social structure inherited from Spain and Portugal remained virtually intact typified by the *hacienda* or great landed estate. The Church, allied with the Crown in the colonial period, continued to exercise a strong conservative influence [5] and the military, greatly strengthened by the prolonged wars, was another privileged institution and one that prejudiced the establishment of effective civilian government.

The vast size of many of the new states, problems of communication, economic dislocation brought about by the wars, lack of experience in administration on the part of the new rulers and the illiteracy of the masses all contributed to make stable government extremely difficult. Few of the heroes of independence were able to govern successfully when peace came to their countries. Simón Bolívar (1783–1830) [Key], the greatest of them, died in self-imposed exile; José de San Martín (1778–1850) [6], the other outstanding liberator of Spanish America, decided to retire to Europe. The characteristic ruler of the new countries was the *caudillo*, or military dictator.

Relationships between countries

Relations between the Latin American countries following independence were generally neither close nor friendly. While Portuguese America remained intact (as Brazil), Spanish America had disintegrated along the lines of the old imperial administrative divisions. These divisions were the accepted basis for the new states, but there were often disputes over ill-defined boundaries.

Geography and history have combined to isolate the countries of Latin America from each other. Formidable physical barriers have been a major cause of this isolation, as

1 On the eve of the wars of independence (c. 1800) Latin America was divided between Spain and Portugal. The newly independent states agreed among themselves to keep their national boundaries generally in line with the old colonial administrative divisions. But because these were often not clearly demarcated, territorial disputes inevitably arose. The Banda Oriental (the east bank of the Río de la Plata) had been a particular bone of contention between Spain and Portugal and continued to be such between Argentina and Brazil after independence. Following a war between these countries (1825–8) and diplomatic intervention by Britain, the disputed territory became a buffer state – the new Republic of Uruguay.

2 Britain's significant influence on the newly independent countries of Latin America was exerted primarily through commerce and finance. The massive inflow of British capital reached a peak from 1904–13, when it accounted for at least 20% of all British investment abroad.

■ Total investment
□ Total investment in government bonds
▨ Total investment in economic enterprises
▨ Share of government bonds and economic enterprises invested in Argentina, Brazil, Chile, Mexico, Peru, Uruguay

Figures in £ millions

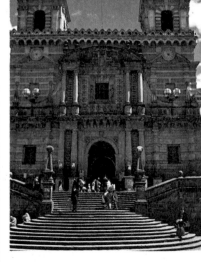

4 Native Indians generally viewed Latin American independence as no more than a change of masters. Many who had been subject to the old forms of colonial bondage became *peones* (peasant labourers) on the great estates.

3 Joseph Bonaparte (1768–1844) was imposed on Spain by his elder brother Napoleon after the invasion of the Iberian Peninsula (1807–8). This forced the issue of Latin American independence. When the French deposed Ferdinand VII (1784–1833) of Spain and then threatened Portugal, the Spanish Americans at first pledged loyalty to Ferdinand but later declared for independence. The Portuguese royal family fled briefly to Brazil and the king's son stayed as regent of Brazil, declaring it independent in 1822.

5 A church in Quito, capital of Ecuador, with an ornate and richly sculptured structure reflects the power and wealth of the Church in Latin America, both in colonial and modern times. But Church-state relations were generally uneasy following independence.

well as regionalism within individual countries. During the colonial era the viceroyalties, captaincies-general and presidencies into which the Spanish American Empire was divided were linked to the mother country rather than to each other. Since independence, relations with powers outside the region generally have been much more important than those among the Latin American countries themselves.

Colonial trading patterns continued after independence. Most countries had to rely on exporting one or two primary products and on importing manufactured goods.

Dependence on other countries

The new states of Latin America thus became economically and financially dependent upon powerful external countries. During the nineteenth century Great Britain was the major economic power in Latin America [2]. British capital played a key role in the economic development of Argentina in the latter part of the century. Her naval power forced Brazil to acquiesce in efforts to stamp out the slave trade. The eventual abolition of slavery itself was one of the main causes of the overthrow of the Brazilian emperor and the establishment of a republic in 1889.

By that time the United States had greatly increased its territory at the expense of Mexico, which it defeated in war (1846–8). Even earlier, in 1823, President Monroe (1758–1831) had enunciated his famous "Doctrine". This warned European powers against incursions or further colonization in Latin America and implied that the United States had a special relationship with Latin America. By the end of the nineteenth century the United States, with military strength, was able to compel respect for the Monroe Doctrine when its own interests were at stake. At the same time it promoted "pan-Americanism", embodying the idea that the countries of the Americas shared a community of interests and a special "system" of international relations: the inter-American system. A conference of the United States and Latin American countries in Washington (1889–90) set up the International Union of American Republics – renamed the Pan American Union in 1910.

KEY

Simón Bolívar, known throughout the continent as "The Liberator", was the greatest hero of Latin American independence. He played a leading part in winning freedom for his native land Venezuela, as well as Colombia, Ecuador, Peru and Bolivia, the country named after him. Bolívar brought together the first three of these countries in one state, the republic of Colombia, and he inspired the Congress of Panama (1826) with the principal aim of establishing a league of Spanish-American nations. But the league did not materialize: Greater Colombia split into its constituent states, and Bolívar died, deeply disillusioned, in 1830.

6 José de San Martín [right] was the outstanding liberator of southern South America. He assured independence for Argentina and gained it for Chile and part of Peru (including Lima, the capital). While the liberation of Peru, the last great stronghold of Spanish power, was incomplete, San Martín had a famous meeting with Bolívar at Guayaquil in Ecuador (July 1822) to discuss the future of Spanish America. San Martín then withdrew, leaving the field to Bolívar.

7 San Martín's "Army of the Andes" crossed the mountains through the Uspallata pass at a height of 3,799m (12,464ft) – an extraordinary military achievement. The army was on its way to liberate Chile, in co-operation with the Chilean patriot Bernardo O'Higgins (1778–1842). The Spanish forces in Chile were taken completely by surprise and routed at Chacabuco on 12 February 1817. In the following April a victory at Maipú, ensured the independence of Chile.

8 Bolívar [right] triumphantly accepts the surrender of the Spanish at the Battle of Boyacá (1819), assuring Colombia's independence.

9 Latin America in 1903 looked much as it does today. Mexico had long before lost more than half its national territory (the former Viceroyalty of New Spain) to the United States. Cuba and Panama had become nominally independent, although virtually protectorates of the United States, in 1902 and 1903 respectively. Paraguay had declared itself independent in 1842. Bolivia had lost its coastal territory to Chile in the War of the Pacific (1879–83) and was now landlocked. Central America had dissolved into its constituent states (Costa Rica, El Salvador, Guatemala, Honduras and Nicaragua) as early as 1838.

Latin American states 1828:
- Republic of Mexico
- United Provinces of Central America
- British possessions
- Cuba (Sp)
- Republic of Haiti
- Republic of Greater Colombia
- Peru
- Demerara (Brit)
- Dutch and French Guiana
- Empire of Brazil
- Bolivia
- Paraguay
- Cisplatine province
- Argentine Confederation
- Chile
- Patagonia
- Boundaries 1903

0   1,500km

129

The Industrial Revolution

The first 70 years of the nineteenth century saw unprecedented economic development in Britain as forces unleashed at the end of the eighteenth century created the first urban industrial society. Population growth and urban development followed an acceleration of industrialization based on a great expansion of trade, the widespread application of the factory system to production and the harnessing of steam-driven machinery to an increasing range of processes. Steam power was also applied to transport with the development of railways and the first steamships. Urban life prompted Britain to develop many social and political institutions that were to become standard in other countries as the Industrial Revolution spread to Europe and the United States.

The British lead

Britain's economic development between 1800 and 1870 was startling, even compared with the progress of the late eighteenth century. There were giant increases in production. Output of pig iron grew 60 times, coal output ten times and total trade by the same amount. Britain maintained and increased her lead over other countries by advances in mechanization and factory production. In a real sense Britain had become the "workshop of the world" by the time of the Crystal Palace Exhibition [Key] in 1851 when great industrial expertise was on display.

Britain supplied a large percentage of the world's textiles, iron and machinery, and a massive increase in her export income was stimulated by the development of "free trade", especially during the 1841–6 ministry of Robert Peel (1788–1850). After 1850 trade expanded even more rapidly than it had in the first half of the century, encouraging further economic development. New industries such as steel (based partly upon the newly discovered Bessemer process) and shipbuilding began to balance Britain's dependence on exports of textiles [10] and iron products.

The development of railways after the opening of the Stockton and Darlington Railway in 1825 gave a major boost to the economy, making it possible to move bulky goods cheaply and stimulating the iron and steel industries. The railways served to concentrate production still further, as raw materials could be brought long distances and finished goods sent to ports many miles away. During the boom years of "railway mania" in 1845–7 a basic railway network covering the major towns, industrial areas and ports had been laid out by railway pioneers such as George Stephenson, Isambard Kingdom Brunel, George Hudson and Thomas Brassey. In addition, the development of railways played an important part in refining investment and banking procedures.

Financial organization

As the pace of industrial expansion quickened, the need arose for a more elaborate banking system. In Britain the less reliable "country" banks were more and more superseded by "joint-stock" banks after 1826. The Bank Charter Act of 1844 secured the role of the Bank of England as the central note-issuing authority and guarantor of the rest of the banking system. Company finance and formation were regulated by a series of limited liability and company acts in the

1 Europe's population rose steadily during the 19th century, mainly because of a falling death-rate through improvements in medicine, diet and living conditions. Birth-rates also tended to rise with industrialization and urbanization. As a result, the total population of Europe almost doubled in the course of the century, quickening migration from the countryside to the increasingly crowded urban centres.

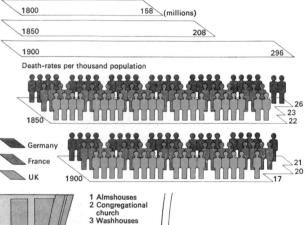

1 European total population (excluding Russia)
1800 — 158 (millions)
1850 — 208
1900 — 296

Death-rates per thousand population

1850 — 26 / 23 / 22
1900 — 21 / 20 / 17

Germany
France
UK

2 Industrial output was rising in many parts of Europe by the middle of the 19th century. Germany and France began to take a significant share in producing iron, coal and textiles and smaller countries such as Belgium and Switzerland were also beginning to develop important industrial sectors. European industrialization still lagged behind that of Britain and was inhibited to some extent by Britain's marketing dominance.

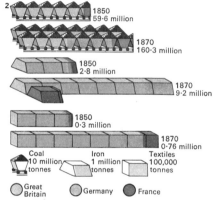

1850 — 59·6 million
1870 — 160·3 million
1850 — 2·8 million
1870 — 9·2 million
1850 — 0·3 million
1870 — 0·76 million

Coal 10 million tonnes
Iron 1 million tonnes
Textiles 100,000 tonnes

Great Britain | Germany | France

1 Almshouses
2 Congregational church
3 Washhouses
4 Wesleyan chapel
5 Factory school
6 Factory

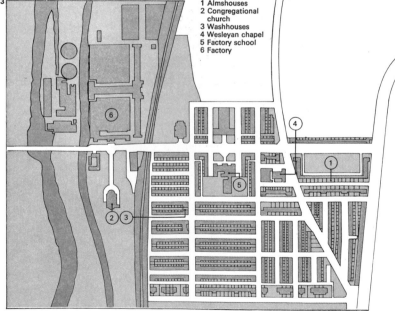

3 New industrial towns, such as Saltaire, in Yorkshire, England, provided shelter and adequate living conditions for large numbers of workers. By the middle of the 19th century factory owners and municipal authorities began to create some order out of the squalor of early factory towns. Regular grid-iron patterns of workers' housing were built, providing the basic amenities of sanitation and water.

4 Riots and strikes in England during the 1840s accompanied efforts by the Chartist movement to win urban workers the vote. Industrialization brought many such political movements and played a part in the European revolutions of 1848.

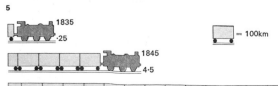

1835 — ·25
1845 — 4·5
1870 — 31·7

= 100km

5 Railway expansion in Belgium between 1835 and 1870 was typical of the rapid developments that took place in Europe in the middle and late nineteenth century. British engineers, contractors and equipment were often employed in an effort to overtake the British lead. Although railways developed more slowly on the Continent, Britain had opened a major trunk route system for carrying goods and people by 1847. The diagram represents length of rail track laid.

middle of the nineteenth century. The growth of trade led to the expansion of the Stock Exchange and the rise of provincial exchanges [8] to deal in specific commodities. By 1870 Britain was not only the centre of the world's industry and trade but its financial capital. Personal wealth increased rapidly [7].

Population growth
Economic and industrial development was accompanied throughout Europe by population growth [1]. Britain's population increased most rapidly of all, doubling between 1801 and 1851. By the middle of the century Britain was no longer a predominantly rural nation, for more than half its people lived in towns [3]. In 1801 there were only 14 European towns with more than 100,000 inhabitants, but by 1870 there were more than 100.

Urban development brought with it a wide range of social and political problems. To deal with these Britain, as the first industrial nation, pioneered many social institutions fundamental to modern life. Measures to regulate public health, provide basic

sanitary and housing amenities and preserve public order through the formation of professional police (the "Peelers") were copied by other countries. Similarly, the introduction of a reliable, cheap postal service [9], the rise of cheap newspapers and the development of cheap railway travel did something to offset the human misery that often accompanied urban development and industrial advance.

Factory Acts [6] regulated child and female labour, as well as hours of work, from the 1830s. Under early pioneers such as Robert Owen (1771–1858) and Robert Applegarth, industrial workers began to organize themselves into trade unions, political associations and the co-operative movement [4], in order to improve their status.

In Europe the gathering pace of industrial development was shown in the growth of railways [5], textile industries and iron and coal production [2] by 1870. Belgium, France and Germany made the largest strides, and although far behind Britain, both Germany and the United States were poised for rapid industrial development in the latter years of the nineteenth century.

KEY

The Great Exhibition of 1851, in London, marked a high point in Victorian industrialization. Organized to show the progress in trade and manufactures achieved since the first days of the Industrial Revolution, it became a symbol of British manufacturing ingenuity and dominance of world trade, although it exhibited industrial goods from many other countries. It was intended to display the virtues of free trade (laissez-faire) as an agent of economic progress. To house it, a revolutionary building of glass and iron was designed by Joseph Paxton and built in only seven months. The Royal Society of Arts sponsored the exhibition with the backing of Albert, the Prince Consort.

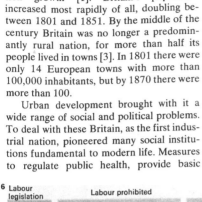

6 Labour legislation

	Labour prohibited		Length of working day	
1833 Factory Act	Children under 9	20·30 – 05·30	9 hrs	12 hrs
1842 Mines Act	Children under 10	Women		
1844 Factory Act	Apprentices under 10		6½ hrs	12 hrs
1847 Factory Act	18·00 – 06·00		10 hrs	10 hrs
1850 Factory Act			10½ hrs	

24-hour day
Labour prohibited
Labour permitted
Working day
Men — Women
Children 13-18 — Under 13

6 Exploitation of child and female labour, with long hours, low wages and poor conditions, was a major abuse of the Industrial Revolution. In the middle of the 19th century, humanitarian concern in Britain led to the passing of Factory Acts to protect women and children.

7

£1,000+
£300-1,000
£100-300
£90-300
£30-90
£30

Income per annum

1·5
0·5
8·6
22·0
27·7
39·7% of population

Less skilled and farm workers
Lower middle-class and skilled workers
Lower middle-class
Middle-class
Upper-class

7 Incomes and social status in Britain changed with the rise of the middle and professional classes and the creation of a new class of manufacturers. But in the mid-19th century the largest group still earned less than £30 a year.

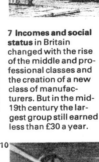

8 The Cotton Exchange in Manchester was one of a number of major commercial institutions set up throughout Britain to deal in particular commodities. The growth of large-scale industry and the demands of a more complex society

forced rapid developments in finance and banking. The Stock Exchange, which had become the centre for financial dealings in the 18th century, continued to expand, doubling in size during the 1860s alone.

9 A cheap postal system was one of the many new social amenities made possible by growing community wealth and a more ordered urban society. In Britain, the railway system permitted rapid movement of mail and a "penny post" was introduced by Rowland Hill in 1840 [A]. The British Post Office introduced the first of its distinctive red letter boxes in London in 1855 [B]. A telegraph system came into use in the middle of the century, with undersea cables

providing the first international means of communication. By 1861, 18,000km (12,250 miles) of cable had been laid.

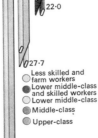

10 The cotton mill was the symbol of the 19th-century industrial town. Cotton was the most completely industrialized sector of the economy, being almost entirely mechanized, steampowered and factorybased, and was one of

the first industries to develop in Europe. Mills were gaunt, utilitarian structures, housing long banks of spinning and weaving machines, tended largely by women and children. Conditions were often dangerous

with many accidents; hours were long, even for very young children, and discipline was strict. In Britain by 1851 over half of the population lived in urban rather than rural areas. Factory conditions improved only slowly.

131

The urban consequences of industrialization

Pre-industrial Britain was a predominantly rural society in which there was only one large city, London, and few other large towns. In 1700 London had a population of more than half a million, but only six towns had populations of more than 10,000. Many parts of the country supported only villages and small market towns with populations of fewer than 5,000. Population growth from the mid-eighteenth century combined with the expansion of industry transformed Britain into a predominantly urban nation.

The growth of towns
By the middle of the nineteenth century, there were more than 70 towns in Britain with populations of more than 10,000, eight with more than 100,000 and Glasgow, Birmingham, Manchester and Liverpool had more than 250,000 inhabitants. By 1851 more than half the population lived in urban areas, compared with about a sixth in 1700 [1]. This growth continued until the eve of World War II, when more than four-fifths of the total population of Britain lived in urban areas. Only in the mid-twentieth century has

the spread of urbanization in Britain been reversed. Continued suburban development and the growth of car ownership has permitted more people to live outside urban areas in the years since 1945 [5].

One major impact of population growth and industrialization was rapid urbanization. Population in Britain rose three-fold between the middle of the eighteenth century and the middle of the nineteenth, from more than 7.5 million to more than 21 million. Although population growth occurred in the countryside as well as in the towns, urban centres expanded both from internal increase and migration from rural areas. London received between eight and twelve thousand immigrants a year by the end of the eighteenth century. In addition, the redistribution of population was changed – new industrial regions such as Clydeside and Lancashire became principal centres of growth.

New industries often recruited substantial portions of their labour force from the surrounding countryside. Short-distance migration, of not much more than 30 or 40km (20 or 30 miles) in most cases, was the

general rule within Britain. Some immigrants, however, did come from farther afield – from Scotland, Ireland, and rural Wales.

Local government created
The rapidity of growth is well illustrated by Manchester. A population of 75,000 in 1801 had grown to nearly 750,000 inhabitants by the eve of World War I. These tremendous increases in urban population almost completely swamped the provision of social amenities and local government. Until 1835, Manchester was still governed as though it were a rural parish, although it had 250,000 inhabitants. Slowly, the structure of local government was created to deal with these problems. The 1835 Municipal Corporations Act provided a basic framework for local government, and during the century most towns were given elected councils and the apparatus of local government [Key].

Conditions in the early industrial towns were often cramped, unhealthy, and insanitary [3]. Rapid expansion meant that families were crowded into cheap lodgings, cellars, and small courts. Piped water sup-

1 In 1700 only an estimated 16 per cent of the population in Britain lived in towns of more than 5,000 people. The Industrial Revolution and its attendant dramatic population growth in the 18th century created a predominantly urban society by 1900, when 77 per cent of the population lived in towns. This growth of the new towns and cities within 200 years bore little relation to the pattern of towns in pre-industrial Britain. Instead the expansion was almost entirely dictated by economic necessity. Some of the most spectacular growth took place in parts of the country that had been least densely populated in the pre-industrial era, such as Lancashire, Yorkshire, north-east England, South Wales and the Lowlands of Scotland. These industrial regions dominated the UK economy until the economic slump of the Depression in the 1920s and 1930s.

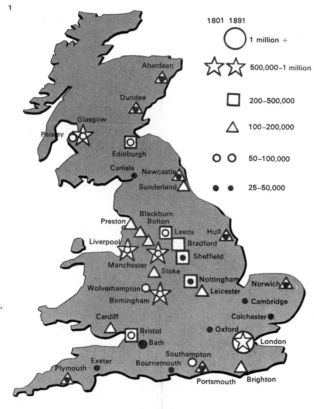

1801 1891

○ 1 million +

☆ ☆ 500,000–1 million

□ 200–500,000

△ 100–200,000

○ ○ 50–100,000

• • 25–50,000

2 The human conditions behind the creation of the first industrial nation were tragic. The unprecedented changes wrought by the Industrial Revolution on Britain's demographic character brought an equally dramatic decline in the social conditions for the majority of the population. Glasgow, an expanding city of more than 100,000 people, had only 40 sewers in 1815. This horrific level of sanitation and hygiene caused an increase in the death rate, and the city's population level would actually have declined in the 1820s and 1830s had it not been supplemented by steady immigration.

3 Cramped "back-to-back" housing was constructed to accommodate the expanding populations of the early industrial towns. The growth of some old towns was actually restricted by local landowners who feared that their power would be undermined by the new industrial masses. This led to chronic overcrowding within the boundaries of the old towns. Only in the mid-19th century did the government begin to introduce legislation to clear and improve insanitary areas.

4 Middlesbrough was literally a creation of the Industrial Revolution. In 1801 it was a tiny group of houses of only 25 inhabitants; but by 1901 the population was more than 90,000, with iron, and later steel, as the principal industry. Without the railways, in this case the Stockton and Darlington line, the town would probably never have existed. The carefully planned growth of the streets and houses, still evident today in this aerial view, was the product of its Quaker founders, who first recognized its great commercial potential at the terminus of the new railway line. In the space of 100 years, Middlesbrough had become one of the commercial prodigies of the 19th century.

plies and sanitary services were often totally inadequate or non-existent, and resulted in disease and high mortality rates, especially among young children. In 1842 the average life expectancy for children of labouring families in Manchester was 17 years, compared with 38 in rural Rutland. Cholera epidemics in 1831–3, 1847–8, and 1865–6 helped to focus attention upon the need for improvement in sanitary conditions. The first Public Health Act was passed in 1848 and a Board of Health was set up to deal with some of the problems of the industrial towns. But industrialization was not responsible for all the squalor and overcrowding to be found in the towns. Pre-industrial London, for example, had had its unsavoury stretches.

Even when new housing was constructed it was often built cheaply by factory owners or speculative builders. Small, terraced houses, often without adequate light or ventilation, with poor foundations and of flimsy construction, soon infested by damp and vermin, created a legacy of slum housing that survived well into the twentieth century in many industrial towns. Indeed it was only

after the destruction brought about by the blitz in World War II that extensive rebuilding of nineteenth-century slums in Britain's cities was carried out [7].

Social concern and planning

Towards the end of the nineteenth century philanthropists and social reformers, conscious of the destructive physical and social effects of industrialization put forward ideas for limited, planned towns and cities. Robert Owen (1771–1858) had attempted to create a "model" community at New Lanark and the first proper "garden cities" at Letchworth (1903) and Welwyn (1920) show a similar concern for careful regulation of the growth and structure of towns and cities. In 1895–6 the first industrial estate, at Trafford Park in Manchester, was built; railways, canals and other transport now enabled a separation to be made between work and home, and encouraged a concentration of industry that was socially and economically attractive. On a smaller scale, the houses built by knitting-machine pioneer Jedediah Strutt (1726–97) can be seen to this day.

Manchester Town Hall, designed by Alfred Waterhouse (1830–1905), symbolizes the civic pride of the urban civilization created by the Industrial Revolution. The nineteenth century saw the creation of local authorities to deal with the intense problems caused by uncontrolled growth.

5 Railways not only led to the spread of towns into the countryside, the creation of "suburbia", but they also resulted in the creation of holiday resorts for the industrial workforce. Blackpool and Scarborough are examples of seaside resorts that developed in the 19th century a short train ride away from industrial regions. Here holidaymakers are shown leaving London for Cornwall in August 1924.

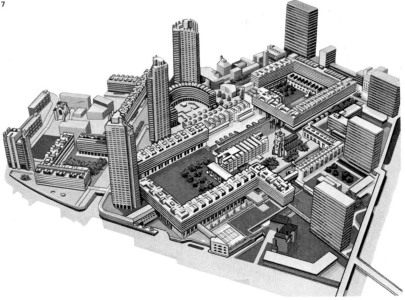

6 Industrialization has created a more affluent society. Previously the predominantly agricultural population had been almost entirely dependent upon fluctuations in harvest levels. Until 1850 it is true to say that the overall standard of living did not decline, although it was subject to severe fluctuations and regional discrepancies. After that time, the standard of living of the population rose, with higher real wages, and kept to a more consistent level. This is shown in the provision of public amenities such as schools, roads and hospitals as well as in the level of personal consumption.

7 London's Barbican housing project is a fine example of the redevelopment that has taken place since the blitz destroyed large areas in many of Britain's cities. Historic features such as St Giles's Church have been sensitively incorporated into the scheme; and pedestrians and traffic have been separated. The complex also includes shops, a theatre, restaurants and a concert hall.

8 The Alton Estate at Roehampton in London illustrates one of the more successful attempts to rehouse the population of the overcrowded inner city areas in an attractive environment. Built between 1952 and 1961, the 11-storey blocks are carefully grouped among four-storey buildings and terraced houses with plenty of open spaces and trees situated on the estate.

The rural consequences of industrialization

The Industrial Revolution had profound consequences for agriculture and rural life. Population growth and increasing urbanization stimulated a demand for foodstuffs of every kind, which in turn made necessary a drastic expansion and development of agriculture. This involved the reclamation of marginal and waste land, the reorganization of landholding through enclosure, the introduction of new crops and techniques, the scientific breeding of healthier and bigger animals, and a more efficient, capitalistic type of farming. The result was a sufficient increase in domestic agricultural production to satisfy the demands of an expanding population until the last quarter of the nineteenth century, when cheap foreign foodstuffs became generally available.

Unemployment on the land

The expansion of agriculture was not sufficient to absorb all population growth on the land. Although the number of families engaged in agriculture rose from 697,000 in 1811 to 761,000 in 1831, many more were forced by sheer economic circumstances to swell the workforce of the industrial towns.

Those who remained were often faced with poor prospects. In the rural south, the system of subsidizing wages from parish rates, introduced by the magistrates of Speenhamland in Berkshire in 1795, discouraged farmers from paying economic wages. Moreover, population growth created conditions of chronic rural unemployment, which depressed farm wage levels to near subsistence level. The harsher New Poor Law of 1834 gave farm labourers the choice of low wages or even worse conditions in the workhouse. By the end of the century, the rural counties still had the highest levels of poverty in the country, often as bad as the worst urban slum areas. Cottage industry too, especially handloom weaving, was badly hit by competition from the factories. Although enclosure did not immediately reduce the agricultural labour force, often actually increasing the demand for labour, wages on the land remained persistently lower than those in industry.

By the turn of the century a drift from the land was accelerated by the depression in prices for farm produce. By 1901, less than ten per cent of the total labour force in the country was involved in agriculture [5].

"High farming" period

Mechanization had not played an important part in the agricultural improvements of the eighteenth and early nineteenth centuries. Seed drills and threshing machines had some success, but the latter aroused opposition in the "Captain Swing" disturbances of 1830–32. The mid-Victorian "high farming" period saw the introduction of more elaborate machinery, including the use of traction engines for steam ploughing. These machines were expensive and not suited to every type of soil, but many new types of apparatus were in use by 1870.

The introduction of the internal combustion engine in the twentieth century had a dramatic impact on farming. Tractors proved useful for a wide range of tasks and, by 1939, there were 55,000 in use. By 1945, there were more than 200,000 tractors working in Britain and more than 50,000 combine harvesters [8]. Electricity was also being

1 The Nant-y-Glo ironworks in Wales in an early 19th-century picture presents a prospect soon to become too familiar — industrial pollution. While it was occasional and localized, pollution could be ignored or sometimes enjoyed as a "sublime" vision of hellishness. Despite the unhealthiness and squalor of the conditions in which they worked and were housed, to many in the most poverty-stricken areas industry brought a welcome opportunity to earn a living. Ironworks in South Wales and the coalfields in the valleys attracted labour from the surrounding regions and some men came on foot from North Wales. Factory life was even thought preferable to farming.

2 The map shows the routes of the earliest railways in Britain, initiated by the opening in 1825 of the famous Stockton-Darlington railway. The railways were in fact only the third wave of improvements in transport in Britain since the 17th century. The building of turnpike roads and of canals had already done much to transform communications and trade, and made travel itself more convenient and enjoyable – the 18th century was a golden age of British tourism. The success of the Stockton-Darlington railway – it more than halved the cost of coal in Stockton – initiated a railway boom, that bound the once distant provinces into an interdependent trading grid, establishing industries far from cities and ports.

Stockton to Darlington 1825
Liverpool to Manchester 1830
Railways by 1844

0   100km

3 John Kay, inventor of the flying shuttle in 1733, is wrapped in a sheet so as to make good his escape from the wrath of rioters at his window. The flying shuttle put out of a job those who previously had thrown the hand-shuttles, and enabled a loom to be worked by one weaver alone. By undermining the rural cottage industries, this and other inventions concentrated within the town the main sources of employment. These rioters were members of an urban workforce whose divorce from the land would soon be politically significant.

4 An expanding railway network was established by 1851. The bridges, tunnels and stations created by the railway engineers proved that the transformed landscape was nowhere inaccessible. But although the influx of trade brought whole new towns, such as Swindon, into being in the Midlands, the more backward parts — much of Wales, Scotland and Ireland — were unaffected. The new habits of leisure travel induced by railways could be seen in the success of the tours organized by Thomas Cook (1808–92).

Railways by 1851

0   100km

used for milking and heating. Technology was applied to a wide range of farming techniques. Animal husbandry was now more scientific and embraced battery farming and complex fertilizers and feedstuffs. The dwindling workforce became much more highly skilled as manual labour was taken over by machinery.

Rural enfranchisement

Social relations on the land were much influenced by the changes in agriculture. Very gradually since the sixteenth century the rural "middle class" of tenant-farmers and yeomen was displaced by the larger landowners and farmers, who employed landless wage-labourers. The dominance of squire and parson was undermined by the enfranchisement of the rural worker and reorganization of local government. In 1884, most agricultural labourers received the vote. The Ballot Act of 1872 also removed them from the more obvious forms of landlord domination by introducing the secret ballot. The establishment of county councils in 1888, and parish councils in 1894,

aided the decline in the influence of the landlord. The early successes of Joseph Arch's Agricultural Trade Union in the 1870s illustrated the permeation of union organization among the agricultural labourers; its progress was nevertheless much slower than among industrial workers.

Many rural areas were brought into the industrial age only with the coming of the railways in the late Victorian and Edwardian eras [2, 4]. The last phase of railway expansion brought branch lines to many hitherto untouched areas. This trend was reversed following the Beeching Report in 1963 which recommended cuts of 8,000km (5,000 miles) of railway. Subsequently, reduction in public transport further isolated many towns and villages. As a result, the motor car became a necessity for those living and working out of town.

The motor car also enabled city-dwellers to enjoy rural pleasures more easily. Large areas of land were set aside as national parks, to be preserved from urban encroachment, while other parts of the countryside were developed for tourists [7, 9].

A Yorkshire miner of 1814 retains a rural look against an early industrial background. Behind him the steam-driven pithead winding-gear brings coal and miners to the surface, and a Blenkinsop locomotive hauls tubs of coal as hills stretch behind. During those early days of industrialization, mining and textile communities were hardly different from farming villages, slightly larger but not yet obtrusive. With the expansion of industry accompanied by a rise in population, factories and housing began to encroach on the rural landscape so much that the countryside in many places became a mere interval between towns. Urban "sprawl" has continued to this day.

5 The proportion of workers employed in industry and services and in agriculture altered greatly between 1801 and 1901. This comparison reveals a clear drift away from the land into the cities; a trend that continues.

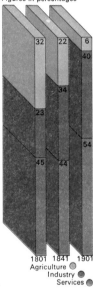

5 Figures in percentages

32 · 22 · 6
40
34
23 · 54
45 · 44

1801 · 1841 · 1901
Agriculture ●
Industry ●
Services ●

6 The destruction of the country house is a recent consequence of industrialization. In previous centuries the country house was the centre from which all agricultural wealth was created, and the unit of local power. Its architecture was an expression of its owner's local status and national role, even if his money came originally from trade or the colonies. After industrialization the country house lost its economic and political vitality and importance.

7 Traffic jams are a consequence of the countryside's role as the playground of the cities. One cause was acceptance by industry of holidays as periods of universal shutdown.

8 Industrialization of the farm itself is one of the inevitable consequences of the mechanization of the entire economy. The trend towards investment in machinery to do the work of many men has made machines such as combine harvesters a commonplace on the land. To obtain sufficient returns on capital outlay farms have had to expand greatly.

9 Giraffes quench their thirst at Longleat, Wiltshire, one of the most popular stately homes in Britain. If the opening of great houses and their parks to the public has made possible their upkeep, it has also spoilt them. The traditional English countryside has lost its essential rusticity, and even moors and mountains, once romantic dreamlands, are now "amenities".

1250-1400 The Mongols unify Asia

Principal events

In Europe the crusading mentality gave way to a more flexible, commercial society, epitomized by the rise of the Italian city states, the Hanseatic League of trading towns in the north and merchant and trade guilds. Kings came to depend more closely on popular support and called parliaments in which they consulted a wider section of the population, including townsmen. After 1300, the growth of population and prosperity gave way to famine and plague which reduced many towns and introduced a period of retrenchment. The population decline, however, increased the bargaining power of the labourers, later enabling the peasantry to escape serfdom.

The Mongols brought prosperity and trade to much of Asia, but their empire was fragmented by religious conflict. Their benevolent rule in China was replaced by the native Ming dynasty in 1368.

1250-65

Gold currencies were introduced in Florence and Genoa, 1252, and bankers, such as the Bardi in Florence, flourished.
Chinese silk became available in Europe in 1257 along the silk route opened up as a result of Mongol expansion.
Kublai Khan, *r.* 1260-94, set up the Yüan dynasty in China.
In England, de Montfort's Parliaments, 1264-5, reflected the improved status of townsmen and lesser knights.

1265-80

Louis IX of France, *r.* 1226-70, the most powerful and respected monarch in Europe, died in Tunis on the ninth and last Crusade.
Mongol peaceful rule in Asia inspired a Venetian trader, **Marco Polo**, 1254-1324, to visit China in 1271-95.
Rudolf of Hapsburg, from an old Swabian family, was elected King of Germany in 1273 and thus became founder of the Hapsburg dynasty.

1280-95

The defeat of the Mongol invasions of Japan in 1274 and 1281 strengthened the Japanese military clans.
The Danish Magna Carta, 1282, united royal power.
Tripoli and Acre fell to the Mamelukes, 1289-91.
The Yüan dynasty in China restored canals and built roads.
Osman, 1259-1326, founded the Turkish Ottoman principality in Bithynia in 1290.
The western Mongols rejected the Khan's authority in 1295.

1295-1310

Venice was governed by a narrow oligarchy of merchants who consolidated their power by crushing the popular and patrician revolts of 1300 and 1310.
A conflict over papal authority led **Philip IV**, *r.* 1285-1314, of France to call one of the first Estates-General in 1302 to appeal for national support.
Military anarchy in Italy drove the papacy to Avignon in 1309.
The African Empire of Mali, based in Sudan, flourished.

National events

Although Parliament was first called to voice responsible opinion in support of Simon de Montfort, *c.* 1208-65, its powers gradually grew as the monarchy needed extra taxation for war. In spite of the ravages of the plague England became more prosperous as a result of war with France.

Opposition to Henry III led to civil war, 1264-5, in which de Montfort, the rebel leader, called a broadly based Parliament, including townsmen.

Edward I, *r.* 1272-1307, reformed the common law in the Statute of Westminster, 1275, and encouraged the development of the woollen trade in London.

Edward conquered Wales by 1284 and campaigned in Scotland without lasting success. He expelled the Jews in 1290.

Edward summoned the "Model Parliament", which provided a convenient means of carrying royal decisions to the country.

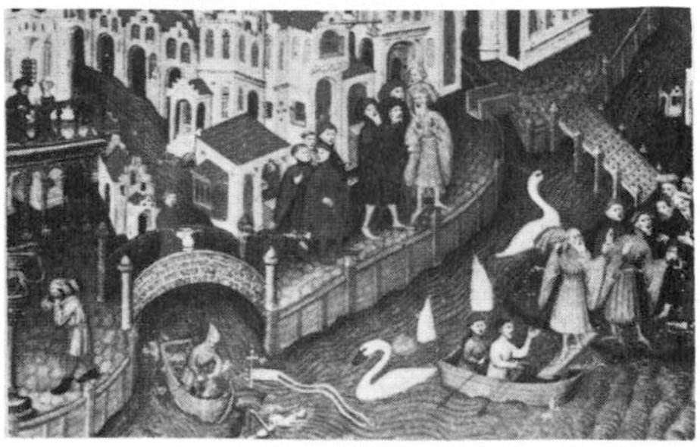

The harbour of Venice, late 12thc.

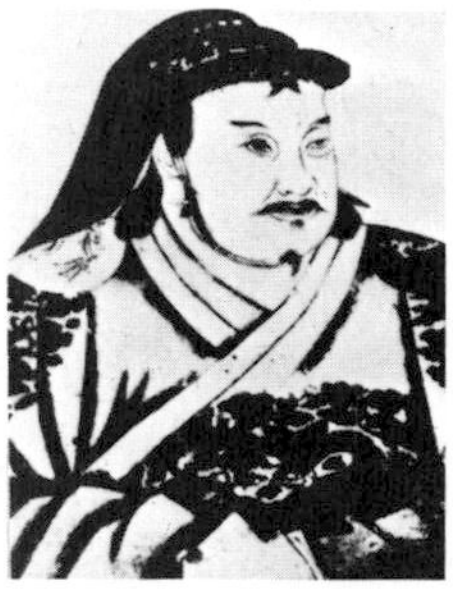

Kublai Khan

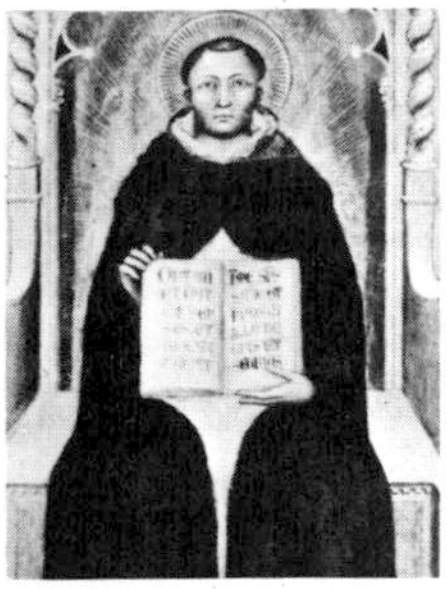

St Thomas Aquinas

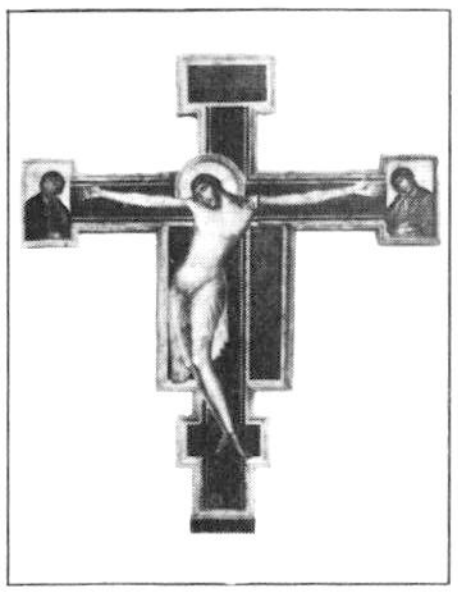

"S. Croce Crucifix", 1283

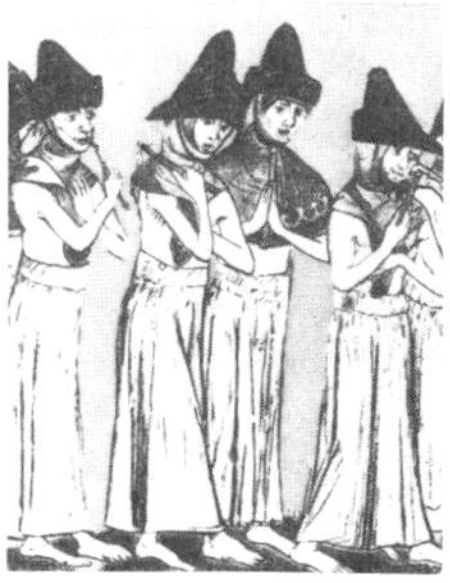

The Black Death: flagellants

Religion and philosophy

The scholastic tradition in European philosophy, which sought to strengthen religious faith with the help of reason, culminated in the work of Thomas Aquinas, Duns Scotus and William of Ockham, who all looked to the work of Plato and Aristotle. Ockham, however, was also an empiricist, disputing the self-evidence of the principles of Aristotelian logic, like the final cause, and of Christian teachings, like the existence of God.

The reign of Pope Boniface VIII marked the summit of papal power. Following the move to Avignon, 1305, the power of the papacy declined.

The vernacular writings of Langland and Wycliffe, both Englishmen, foreshadowed the Reformation in condemning priestly corruption while advocating spiritual as well as social equality.

The Islamic world produced its most original thinker, the scholar Ibn Khaldun.

St Thomas Aquinas, *c.* 1225-74, the greatest scholastic philosopher, stated his belief in the power of reason in *Summa contra Gentiles*, 1264, in which he presented arguments designed to convince the non-believer of the power and truth displayed in Christianity. This work, together with his *Summa Theologica*, 1266-73, was influential in giving a strong Aristotelian basis to Catholic philosophy.

Roger Bacon, *c.* 1214-92, a Franciscan philosopher interested in science, magic and mathematics, in 1272 wrote *Compendium Studii Philosophiae*, attacking clerical influence. He was unusual in valuing experiment as a worthwhile and useful source of knowledge.
Madhava, 1197-1276, an Indian thinker whose life was remarkably similar to that of Christ, denied the Sankara doctrine of the illusory nature of the world.

Duns Scotus, *c.* 1265-1308, an English scholastic philosopher and a Fransciscan monk, drew on the work of Plato. He was a realist, denying the nominalist view that the qualities we perceive, such as the colour green, are merely products of thought and do not exist in the real world. He rejected the idea of predestination and inclined to the Pelagian view that man can alter his fate by his conduct.

Pope Boniface VIII instituted the Jubilee year of 1300, when plenary indulgence was granted to those visiting Rome.
The papacy moved to Avignon in 1309, under Clement V, where it remained for nearly 70 years. The French influence over the papacy in this period marked the beginning of the decline in its temporal power.

Literature 1250-1400

Italian writers of the early Renaissance, particularly Dante, Petrarch and Boccaccio, drew on the passionate and poetical faith of St Francis, the philosophical theology of Aquinas and the new lyricism of the French troubadours to forge a brilliant literature. Honoured by the princes of the Italian states, they explored in allegories, love poems and philosophical writings the contradictions between classical humanism and Christian ideals. Italian vernacular poetry and prose was the latest to emerge among the Romance languages, but the work of writers such as Boccaccio opened the way to the vivid portrayal of contemporary life that marked the work of Chaucer in England and became characteristic of Renaissance literature.

Laudi (praises to God) became a common form of religious song in Italy during the period following the death of **St Francis**, 1226. The Franciscan friar **Jacapone da Todi**, *c.* 1230-1306, was the greatest poet of this style. Written in an Umbrian dialect, his ardent mystical laudi counterposed a love of God with a harsh awareness of the secular world.

The ghazal – a 7th-century form of Arabic love poetry celebrating mystical and worldly love in mono-rhymed verses without logical sequence – was developed by Persian Sufi mystics, notably **Rumi**, 1207-73, in his *Divan*.
Roman de la Rose, a French poem of 22,000 lines in 8-syllable couplets, completed by 1280, included an elaborate allegory on the psychology of love.

One of the major figures in Catalan literature, Raymon Lully, 1232-1315, was a poet, mystic, philosopher and theologian who produced 243 works. *Blanquerna*, 1289, is notable as a philosophical study of Utopia and the forerunner of the novel.
The exploits of the 13th-century Tannhäuser, a knight and poet of the **Minnesinger** school, were described in legend and ballad.

Marco Polo recorded in a Genoese prison, *c.* 1298, the story of his travels in China and Asia. His account was the basis of Western knowledge of China.
Heinrich von Meissen, *c.* 1250-1318, was a representative of the school of middle-class poets who succeeded the knightly Minnesingers, adapting Minnesinger traditions to poems dealing with theology and philosophy.

Art and architecture

Art and architecture in Europe between 1250 and 1400 show their initial indebtedness to France, a nation that had achieved success both politically and artistically. German patrons sent for architects to build "in the French manner", while Italian masons grafted details from Rayonnant Gothic architecture onto buildings that were essentially the piled masses of Italian Romanesque. Everywhere much time, skill and money were lavished to make buildings bigger and more ornate and objects more intricate and naturalistic, both in religious and secular spheres. The period saw the "birth" of Italian painting in the works of Cimabue, Giotto and Duccio and the beginnings of modern sculpture with Nicola Pisano and his son, Giovanni.

Cultures in South-East Asia became more distinct, yet borrowed freely from each other. Comparatively little survives from India at this time.

The French Rayonnant Gothic style, characterized by circular windows with wheel tracery, was exemplified on the western façade of **Rheims Cathedral**, begun in 1255, and also in Spain at **Leon Cathedral**, 1255-1303. The choir of **Old St Paul's**, London, begun in 1256, also incorporated French features.
Nicola Pisano, *c.* 1225-*c.* 84, the greatest sculptor of his generation, completed a font for the baptistery at Pisa, 1260.

The influence of the Four Great Masters on landscape painting of the Mongol **Yüan dynasty** in China, 1264-1368, brought a greater robustness and broader colour spectrum to this important art form.
The Benin (Nigeria) bronzecasters' "lost wax" technique was developed in the late 13th century, introduced by tradition from Ife.

Cimabue, *c.* 1240-1302, one of the first great Italian painters, worked towards the realistic depiction of physical form and human emotion, as in his "Sta Croce crucifix", 1283.
In England one of the earliest lierne vaults, characterized by small ribs running from one major rib to another, was built at **Pershore Abbey**, Worcs., 1288. Lierne vaults became a purely decorative, typically English device.

The frescoes by Giotto, 1266-1337, in the Arena (Scrovegni) chapel in Padua, painted *c.* 1305, show solidity, naturalistic detail and perspective, and represent the turning point in Italian painting. By contrast **Duccio di Buoninsegna**, *c.* 1260-1315, the first great Sienese painter, summed up the mastery of the Byzantine tradition in his "Maesta" for Siena Cathedral, commissioned in 1308.

Music

Late medieval European music was increasingly complex and brilliant, requiring more exact systems of notation. The beginning of the Renaissance produced an easing of the Church's nearly exclusive hold on serious composition and, as patrons began to sponsor secular music, compositions began to show signs of greater individuality and independence.

The motet, a polyphonic form with different words sung simultaneously in the various parts, in which the *cantus firmus* was reduced to a repeated rhythmic phrase, developed after *c.* 1250.

Notation was developed for shorter time values as intricate parts were introduced to overlie lines of long notes. The new notation helped to clarify the time relationship between the parts.

In China, during the Yüan dynasty, 1264-1368, music was encouraged. Opera developed in the theatre with recitative (musically declaimed words), arias and melodies for set moods.

The madrigal emerged in Italy. Usually set for two or more voices, it was in a strict poetic structure corresponding to the *formes fixes* of France. It was unrelated to the 16th-century madrigal.

Science and technology

European trade and industry, although violently arrested in the mid-14th century by the Black Death, expanded rapidly in the first century of this period. Italian galleys carried cargoes of glass, silk and finished metal goods to northern Europe and elsewhere, returning laden with textiles from the Hanseatic cloth towns and metals from the mines of central Europe.

Intellectual life, including that of the newly founded universities of Oxford and Paris, was also vigorous. Although in science Scholasticism was still the rule, signs of a breakthrough to a more experimental approach began with the works of Oresme and Buridan in Paris and William of Ockham in England, whose ideas conflicted with those of the scholastic's ultimate scientific authority, Aristotle.

By the end of this period Arab science was limited to the teachings of a few wandering scholars, and China, the home of accurate scientific reasoning and technology, had declined due to an unwieldy bureaucracy.

Gold florins were first struck in Florence in 1252.
The first cannons, employed by the Moors perhaps as early as 1250, were simply iron buckets charged with gunpowder and filled with stones. They were ignited by means of a touch-hole near the bottom of the bucket.
Vincent of Beauvais, *d.* 1264 was a major encyclopedist. His *Speculum Majus*, unequalled in length until the 18th century, summarized the scientific and philosophical views of the major scholastic writers.

Commercial fishing, encouraged by the many meatless fastdays of the Christian calendar, grew rapidly during the Middle Ages in Europe. The Hanseatic League fishery, in the Baltic, reached its peak, 1275-1350, with catches of 13,000 tonnes of herring a year.
The spinning wheel may have been invented by 1280 but was not commonly introduced into Europe until the 14th century, when it replaced the distaff and loose spindle. It is pictured in the Luttrell Psalter of 1338.

Spectacles, with convex lenses, were first recorded by an Englishman, Roger Bacon, 1286. By the early 14th century they were factory-made in Venice.
Albertus Magnus, *c.* 1200-80, a German encyclopedist, classified plants by their structures.

Stanches, or navigation weirs, which maintain a depth of water for ships, were built in European rivers and canals and include one built on the Thames in 1306.
Linen clothes were widely worn in the 14th century for the first time. This led to an improvement in personal cleanliness and an associated decline in diseases such as leprosy.
Gunpowder for artillery appeared in Europe *c.* 1300.
Watermarks were first used in papermaking in Italy in the late 13th century.

1310-25

Bad harvests in 1315 brought famine to much of Europe, slowing population growth. **In north India**, where Muslim dynasties ruled from Delhi since 1206, a Turkish Tughluk dynasty was founded in 1320. **In Mexico the Aztecs** founded the capital Tenochtitlan in 1325 and began to colonize Central America. **Uzbeg**, *r.* 1312-41, converted the Mongol Golden Horde to Islam and brought Mongol prosperity to its height.

1325-40

The Ottoman Empire expanded into Thrace, 1326-61, threatening Constantinople. **The Hundred Years War** of England and France broke out in 1337 as a result of the rival claims to the French throne of **Edward III**, *r.* 1327-77, and **Philip of Valois**, *r.* 1328-50. **The Hanseatic League** grew politically powerful *c.* 1340. **Victory at Rio Salado** in 1340 by Alfonso XI of Castile, *r.* 1312-50, ended the African threat to Spain.

1340-55

Italian economic decline followed the fall of the Bardi bankers after the English monarchy repudiated its debts. **Cola de Rienzo**, 1313-54, was murdered after his attempt to set up a Roman republic independent of the papacy. **The Black Death** destroyed up to half Europe's population between 1348 and 1352, totally disrupting commerce. **During the Hundred Years War** England profited from pillage and the ransom of captives.

1355-70

The Holy Roman Empire was changed by papal decree, the **Golden Bull**, from a monarchy to an aristocratic federation. **The ransom of John II** of France by England provoked the **Jacquerie**, a peasant revolt against war taxes which was violently suppressed in 1358. **The Ming dynasty** in China was created after a popular revolt against the Mongols, 1368.

1370-85

The Ottomans took Adrianople. **Rival popes** were created in Rome and Avignon, 1378, after the breakdown of negotiations over plans to reform the papacy. **Popular revolts** in Florence in 1378 and England in 1381 were suppressed. **Constitutional reform** in Florence marked the beginning of Florentine power in 1382. **Moscow** emerged as the focus of Russian opposition to the Mongols after the defeat of the Tatars at Kulikovo in 1380.

1385-1400

Portugal assured its independence by defeating Castile at Aljubarota in 1385. **Tamerlane**, *r.* 1369-1405, conquered Central Asia and defeated the Golden Horde, 1391, destroying the kingdom of Delhi in 1398 and delaying the Ottoman advance westwards into Europe, despite a victory over the Serbian alliance in 1398. **The Ming dynasty** began to develop a naval empire *c.* 1400. **Japanese prosperity** was primarily based on piracy *c.* 1400.

Robert Bruce, *r.* 1306-29, assured Scottish independence at Bannockburn in 1314 by defeating **Edward II**, *r.* 1307-27.

The nobility deposed and killed Edward II, 1327. **The need to defend the interests of the woollen trade** in Flanders helped to bring war with France, 1337.

The Black Death quickened the decline of serfdom and **Edward III**, *r.* 1327-77, attempted unsuccessfully to control wage rates and labour problems.

English pillaging in France brought new wealth to all classes and professional soldiers emerged in the army alongside the feudal nobility.

The Peasants' Revolt, 1381, failed in its attempt to end villeinage immediately. **Parliament** claimed the right to impeach royal ministers, 1376.

Richard II's absolutist reign, 1377-99, was ended by noble opposition led by Henry of Bolingbroke, 1367-1413, who became Henry IV, 1399.

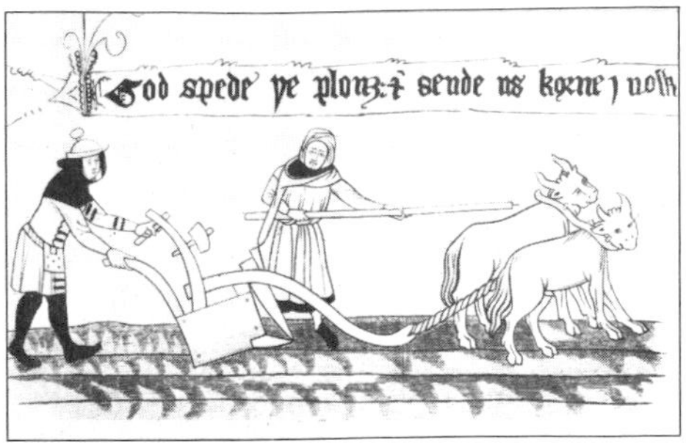

Piers Plowman frontispiece

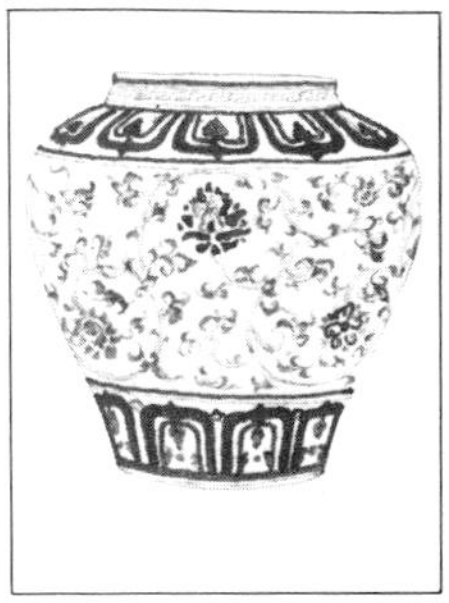

Ming vase

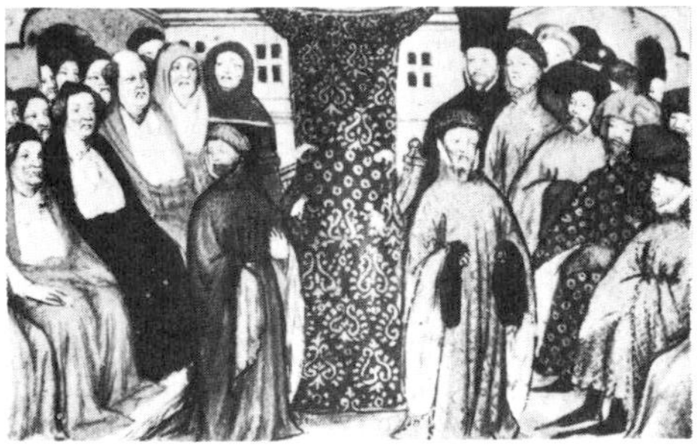

The English Parliament deposing Richard II

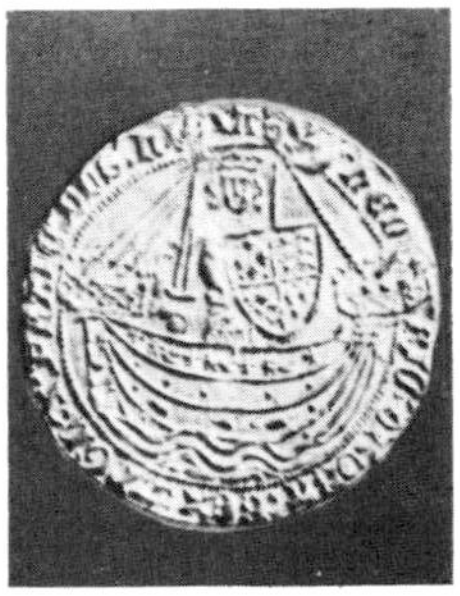

English gold coin, *c.* 1400

Giovanni Monte Corvino, 1247-1328, established the first Christian missions in China and baptized **Khaistan Kuluk**, *r.* 1307-11, the third great Khan of the Chinese Yüan dynasty. **Marsiglio of Padua**, *c.* 1275-1342, wrote *Defensor Pacis*, 1324, a famous treatise espousing the supremacy of lay power over the Church and claimed that all power derives from the people, for whom the ruler is a delegate.

William of Ockham, *c.* 1300-*c.* 47, an Englishman, was the last of the great scholastic Franciscan philosophers. He broke with the Aristotelian realism of **Aquinas** and took a nominalist position. His importance lies in his development of a sophisticated logic and epistemology of more than a purely theological significance, which was to have a great effect on later secular philosophy.

The Flagellant movement arose in response to fear of the Black Death, but was condemned by **Pope Clement VI**, 1349. The Flagellants sought to avoid divine wrath by whipping themselves thrice daily. They began in Italy and spread to Germany and the Low Countries, where they toured the countryside proclaiming flagellation as the way to salvation.

The Sufi branch of Islam spread into India, Malaya and Africa south of the Sahara. *Piers Plowman*, a vernacular poem probably by the English parson **Langland** *c.* 1362, attacked corruption in the state and Church. The poem is an appeal on behalf of the poor and a plea for spiritual equality.

John Wycliffe, *c.* 1328-84, and his followers the Lollards, a religious group with noble supporters in England, spread ideas that were unacceptable until the Reformation. In *On Civil Dominion*, 1376, Wycliffe proposed a propertyless Church and argued for direct access to God for individuals. **In the Netherlands disciples of Gerhard Grote**, 1340-84, who espoused a non-ritualized, humane Christianity, formed the Brethren of the Common Life.

Ibn Khaldun, 1322-1406, the Islamic scholar, was unique in the medieval era. The greatest social thinker until modern times, he based a theory of society on social cohesion and a cyclical pattern of growth and decay. In his masterwork, the *Muquaddimah*, he outlined a philosophy of history and laid the foundations for what he called "a science of culture".

The theme of spiritual love developed by such Tuscan poets as **Guido Calvacanti**, 1260-1300, was given expression by **Dante Alighieri**, 1265-1321. In his *Divina Commedia*, begun *c.* 1307, he describes his journey through *Inferno*, *Purgatorio* and *Paradiso*, giving insight on medieval views and religious beliefs. It made Tuscan Italy's literary medium.

Petrarch (Francesco Petrarca), 1304-74, gave passionate form to Italian love poetry in his "Canzoniere", sonnets and madrigals inspired by his unrequited love for Laura. An admirer of Roman and Greek ideals, his humanistic outlook influenced other writers. **The Persian mystic poet Hafiz**, 1320-88, used complex lyrical imagery in ghazal form.

The Italian novella was developed by **Giovanni Boccaccio**, 1313-75, in *The Decameron*, *c.* 1348-53, a collection of 100 witty and bawdy tales set in the time of the Black Death. Their humanism and breadth of social and psychological observation had an enormous influence on Renaissance literature everywhere. Boccaccio was influenced by Graeco-Roman styles.

A great Christian allegorical poem, *Piers Plowman*, attributed to **William Langland**, *c.* 1332-1400, brought to Middle English the alliterative tradition of Anglo-Saxon verse in a series of 11 dream visions. **A more mysterious allegory** was the anonymous *Gawain and the Green Knight*, *c.* 1370, an Arthurian romance. *Pearl* was found in the same manuscript.

The No play emerged in Japan in a classic form established by **Kanami Motokiyo**, 1333-84, and his son **Zeami Motokiyo**, 1363-1443, who wrote most of the 100 plays that survive from this period. No drama is formal in style, incorporates music and dancing and is performed without scenery by males who wear masks to portray women, old men or supernatural beings.

The first truly native English poetry was created by **Geoffrey Chaucer**, *c.* 1345-1400, influenced by French and Italian styles. His best works include *Troilus and Criseyde*, *c.* 1385, and *Canterbury Tales*, *c.* 1395. ***Confessio Amantis***, *c.* 1390, by English poet **John Gower**, 1325-1408, told moralistic stories of courtly love.

The Paris school of manuscript illumination flowed in the work of **Master Honoré**, *d.* 1318. **Second generation "decorated" Gothic** architecture in England developed with the building of Ely Cathedral Lady Chapel, 1321-48, whose undulating blind arcading and curvilinear tracery derived from geometrical forms. **Giovanni Pisano**, *c.* 1250-*c.* 1320, completed the pulpit in Pisa Cathedral, 1310, synthesizing Gothic and classical elements.

In the Muromachi (Ashikaga) period in Japan, 1338-1573, painters followed previous traditions such as continuous narrative scrolls. Renewal of contact with China and Korea introduced new techniques such as the art of painting. **The Perpendicular style** of architecture in England first appeared in Gloucester Cathedral cloister, where the ribs of the vault spread out into fan-vaulting.

Italian painting followed the Sienese tradition in the works of **Simone Martini**, *c.* 1284-1344, and of **Pietro and Ambrogio Lorenzetti**, both active in the first half of the 14th century. Papal patronage in the palace of Avignon brought numerous Italian artists to France. Giotto's earlier detailed studies of nature influenced the decoration of the **Tour des Anges**, *c.* 1340, by **Matteo Giovanetti**.

Potters of the Ming dynasty in China, 1368-1644, discovered underglaze painting using imported Persian cobalt. Their harmonious blue designs on white ground balanced their favourite opulent shapes and sinuous line. **Italian architecture's** continuity with Romanesque was shown in the new design for the east end of Florence Cathedral by **Francesco Talenti**. Only external details such as windows are borrowed Gothic.

English Perpendicular architecture matured. Canterbury Cathedral nave had smoothly shafted columns rising to the lierne vaults. **The Hindu Vijanagar dynasty** of the Deccan, India, 1336-*c.* 1614, favoured an almost baroque style. Groups of small buildings were characteristic and columns were often sculptured with groups of figures and animals.

The rebuilding of Milan Cathedral, 1387, in the northern Late Gothic style showed the influence of and enthusiasm for French ideas. Building continued throughout the Renaissance. **Tamerlane's mausolea** at Samarkand, built in the decade after Baghdad's capture, 1393, inspired Timurid architects, 1405-1500, by their tall domes on high drums and colourful glazed relief-tile decoration.

Ars nova was a term coined by **Phillipe de Vitry**, 1291-1361, to describe new and freer forms of music. The earlier forms became known as *ars antiqua*. Religious music still favoured triple time as symbolic of the Trinity, but growing acceptance of **duple** (beats in groups of two) time advocated in *ars nova* implied an acknowledgment of the equality of secular music.

Guillaume de Machaut, *c.* 1300-77, was the chief figure of *ars nova*. The complex forms he used involved modulation (changing key), intricate cross-rhythms and great independence of line.

Meistersinger in Germany took over the lyric art of the aristocratic Minnesinger. Meistersinger were traders and craftsmen who founded guilds to set and keep up standards for their art.

Dissonances and great embellishment in music were part of the general concern with richness and diversity seen in European art of the time. Paris produced the best examples.

Drainage mills, windmills which operate drainage scoops, were invented in the 14th century. (In the 16th century the Dutch used such mills for recovering land for agriculture.) **Chaulmoogra oil**, for the treatment of leprosy, was first seen in 14th-century China. It was the only effective treatment for leprosy until the 20th century.

Salt-glazing of pottery was practised in the Rhineland from the 14th century. The potter threw salt over wares in the final stages of firing in the kiln; this produced a fine glaze which sealed off the wares. **The cross staff**, a primitive form of sextant, was popularized for use in navigation by **Levi ben Gerson** of Provence, 1288-1344.

The Black Death of 1348-52 caused a severe decline in European trade and power, badly affecting labour-intensive industries such as agriculture, mining and fishing, which did not recover for over a century. **Double-entry book-keeping** methods are known to have been used by the Massari family of Genoa *c.* 1340, although they were probably used before that by the Hanseatic League, the Medicis and the Fuggers. **Iron cannons** were used by the Germans from 1350 onwards.

Oresme, *c.* 1325-82, and **Buridan**, 1300-58, in Paris, criticized Aristotle's doctrine of motion. They were influenced by the idea of *impetus*, conceived by **Philoponus**, *c.* 530, and later developed into a theory of motion by Galileo. **Mechanically wound** steel crossbows were developed.

Lock gates on Dutch canals date from at least 1373. By 1400, locks were an integral part of navigation and drainage systems of Italy and Germany. **Geoffrey Chaucer**, an English writer, *c.* 1345-1400, described what may be the first scientific work in English, *The Equatorial Planetarie*, which deals with a device for predicting the paths and positions of planets. **Forged iron guns** weighing 272kg (600lb) were used by Richard II, *r.* 1377-99, to defend the Tower of London.

Weight-driven clocks, often employing elaborate striking mechanisms, appear in Europe at this time. The earliest surviving clock in England is in Salisbury Cathedral, installed in 1386. **Arab observatories** were among the last achievements of Arab science and include that of **Ulugh-Beg**, 1394-1449, the grandson of Tamerlane, in Samarkand. His astronomical tables were used by Western astronomers until the Renaissance.

1400-1500 Printing and discovery

Principal events

In spite of a generally static economic climate the move towards national sovereignty increased at the expense of papal authority. The process of the consolidation of the European states continued and the power of the monarchs over the nobility grew gradually with the help of ostentatious artistic patronage and ambitious foreign wars. In Spain, united under Ferdinand and Isabella, the Moors were finally expelled and Ivan I established the power of Moscow by bargaining with the Tatars.

Byzantium fell to the Ottoman Turks in 1453, closing the eastern Mediterranean to Christian traffic, but European expansion began to the west as the Spanish and Portuguese thrones sponsored the exploration of alternative routes to India round the coast of Africa.

In China, the Ming dynasty made contact by sea with India and Africa and fought to protect its weak northern frontiers.

1400-10

Tamerlane's victory at Angora in 1402 brought temporary disorder to the Ottoman Empire. **Chinese naval expeditions** to India and Africa for commercial and military prestige began in 1403. **Burgundian ambitions** led to a French civil war with the Armagnacs in 1404. **Venice seized Vicenza**, Padua and Verona, to become the dominant power in northern Italy. **Florence** won access to the sea by buying Pisa in 1405.

1410-20

Mehmet I, *r.* 1413-21, reunited the Ottoman Empire and consolidated power in the Balkans. **Henry V of England**, *r.* 1413-22, captured Normandy, 1417-19, after his victory at Agincourt in 1415. **The papal schism** was ended at the Council of Constance, 1414-17, where **Huss**, 1369-1415, the Bohemian religious reformer, was burnt for heresy. **Henry the Navigator**, 1394-1460, began his systematic exploration of the African coast.

1420-30

The Bohemian Hussites under **John Ziska**, *c.* 1370-1424, were defeated in a series of imperial crusades, 1420-33. **Henry V** of England was recognized as heir to the French throne, 1420. **Joan of Arc**, *c.* 1412-31, then inspired a new French national unity in support of **Charles VII**, *r.* 1422-61. **Peking** became the Ming capital in 1421. **Murad II**, *r.* 1421-51, led an Ottoman attack on Constantinople in 1422.

1430-40

Alfonso V of Aragon, *r.* 1416-58, campaigned in Italy and took Naples in 1435. **The banking and wool merchant Medici family** controlled Florence, 1434-94. **Hapsburg control** of the Holy Roman Empire became virtually hereditary with **Albert II**, *r.* 1438-9. **John VIII**, *r.* 1425-48, of Byzantium, inspired serious opposition by accepting the primacy of the pope in 1439.

National events

Unstable royal authority resulted in civil war, the Wars of the Roses. Traditional feudal ties were breaking down and a strong independent yeomanry emerged. Although Henry Tudor introduced few innovations, his reign prepared the way for the later assertion of royal authority.

Henry IV, *r.* 1399-1413, whose seizure of power had relied on Parliament, suffered from parliamentary demands to supervise his expenditure.

Henry V, *r.* 1413-22, united Parliament and the country behind his nationalist appeal for a successful invasion of France.

The weakness of **Henry VI**, *r.* 1422-61 intermittently, resulted in a rise in the activity of noble factions.

The rise of **"bastard feudalism"** reflected the short-term political interest of the rising knightly classes.

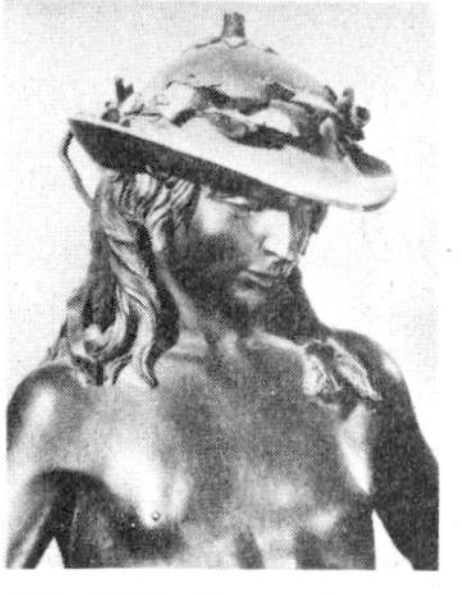

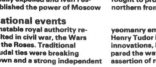

"David" by Donatello

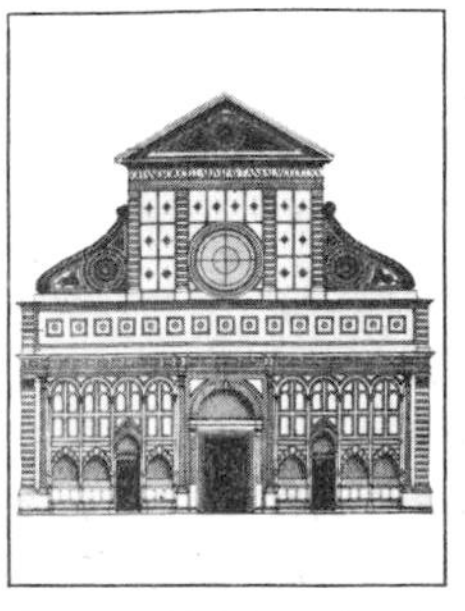

Façade of S. Maria Novella

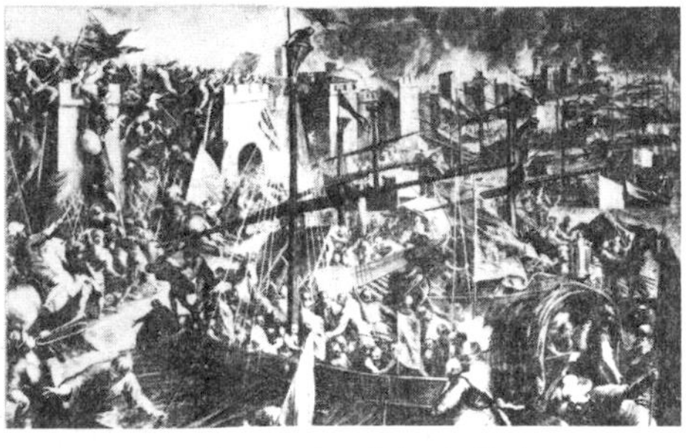

The conquest of Constantinople by the Turks

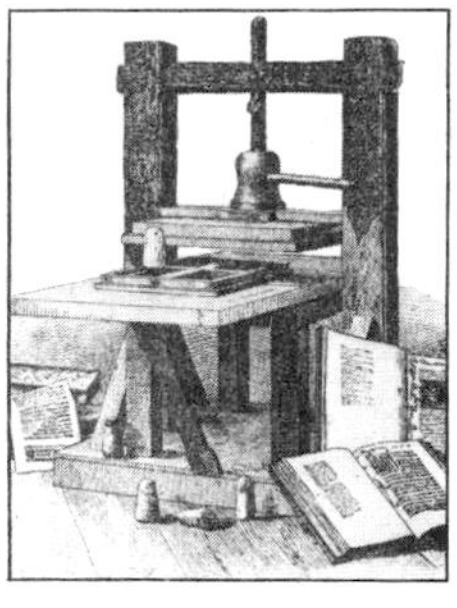

Gutenberg's printing press

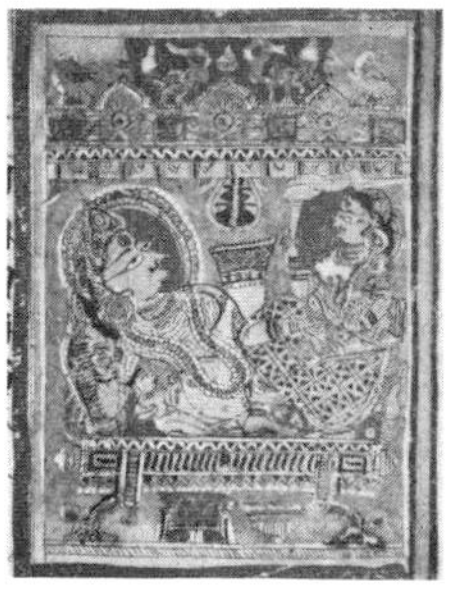

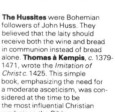

Jain manuscript, 14th.-15thc.

Religion and philosophy

The relationship of Church and state was a major subject of controversy in 15th-century Europe, while the corrupt practices and moral laxity of the established religious orders came under attack. Reformers and critics of religious authority spelt out many of the themes that would be elaborated in the Protestant Reformation of the next century.

Savonarola, an Italian monk, denounced corruption in Florence and the abuse of political power, calling for a regeneration of spiritual values and a steadfast devotion to asceticism.

In Bohemia the Hussites identified religious reforms with Bohemian nationalism while humanist writers in Italy, England and Holland argued for the separation of religious and secular law and the freedom of conscience of the individual. In another sense the power of the universal Church was challenged in Spain where the crown set up the Spanish Inquisition.

The Chinese emperor Ch'eng-Jsu, *r.* 1403-24, sponsored the publication of an 11,095-volume encyclopedia in 1403. **The Council of Pisa**, 1409, attempted to resolve the Great Schism in the papacy. This had arisen in 1378, with Urban VI in Rome and Clement VII in Avignon as rival claimants, backed by the empire and France. **John XXII**, however, the compromise candidate, satisfied no one and the schism continued until 1417.

Pope Martin V, *r.* 1417-31, whose election ended the Great Schism, moved the papacy permanently to Rome in 1420 and consolidated Church unity. **John Huss**, *c.* 1369-1415, a Bohemian follower of Wycliffe, criticized the papacy for the sale of indulgences (absolutions from sin) and urged a literal interpretation of the Bible. He denied the infallibility of an immoral pope, and claimed the supremacy of the state over the Church.

The Hussites were Bohemian followers of John Huss. They believed that the laity should receive both the wine and bread in communion instead of bread alone. **Thomas à Kempis**, *c.* 1379-1471, wrote the *Imitation of Christ c.* 1425. This simple book, emphasizing the need for a moderate asceticism, was considered at the time to be the most influential Christian work since the Bible.

Nicholas of Cusa, 1401-64, in his *De Concordantia Catholica*, 1433, argued for the General Council's authority over the pope. However, the council's lack of power led him to reverse his position by 1437. Cusa also contributed to the sciences and philosophy. He wrote *Of Learned Ignorance*, in 1440, arguing against the possibility of ever attaining eternal truths.

Literature

Compared with the vitality and initiative of Boccaccio and Chaucer, European writers of the early 15th century produced less distinctive work. Learning rather than literature held sway and the revival of interest in classical studies led by the Humanist scholars in Italy had its main impact only after 1454, when the development of printing by Gutenberg in Germany produced a rapidly increasing flow of books. Two outstanding writers who drew on medieval traditions were Villon, France's first great lyrical poet, and Malory, who dominated English prose with an adaptation of Arthurian legend. Lively vernacular poetry emerged in Scotland with Henryson and Dunbar and also in Florence and Naples late in the century.

The Mabinogion collection of Celtic tales and heroic legends was preserved in the Welsh *Red Book of Hergest*, *c.* 1375-1425. These anonymous stories contained a wealth of ancient mythology. They fused narrative with dialogue, conveying the vitality of the oral tradition from which these tales emerged, probably during the 11th century.

Miracle plays based on biblical themes or the lives of saints were enacted in popular style in England and Europe. **John Lydgate**, *c.* 1370-1451, English imitator of Chaucer and Boccaccio, wrote the *Troy Book* and *Siege of Thebes*, *c.* 1420. **Perez de Guzman**, *c.* 1376-*c.* 1460, Spanish historian and poet, examined the theory of history and role of the historian.

Alain Chartier, *c.* 1390-1440, wrote the allegorical poem *La Belle Dame Sans Merci* in 1424. An attack on courtly love, it reflected political unrest in France after the defeat at Agincourt. In *Le Quadrilogue invectif*, 1422, a political pamphlet, he called for French solidarity to combat the turmoil of the Hundred Years War, using prose form to convey his plea.

The Italian Leon Battista Alberti, 1404-72, a brilliant Renaissance figure who was an architect, sculptor and musician, wrote *Della Famiglia*, 1434, containing a theoretical treatise within a discussion of household affairs. Styled on Latin models, it displayed a pessimistic view of contemporary life. He also published works on ethics, jurisprudence and architecture.

Art and architecture

Fifteenth-century European art was profoundly affected by the artistic Renaissance that emerged in Italy – a stylistic revolution characterized by a revival of interest in Greek and Roman antiquities that brought with it a new interest in the anatomy of the human form, in proportion and in perspective, combined with a new sense of human dignity and confidence. Beginning in Florence, and fostered by widespread court patronage both ecclesiastical and secular, it spread rapidly to other parts of Italy and culminated at the end of the century in the masterpieces of Mantegna, Botticelli, Bellini, Leonardo, Michelangelo and Bramante.

The Gothic style in architecture still flourished even in Italy and took new forms with the Perpendicular style in England, while International Gothic brought a new realism to European painting and sculpture.

The International Gothic style introduced a new realism into the painting of landscape, costume and animals, exemplified in the wings of the altarpiece at Dijon, 1399, by **Melchior Broederlam**, *d. c.* 1410. **Gothic and Renaissance styles** were linked in the bronze doors of the Florence Baptistery sculptured by **Lorenzo Ghiberti**, 1378-1455, from 1403 to 1452. **Burgundian sculpture** was characterized by the "Well of Moses", 1401, by **Claus Sluter**, *d.* 1406.

The Duc de Berry commissioned the *Très Riches Heures*, *c.* 1415, from the Limbourg brothers. His extensive patronage included the less-known *Très Belles Heures* and he built twelve elegant castles. **The design for Innocenti (Foundling) Hospital** in Florence, 1419, by **Filippo Brunelleschi**, 1377-1446, began the architectural Renaissance in Italy and established Brunelleschi's reputation as one of the finest Renaissance architects.

Masaccio, *c.* 1401-28, the first of the great *quattrocento* painters, used simplicity, naturalism and light in a new way in his Brancacci Chapel frescoes, Florence, 1425-8. **One of the masterpieces** of the International Gothic style in Italy was the "Adoration of the Magi", 1423, by **Gentile da Fabriano**, *c.* 1370-1427.

Donatello, 1386-1466, an Italian and one of the greatest figures of 15th-century art, executed his classic bronze masterpiece "David" *c.* 1435. **Flemish painting** was revolutionized by **Jan van Eyck**, *d.* 1441, who not only perfected an oil painting technique using brilliant colour and subtle light effects but also brought an everyday realism to such works as "Adoration of the Lamb", 1432.

Music

European music was dominated by the brilliance of the Franco-Flemish composers, the first great musical school. The Church favoured an international style of music and would admit no other styles, but national composers successfully challenged the Franco-Flemish school in the quality of their work, especially in the field of polyphonic songs.

Under the Ming dynasty, 1368-1644, music declined in China. Long pieces, interspersing new material with a refrain, were played on the zither and tunes modulated for special effect.

Composers set parts to imitate each other. Polyphony related melodies to the *cantus firmus*, and **counterpoint** used rhythmically related tunes to combat the turgid rhythm of much polyphonic music.

Choral polyphony using four independent parts now grew up. The voices (parts) were finely blended and the harmony euphonious, avoiding the dissonances common in earlier music.

Secular polyphony developed as part-songs were combined with the four-part texture of "learned" music. This is a style that still lives on in barber-shop quartet singing in the United States.

Science

Important changes occurred in the economic and industrial organization of Europe. The Hundred Years War ended and with the Renaissance feudal methods of exchange gave way to more dynamic systems of trade. Technological change – in agriculture, mining, textiles and glassmaking – continued, bringing a steady expansion of industry. The breakthrough of the century was the creation of Gutenberg's book-printing industry at Nuremberg.

Ships and navigational instruments had been undergoing steady improvement and by the end of the century provided explorers with the means to sail to all parts of the globe. Maritime successes stimulated the founding of schools of navigation, which produced men trained in mathematics and curious about science but relatively untrammelled by the religious ideas that had ruled the minds of educated people of earlier medieval times.

Technical treatises on military engineering and ballistics abounded in the early 15th century, especially in Germany and Italy. Among the most famous was the *Bellifortis* of 1405 by **Conrad Kyeser**, a German. **Archimedean screws**, used for lifting water in Dutch polder dams, are known from 1408. **Perspective**, used first in painting but later in scientific and architectural drawings, was discovered in the early 15th century by **Filippo Brunelleschi**, 1377-1446.

Drift nets up to 110m (360ft) long, towed behind fishing boats, were introduced by the Dutch fishing industry in 1416. These nets greatly improved the size of herring catches. The fish were preserved by a salting process improved by the Dutch. **Navigation** was studied by experts from many nations at the court of **Henry the Navigator**, 1394-1460.

Nicholas of Cusa, 1401-64, wrote that the Earth, and not the heavens, revolved daily, a refutation of the accepted Ptolemaic astronomical system. Nicholas's idea was based upon philosophic notions and not on observable scientific data. **Hollow-post mills**, invented *c.* 1430 in Holland, were an improved form of windmill in which the size of the rotating sail arms was reduced and a shaft was passed from them through a hollow post to drive machinery in a building below.

Textile industries in the 15th century used **alum** to fix vegetable dyes, such as indigo, madder and saffron, to cloth. Black dyes were made at this time by mixing green vitriol (iron sulphate) with oak galls to make the intensely black iron stannate. In textile finishing, **gig-mills** (as first drawn by Leonardo da Vinci) were being used to raise the nap of cloth into a woolly texture.

1440-50

After losing Serbia, the Ottoman Turks defeated a Hungarian crusade against them in 1444.
Charles VII created a French standing army free from feudal obligations.
Wars in Italy caused a rise in diplomatic activity, and artistic patronage became a major factor in a ruler's prestige *c.* 1440.
Japan, under Ashikaga rule since 1336, underwent a period of cultural refinement *c.* 1440.

1450-60

The alliance of Florence, Naples and Milan, 1450, inspired by Medici diplomacy, ensured the balance of power among the Italian states.
The fall of Constantinople in 1453 to the Ottoman ruler **Mehmet II**, *r.* 1451-81, ended 1,000 years of Byzantine rule.
George Podiebrad, 1420-71, ended the Bohemian religious wars with conciliatory policies.
The Wars of the Roses between the houses of Lancaster and York began in England, 1455.

1460-70

Venice fought the Turks for control of the Mediterranean, 1463-79.
Louis XI, *r.* 1461-83, aided French unification by ending provincial and urban privileges.
The Onin War, 1467-77, resulted from a succession dispute among the Ashikaga in Japan. This was a prelude to a century of war.
The kingdom of Songhay, based on the Middle Niger region, reached its zenith under **Sonni Ali**, *r.* 1464-92.

1470-80

Ivan the Great, *r.* 1462-1505, adopted the title of tsar in 1472 and subjected Novgorod to Muscovite rule in 1478.
Burgundy was reunited with France, 1477.
In spite of the Pazzi plot to assassinate him, **Lorenzo de' Medici**, 1449-92, ruled in Florence and exhausted the stagnant economy with his flamboyant foreign policy.
The marriage of Ferdinand and Isabella united Aragon and Castile in 1479.

1480-90

Ivan the Great ended the Tatar threat to Moscow, 1480, and annexed Tver in 1485.
The Spanish Church and the **Inquisition** came under royal control after a concordat with the pope in 1482.
The Portuguese Bartolomew Diaz, 1450-1500, rounded the Cape of Good Hope, 1478-8.
The Wars of the Roses ended with the dominance of **Henry VII** (Tudor), *r.* 1485-1509 who established royal independence from baronial support.

1490-1500

Spain captured Granada, the last Moorish outpost, and expelled 200,000 Jews, 1492.
Columbus, with Spanish support, discovered the Bahamas and Cuba, 1492, on his search for a western route to India.
Vasco da Gama reached India around Africa, 1497-8.
Charles VIII of France, *r.* 1483-98, invaded Italy, 1495, but was expelled by an alliance including the empire, the papacy and Venice formed to protect Italy from foreign domination.

The flourishing woollen industry moved away from the towns, where economic decline had made the guilds increasingly restrictive.

The widespread enclosure of common land to promote sheep farming began in 1453. A strong independent smallholder class developed.

Edward IV, *r.* 1461-83, a Yorkist, won the throne from Henry VI in the Wars of the Roses, relying on popular support in London for his authority.

After Henry's brief restoration, 1470-1, **Edward IV** continued to rule parsimoniously in order to assert royal independence from nobility and Parliament.

After a revival of the wars, **Henry VII**, *r.* 1485-1509, the first Tudor king, brought permanent peace by uniting the rival families in his marriage.

Henry VII ensured his military control over England and asserted royal authority over the nobility in the new Star Chamber court.

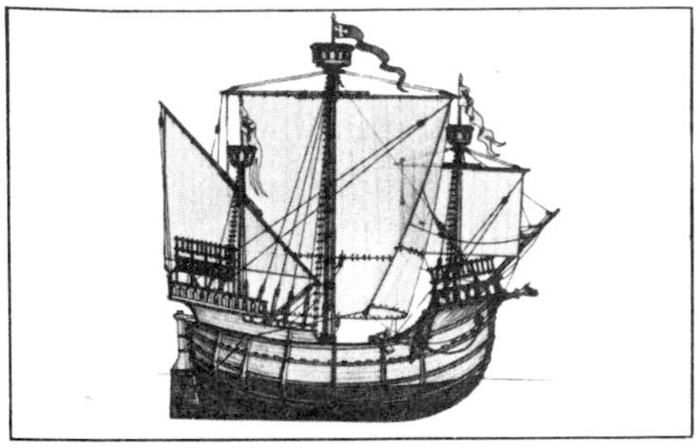

Carrack, 15thc.

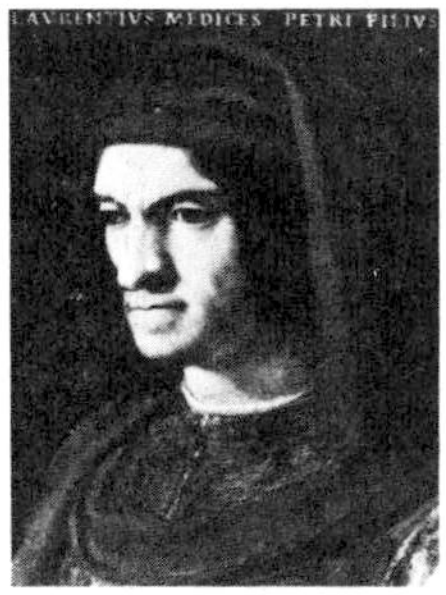

Lorenzo de Medici

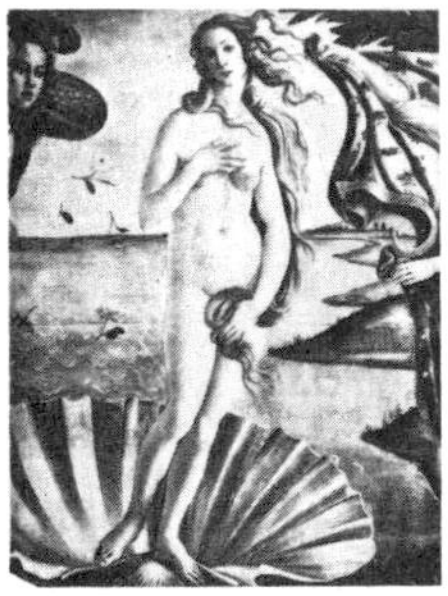

"Venus" by Botticelli

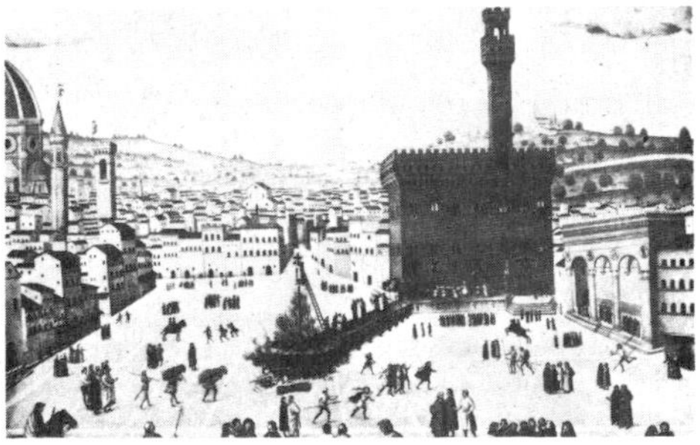

The burning of Savonarola in Florence

In 1440, **Lorenzo Valla**, 1407-57, attacked papal political claims by asserting that the *Donations of Constantine*, an anonymous document that supposedly granted universal temporal power to the papacy, was a forgery. As a humanist of the Italian Renaissance, Valla accused the medieval philosophers of deliberately misunderstanding and poorly interpreting the works of Plato and Aristotle.

The Indian mystic Kabir, 1440-1518, attempted to merge some aspects of the Hindu creed with Sufist Muslim ideas. Kabir, originally a weaver from Benares, rejected Hindu beliefs in idols and castes but accepted the institutions of reincarnation and eventual release. His followers were known as **Kabirpanthis**. This movement was a forerunner of the movement of Sikhism.
The first printed Bible was produced in Mainz in 1456.

The Unitas Fratrum (Bohemian Brethren), founded by Peter of Chelchich, *d.* 1460, broke with the Utraquists in 1467. They were a militantly democratic sect who, like the Taborites, rejected subordination to Rome.

Sir John Fortescue, *c.* 1385-*c.* 1479, in *De Laudibus Legum Angliae*; *c.* 1470, praised English over Roman law and introduced the principle of "innocent until proven guilty".
Set up in 1478 by Ferdinand and Isabella with the reluctant permission of the pope, who regarded it as a breach of Church privilege, **the Spanish Inquisition** persecuted converted Jews and Muslims as well as Catholic intellectuals, among them Ignatius de Loyola.

Rodolphus Agricola, *c.* 1443-85, was an early Dutch humanist who influenced Erasmus In his lectures at Heidelberg, given from 1484, he expounded a philosophy emphasizing the freedom of the individual and the intellectual and physical development of the self.
The existence of witchcraft was admitted by the Church in 1484 and its practices condemned. *Malleus Maleficarum*, 1487, described witchcraft and encouraged its suppression.

The French statesman **Phillippe de Comines**, 1445-1509, argued that taxes needed sanction of the Estates-General, the representative body of nobles, gentry and clergy.
With the defeat of the Medicis in Florence, **Savonarola**, 1452-98, established city rule free from corruption and along democratic lines. His sermons criticizing aristocratic and papal corruption led to his death at the stake in 1498.

Bengali literature, which had existed in India since the 10th century, was enriched by the rhymed version of *Ramayana*, made *c.* 1440 by Kirttivasa, *b.* 1385, and by the lyrical *Song of Krishna* by **Chandidas**, 1417-77.
In Spain, the Marquis of Santillana, 1398-1458, wrote Italian-style sonnets that enriched the poetic tradition.

Medieval French verse forms were infused with vigour and blunt realism in the lyrical poetry of **François Villon**, 1430-*c.* 63, in which he recalls his wasted life. He was awaiting execution when he wrote *Ballad of a Hanged Man*.
Diego de San Pedro, *fl.* 1450, was best known for his sentimental novels that influenced the evolution of the Spanish novel.

Scottish poetry flourished with *The Testament of Cresseid* by **Robert Henryson**, *c.* 1425-1508, a tragic and powerful sequel to Chaucer's poem. **William Dunbar**, *c.* 1460-1520, was less earnest but more versatile. His *Dance of the Seven Deadly Synnis* is similar to Villon in its macabre vigour. The Scottish poets combined romance and satire with idiomatic language.

Arthurian legend was unified in the epic prose romance *Morte d'Arthur*, 1469-70, by **Sir Thomas Malory**, *d.* 1471. Its admirably plain style and its creative adaptation of medievalism to modern thought deeply influenced later writers. It was published in 1485 by **William Caxton**, a key figure in the development of English printing, which he began in 1476.

Humanist poetry emerged in Italy where **Luigi Pulci**, 1432-84, treated the heroic Charlemagne theme irreverently in *Morgante*, *c.* 1480. Another Florentine poet, **Angelo Poliziano**, 1454-94, wrote the first secular play *Orfeo*, 1480.
Matteo Maria Boiardo, *c.* 1441-94, wrote Latin eulogies and lyric love poems including his epic *Orlando Inammorato*.

German satirical writing reached the common man in the popular and influential *Ship of Fools*, 1494, by **Sebastian Brant**, 1458-1521, which mocked vice in rhyming couplets.
In Persia, the death of the poet and mystic **Jami**, 1414-92, ended the classical period of Persian Sufi poetry. He was notable for such romantic verse as "Salaman u Absal".

In Italy Domenico Veneziano, *d.* 1461, represented the most advanced stage of mid-century Florentine painting in his "St Lucy" altarpiece, 1445.
Rogier van der Weyden, 1400-64, a major mid-15th century Flemish artist, produced a more emotional style than van Eyck. His great "Deposition" was painted *c.* 1435.
Fra Angelico, *c.* 1387-1455, and **Fra Filippo Lippi**, *c.* 1406-69, both linked Gothic and Renaissance styles.

The study of perspective absorbed **Paolo Uccello**, *c.* 1397-1475, whose famous "Battles", 1454-7, also possess an eerie, dream-like atmosphere.
The frescoes of S. Francesco Arrezzo, 1452, by **Piero della Francesca**, *c.* 1410-92, were outside the mainstream of Italian painting and closer to the diffused naturalism of Flemish art with their mathematical precision and use of light and shade.

Leon Battista Alberti, 1404-72, writer, musician, painter and architect, crystallized Renaissance ideas on architectural proportions and harmonious design. His use of classical elements for the church of San Sebastiano, Mantua, 1470, deprived it of an "ecclesiastical" flavour.
Hans Memling, *c.* 1440-94, a German painter settled in Bruges, was, after 1465, a successful Flemish painter and influenced later Italian art.

The equestrian monument to Bartolomeo Colleone, in Venice, commissioned in 1479 and executed by **Andrea del Verrocchio**, *c.* 1434-88, showed a masterly rendering of movement and a use of light and shade that anticipates Michelangelo.
In Mantua Andrea Mantegna, 1431-1506, painted his fresco "Camera degli Sposi" 1474, and in Florence **Sandro Botticelli**, 1445-1510, produced his "Spring", *c.* 1478, with abstract colours and unreal light.

English Perpendicular Gothic style with its extremely intricate vaulting is seen in the **Divinity School** at Oxford University, completed 1480.
The rebirth of Venetian painting began with **Giovanni Bellini**, *c.* 1430-1516, whose "Madonna and Saints", 1488, has resonant colours and novel lighting.
Medici patronage in Florence produced the first great Renaissance villa, **Poggio a Caiano**, begun *c.* 1482 by **Giuliano da Sangallo**, 1445-1516.

The two giants of the Italian **Renaissance** emerged. **Leonardo da Vinci**, 1452-1519, painted his "Last Supper" in the refectory of Sta Maria delle Grazie, Milan, in 1495-8. His rival **Michelangelo**, 1475-1564, sculpted the St Peter's "Pietà" in 1499 when 24 years old.
Donato Bramante, 1444-1514, one of the greatest architects of the High Renaissance, designed the spacious gallery of **Sta Maria delle Grazie**, Milan, dating from 1492.

The use of the interval of a third (long established in England) standardized harmony in polyphony but the increasing preoccupation with harmony itself led to dull and static rhythms.

National forms evolved in polyphonic song, with the *frottola* in Italy and the *lied* in Germany matching the richness of the established *chanson* in France.

The Franco-Flemish school included Guillaume Dufay, *c.* 1400-74, Jean d'Ockeghem, *c.* 1430-95, and Josquin des Prés, *c.* 1450-1521, who often used popular tunes in his work.

The mass attained a great variety of structure, although the use of the *cantus firmus* throughout, in many ingenious modifications, brought unity to the form.

Keyboard instruments improved in Europe. A Flemish painting of 1484 depicts an organ with a chromatic keyboard. The clavichord (a forerunner of the piano) had a range of up to four octaves.

Music printing began in Germany but was developed fully in Venice by **Ottaviano dei Petrucci**, who patented his process in 1498. His technique led to the birth of music publishing.

Johann Gutenberg, *c.* 1400-68, of Strasbourg, began printing with movable metal type, a process invented in Korea in the 15th century. Gutenberg's books were the first to be printed in this way in the West, yet no printed work bearing his name exists. Letters were cast in type metal, composed into sentences on a type stick and set up as pages of type before being inked for the press. It is possible that Gutenberg designed his press along the lines of wine and linen presses.

Instrument-making in Europe became centred on Nuremberg *c.* 1450, and Augsburg *c.* 1475.
Calendar reform was undertaken *c.* 1450 under the direction of the astronomer **Puerbach**, 1423-61. The Julian calendar, commissioned by Julius Caesar and accurate to 1 day in 128 years, was wrong by 10 days in 1450. However, revision was not finished until 1582.
Quadrants, for determining latitude at sea, were used by European seafarers *c.* 1456.

Carracks, the earliest form of modern sailing ships, are illustrated on a French seal of 1466. These ships had three or four masts, raised decks fore and aft, and a stern rudder and tiller for steering; by 1500 they weighed as much as 600 tonnes. They supplanted the trading galleys for ocean voyages, and a military version followed – the galleon.

Rifles were first made *c.* 1475, according to armoury records in Turin and Nuremberg. These were muzzle loaders, in which the lead bullet was made slightly larger than the bore so that it had to be forced into the barrel, giving a tight fit.
Tables for navigation were revised by the German astronomer **Johann Müller**, 1436-76.

The voyages of Diaz, Vasco da Gama, Columbus and Magellan, in the late 14th and 15th centuries, encouraged the founding of navigation schools in Portugal and Spain. These schools produced a new group of expertly trained mathematical and nautical technicians, which greatly influenced the standing of science in Europe.

Leonardo da Vinci, 1452-1519, painter, sculptor, architect, engineer and scientist, began service as a military engineer with Cesare Borgia, 1476-1507, in 1499. Working mainly in Milan and Florence, his scientific drawings included animal, human and plant anatomy, rocks and optical systems. He also conceived and drew a helicopter, a mobile canal cutter and several kinds of pumps. However, most of his designs were never built, as mechanics lagged behind his inventiveness.

1500-1600 The Reformation

Principal events

The Reformation brought a new dimension to Europe's dynastic wars and social conflicts. As the Italian states declined, Spain, invigorated by wealth from the New World, led the Catholic offensive against England, the Netherlands and the Protestant German princes. Royal authority increased with the decline of papal authority, but the religious and political debates, and the new wealth from confiscation of church lands, enabled an eloquent and powerful middle class to challenge royal power.

European expansion continued. Much of the American coastline and the Far East was reached by all the major powers although only the American civilizations succumbed to the explorers. Japan experienced vigorous expansion and the Moguls brought a stable and flourishing culture to India with the establishment of an extensive empire under Babur and Akbar.

1500-10

The Italian wars provided an opportunity for conflict between the Hapsburgs and the Valois (French kings) until 1559. This caused a decline in the prosperity and autonomy of the Italian cities. **The Portuguese** claimed Brazil and established regular trade with India, 1500. The Spanish introduced African slaves to the West Indies, 1501. **Ashikaga prestige** in Japan was in decline.

1510-20

Russia took Smolensk from Poland in 1514. **Charles V**, 1500-58, created the Hapsburg Empire, inheriting the Spanish crown, 1516, and being proclaimed Holy Roman emperor in 1519. **Ferdinand Magellan**, *c.* 1480-1521, sailed through the Pacific Ocean, 1519-21, and **Hernán Cortés**, 1485-1547, conquered the Aztecs in Mexico, 1519-21. **Portugal** controlled the import of spices from the East Indies *c.* 1520.

1520-30

Portuguese traders reached China, 1520-1. **Frederick III of Saxony**, *r.* 1486-1525, led the princely support for Luther, 1483-1546. **Peasant revolts** in Swabia, inspired by Luther's example and by discontent with feudal obligations, were ruthlessly suppressed in 1525. **Babur**, 1483-1530, founded the brilliant Mogul Empire in north India in 1526. **The Medici** were driven out of Florence in 1527.

1530-40

Protestantism spread throughout northern Europe. **Henry VIII** of England, *r.* 1509-47, dissolved the monasteries, 1536-9. **Francisco Pizarro**, *c.* 1471-1541, a Spaniard, conquered Peru for booty, 1531-6. **The Afghan Sher Khan**, *r.* 1539-45, expelled the Mogul emperor Humayan and reformed the administration. **Suleiman the Magnificent**, *r.* 1520-66, brought Ottoman power to its zenith.

National events

The power of Parliament increased steadily as a series of changes in religious policy and threats from abroad caused the monarchy to rely increasingly on the support of the newly educated gentry class. In the same period, the political power of the nobility began to decline.

Henry VII's thrift made him virtually independent of Parliament, although his methods of taxation such as "Morton's Fork" were unpopular.

Henry VIII, *r.* 1509-47, ruled as a magnificent Renaissance prince, engaging in costly dynastic wars with France until 1520.

Henry's desire for a divorce from Catherine of Aragon was thwarted by political opposition from her nephew the emperor and from the pope, 1525-9.

Henry defied the pope and remarried, 1533. His reliance on Parliament to claim supremacy over the Church greatly increased its prestige.

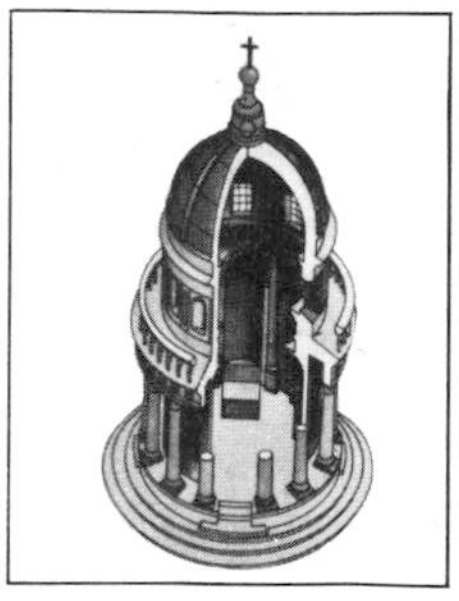

Tempietto of S. Pietro

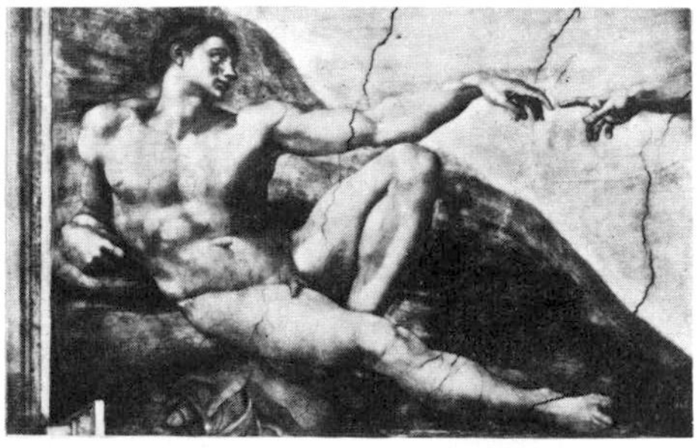

Sistine chapel frescoes: the "Birth of Adam"

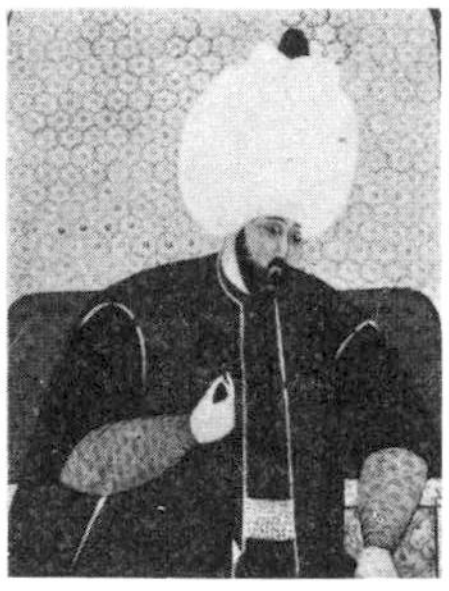

Ottoman Emperor Selim I

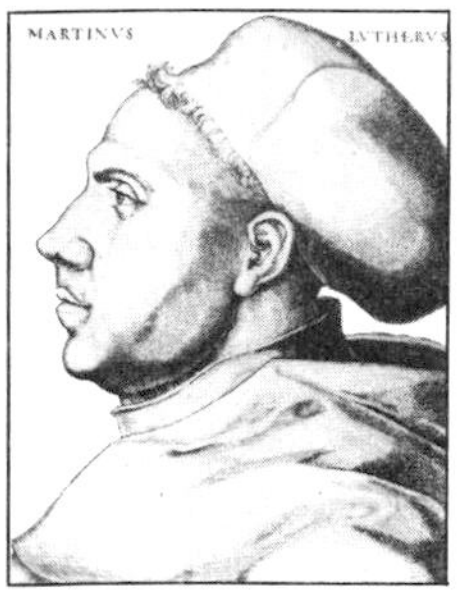

Martin Luther

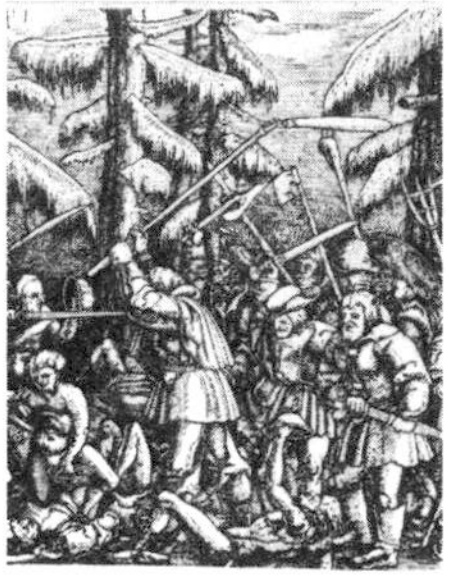

The German Peasants' war

Religion and philosophy

The Protestant Reformation took place in western Europe, arising from objections to many of the doctrines and practices of the medieval Church. Reformers attacked the worldliness of clergy, the stifling of intellectual progress and the inability of the Church to provide spiritual leadership. Luther stated that faith alone was the basis of salvation, believing that no intermediary between man and God could alter his salvation. Calvin in Geneva also rejected the power of his Church to alter who was saved and who damned by God. The general questioning of religious authority gave a new dimension to the already critical question of the relation of Church and state, leading for example in England to rapid changes in official religion. By 1600 the Reformation had spread to almost all of northwest Europe, and there were also large numbers of Protestants in France, Poland and Hungary.

Erasmus, *c.* 1466-1536, a humanist scholar, wrote *In Praise of Folly*, 1509, which satired church corruption and scholastic philosophy.

The ***Utopia***, 1516, of **Thomas More**, *c.* 1478-1535, depicted an imaginary island lacking the evils of Europe. **Machiavelli**, 1469-1527, wrote *The Prince*, 1513, the first ruthlessly pragmatic analysis of politics. **Martin Luther**, 1483-1546, affixed his *95 Theses* to the door of Wittenberg Castle Church in 1517. **Sikhism**, a combination of Hinduism and Islam, was founded *c.* 1519 by **Nanak**, 1469-1533.

Luther was excommunicated in 1520. At the Diet of Worms, 1521, he argued for "justification by faith alone", the doctrine that no intermediary priest can aid salvation. Luther's attacks on the Catholic Church led to a rejection of papal authority and marked the start of the Protestant Reformation. This doctrine was adopted by many princes for its political implications. Luther translated the Bible into the vernacular *c.* 1525.

The Anabaptists, who prophesied the imminent end of the world, gained control of Munster in Germany in 1534. **The Memonites**, a Dutch sect, shared the Anabaptists' belief in pacifism and pastoralism. **In 1534 Henry VIII of England** assumed full authority over the English Church. **Ignatius de Loyola**, 1491-1556, formed the Catholic Jesuit order in 1540.

Literature

The spread of the Renaissance in the sixteenth century brought moments of great brilliance to national literatures, particularly those of England, France, Italy, Spain and Portugal. In England, the work of Wyatt and the Elizabethan poets and dramatists culminated in the genius of Shakespeare, who created a body of lyric poetry and drama of unmatched scope and power. Rabelais and Montaigne dominated French writing and poets such as Ronsard began the move towards classical themes in French literature. Pastoral idealism found expression in the Iberian Peninsula and Italy, and epic poetry flourished.

In China the novel form emerged and, in both India and Turkey, Islamic influence revitalized literary traditions.

Commedia dell'arte developed from earlier peasant traditions in Italy. Actors improvised farce from a set scenario using stock characters such as Pedrillo, who became the French Pierrot, and the stupid but agile Harlequin. This boisterous form of theatre had little literary merit but influenced later drama, especially the comedies of **Molière** in France.

The Portuguese dramatist **Gil Vicente**, 1470-1536, wrote naturalistic plays, full of intrigue and psychological insight. The innovate English poet and humanist **John Skelton**, 1460-1529, wrote scathing attacks on the court and clergy. His German contemporary **Ulrich von Hutten**, 1488-1523, used dialogues to champion the cause of the Reformation.

Italian court life and etiquette were vividly portrayed in the *Libro del Cortegiano*, 1528, by **Baldassare Castiglione**, 1478-1529. **Portuguese poetry** reached its peak with the epic *The Lusiads*, 1572, by **Luis Camoes**, *c.* 1524-80.

Ludovico Ariosto, 1474-1533, poet, dramatist and satirist, published *Orlando Furioso*, 1532, the greatest Italian epic of romantic chivalry. **Meistersang**, a form of poetic song based on minstrel tradition, was popular in Germany. It was enlivened by the work of the devout Lutheran poet **Hans Sachs**, 1494-1576, a cobbler with a talent for comic verse.

Art and architecture

With the work of Michelangelo, Leonardo, Raphael and Bramante in the early 16th century, Italian Renaissance art reached a climax in the development of perspective, the analysis of the human form and the celebration of classical models. By 1520, however, this peak was past. Mannerism followed with its lack of harmony, distorted forms and search for novelty. Later in the century, the naturalistic experiments of Caravaggio, and Carracci's reassertion of classical canons in new dramatic compositions, pointed towards a new style – Baroque. Italy remained the official arbiter of taste in Europe, but the styles were more readily absorbed by the still solidly Catholic France and Spain. In the Protestant north the Reformation replaced Church patronage with that of merchants, encouraging the growth of secular art forms. Exploration in the New World carried European art abroad.

The Renaissance reached its height in Florence and Rome *c.* 1500-20. **Leonardo da Vinci**, 1452-1519, painted the "Mona Lisa", 1503-6, achieving a more naturalistic effect by leaving outlines blurred. **Michelangelo**, 1475-1564, also in Florence at this time, completed the statue of "David", 1504. **Donato Bramante**, 1444-1514, built the Tempietto of S. Pietro, Rome, 1502, and was invited by Pope Julius II to design the new St. Peter's, 1506.

Michelangelo in Rome completed the Sistine Chapel frescoes, 1512, and **Raphael**, 1483-1520, the Stanza frescoes in 1514, with their dazzling use of perspective. **Leonardo** left for Amboise, France, 1516. **English Gothic art** in its final stage was seen in Henry VII's Westminster Chapel, 1503-19. His tomb in the chapel by **Torrigiano**, 1472-1528, was the first use of Italian Renaissance motifs in England.

German painting showed two trends: **Grunewald**, 1480-1528, painted the Isenheim altarpiece, *c.* 1512-16, in the late Gothic style but **Dürer**, 1471-1528, who had visited Italy, made use of Rennaissance ideals in his "Four Apostles", 1526. **Venetian painting** broke from the Renaissance emphasis on drawing and perfect form. The Pesaro altarpiece, 1519-26, by **Titian**, *c.* 1487-1576, used a dramatic juxtaposition of contrasting colours and diagonals.

The Reformation had interrupted patronage in Basel and forced **Hans Holbein**, 1497-1543, to seek work in England, where he arrived in 1526 with a letter of introduction from Erasmus to Sir Thomas More. After 1532 he settled there and painted court portraits. **The Wu school** in China, including **Wen Cheng-ming**, 1470-1559, and **T'ang Yin**, 1470-1523, worked away from the Imperial Academy, painting ink landscapes with genre scenes.

Music

The growing Protestant Church in Europe redefined the liturgy for its own use and sacred music began to be performed by lay people in church and in their homes, widening the basis of religious music. City councils and individual patrons established their own groups of musicians, raising instrumental music to the same status as choral music.

The single or solo line drew the interest of composers of the early 1500s, reacting to the increasing complexity of polyphony. Their interest is seen in their airs and lute songs.

The fantasia, toccata and variations and the ricercar (forerunner of the fugue) were new instrumental forms devised to exploit the individual qualities of musical instruments.

German hymns or chorales were composed in the 1520s and were firmly established by the end of the century. Set in four or five parts, they were often written to existing popular tunes.

Consorts of instruments (viols or recorders) were cultural perquisites found in many wealthy homes. Families of instruments were usually played separately to give euphonious sonorities.

Science

A scientific revolution began in Europe in the 16th century and with it a long-held conception of the nature of the universe died. The century began with the later work of Leonardo da Vinci – a series of brilliant inventions which came to little because the scientific principles needed to realize them were hardly known – and culminated in Kepler's exact scientific calculations, based on Copernicus' idea of a Sun-centred universe and the precise astronomical observations of Tycho Brahe. This work finally destroyed the Aristotelian picture of the universe as a group of perfect crystal spheres centring on, and revolving about, the Earth, and opened the way for Galileo.

Advances were also made in medical science, particularly in anatomy, chemistry, larger-scale iron production and mining technology. Despite opposition from the Church, by 1600 science was firmly based on the experimental method and had turned its back on theology.

T.B. von Hohenheim Paracelsus, *c.* 1493-1541, professor of medicine at Basel, made advances in chemistry although his system of iatrochemistry (chemical doctoring) was a mixture of observed fact and superstition. **The coach** was invented in Hungary, probably in the early 16th century, and appeared in England in the 1580s. **Dissection** of the human cadaver has been practised for a century in Europe but systematic dissections in the schools of Padua, date from the early 16th century.

Coins containing copper mixed with gold or silver came into use in Europe in the early 16th century as a result of the great increase in prices caused in part by large imports of Spanish silver from Peru. **Henry VIII of England**, *r.* 1509-47, in particular, debased the currency in this way. Although later recoinage partly improved the real value of money, alloying became the rule. **A mass production technique** for casting small brass objects was practised in Italy at this time.

Blast furnaces, able to produce large quantities of cast iron, gradually evolved from earlier Stückofen. Cast iron so made was mostly used in weaponry, an industry in which England led Europe, selling to any customer who could pay the price, whether friend or enemy. **Coal** became a major fuel in mid-16th century industrial Europe as the price of wood soared and forests disappeared. Coal mines opened in Liège and Newcastle.

Telesio, an Italian who lived 1509-88, proposed the first system of physics to rival Aristotle's. His theory argued that heat and cold were the motive powers of the universe, an idea which influenced the work of the English philosopher **Francis Bacon**, 1561-1626. **Andreas Vesalius**, 1514-64, advanced knowledge of internal anatomy in his book *De Humani Corporis Fabrica*, 1543. He accepted the chair of anatomy in Padua, 1537, and shocked the Church by dissecting corpses.

1540-50

Jean Calvin, 1509-64, established a puritan theocracy at Geneva in 1541.
The Catholic Counter-Reformation inspired Charles V to conduct the Schmalkaldic War, 1546-7, against the Protestant princes.
Brittany was united with France in 1547.
The Portuguese were the first Europeans in Japan, 1542, where the Jesuit **Francis Xavier**, 1506-52, founded a mission in 1549.

The sale of the monastic lands encouraged the rise of the middle gentry class. Inflation was accelerated by debased coinage and hit the poorest classes.

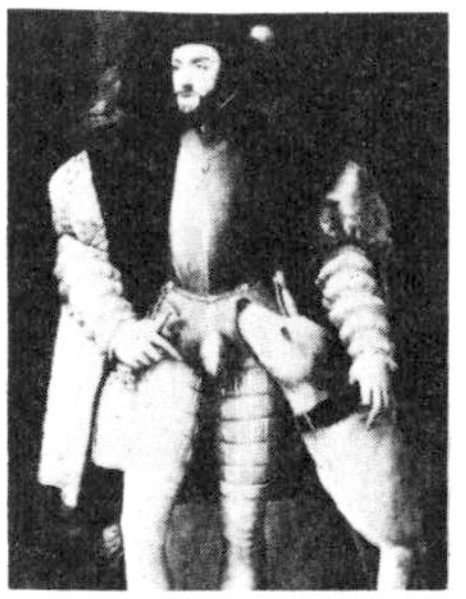

"Charles V" by Titian

Jean Calvin 1509-64, promoted the Reformation in Geneva, 1541. He espoused the doctrine of predestination – that God had already elected those to be saved but it was believed that exemplary conduct signified election.
Decrees issued by the Council of Trent on Church reform in 1545, initiated the Catholic, or Counter, Reformation.
Thomas Cranmer, 1489-1556, issued the Church of England's *Book of Common Prayer*, 1549.

La Pléiade, a group of seven French poets, of whom the greatest was **Pierre de Ronsard**, 1524-85, established the Alexandrine metre of a 12-syllable line and emphasized the dignity of the French language while turning to classical themes. Their manifesto was written by **Joachim du Bellay**, 1522-60, in *Défense et Illustration de la Langue Française*, 1549.

French Renaissance art copied Italian models as the painters **Rosso**, 1494-1540, and **Primaticcio**, 1504-*c*. 70, and the architects **Vignola**, 1507-73, and **Serlio**, 1475-1554, came to France to work on the Palace of Fontainebleau, 1528-60.
Mannerist painting in Italy, like the "Madonna with the Long Neck", 1534-6, by **Girolamo Parmigianino**, 1503-40, shows an elongation of figures, lack of harmony and a search for the new and unusual.

The lute became popular as an accompanying instrument. It could be used to accompany the new contrapuntal madrigal style that grew up in Italy after 1530. Later, the English adopted it.

A Sun-centred universe was proposed in the book *De Revolutionibus Orbium Caelestium* by **Nicolas Copernicus**, 1473-1543, published in the year of his death. In this revolutionary work, the Earth, Moon and planets, and outside them the stars, orbited around the Sun in circles. This theory is the basis of modern cosmology.
Zoological and botanical works were published in the mid-16th century by the French biologists **Gesner**, 1516-65, **Belon**, 1517-64, and **Rondelet**, 1507-66.

1550-60

The Peace of Augsburg, 1555, permitted each German prince to decide the religion of his subjects
After Charles V's abdication in 1556, **Philip II of Spain**, *r*. 1556-98, took over the Catholic offensive, while **Elizabeth I**, *r*. 1558-1603, confirmed England's Protestantism.
The influx of American silver to Spain accelerated inflation and caused hardship to the poor, but encouraged the rise of a European middle class.

Edward VI, *r*. 1547-53, faced peasant risings, 1549-50, and introduced a Protestant prayer book. **Mary**, *r*. 1553-8, restored Catholicism, burning heretics.

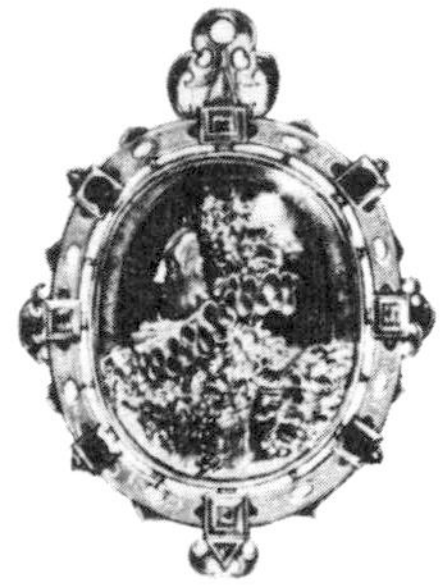

Elizabeth I: Armada jewel

Many English Protestant bishops, including Cranmer, were burned at the stake in the reign of Queen Mary. Elizabeth, her successor, re-established the Protestant Church but continued to burn heretics.
The Holy Roman Empire acknowledged Lutheranism in the Peace of Augsburg, 1555.
Protestantism in Scotland was united by the Calvinist **John Knox**, 1513-72, and became the national faith by Act of Parliament in 1560.

One of the great comic prose works of world literature, *Gargantua and Pantagruel* was completed in 1552 by **Francois Rabelais**, *c*. 1494-*c*. 1553. This bawdy, satirical tale of two grotesque giants was an erudite allegory vigorously attacking established institutions and conventional wisdom, mocking superstitious fears and defending free will.

The historian and painter **Vasari**, 1511-74, published the *Lives of the most excellent Painters, Sculptors and Architects* in 1550. **Palladio**, 1508-80, designed the Villa Rotunda, Vicenza, *c*. 1550, beginning work *c*. 1566. With its four porticoes and symmetrical plan, it is an example of his search for classical and harmonious proportions. **Benin bronze figures** of West Africa adopted freer poses as a result of contact with Portuguese culture.

Sacred polyphony declined in influence after the Council of Trent, 1545-63, regularized the musical forms suitable for the mass of the Roman Catholic Church.

Georg Bauer (Agricola), 1494-1555, a German doctor, gave a full description of mining, smelting and chemistry in *De Re Metallica*, published at Basel in 1556. Agricola's book is still the major source on the state of technology in the later Middle Ages.
Discoveries of metals in the 16th century included that of mercury, *c*. 1550, in Peru. Zinc, bismuth, cobalt and nickel were other metals used in alloys or mixtures.

1560-70

The French wars of religion began, 1562, between the Catholics and the Protestant Huguenots (mostly nobles and townsmen in west and south France).
The Calvinist and predominantly mercantile Dutch provinces began a long war of independence from Spain, 1568.
Nobunaga, 1534-82, introduced a dynamic period of Japanese centralization and expansion.
Akbar, *r*. 1556-1605, expanded the Mogul Empire and created a tolerant cosmopolitan culture.

Under Elizabeth I, *r*. 1558-1603, Protestantism was reinstated. The Statute of Apprentices marked the end of the authority of trade guilds.

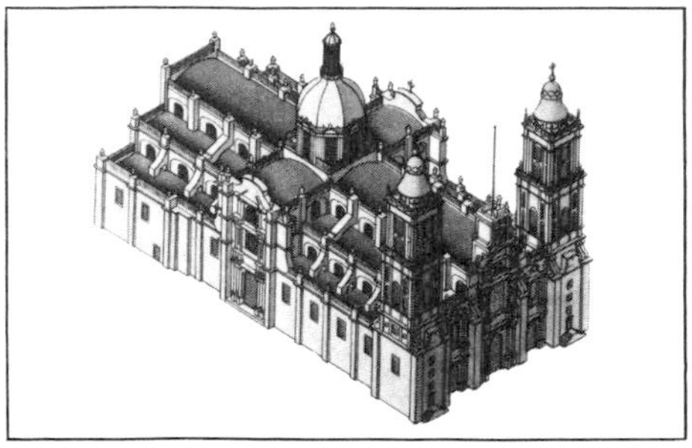

Renaissance Mexico city cathedral

The adoption of the 39 Articles in 1563, combining Protestant doctrine with Catholic church organization, finally established the Church of England. There were many dissenting groups, among them the Puritans, who opposed church ritual, the Separatists, who rejected Anglicanism entirely, the Presbyterians, who had synods instead of bishops, and the Brownists, a communistic sect. All but the Brownists and Catholics were tolerated.

The English poets **Thomas Wyatt**, 1503-42, and the **Earl of Surrey**, *c*. 1517-47, wrote in sonnets and blank verse – forms perfected by the Elizabethan poets **Shakespeare, Walter Raleigh**, 1552-1618, and **Edmund Spenser**, 1552-99.

Flemish painting saw the emergence of the individualist **Pieter Bruegel the Elder**, *c*. 1520-69, one of the greatest landscape painters and a remarkable satirist, whose series "The Months" dates from 1565.
Indian Mogul art assimilated the Persian tradition of miniature painting, which emphasized sumptuous decoration and lively colour patterns. This was combined with indigenous styles in the illustrations of Akbar's life in the *Akbar-nama*.

Japanese music began to win its individual character with the popularization of national forms of vertical bamboo pipe *(shakuhachi)*, three-stringed guitar *(samisen)* and zither *(koto)*.

Letter symbols for algebra and trigonometry were pioneered by **Vieta**, a French mathematician, 1540-1603. Words had previously been used for variables; the substitution of letters such as *x* and *y* greatly speeded up calculations and also removed many previous ambiguities.
Gerhard Kremer Mercator, 1512-94, published a map, 1568, using a projection of the world that has since borne his name.
The potato was introduced to Europe from South America by the Spaniards *c*. 1570.

1570-80

A European alliance defeated the Ottoman fleet at **Lepanto** in 1571, but Venice failed to use the opportunity to regain control of the eastern Mediterranean.
The Portuguese began their settlement of Angola, 1574.
The Dutch provinces, with increasing involvement in trade outside Europe, united in opposition to Spain, 1579.
Drake, *c*. 1540-96, an Englishman, circumnavigated the world, 1577-80.

Calvinists frequently attacked Elizabeth's religious policy in Parliament.
The Dutch wars upset English trade in the Low Countries.

Jean Bodin, 1530-96, a major French political theorist, published his *Six Books of the Commonwealth* in 1576, arguing that the basis of any society was the family. His most important contribution was an analysis of sovereignty. He argued that in any state sovereignty was necessary to prevent anarchy and that the exercise of monarchical power in conformity with the natural law was unquestionable, as it had divine authorization.

Michel de Montaigne, 1533-92, began his *Essays* in 1580.
In China the realistic, erotic novel the *The Golden Lotus* was published *c*. 1575.
John Lyly, *c*. 1554-1606, wrote *Euphues*, 1578-80, an early novel of manners.
Torquato Tasso, 1544-95, published *Jerusalem Liberated* in 1575 and the pastoral romance *Aminta* in 1573.

The brilliant Monoyama period in Japan, 1573-1615, is seen in the castle at Azuchi, built for **Nobunaga**, 1576-9, which contained large rooms decorated with murals. Screens painted with strong colours on gold ground came into fashion.
Spanish colonial architecture in the late 16th century, like Mexico Cathedral, 1563-1667, was based on contemporary Spanish mannerist styles but derived a pre-Columbian flavour from the native Indian labour.

Javanese fleeing the spread of Islam reached Bali and kept early traditions of Indonesian music in the works for the gamelan orchestra (mostly tuned percussion instruments).

Sir Thomas Gresham, 1519-79, established by will the first British institute for teaching science, which later housed the Royal Society.
Chinese pharmacology was summed up by **Li Shih-Chen** in his *Great Pharmacopoeia*, 1578. Chinese medicine was completely conservative and few new treatments were reported.

1580-90

Portugal and Spain were united on the death of Philip I of Portugal, 1580.
England assisted the Dutch revolt in 1585, executed the Catholic **Mary, Queen of Scots** in 1587 and defeated the **Spanish Armada** in 1588.
Pope Sixtus V, *r*. 1585-90, a supporter of the Counter-Reformation, began the internal reform of the papacy.
Hideyoshi, *r*. 1584-98, expelled the Portuguese missionaries in 1587.

War was declared with Spain in 1587. A newly constructed English fleet defeated an invasion by the Spanish Armada, 1588.

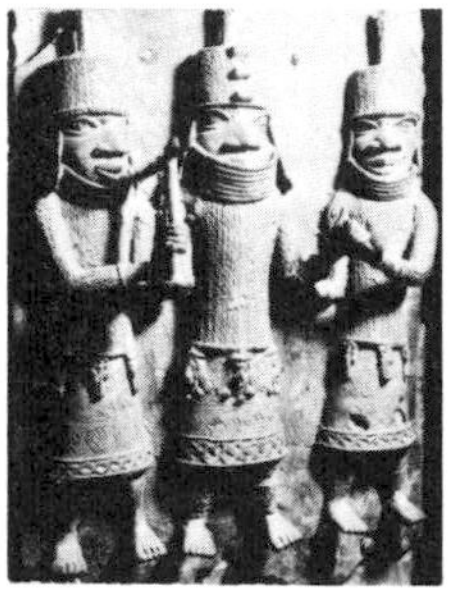

Benin bronzes, 16thc.

Akbar, the greatest Mogul emperor of India, *r*. 1556-1605, attempted to establish "**Din Illahl**" as a universal religion acceptable to his many Hindu subjects. Vegetarianism and other Hindu practices were supported by Akbar. Although the Din Illahl movement was influential for some time after Akbar's death it was discouraged by **Emperor Aurungzebe**, *r*. 1658-1707, and eventually collapsed under the 18th-century Muslim revival.

English drama entered its great period. **Christopher Marlowe**, 1564-93, in his *Dr Faustus*, *c*. 1588, perfected the blank verse of *The Spanish Tragedy* by **Thomas Kyd**, 1558-94.
Sir Philip Sidney, 1554-86, in his verse-prose *Arcadia*, 1590, drew on a tradition of pastoral romance established in Spain by **Jorge de Montemayor**, *c*. 1520-61, in his *Diana*.

English court portraiture and domestic architecture was given impetus by the Reformation.
Longleat, Wilts., 1567-80, was a house built in the rectangular style with large expanses of windows by **Smythson**, *c*. 1536-1614.
The Mannerist style emphasizing the bizarre and the tortuous spread through Europe; to Spain with **El Greco**, 1541-1614, to Germany in the works of artists like **Spranger**, 1546-1611, and to France with the second **Fontainebleau School.**

Equal temperament (based on equal half-tone divisions) was proposed by Prince Tsai-Yu in his *Handbook of Music*. It predated the West's recognition of its importance to harmony.

Decimals were introduced to mathematical calculations in physics by **Simon Stevin**, 1585.
Tycho Brahe, 1546-1601, and his assistant **Johannes Kepler**, 1571-1630, extended Copernican theory. Brahe made accurate observations of planetary movements. Using these results, Kepler calculated the actual orbits of the planets, which he found to be ellipses and not perfect circles. Kepler's results established astronomy as an observational science, free from any religious considerations.

1590-1600

Henry IV, *r*. 1589-1610, ended the French wars of religion and granted equal rights to Catholics and Huguenots in the **Edict of Nantes**, 1598.
The Dutch took over much of Portugal's former trade with the East Indies, 1595.
Japan invaded Korea, 1592-3 and 1597-8, but was expelled by the Chinese.
Spanish power gradually declined owing to the stagnation of her internal economy and the lack of a middle class.

Economic depression and the need for taxation to pay for the war with Spain served to make Elizabeth increasingly dependent on Parliament.

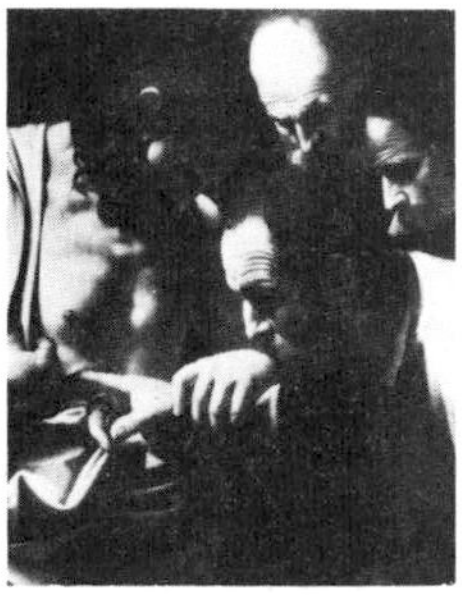

Work by Caravaggio

A Protestant movement, opposed to Calvinism, grew up in the United Provinces, denying the doctrine of predestination and arguing for religious tolerance. The movement came to be called **Arminianism**, after **Jacobus Arminius**, 1560-1609, who defended the Arminians in a controversy with his colleague **Gomarus.**
The Edict of Nantes, 1598, granted liberty of worship to the Huguenots, the French Protestant sect.

William Shakespeare, 1564-1616, consummate master of the English language, began *c*. 1591 to produce a stream of historical dramas and comedies revealing a remarkable range of human experience and thought. By 1600 he had written some 20 plays, including the comedies *As You Like It* and *A Midsummer Night's Dream* and the romantic tragedy *Romeo and Juliet*.

The precursors of Italian baroque painting were radically opposed to each other. "The Loves of the Gods", 1597, in the Palazzo Farnese by **Annibale Carracci**, 1560-1609, returned to the classical ideals, but with an emotional, anecdotal appeal and complex composition. "Doubting Thomas", *c*. 1600, by **Caravaggio**, 1571-1610, introduced a vivid realism and simplicity seen in the portrayal of Christ and the Apostles as ordinary men.

Sonata Pian'e Forte, 1597, by Giovanni Gabrielli, 1557-1612, was composed for two consorts, the first ensemble piece in which instrumentation was specified. It also used changes of volume.

Galileo, 1564-1642, wrote in 1597 stating his agreement with the Copernican system. Three years later, **Giordano Bruno** was burned by the Inquisition as a heretic for propagating the same idea.

1600-1660 Galileo and the new science

Principal events

The political and religious tensions generated by the Reformation in the previous century were brought to a head in the Thirty Years War, which involved most of the European powers and left the Holy Roman Empire in particular devastated from constant military activity. Although England remained out of the war, the same conflicts over religion and constitutional authority led to the execution of Charles I in 1649, but the establishment of the Commonwealth proved no solution.

Colonial trade expanded throughout the world bringing skirmishes and trade wars in India, America and Europe as the European powers jostled for supremacy, regarding control of trade as a tangible form of political power.

In China the Manchu dynasty brought strength and prosperity, while Japan withdrew into isolation after experiencing the disruptive impact of Christianity and European trade.

1600-6

Power struggles in Japan resulted in the Tokugawa (Edo) period, 1603, which advanced education and economic growth. **Charles IX**, *r.* 1604-11, a Protestant, succeeded to the Swedish throne after the deposition of his Catholic predecessor.
A period of anarchy in Russia resulting from rivalry between the boyars (nobility) began under **Boris Godunov**, *r.* 1598-1605, who was opposed by a pretender, the false **Dmitry.**

1606-12

In Japan the Tokugawa introduced **Confucianism** as the official religion, 1608, and Dutch traders arrived, 1609, rivalling the Spanish and Portuguese in the Far East.
The settlement of the French wars of religion was threatened by the murder of **Henry IV**, *r.* 1589-1610.

1612-18

The influence of the English East India Company extended to India, ousting the Portuguese as a rival to the Dutch.
Persecution of Christianity began in Japan, 1612, although trade with Europe increased.
The accession of Mikhail Romanov, *r.* 1613-45, in Russia established royal authority by ending local autonomy and strengthening serfdom.
A group of Tungus tribes in Manchuria grew powerful under **Nurhachi**, 1615-16.

1618-24

The Thirty Years War began in 1618 after a nationalist and Protestant revolt in Bohemia. By 1619 **Emperor Ferdinand**, *r.* 1619-37, had restored Catholicism in Bohemia.
Spanish troops invaded the Protestant Palatinate to ensure a route to the Netherlands.
The Pilgrim Fathers landed in North America in 1620.
Batavia was established by the Dutch as the centre of their Eastern spice trade, 1619.

National events

The Protestant gentry objected to the Stuart kings' claim to rule by divine right, and to the use of feudal levies to circumvent Parliamentary control over royal expenditure. Civil war followed and, after the execution of Charles I, Cromwell set up a shortlived Puritan Commonwealth.

The Gunpowder Plot, 1605, was a Catholic attempt to blow up the Houses of Parliament.
James I, *r.* 1603-25, ended the war with Spain in 1604.

James I encouraged colonial development in North America.
A regular financial grant to the king was discussed in Parliament but was never agreed.

Walter Raleigh, 1552-1618, was executed to placate Spain after the failure of his expedition in search of El Dorado.

Edward Coke, 1552-1634, supported the common law against absolute monarchy.
Francis Bacon was impeached for corruption, 1621.

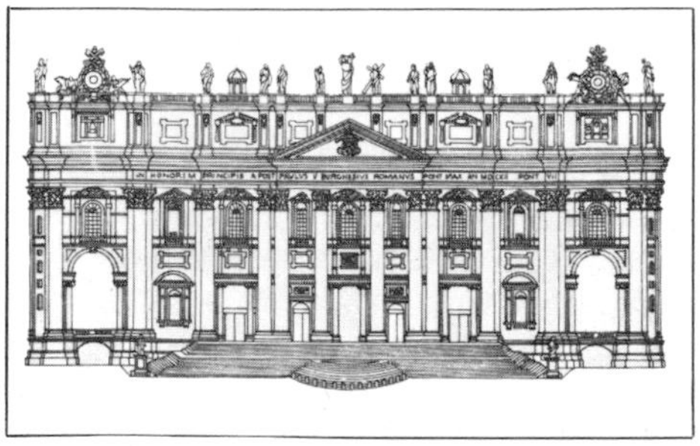

Baroque: façade of St. Peter's Rome by Maderna

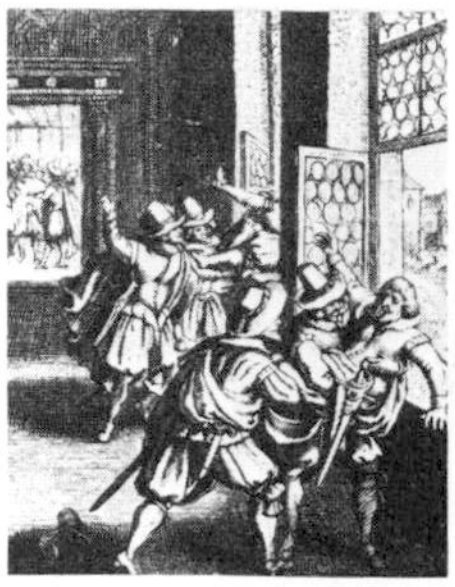

Defenestration of Prague

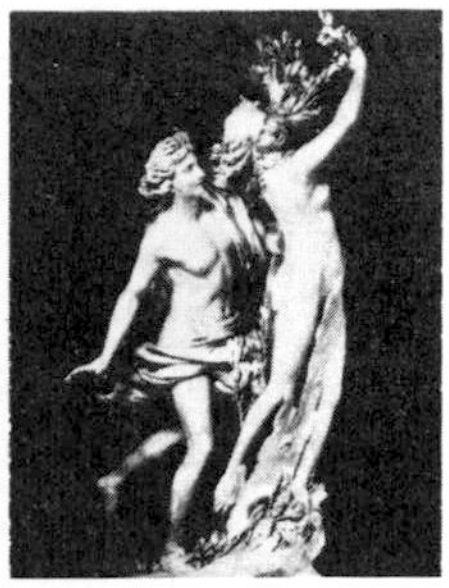

"Apollo and Daphne"

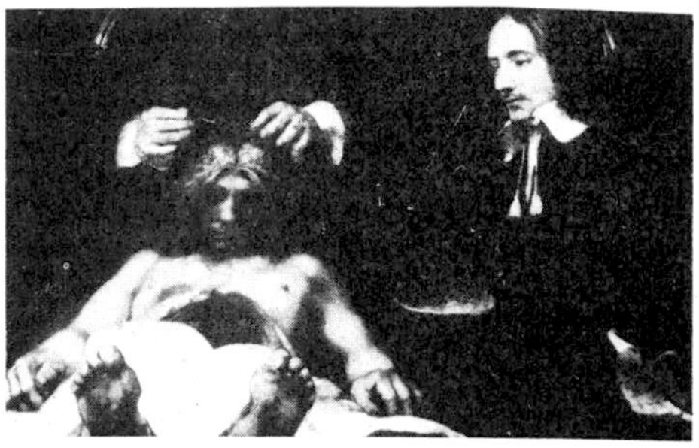

"The Anatomy Lesson" by Rembrandt

Religion and philosophy

As the basic assumptions and methodology of the natural sciences underwent a dramatic change with Galileo's suggestion that the workings of natural phenomena could be described exactly, philosophical and religious thought was also transformed. Theories of society based on the natural condition of man were common and resulted in the concept of the social contract, which could be renounced if the ruler rejected his duties to his subjects. Such ideas were used to justify widespread political revolts.

Descartes and Hobbes laid the foundations of modern philosophy by attempting to return to first principles, using only scientific or mathematical tools, and the same reliance on reason brought the beginnings of Deism, which would become popular in the 18th century.

In England in the Civil War, utopian ideas linking political and religious aims abounded.

Faustus Socinus, 1539-1604, in Poland, argued that Christ, though sinless, was not divine. He inspired the **Polish Unitarian movement**, which denied the existence of the Holy Trinity.
Johannes Althusius, 1557-1638, a Dutch Calvinist, said in 1603 that voluntary agreement should be the basis of political association. He advocated federalism and republican government.
The Tung-lin Academy, founded in China, 1604, revived Confucianism and attacked graft.

John Dee, 1527-1608, Elizabeth of England's astrologer, helped to revive interest in mathematics in England. As a magician and scientist he was a leading representative of the Hermetic tradition of alchemical study. This tradition, which sought to establish mystical connection among empirical phenomena with the help of experimentation, influenced the Cambridge Platonists and the development of Newtonian science.

Francisco Suarez, 1548-1617, a Spanish Jesuit, argued in *On Laws*, 1612, that a contract between ruler and subject was the basis of sovereignty. He hoped to refute James I of England's claim to rule by divine right.
The Dutch rejected Arminianism at the Synod of Dort, 1618. But after the publication of Arminius' works in 1629, they were granted freedom of worship in the United Provinces.

Francis Bacon, 1561-1626, elaborated a sophisticated method of establishing scientific truths, using observation and experiment to test hypotheses, in *Novum Organum*, 1620. He argued for the usefulness of scientific knowledge in giving man mastery over nature and conceived a scientific Utopia in *The New Atlantis*, 1627, a book that foreshadowed later developments in mid-17th century scientific thought.

Literature

The Elizabethan age in English literature culminated in the later work of William Shakespeare whose plays and sonnets epitomize the innovation and humanism of the Renaissance, while in Spain Cervantes wrote his picaresque *Don Quixote*. As the century wore on the religious and political conflicts between Royalists and Puritans were reflected in English literature with the poetry of Marvell and the genius of Milton.

In France an effort to systematize the rules of language and literature was made by the newly founded Académie Française, which would stand until the 19th century, and an interest in classical models produced the tightly organized psychological dramas of Corneille and the accomplished verse of Malherbe.

Miguel de Cervantes, 1547-1616, blended and transcended the realistic and idealistic veins of Spanish prose writing in *Don Quixote*, published in two parts in 1605 and 1615. Its satirical theme of an amiable landowner who fancies himself an adventurous knight had a universality and a delicate juxtaposition of humour and sadness that influenced many later novelists.

Ben Jonson, *c.* 1572-1637, poet, critic and playwright, wrote *Volpone*, 1607, *The Alchemist*, 1610, and other comedies notable for their honesty. Other English dramatists were **John Webster**, 1580-1625, with *The White Devil*, 1608, **Thomas Middleton**, 1570-1627, **Thomas Dekker**, *c.* 1570-*c.* 1632, and the prolific **Francis Beaumont** and **John Fletcher**, *fl.* 1606-16.

Shakespeare's profound tragedies, including *Hamlet*, *Lear* and *Othello*, dealt with heroes trapped as much by the human condition as by their individual flaws of character. In 1608 he began writing his last, enigmatic plays, in which a spirit of reconciliation appears, among them *The Tempest*, *c.* 1612. His *Sonnets*, were printed in 1609.

The English metaphysical poets, who included **George Herbert**, 1593-1633, explored the unity of flesh and spirit in a style that influenced modern poetry. Erudition, wit, reason and passion were best combined in the devotional and love poems of **John Donne**, 1572-1631, (*Anniversaries*), who as Dean of St Paul's from 1621 preached a series of fine sermons.

Art and architecture

Baroque art emerged in Italy in the 1600s and reached its peak in the mid-17th century in the works of Bernini, Pietro da Cortona and Borromini. Its stylistic emphasis was on unity of composition, so that the parts were subordinate to the whole, an effect most expertly achieved in sculpture and architecture. Throughout the 17th century, Baroque spread from its basically Roman origins to Catholic Europe but had least influence in northern Protestant countries in spite of the achievement of Rubens and Van Dyck.

Bourgeois Dutch art flourished during the long war of independence from Spain, while native English painting was relatively unaffected by European developments, although Charles I patronised many continental artists. In France the tradition of rationalism produced the restrained classicism of Poussin and Claude.

Indian art flourished at the height of Mogul power.

Parisian town planning, like the Place Royale, 1605, with its smaller terraced houses, was the result of Henry IV's policy to support the new merchant classes and improve traffic circulation.
Painting in China within the traditional schools was dominated by literati and theorists, like **Tung Ch'i-ch'ang**, 1555-1636, who, in his "Dwelling in the Ch'ing-pien Mountains", emphasized the spiritual message of landscape.

Art and architecture in Mogul India reached its greatest achievement during the reigns of **Jahangir**, *r.* 1605-27, and **Shah Jehan**, *r.* 1628-58. Painting was characterized by the realism and vigour of Jahangir's picture albums, which were primarily portraits and depictions of the hunt. **The Taj Mahal**, 1632-43, the most renowned structure in India, was built by Shah Jehan as a mausoleum for his dead wife.

Italian baroque painting was dominated by the influence of the Carracci and Caravaggio. **Guido Reni**, 1575-1642, painted "Aurora", 1613, in the Carracci style. In Flanders, **Peter Paul Rubens**, 1577-1640, shows the influence of Caravaggio in his work "Descent from the Cross", 1611-14.
Palladian architecture was introduced to England by **Inigo Jones**, 1573-1652, whose Queen's House, Greenwich, 1616, is thoroughly classical.

The baroque style was epitomized in the magnificent sculptures of **Gianlorenzo Bernini**, 1598-1680, whose "Apollo and Daphne", 1622-5, established him as the greatest sculptor since Michelangelo.
Reality, allegory and myth are combined in one of **Rubens** masterpieces, the gigantic Medici cycle painted for the Luxembourg Palace, Paris, 1622-5.

Music

Many of the forms of music current today had their beginnings in 17th-century Europe. The suite was developing to provide the basis of the later sonata, and opera and ballet were evolving from court entertainments. Italy was the centre of the stage, and interest in the solo line pressed forward the development of a new style of madrigal and fine singing styles.

Dances for lutes and consorts became popular, providing musical forms such as the *pavane*, *galliard*, *allemande* and *gavotte*, which were later gathered into composite pieces called suites.

La Favola d'Orfeo, 1607, by Claudio Monteverdi, 1567-1643, is the earliest European opera extant. The form arose from a search for a new way to express the ideals of classical drama.

The violin made its orchestral appearance in the *Vingt-quatre violons du roi*, set up by Louis XIII, *r.* 1610-43, as a court band. Later, bands of several consorts had up to 35 players.

Figured bass developed in Italian lute songs. Beneath the melody was written a base line with figures and signs to indicate the harmony of the inner parts without writing chords in full.

Science and technology

Religious dissent marked this period in Europe and from it rose the beginnings of modern science. The century was only a few weeks old when the Italian Giordano Bruno was burnt at the stake for heresy. He had conceived of the universe as infinite in time and space and filled with a multitude of suns each bearing planets, everything being in constant motion. His views were a major threat to orthodox theology at a time when the Catholic Church was threatened by the Reformation. Bruno's death probably persuaded Galileo, another Italian, to retract his belief that the Earth moves, and helped to shift the scene of progress towards the Protestant countries of Northern Europe.

The concept of scientific method was established and practical endeavour stimulated invention and enquiry. For example, the pumps required to clear water from mines prompted the investigation of air pressure and helped understanding of the heart's action.

De Magnete, a study of magnetism and electricity, was published in 1600 by an Englishman, **William Gilbert**, 1504-1603. He suggested that the Earth was a giant magnet with its own magnetic field.
Galileo Galilei, 1564-1642, studied the motions of falling bodies and discovered that they accelerated constantly towards the Earth. Galileo, the father of experimental science, drew conclusions from observation and experiment only without theological speculations.

The telescope was invented by the Dutchman Hans Lippershey, *c.* 1570-1619, in 1608.
Astronomia Nova, published in 1609 by Johannes Kepler, 1571-1630, argued that the planets moved around the Sun in ellipses and at varying speeds.
The moons of Jupiter and phases of Venus were discovered by Galileo in 1610.

The Art of Glass Making, 1612, by the Italian Antonio Neri, was one of many handbooks that helped the spread of technology.
John Napier, 1550-1617, introduced logarithms in 1614. Logarithmic tables prepared by **Henry Briggs**, 1561-1631, greatly facilitated their use.
Sanctorius, 1561-1636, founded the study of metabolism with his *De Medicina Statica*, 1614. He weighed himself over thirty years, recording changes in weight, pulse and temperature.

Harmonice Mundi, 1619, by Kepler, returned to the ancient concept of the harmony of the spheres in trying to find a relationship between music and astronomy. This work nevertheless contained a third law of planetary motion.
Francis Bacon published *Novum Organum*, 1620, in which theories are drawn from hypothesis and tested by observation and experiment.

1624-30

England, the United Provinces, Denmark and France allied against the Hapsburgs, 1625.
In France, Richelieu, 1585-1642, rebuilt royal power, attacking the Huguenots, 1628.
French settlements in the West Indies began in 1625, exporting sugar and tobacco, and emigration to Canada was encouraged among traders and fishermen.
The Tungus Manchus overran Korea, ousting the Ming dynasty from the Liao Basin, 1627.

1630-36

The Dutch East India Company seized part of Brazil for its sugar and silver, 1630.
Gustavus Adolphus, *r.* 1611-32, of Sweden invaded the Holy Roman Empire, 1630, to protect the Protestant cause against ruthless Catholic suppression.
Magdeburg was sacked in 1631 by the Catholic general **Tilly**, 1559-1632.
The war in Europe dislocated previous patterns of trade and industry and the search for colonial wealth increased.

1636-42

After the Shimabara revolt of the Christian peasantry, 1637, Japan cut her foreign trade and cultural contacts.
France first entered the Thirty Years War in 1639.
Spain was weakened by the establishment of Portuguese independence and a Catalan nationalist revolt in 1640.
England was close to civil war in 1641 after constitutional opposition to royal absolutism.

1642-8

The New England Confederacy was founded in 1643 for defence against the Indians.
The Manchus set up the **Ta Ch'ing** dynasty at Mukden 1644, replacing the Ming dynasty.
The English Civil War, 1642-6, resulted in military victory for Parliament and the puritans after the reorganization of their army, in 1645. Attempts to find a constitutional settlement failed.
France confirmed her new military superiority by defeating Spain at Rocroi, 1647.

1648-54

The Peace of Westphalia ended the Thirty Years War in 1648 with every participant exhausted.
The Fronde, a series of noble and peasant uprisings in France, tried to substitute government by law for royal power and voiced economic grievances but was crushed, 1648-53.
Charles I, *r.* 1625-49, of England was executed and a Commonwealth set up under **Oliver Cromwell**, 1599-1658. His Navigation Act, 1651, led to war with the Dutch, 1652.

1654-60

The rise of Brandenburg and Russia as military powers brought a new conflict in the Baltic and Poland, 1655-60.
The Venetians drove the Turks from the Dardanelles, 1656, following a period of anarchy among the Ottomans.
Anarchy after Cromwell's death led to the restoration of the English monarchy, 1660.
The war between France and Spain ended, 1659, emphasizing the Spanish decline and the rise of French power.

Charles I, *r.* 1625-49, wed the Catholic **Henrietta Maria**, 1625, and led an abortive expedition to assist the Huguenots, 1627.

Charles ruled without Parliament, 1629-40, relying in part on feudal dues for finances. **Thomas Strafford**, 1593-1641, ruthlessly subdued Ireland.

Charles recalled Parliament, 1640, to finance an expedition to end Scottish religious revolt. He faced attacks on his economic and religious policies.

Charles raised the royal standard at Nottingham and sparked off the Civil War, 1642. The superiority of Cromwell's army forced him to surrender, 1646.

Charles was executed in 1649. **The Navigation Act**, 1651, made the colonies economically dependent on the mother country.

Cromwell's dependence on the army was not popular and after his death anarchy followed. The monarchy was restored in 1660.

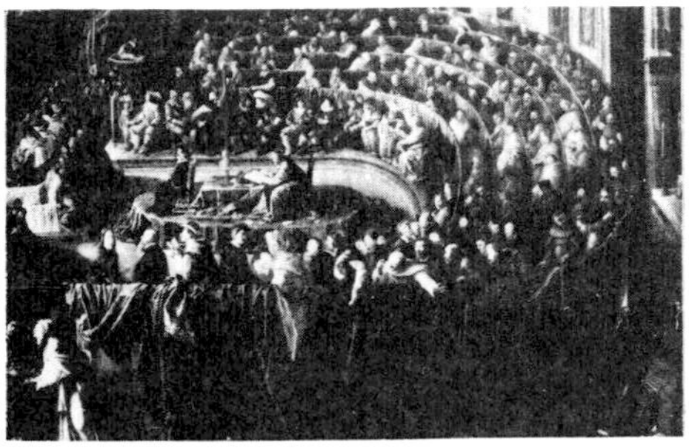

The trial of Galileo

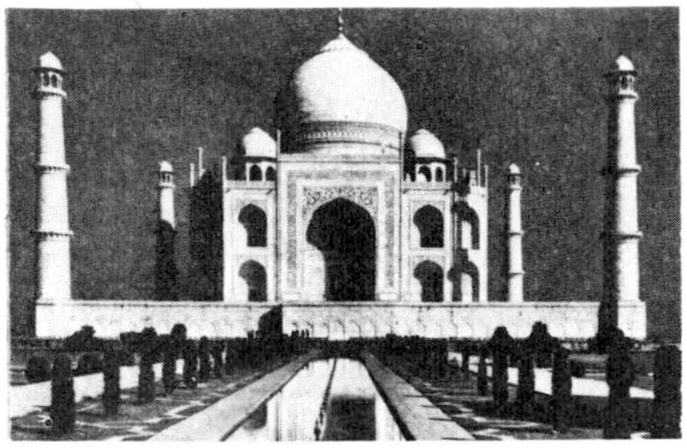

The Taj Mahal

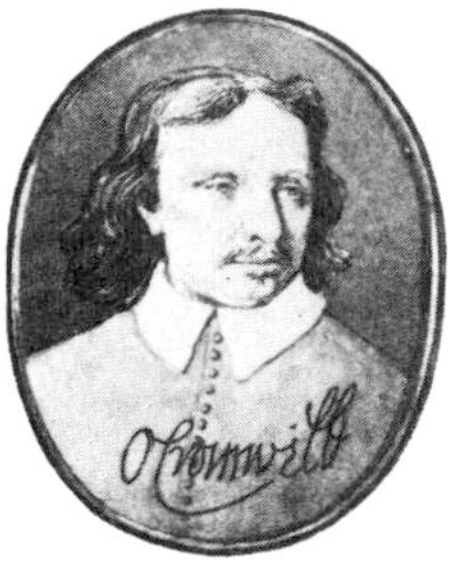

Oliver Cromwell

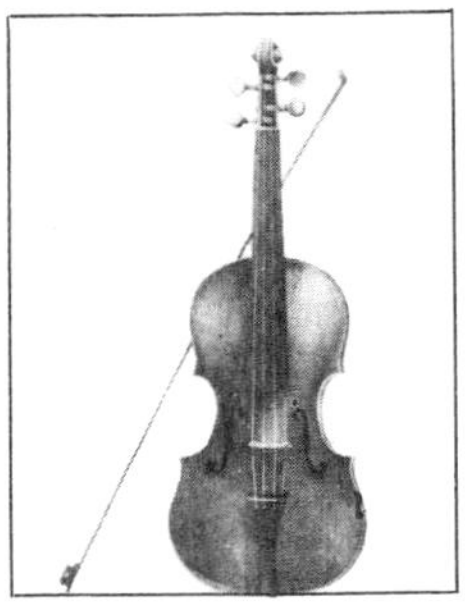

Late 17thc. violin

Herbert of Cherbury, 1583-1648, attempted to establish a belief in God based on rational enquiry rather than faith in *On Truth*, 1624. His belief that the basic tenets of religion were reasonable and universal was central to the growth of Deism. **Hugo Grotius**, 1583-1645, a Dutchman, developed the theory of international law in *On Law*, 1625. He aimed to make war more humane, arguing that nations, like individuals, are bound by natural law.

Galileo Galilei, 1564-1642, an Italian, began modern science by uniting mathematics with physics. He distinguished real or "primary" qualities such as mass, from subjective "secondary" qualities such as colour. The religious opposition to his work highlighted the challenge of experimental science to the Aristotelian world-view, both philosophically and politically.

Cornelius Jansen, 1585-1638, a Frenchman, attacked the Jesuits and proclaimed strict predestinarianism, while staying within the Catholic Church, in the *Augustinus*, 1640. **Blaise Pascal**, 1623-62, supported the Jansenist movement in France, where it appealed to the nationalist opposition to papal power. The Jesuits rejected these views because they implied the denial both of free will and of the universality of redemption.

René Descartes, 1596-1650, who founded modern philosophy, attempted to establish a philosophical system from first principles alone, relying on mathematical logic and using systematic doubt as his method. He espoused a total dualism between mind and matter, arguing that the physical world was governed by deterministic laws, while the clarity and distinctness of ideas established their truth independently of any experience.

Utopian social and religious ideas flourished in England after the civil war. **George Fox**, 1624-91, founded the pacifist and egalitarian Friends, or **Quakers**, in 1652, while the **Diggers**, an agrarian communistic group, believed that religious ideas had diverted man from asserting his political rights in this world. **The Levellers**, another Puritan group, led by John Lilburne, 1614-57, demanded an egalitarian and republican society.

In *De Corpore*, 1655, Thomas Hobbes, 1588-1679, following Descartes' mathematical method, suggested that the universe comprises material particles moving in a void. This atomism also occurred in his political tract, *Leviathan*, 1651, in which he argued that in a state of nature men would fight because of their natural selfishness; they could only escape by means of a contract whereby they renounced their freedom to a supreme ruler.

Spanish drama was dominated by the popular and prolific **Lope de Vega**, 1562-1635, whose ingeniously plotted verse plays mixed comedy and tragedy. **Pedro Calderón**, 1600-81, added deeper characterization in plays that reflected the richly ornate **culteranismo** style of the poet and satirist Luis de Gongora, 1561-1627.

The Passion play at Oberammergau, Bavaria, the most famous survival of its genre, was inaugurated in 1634. It has been performed every ten years except for three wartime interruptions.

French writers applied strict classical rules under the influence of **François de Malherbe**, 1555-1628. **Pierre Corneille**, 1606-84, successfully adapted these in a series of tragedies in Alexandrine couplets, starting with *El Cid*, 1637. His artificial but powerful plays based on Spanish and Roman heroes made drama the chief form of French classical literature.

English prose had acquired a new eloquence in *Anatomy of Melancholy* by **Robert Burton**, 1577-1640. This tradition was extended by **Sir Thomas Browne**, 1605-82, whose *Religio Medici*, 1643, was a reflective study of a doctor's spiritual life. An equally individualistic writer, **Izaak Walton**, 1593-1683, began to write *The Compleat Angler*.

English poetry reflected the political conflict of Puritans and Royalists. The Cavalier lyricists included **Sir John Suckling**, 1609-42, **Robert Herrick**, 1591-1674, and **Richard Lovelace**, 1618-57, whose best work was collected in *Lucasta*, 1649. On the Puritan side, **Andrew Marvell**, 1621-78, wrote poems on nature during the 1650s.

The greatest Dutch poet, Joost van den Vondel, 1587-1679, turned from satire to write his religious drama *Lucifer*, 1654. **In Germany**, literature revived after the Thirty Years War, 1618-48. Poetry was much influenced by Lutheranism and the poet and mystic **Paul Gerhardt**, 1607-76, wrote outstanding hymns, including "O sacred head sore wounded".

Classicism in French painting was developed by **Nicolas Poussin**, *c.* 1594-1665, whose "Triumph of David", 1626, shows an abstraction and modelling based on antique ideals. **Realism** and the skilful use of colour and light began to appear in Spanish painting in such works as the "Scenes from the life of St Bonaventura", 1629-30, by **José Ribera**, 1591-1652, and in the works of **Francisco de Zurbarán**, 1598-1664.

Roman high baroque painting was represented in the works of **Pietro da Cortona**, 1596-1669, whose masterpiece, the ceiling of the Gran Salone, Palazzo Barberini, painted in 1633-9, was a skilful illusion, its centre seemingly open to the sky. **Anthony van Dyck**, 1599-1641, working at the English court, brought sophistication and elegance to English portraiture in the "Equestrian portrait of Charles I", 1633.

Dutch art found its greatest painter in Rembrandt van Rijn, 1606-69, whose psychological insight and technical virtuosity produced "The Night Watch", 1642. **Jan Vermeer**, 1632-75, painted domestic interiors and **Frans Hals**, *c.* 1581-1666, lively portraits. **The greatest of the baroque architects, Francesco Borromini**, 1599-1667, produced his masterpiece of spatial ingenuity, **S. Carlo alle Quattro Fontane**, 1634-44.

French landscape painting as developed by **Claude Lorrain**, 1600-82, involved the formal arrangement of trees and a panoramic background as the setting for diminutive foreground figures, as in "Hagar and the Angel", 1646. **Individualist schools in China** broke away from traditional painting. **Kung Hsien**, *c.* 1620-89, painted vast landscapes of great originality, such as his "A Thousand Peaks and a Myriad Rivers".

French classical architecture was initially developed by **Francois Mansart**, 1598-1666, whose Château of Maisons Laffitte, with its elegance, clarity and cool restraint, epitomized his subtly proportioned style. **Classical compositions** and the use of indirect lighting are combined in the highly personal style of **Georges de la Tour**, 1593-1652, whose "St Sebastian", *c.* 1650, suggests the influence of Caravaggio.

Realism and a superlative handling of colour distinguish the works of the Spanish court painter **Diego de Velazquez**, 1599-1660. His "Las Meninas", 1656, an informal royal group, represents the culmination of his remarkable style. **Bernini's genius as an architect** was affirmed in his Piazza of St Peter's, begun in 1656, which was both simple and original in design and reflected the dignity and grandeur of Mother Church.

Fugue developed, principally in Germany, as a contrapuntal treatment of one main theme. It remained the dominant form for solo organ until the 1700s but also had wider applications.

Bel canto, a lyrical and agile style of singing, developed in Italy. *Castrati*, men castrated before puberty, were renowned for their high, sweet, powerful voices, often used in opera.

Dynamic markings, such as *p* (piano) and *f* (forte), were used for the first time in 1638 by **Domenico Mazzochi**, 1592-1665, in Italy. He was quickly followed by other composers.

Ballet developed at the French court in the reign of Louis XIV, *r.* 1643-1715, who first danced it in 1651. Brought from Italy, ballet had been known at the French court since *c.* 1581.

The violin was perfected in Italy by the Amati, Stradivari and Guarneri families from 1650 to 1740. The great brilliance of violin tone soon overwhelmed the softer viols, which died out.

The koto became the national instrument of Japan. Its strings and movable bridge produced various five-note scales. Its solo music was often composed in the form of variations.

Johann Glauber, *c.* 1603-68, discovered many chemical compounds, including benzene, acetone and hydrochloric acid. **William Harvey**, 1578-1657, discovered the circulation of the blood in 1628, but this was not confirmed until later improvements in the microscope took place. By studying valves Harvey realized that blood must flow in one direction only. His mechanistic view of man perfectly complemented Galileo's mechanistic universe.

In ***Dialogues concerning two World Systems***, published in 1632, Galileo presented the evidence for a heliocentric solar system in which the Earth moves. In 1633 Galileo was forced by Inquisition to retract his views. **Fen drainage** in England since the 1620s had increased farm land. Fertilizer experiments also aided agriculture. English trade and industry prospered, especially coal production, iron mining and metallurgy. **The slide rule** was invented in 1632 by Oughtred, 1575-1660.

Discours de la Méthode, 1637, by René Descartes, 1596-1650, established the deductive method, by which theories are deduced from observations and experimentally tested for validity. He also invented co-ordinate geometry, in which position can be described mathematically, an advance vital to the growth of engineering and the calculus. ***Two New Sciences***, published by Galileo, 1638, dealt with dynamics and established, more than any other work, experimental science.

Blaise Pascal, 1623-62, invented an adding machine in 1642. He also discovered the principles of hydraulics and investigated the theory of probability, showing that chance can be assessed mathematically. **Evangelista Torricelli**, 1608-47, demonstrated in 1643 that air pressure is sufficient to hold up a column of mercury about 76 cm high, thus producing the first barometer. This discovery laid down the fundamental principles of hydromechanics.

The air pump, developed *c.* 1650 by Otto von Guericke, 1602-86, was used to show that sound cannot cross a vacuum. In 1654 Guericke conducted a famous experiment in which two teams of horses tried and failed to separate two evacuated hemispheres, thus demonstrating the power of air pressure, later to be harnessed in the first steam engines.

Christiaan Huygens, 1629-95, a Dutchman, invented the pendulum clock from 1656. **Academia del Cimento**, the first scientific research institute, was founded in Florence, 1657.

1660-1720 The age of Louis XIV

Principal events

Louis XIV's schemes for the expansion of France brought him into conflict with the major European powers. The spectacle of his rule as an absolute monarch dominated 17th-century European politics, arousing the envy of lesser rulers including James II of England who was expelled in 1688 for trying to emulate him. This second English Revolution finally confirmed the victory of Protestantism and the rule of Parliament which would serve to inspire the Enlightenment thinkers of the following century, particularly in France itself.

Outside Europe the major powers fought for colonies – valued for their dual role as sources of raw materials and luxury goods like tobacco, sugar and spices and as markets for the produce of the home country.

The Mogul Empire in India declined after Aurungzebe had made the dynasty unpopular with his policy of intolerance towards Hinduism.

1660-66

Louis XIV began his personal rule in 1661 marked by a suppression of noble authority and the creation of a bureaucracy for local government.
K'ang Hsi, *r.* 1662-1722, introduced a period of Chinese cultural splendour.
The English acquired Bombay in 1661 and took New Amsterdam from the Dutch in 1664.
The Spanish colonies became a prize sought after by the major naval powers in the reign of **Charles II**, 1665-1700.

1666-72

Louis XIV invaded the Spanish Netherlands but was opposed by the United Provinces, 1667-8.
The English and Dutch fought an indecisive trade war, 1665-7.
Russia defeated Poland for the Ukraine, 1654-67.
The Mogul Emperor Aurungzebe revoked Hindu toleration in 1669, causing unrest in India.
The English founded the Hudson Bay Company for the exploration of North America.

1672-8

The French again attacked the Dutch in 1672, backed by riches gained through the mercantilist economic policy of **Jean Baptiste Colbert**, 1619-83. They were opposed by Spain and the empire, who feared French strength in the north.
A two-party system emerged in England in the 1670s.

1678-84

Brandenburg sent an expedition to West Africa in 1680.
Louis XIV moved his court to Versailles to consolidate his independence from the nobility and the Parisians, 1682.
K'ang Hsi took Formosa, 1683, which had been wrested from the Dutch by a Chinese pirate in 1661.
The Turks besieged Vienna, 1683, but were defeated at **Mohacs**, 1687.
Robert de la Salle explored the Mississippi for France.

National events

Attempts by Charles II to establish absolute power and by James II to restore Catholicism led to the Glorious Revolution of 1688. This brought the final victory of the constitutional idea and the supremacy of Parliament over the monarch. Protestantism was supreme and the rights of the gentry assured.

Charles II, *r.* 1660-85, restored peace, confirmed the supremacy of the Anglican Church in 1661 and promoted the growth of overseas trade.

London was rebuilt following the **Plague** and the **Great Fire**, 1665-6. Charles distrusted Parliament and made a secret alliance with Louis XIV.

Parliament forced through the **Test Act**, 1673, which aimed to prevent Catholics from attaining office, hoping thereby to exclude James from the throne.

After the scare of a Catholic coup (**The Popish Plot**), 1678-81, further attempts to exclude James failed. Charles revoked London's charter in 1683.

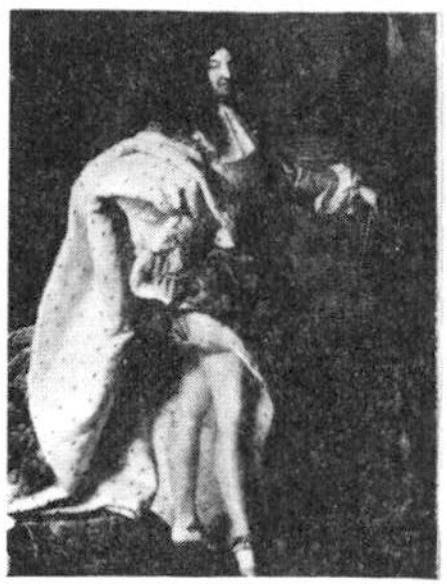
Louis XIV

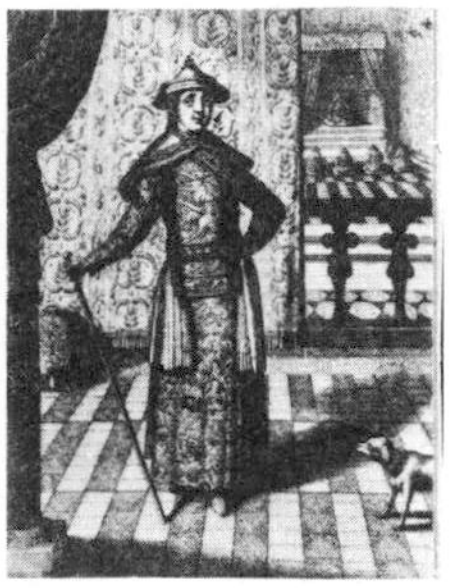
Chinese Emperor K'ang-hsi

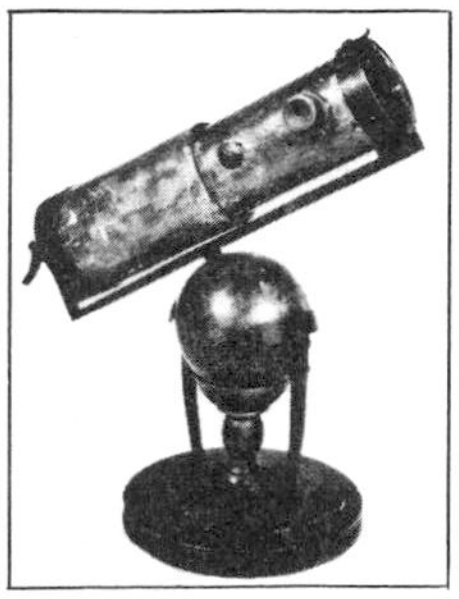
Newton's first telescope

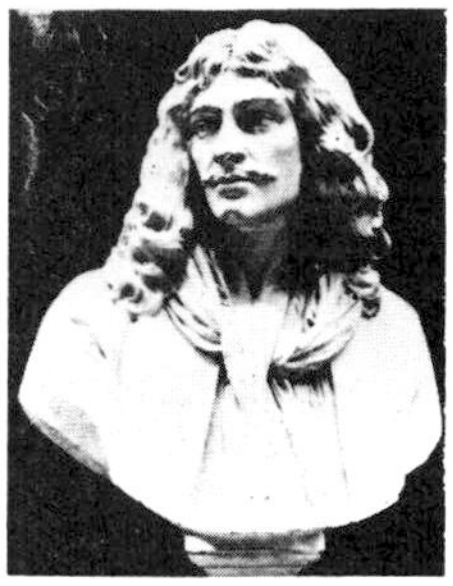
Molière

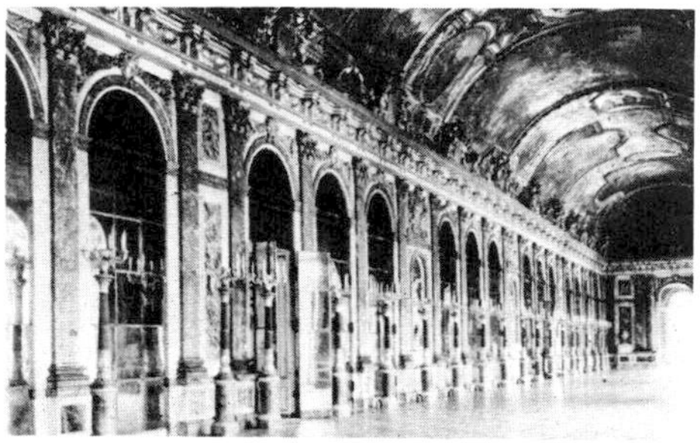
Versailles: the Hall of Mirrors

Religion and philosophy

European theories of knowledge and politics underwent important changes in the latter half of the 17th century, at a time when Newton's revolutionary ideas on the workings of the universe were transforming Western science. In Britain Newton himself, Locke and Berkeley took the empiricist position that knowledge was obtained by experience alone, in direct contrast to the rationalist views of thinkers like Spinoza and Leibniz who argued that the world could be obtained by deductions from certain key principles like the nature of substance. Empiricism would dominate British philosophy hereafter and was to have a major influence on the thinkers of the French Enlightenment. Among political theorists, Locke and Pufendorf argued that political authority depended upon consent and took the form of a contract between the people and the king.

Mercantilists, such as **Thomas Mun**, 1571-1641, in England and **Jean Baptiste Colbert**, 1619-83, in France held that governmental regulation of the economy was necessary to increase the power of the state, since a nation's economic power depended on the bullion at its disposal. A key factor was the monopolization of colonial trade by the mother country.

The Swede Pufendorf, 1632-94, based his concept of natural law on "socialitas", the essentially social nature of man. He believed that agreement was the basis of political relationships and that human dignity implied the equality of all men.
The Old Believers broke with the Russian Church in 1667 to counteract the reforms of the patriarch **Nikon**, 1605-81, who introduced Greek practices and reformed the parish clergy.

Spinoza, 1632-77, a Portuguese Jew, attempted to find a rational explanation of the universe and argued that since God cannot be other than He is then the world, His creation, cannot be other than it is. In his *Ethics*, 1675, he held that free will was an illusion which would be dispelled by man's recognition that the world was completely determined. He supported democracy as the most natural form of government, and rejected Descartes' dualism of mind and body.

Ralph Cudworth, 1617-88, an Englishman, published his *True Intellectual System*, 1678, admitting mental as well as material forces to science. He belonged to the **Cambridge Platonist** group of Christian humanists associated with the religiously tolerant "Latitudinarian" followers of Arminius.
Jacques Bossuet, 1627-1704, upheld Louis XIV's absolute monarchy against Protestantism, arguing that any legally formed government is sacred.

Literature

Neo-classical drama, based on logic and Graeco-Roman stylistic rules, reached a peak in France in the tragedies of Racine and comedies of Molière. After the comic licence of early Restoration drama, English writers such as Dryden also turned to classical models, laying the ground for the Age of Reason. English journalism began with Addison and Defoe and satire developed with Pope.

The period also saw the publication of the chief work of the two greatest English Puritan writers, Milton and Bunyan, as well as developments in baroque poetry and picaresque prose in Germany and the emergence of new prose and verse forms in France with La Fontaine.

In Japan, Basho emerged as the supreme haiku poet.

German baroque literature was dominated by the influence of **Andreas Gryphius**, 1616-64, whose comedies and religious poems were collected in 1663. Another baroque writer was **Hans Grimmelshausen**, *c.* 1621-76, whose *Simplicissimus*, a graphic account of the experiences of the peasantry in the Thirty Years War, is regarded as the start of the German novel.

The Greek "unities" of action, time and space were given dramatic form in the French classical drama of **Jean Racine**, 1639-99, and **Molière**, 1622-73. Racine's *Andromaque*, 1667, blended poetic style with tragic passion. In comedies such as *Le Misanthrope* and *Tartuffe*, Molière exposed upper and middle class hypocrisies, mastering both plot and dialogue.

John Milton, 1608-74, an English poet who was politically prominent on the Puritan side, published in 1674 his final version of *Paradise Lost*, written, 1658-63, in strong blank verse, showing man as obsessed by sin.
In Mexico, a Spanish nun, **Juana Inez de la Cruz**, published *A Nosegay of Poetic flowers*. Her works are among Latin America's best.

A forerunner of the English novel, *Pilgrim's Progress*, 1678, was an allegorical journey through life, told in plain prose with a wealth of narrative detail that overrode the narrow puritanism of its author, **John Bunyan**, 1628-88.
Madame de La Fayette, 1634-93, wrote *La Princesse de Clèves*, the first French court romance of psychological depth.

Art and architecture

France replaced Italy as the centre of the arts in Europe. They were dominated by the royal patronage of Louis XIV, who rebuilt Versailles using the talents of Lebrun, Le Vau, Hardouin-Mansart and Le Nôtre. Baroque architecture was at its purest in Italy, at its most restrained in England and at its most extravagant in Spain and Portugal. Painting during the latter half of the 17th century produced few masterpieces though the works of Murillo in Spain, Pozzo in Italy, Claude in France and the landscapists in Holland were exceptional. In the American colonies architecture and painting adapted European styles to their own conditions.

The Rococo style emerged in France in the late 17th century, bringing to interior decoration the use of swirls, scrolls and conches in design, and finding a stylistic parallel in the elegant paintings of Watteau, dealing with life at court.

Spanish painting was represented by the works of **Bartolomé Estebán Murillo**, 1617-82, who founded the Seville Academy and became its first president, 1660. Eight of his 11 paintings for the almshouse of St Jorge, 1661-74, are regarded as his masterpieces.
The greatest exponent of Baroque, Gianlorenzo Bernini, 1598-1680, went to Paris to redesign the Louvre, 1665. His plans were rejected, but he made a superb bust of Louis XIV.

Dutch landscape painting was exemplified in "The Avenue of Middelharnis", 1669, by **Meindert Hobbema**, 1638-1709, and in "Windmill at Wijk", *c.* 1670, by **Jacob van Ruisdael**, 1628?-82, a great Dutch landscapist.
The palace of Versailles in France was first remodelled in 1669 by **Louis Le Vau**, 1612-70, France's leading baroque architect. The park and gardens at Versailles were designed by **André Le Nôtre**, 1613-1700, from 1662.

The classical landscape tradition of Poussin in France continued with **Claude Lorrain**, 1600-82, whose "Evening", 1672, expresses a questioning melancholy. **Jules Hardouin-Mansart**, 1646-1708, officially supervised building at Versailles after 1678.
Christopher Wren, 1632-1723, the greatest English architect, began work on St Paul's Cathedral, 1675. It is a classical work with baroque overtones.

The Poussinistes/Rubensistes controversy was sparked off by the French Academy's publication of rules for painting, 1680. **André Félibien**, 1619-95, defended the orthodox view which valued drawing, idealism, formalized rules and the work of Poussin. **Roger de Piles**, 1635-1709, led the revolutionaries and argued the importance of colour, imagination and the works of Rubens. The Academy was officially associated with the ideas of Poussinistes.

Music

Baroque music grew up in Europe in the second half of the 17th century in the princely states of northern Italy and Germany. The freewheeling melodic lines and firm harmonic structure in the works of such composers as Diderik Buxtehude, 1637-1707, and Johann Sebastian Bach, 1685-1750, paralleled the ornamented but firm qualities of Baroque architecture.

The Restoration in England saw the introduction of the first public concerts in the modern sense. But music declined there for two centuries after the death of **Henry Purcell**, 1659-95.

The trio sonata was developed by Germans and Italians, using a quick first movement adapting *aabb* dance form with sections in contrasting moods and keys, and a slow second movement.

The chorale prelude, a free composition based on a hymn tune, exploited the varied capabilities of the organ. **Buxtehude's** chorale preludes influenced young composers such as **Bach**.

Continuo was played on a keyboard instrument – often a harpsichord – filling in the harmony between treble and bass lines, as in the cantatas of **Alessandro Scarlatti**, 1660-1725.

Science and technology

Isaac Newton's account of the workings of the universe surpassed Galileo's and provided a new framework for scientific thought. His exceptional insight into nature found definitions for concepts such as inertia and gravity that cannot easily be sensed. Newton's view of the universe, as one obeying set laws, accorded with the spirit of Protestant enquiry into the purpose of creation, in opposition to the Catholic world of personal salvation and divine intervention. Scientific advance in England and Holland was also stimulated by wealth from their growing trade.

Scientific communities grew up and provided scientists with the means to pool their researches, facilitating the spread of information and ideas internationally, while increasing the scientist's stature by granting him royal patronage. However, the growth of these communities contributed to the new division in men's minds between the impersonal sciences and the humanities.

The Royal Society was founded in London, 1660, and the French **Académie Royale des Sciences**, in 1666.
Marcello Malpighi, 1628-94, used a microscope to discover capillary blood vessels in 1661, thereby confirming Harvey's theory of blood circulation.
Robert Boyle, 1627-91, a British physicist, found that gas pressure varies inversely with volume (Boyle's law, 1662). His book *The Sceptical Chymist*, 1661, defined the concepts of element, alkali and acid.

Isaac Newton, 1642-1727, conceived of gravity, 1664-6, correctly concluding that it obeys an inverse square law. He discovered the spectrum 1666, and invented the reflecting telescope, 1671.
Francesco Redi, *c.* 1626-97, disproved previous theories of the spontaneous generation of lower animals by showing in 1668 that flies are needed to produce the eggs of maggots.
A calculating machine that could multiply and divide was made by Leibniz, 1646-1716, in 1671.

Greenwich Observatory, founded in 1675 principally to improve navigation, marks the standard meridian of longitude.
The speed of light was calculated for the first time in 1675 by **Olavs Roemer**, 1644-1710, and shown to be finite.
A single-lens microscope was made by **Anton van Leeuwenhoek**, 1632-1723, a Dutch biologist who discovered protozoa, 1677, and bacteria, 1683.
The calculus was independently developed by Leibniz and Newton.

The pressure cooker was invented, 1679, by **Denis Papin**, 1647-1712. Papin also experimented on steam engines, using both the vacuum made by condensing cylinders and the power produced by the expansion of steam as water boils.
John Ray, 1627-1705, laid the ground work for modern plant classification in his *Historia Generalis plantarum*.

1684-90

The Edict of Nantes, granting freedom of worship to Huguenots in France, was revoked by Louis XIV in 1685. Many Huguenots emigrated. **Russian eastward expansion** led to conflict with China, 1683-9. **James II of England**, *r.* 1685-8, was expelled for trying to restore Catholicism. **The Bill of Rights**, 1689, confirmed a constitutional monarchy. **In Japan**, the Genroku year period, 1688-1704, saw the rise of a merchant culture.

James II attempted to bring a Catholic restoration and was expelled by an alliance of the landed gentry and merchant classes in 1688.

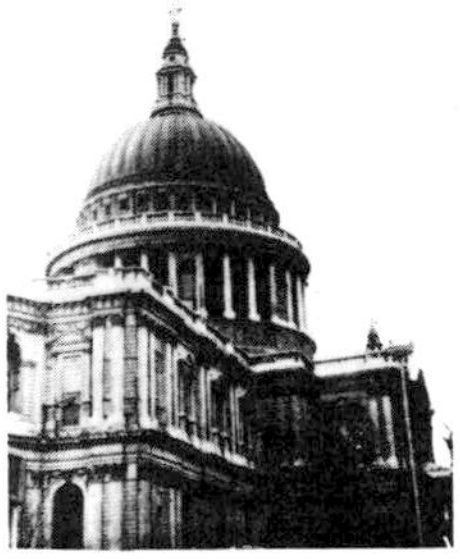

St. Paul's Cathedral

Isaac Newton, 1642-1727, published the *Principia* in 1687. He defended the idea of a gravitational force by arguing that science should merely establish observed regularities, without speculating about underlying mechanisms. His view that the same set of laws, comprehensible with the aid of the physical sciences, apply throughout the universe was fundamental to the development of the mechanistic and optimistic philosophy of the 18th century.

The French poet Jean de La Fontaine, 1621-95, read his *Discours en Vers* to the Academy in 1684. His verse *Fables*, begun in 1668, conveyed human insights through the old tradition of animal stories. **In Japan**, the succinct three-line poetic form called **haiku** reached a peak in the poetry of **Matsuo Basho**, 1644-94.

The arts in France under Louis XIV were dominated by **Charles Lebrun**, 1619-90, who was director from 1663 of the French Academy and was also responsible for the Versailles Galerie des Glaces, completed 1684, and the Salons de la Guerre and de la Paix, 1686. **Venetian architecture** was represented by the Sta Maria della Salute, 1687, by **Baldassare Longhena**, 1598-1682. It was classical in conception but had baroque overtones.

Baroque composers' awareness of modulation through a cycle of fifths brought more harmonic interest to their music, but tuning problems grew when harmony wandered far from the home key.

Newton's *Principia*, probably the most important book in science, was published in 1687. The first section deals with the behaviour of moving bodies and enunciates Newton's three laws of motion, as well as the principles of gravitation. The second deals with the motion of bodies in fluids, and also wave motion. The third utilizes the principles expounded in the earlier sections to explain the motion of bodies on the Earth and in the universe. It was a revolutionary conception.

1690-96

William of Orange, *r.* 1689-1702, who reigned jointly with his wife, James II's daughter **Mary**, brought England into the war against France. **Peter the Great**, *r.* 1689-1725, began his policy of Russian expansion towards Azov for an outlet to the Black Sea and visited western Europe. **English trade in India** grew and a factory was set up in Calcutta in 1690. **European sugar traders** competed in the West Indies.

William III, *r.* 1689-1702, defeated James at the **Boyne** in Ireland, 1690. **The Bank of England** was founded, 1694, to finance William's wars.

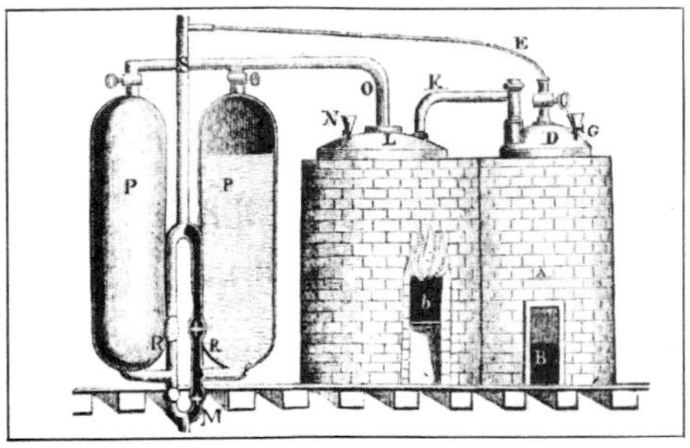

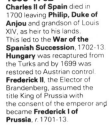

Thomas Savery's steam engine

John Locke, 1632-1704, produced the first thorough empiricist study in *An Essay Concerning Human Understanding*, 1690. He denied the existence of innate knowledge, arguing that the mind was a "tabula rasa" (a blank slate) that was only filled in by sensory experience. His *Two Treatises on Government*, 1690, which justified the English Revolution of 1688, claimed that rulers' legitimacy depended on their protecting the citizens' rights.

Restoration English drama, dominated since 1660 by the influence of the poet, critic, satirist and playwright **John Dryden**, 1631-1700, culminated in *Love for Love*, 1695, by **William Congreve**, 1670-1729. This comedy of manners improved on the comedies of **William Wycherley**, 1640-1716, whose bawdy play *The Country Wife*, 1675, rejected puritan morals.

Spanish Baroque style in architecture was derived from the works of **José Churriguera**, 1665-1725, whose east end of St Esteban, Salamanca, 1693, shows the extravagant surface decoration and richly guilded ornament called Churriguesque. **The leading exponent of the Baroque style of illusionist decoration** in Italy was **Andrea Pozzo**, 1642-1709, whose ceiling of S. Ignazio, Rome, 1691-4, was a masterpiece of perspective and trompe l'oeil.

The concerto was developed by **Arcangelo Corelli**, 1653-1713, and others as a concerto grosso for a group of instruments and orchestra or for a virtuoso solo performer with orchestra.

Christiaan Huygens, 1629-95, a Dutch physicist, put forward a wave theory of light, 1690. Newton at this time proposed a particle theory. Later science would prove them both right.

1696-1702

Charles II of Spain died in 1700 leaving **Philip, Duke of Anjou** and grandson of Louis XIV, as heir to his lands. This led to the **War of the Spanish Succession**, 1702-13. **Hungary** was recaptured from the Turks and by 1699 was restored to Austrian control. **Frederick II**, the Elector of Brandenberg, assumed the title King of Prussia with the consent of the emperor and became **Frederick I of Prussia**, *r.* 1701-13.

The Stock Exchange was founded, 1698. The unpopularity of the war gave the Tories a majority in the Commons, 1701.

Govind Rai, 1666-1708, the tenth Guru of the Sikh religion, began a strategy of armed resistance to Mogul persecution and in 1699 gave the common surname Singh (meaning "lion") to the Sikhs. He also introduced the strict practices of the Sikhs, who were pledged to wear a turban, to carry a knife and never to cut their hair. The Sikhs eventually dominated the Punjab.

John Dryden ended a fruitful career with *Fables Ancient and Modern*, 1699. He also wrote a significant political satire on Monmouth and Shaftesbury, *Absalom and Achitophel*. His clear, elegant verse and prose influenced many, including **Samuel Butler**, 1612-80, whose *Hudibras*, 1663-78, was a satire on Puritanism. *All for Love* was Dryden's best play.

Baroque architecture in England was exemplified in Castle Howard designed by **John Vanbrugh**, 1664-1726, from 1696. He worked with **Nicholas Hawksmoor**, 1661-1736, on this and other buildings. **The beginnings of the Rococo** style were seen in the "arabesques" and "grotesques" designed by **Jean Bérain**, 1640-1711, and **Claude Audran**, 1658-1734.

Fugues in organ music were often paired with a free composition for contrast, giving the prelude and fugue or toccata and fugue found in many works by Buxtehude and Bach.

The first practical steam engine was invented, 1696, by **Thomas Savery**, 1650-1715, a British engineer. **Thomas Newcomen**, 1663-1729, another British engineer, invented the atmospheric steam engine, used until 1934 to pump water from mines. Both engines had a great drawback: the cylinder had to be cooled at each stroke, wasting 99% of the heat from the fuel. **Agriculture** was improved by sowing seeds in rows with a drill invented in 1701 by **Jethro Tull**, 1674-1741, in England.

1702-8

The French won control of the *asiento* contract in 1702, which allowed them to transport Negro slaves to the Spanish colonies. **Portugal** joined the alliance against France, acting as a base for operations in Spain, 1703. **The Duke of Marlborough**, 1650-1722, defeated the French at **Blenheim**, 1704. **After Aurungzebe's death** in 1707, the Mogul Empire disintegrated as local princes asserted their autonomy, seeking assistance from European traders.

England and Scotland were formally united, 1707. England won Gibraltar in 1704, after coming to a trading agreement with Portugal in 1703.

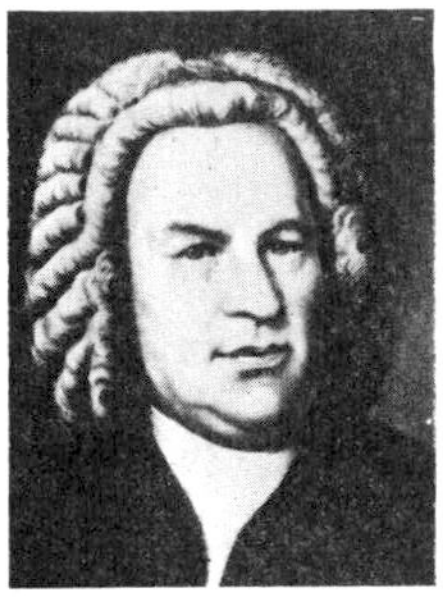

Johann Sebastian Bach

In *The Grumbling Hive*, 1705, **Bernard de Mandeville**, 1670-1733, argued that all individual actions are motivated by self-interest but the net effect of many such actions is the general good. This idea influenced later *laissez-faire* economists. **The Earl of Shaftesbury's** *Letter concerning Enthusiasm*, 1708, helped to popularize **Deism**, or Natural Religion. Deists criticized formal religions, intolerance and extremism.

English journalism arose to satisfy the new middle class market. **Daniel Defoe**, 1660-1731, journalist, novelist, merchant and spy, issued the *Review*, 1704; **Richard Steele** the *Tatler*, 1709; and **Joseph Addison** the *Spectator*, 1711. Addison and Steele were informed and sensible essayists on literary, political and social issues of the period.

The grandeur and formal design of Versailles were emulated throughout Europe in the 18th century with the founding of St Petersburg, Russia, 1703, and in England with Blenheim Palace, 1705, built for the Duke of Marlborough by Vanbrugh.

German suites by Bach and others mixed free forms such as prelude and toccata with dance forms such as *allemande, sarabande, minuet, gavotte* and *gigue*.

Opticks, published by Newton in 1704, encapsulated his work on light. His particle theory of light held great sway for a century before Huygen's wave theory was revived. **Edmond Halley**, 1656-1742, British Astronomer Royal, proposed the idea that comets orbit the Sun and, using Newton's principles, correctly predicted in 1705 the return of the comet that now bears his name.

1708-14

The Sikhs became militant and made the Punjab virtually independent of Mogul rule, 1708. **A mass emigration** of Germans to America began in 1709. **War between the native Brazilians** and the Portuguese erupted after France attacked Rio de Janeiro in the course of the Spanish War of Succession. **The Treaty of Utrecht**, 1713, confirmed that France and Spain should not be united and left Britain in control of the *asiento* slave trade.

The Tories formed a government, 1710, and reduced involvement in the war. They also tried to exclude merchants from Parliament.

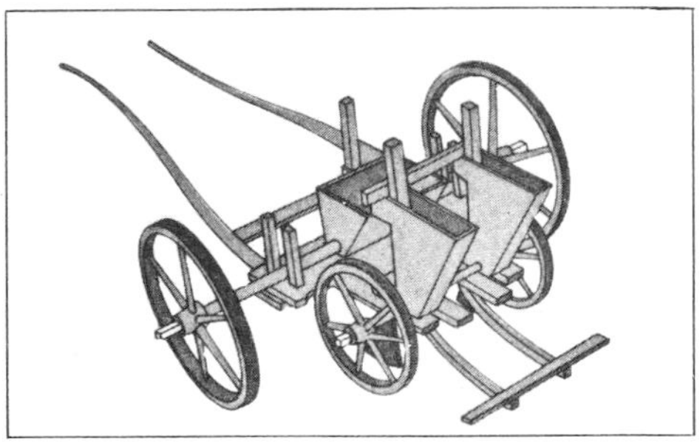

Jethro Tull's seed drill

In *The Principles of Human Knowledge*, 1710, **Bishop Berkeley**, 1685-1753, starting from the belief that all knowledge must come from perception, went beyond Locke and argued for an extreme idealism. He claimed that all we perceive is in the mind alone. As a result, to exist is merely to be perceived, and thus the continuing existence of the external world depends on God's external perception of it. Berkeley thus hoped to refute atheism definitively.

English Classicism found its wittiest poet in **Alexander Pope**, 1688-1744, whose *Rape of The Lock* was published in its full form in 1714. The main defenders of classicism in France were **Nicolas Boileau**, 1636-1711, **Jean de la Bruyère**, 1645-96, and **Jacques Bossuet**, 1627-1704.

European artists, like **Gustavus Hesselius**, 1682-1755, from Sweden, settled in Philadelphia in 1711 and executed realistic portraits and history paintings. **A triumph for Rubensistes** was evident in the vast ceiling of the Chapel at Versailles, 1708, by **Antoine Coypel**, 1661-1722, which is in the manner of Roman baroque illusionism.

The pianoforte was invented. It is usually attributed to the Italian **Bartolommeo Cristofori**, 1655-1731, who in 1709 substituted hammer action for the harpsichord's plucking action.

Jesuit missionaries made an accurate map of China, 1708. **High quality iron** was produced in 1709 by **Abraham Darby**, 1677-1717, a British iron worker. The iron was smelted with coke and moulded in sand for cheap production, making the cast iron steam engine an economic proposition. **Francis Hawksee**, an Englishman, made the first accurate observations of capillary action in glass tubes in 1709. **Prussian blue**, a coloured dye, was produced from 1710.

1714-20

The South Sea Company was set up in 1710 to increase British trade with South America. **The English East India Company** won trading concessions over rival companies from the Mogul emperor in 1717. **Frederick William of Prussia**, *r.* 1713-40, laid the foundations of Prussian military power by setting up a standing army. **Louis XIV** died in 1715, with France's economy exhausted. **Manchu rule in Tibet** was assured by 1720.

George I, *r.* 1714-27, suppressed Jacobite risings in Scotland, 1715.

The metaphysical views of **Gottfried Leibniz**, 1646-1716, were summed up in the *Monadologie*, 1714. He saw the universe as comprising an infinity of "monads", dimensionless entities endowed with souls, in pre-established harmony with each other. Leibniz held that God had chosen this as the best of all possible worlds and that the evil in it was necessary. He also worked influentially in symbolic logic.

The tradition of the picaresque novel (recounting exploits of an adventurer), which derived from Spain, was used by **Alain Le Sage**, 1668-1747, in his *Gil Blas*, 1715. **The romantic Japanese dramatist Chikamatsu Monzaemon**, 1652-1725, wrote *Love Suicides*, the last of many successful plays both in **kabuki** (song-dance) and **jojuri** (puppet) forms.

The "fête galante", a new genre of painting characterized by exquisite scenes of pleasure and dalliance, was introduced by **Antoine Watteau**, 1684-1721, in the "Departure for the Island of Cythera", 1717. **The first phase of the Rococo in France**, 1700-20, largely in sculpture and interior design, was exemplified in the fountains of **Gilles Marie Oppenordt**, 1672-1742, designed about 1715 and showing twisting figures, shells and scrolls.

Italian became the usual operatic language in Europe, though France still kept its own opera. **Georg Friedrich Handel**, 1685-1759, composed Italian opera in England after 1719.

The mercury thermometer was invented in 1714 by **Gabriel Fahrenheit**, a German physicist, 1686-1736. **Jethro Tull** brought the horse-hoe to England from France. **Thomas Lombe**, 1658-1739, an Englishman, patented a machine to make thrown silk in 1718.

1720-1760 Reason and the Enlightenment

Principal events

A series of dynastic and trade wars overtook Europe, adding to the growing conflict between centralized monarchical authority, the nobility and the newly strong mercantile class. In France the supremacy of the monarch over the nobles broke down, producing political stalemate. In Prussia, Russia and Portugal, however, the liberal ideas of the Enlightenment were harnessed to the growth of royal absolutism and industrial reform.

The English moved inland in India into the vacuum of the collapsing Mogul Empire, prized both for the value of its produce and the quality of its culture. Here they competed successfully with the French despite the unwillingness of the English government to take on imperial responsibility. At the same time the American colonies, whose economies were beginning to grow, were becoming impatient with Britain's rigid mercantilist policies.

1720-4

The English South Sea Company and the French Mississippi scheme, which had both aimed to restore royal finances, collapsed in 1720.
The Pragmatic Sanction, 1713, establishing the indivisibility of Austria-Hungary, was accepted in 1720.
In North America, Spain occupied Texas, 1720-2, to prevent a French invasion, and the Piedmont region was colonized by Swiss, Germans and Scots.

1724-8

Peter the Great of Russia died, 1725, having encouraged industrial growth, centralized the administration and subdued the nobility.
The ministry of Fleury, 1653-1743, in France began, 1726, introducing a period of peace and economic growth which led to a strengthening of the middle classes.
The Russian border with China was fixed in 1727.

1728-32

The Anglo-Spanish War, 1727-8, forced Spain to end her siege and confirm England's possession of Gibraltar, 1729.
Anna, *r.* 1730-40, Empress of Russia, founded the Corps of Cadets to encourage the nobles' participation in administration.
By the Treaty of Vienna, 1731, the Holy Roman Empire dissolved the Ostend East India Company, England's colonial trading rival in cotton, spices and saltpetre.

1732-6

England prohibited trade between her American and West Indian colonies by the Molasses Act of 1733.
War over the succession, 1733-5, weakened Poland.
Georgia, the last of the English colonies, was founded in 1733.
The French Compagnie des Indes was firmly established in India by 1735.
Class distinctions between the merchant and military groups in Japan became blurred during a long period of economic decline.

National events

In this period of Whig oligarchy, the constitutional roles of cabinet and prime minister were evolving. Commercial growth was encouraged by the government's fiscal policy and, with the increasing population and new agricultural techniques, prepared the ground for the Industrial Revolution.

Robert Walpole, 1676-1745, became Britain's first prime minister, 1721. His policy of keeping a permanent national debt brought prosperity.

George II, *r.* 1727-60, assigned to power the former opposition to George I. He was much influenced by his wife, **Caroline of Ansbach**.

Agricultural enclosures were beginning to increase the production of food so that it could support the growing urban population.

Walpole's attempt to introduce excise duty on wine and tobacco, 1733, brought great unrest, but the Tories were too weak to overthrow him.

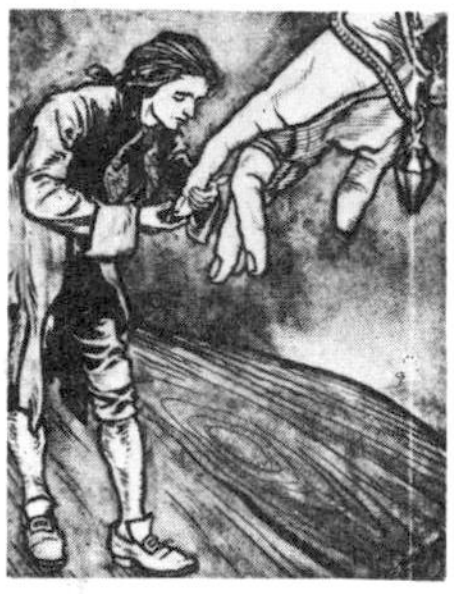

Gulliver's Travels

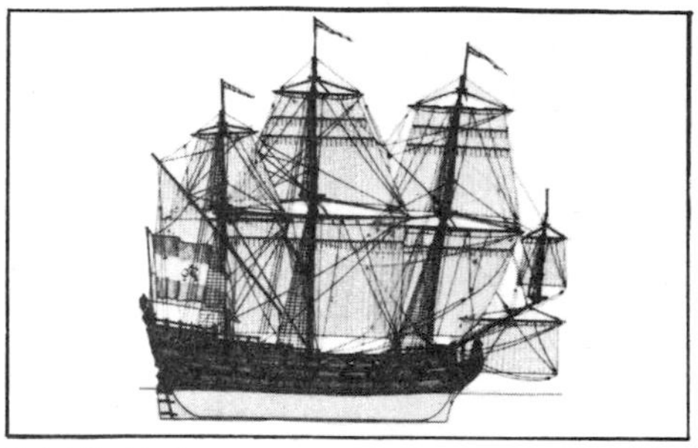

Dutch East Indiaman

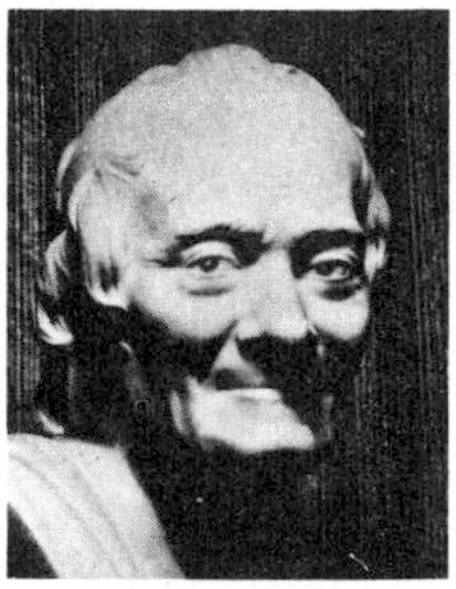

Marble bust of Voltaire

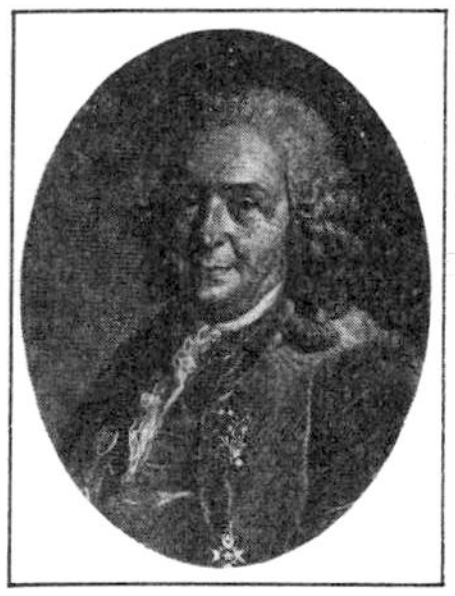

Carl Linnaeus

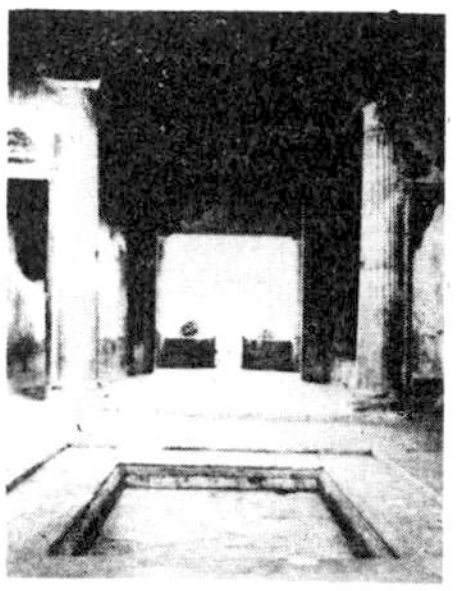

House of Menander, Pompeii

Religion and philosophy

The influence of English empiricist ideas on the philosophical tradition stemming from Descartes led to the great intellectual development known as the French Enlightenment. Montesquieu, Voltaire, Rousseau and other "philosophes" who contributed to the French *Encyclopédie* believed in the power of reason and knowledge to liberate man from restrictive political and religious systems.

On religious questions these thinkers tended towards deism or even atheism, and accepted a materialist conception of the universe. In politics they were liberals. Montesquieu sought to classify social systems and analyse their function. The Physiocrats laid the foundation of scientific economics. Others such as Condillac elaborated the basic ideas of materialist philosophy.

In Britain David Hume showed how empiricism could lead to an extreme scepticism.

Christian Wolff, 1679-1754, a follower of Leibniz, made rationalist anti-traditional philosophy popular in Germany. Puritan Pietists engineered his expulsion from the University of Halle in 1723, but he later became its chancellor.
Ba'al Shem Tov, *c.* 1700-60, founded **Hasidism** in Poland. This vibrant orthodox movement within Judaism stressed the joy of religious practice and expression, and rejected academic formalism and élitism.

Giambattista Vico, 1688-1744, an important forerunner of the modern social scientists, outlined his ideas in *Universal Law*, 1720-1, and elaborated them later in his masterpiece, *The New Science*, 1725. Vico held that societies pass from a bestial stage through a patrician stage ruled by an hereditary elite, to a stage where men are equal. He warned that man was never wholly rid of his bestial aspect and might always regress into barbarism.

Voltaire, 1694-1778, returned to France in 1729 after a two-year visit to England. His *Lettres philosophiques*, 1734, advocating the empiricism of **Isaac Newton** and **John Locke** and the merits of the English political system, had a great influence on the French Enlightenment. Voltaire was a deist, and an active liberal fighting for the exercise of tolerance in both religion and politics.

In his ***Treatise on Human Nature***, written from 1734 to 1737, **David Hume**, 1711-76, argued from empiricist presuppositions that knowledge was unattainable. He said that since connections were unobservable our belief in them was irrational. Hume held that the basis of moral judgement was man's subjective reaction of approval or disapproval of the effects actions have to himself and others.

Literature

European literature was dominated by the critical spirit of the Age of Reason expressed in the work of essayists and satirists such as Pope and Swift in Britain or Voltaire and Montesquieu in France, where polemical writing was in the ascendant. The same desire to grasp social reality, found expression in the English novel, whether in the vein of a new realism, with Defoe or Fielding, in the psychological studies of Laurence Sterne or the picaresque novels of Smollett. In Italy, Goldoni's comedies began a parallel move in the theatre away from stock characterization and towards a greater realism.

The basis of modern Russian poetry was established by Lomonosov.

Daniel Defoe, 1660-1731, a prolific writer and one of the founders of modern journalism, turned to fiction (disguised as fact) and revealed a powerful imagination. His novels, including *Robinson Crusoe*, 1719-20, and *Moll Flanders*, 1722, are noted for their highly realistic descriptions.

Jonathan Swift, 1667-1745, poet, polemicist and churchman, published *Gulliver's Travels*, 1726, a highly imaginative satire on mankind. Swift wrote brilliantly abusive essays.
The Beggar's Opera by John Gay, 1685-1732, was first played in 1728. It uses elements of Italian opera and traditional songs to create a new style of political satire.

German ideas of the Aufklärung (Enlightenment) were summed up in *Critische Dichtkunst*, 1730, a critical work by the playwright **J. C. Gottsched**, 1700-66. He argued that literature must imitate classical models and that its purpose is didactic. But the lyrical poetry of **F. G. Klopstock**, 1724-1803, who took Greek verse as his model, anticipated Romanticism.

The Italian **Scipione Maffei**, 1675-1755, published his erudite study of the history of Verona, *Verona Illustrata*, in 1732.
Montesquieu, 1689-1755, a leading French thinker and satirist, wrote his *Considerations of the Grandeur of the Romans and their Decadence*, 1734, an outstanding piece of socio-political analysis.

Art and architecture

Late manifestations of the more emotional baroque and rococo forms were seen in Austria and Germany as well as in European colonial architecture in the mid-18th century. But as concepts of "good taste" emerged during the Enlightenment, combined with a more exact and careful study of the aesthetics of classical art, the exuberance of the early 18th century became restrained within realist, or neoclassical modes. Interest in fantasy shifted from the Baroque to chinoiserie or rococo "Gothick", in the search for new stylistic forms.

Native Indian art was in decline and European styles were introduced to India by the advancing colonialists. The impact of European expansion in the cultural sphere was also found in China.

In Japan colour printing techniques were developed and the art reached a new peak in the work of Utamaro.

Easter Island was discovered by the Dutch, 1722. Archaeologists have since been baffled by the significance of, and building methods used to erect, the megalithic statues found there.
Austrian art reached its peak in the architecture of palaces, churches and monasteries, especially those of **Lukas von Hildebrandt**, 1688-1745. Known as "Austrian Baroque", this style with its florid shapes and lavish decoration paved the way for late German Baroque.

Indian art was in decline with the collapse of the Mogul Empire and European architectural styles began to be introduced in colonial towns, including Bombay where **St Thomas Cathedral** was built.
Catholic Bavaria accepted Italian baroque forms which in the later work of **Balthasar Neumann**, 1687-1753, took on an almost rococo lightness. His church at Vierzehnheiligen, 1743-72, is richly painted in pink, gold and white.

Palladianism, a revival of interest in the restrained classicism of Vitruvius, Palladio and his English follower Inigo Jones, marked an English reaction against Baroque. It was pioneered by **Colen Campbell**, *d.* 1729, and taken up by **Lord Burlington**, 1694-1753, who encouraged **William Kent**, *d.* 1748, and **Isaac Ware**, *d.* 1766.
Giuseppe Castiglione, 1698-1768, settled in China *c.* 1730, and was the first Western painter to be appreciated there.

Venice took the lead in Italian art with the painting of **Giovanni Tiepolo**, 1696-1770, and **Antonio Canaletto**, 1697-1768.
Servandoni, 1695-1766, began work on the façade of San Sulpice in Paris, 1732. It relied on antique architecture and heralded a reaction against Rococo.

Music

Italian influence on European music waned, except in opera and song. The French evolved instruments and musical theory, but the Germans and Austrians, patronized by their princes, made the most use of these developments and ushered in the classical age of music. In the work of Joseph Haydn, 1732-1809, the symphony found a champion to establish its form.

Traité de l'harmonie, 1722, by **Jean Philippe Rameau**, 1683-1764, provided the foundation of harmonic thought for two centuries, with its clear statement of the function of tonality.

Light opera emerged in Germany, where **Reinhard Keiser**, 1674-1739, wrote operas with catchy tunes. He wrote a comic opera in 1726 which used spoken dialogue rather than recitative.

Virtuoso players such as **Antonio Vivaldi**, *c.* 1675-1741, advanced the techniques of their instruments and led to a distinction between music for professional and amateur players.

Religious cantata and oratorio were developed on a grand scale by **Bach** and **Georg Friedrich Handel**, 1685-1759, to embrace all musical techniques but without the use of operatic staging.

Science and technology

Great technological innovation were created and stimulated by the Industrial Revolution. In England the textile industry, with its need for large-scale bleaching and dyeing processes, gave a boost to practical chemistry and to machine technology. The flying shuttle produced the large quantities of cloth that demanded bleaching, and new methods were invented to provide the great amounts of acid employed in the process. Similarly, the need to transport more raw materials and finished products by sea than ever before encouraged navigational innovation. An early form of the sextant and the first accurate chronometer were invented.

Meanwhile pure scientific research continued in the form of discoveries, particularly in plant physiology and growth. Early work on electricity was performed at Leyden University and in America, providing the basis of later experiments into the nature of electric currents and their potential.

Smallpox inoculations were first administered in the New World during an epidemic in 1721, when **Zabdiel Boylston**, 1679-1766, inoculated 240 persons, of whom all but six survived.

The chronometer was developed from 1726 by John Harrison, 1693-1776, an Englishman, to aid navigation, as longitude could be determined only by time. He invented the compensating pendulum, so that his chronometers would keep perfect time in whatever climate they were used.
Plant physiology was founded by the publication of *Vegetable Staticks*, in 1727, by **Stephen Hales**, 1677-1761. Measuring plant growth and sap production, Hales realized that air is necessary for plants to grow.

Stellar aberration, a change in the position of stars caused by the Earth's motion, was detected in 1729 by an Englishman, **James Bradley**, 1693-1762. This was the first absolute confirmation of Copernicus' theory that the Earth moves around the Sun.
Cobalt was discovered in 1730 by George Brandt, 1694-1768, a Swedish chemist.
The reflecting quadrant, a forerunner of the sextant, aided navigation. It was invented in 1730 by John Hadley, 1682-1744.

Systema Naturae was published by Carl Linnaeus, 1707-78, a Swedish botanist, in 1735. He defined the differences between species and formed the idea of classifying plants and animals into species and genera, classes and orders.
The flying shuttle was invented in England in 1733 by John Kay, 1704-64.
Rubber was found in South America by Charles Marie de la Condamine, 1701-74, while on an expedition to measure the curvature of the Earth, 1735.

1736-40

Russia and Austria clashed with the Turks over their Polish policy. The Russians captured Azov but by the Treaty of Belgrade, 1739, were prevented from keeping a fortified Black Sea base there.
Commercial rivalry in America between England and Spain brought an end to a period of peace for England, with the War of Jenkins' Ear, 1739-41. The war resulted from a dispute over trading rights in the Spanish colonies.

The death of Queen Caroline, 1683-1737, weakened Walpole's authority, which relied in part on favour at court.

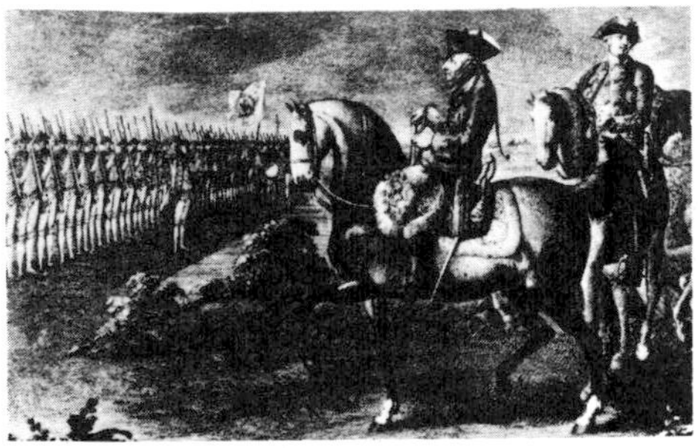

Frederick II of Prussia reviewing troops

John Wesley, 1703-91, an Anglican minister, founded the Methodist movement in England. After a spiritual experience in 1738 Wesley began evangelical open-air preaching and drew up a set of "Rules" for his followers, who formed "bands" – groups for mutual encouragement and for teaching and prayer. They believed in a personal relationship with God and were noted for their good works. The Methodists finally broke with the Church of England in 1795.

Voltaire (F. M. Arouet), 1694-1778, wit, poet, dramatist and epitome of the Enlightenment in his scorn for prejudice and distrust of accepted ideas, wrote the philosophical poems *Le Mondain*, 1736, and *Discours sur l'Homme*, 1738. Stressing the value of experience, he later satirized ideas of human perfectability in *Candide*, 1759, a tale of innocence abused.

French art was divided between the officially accepted art in the rococo vein, like the frivolous, mildly erotic work of **François Boucher**, 1703-70, who had adopted much of Tiepolo's technique, and the more solid realistic genre scenes of **Jean Chardin**, 1699-1779, which reflected a contemporary taste for northern painting, especially 17th century Dutch masters.
Herculaneum was discovered in 1738.

Contrapuntal writing reached a masterful zenith under Bach, with music of great power and intricacy, as in the "Kyrie" from his *Mass in B minor*, 1738.

Daniel Bernoulli, 1700-82, a Frenchman, related fluid flow to pressure in 1738.

1740-4

Frederick II the Great of Prussia, *r.* 1740-86, introduced religious toleration and agricultural reform, consolidated royal authority and reformed the army. In 1740 he occupied Silesia, thus striking the first blow in the War of the Austrian Succession, 1740-8.
Elizabeth of Russia, *r.* 1741-62, gave new authority to the Senate.
The Marathas took Bengal, 1742-4, and disturbed English trade in Bombay.

Commitment to Austria in the war of Austrian Succession led to the fall of Walpole, 1742.

The puritanical Wahhabi movement within Islam was founded by **Muhammed ibn 'Abd al-Wahhab**, 1703-92. He advocated a return to the original principles of Islam, and condemned as polytheistic the decoration of mosques and the cult of saints, which he saw as intervening in the personal and direct relationship between the faithful and God. In 1744 the powerful Saudi family in central Arabia adopted the principles of the Wahhabi sect.

The crowning achievement of Augustan poetry in England, *The Dunciad* of **Alexander Pope**, appeared in its final version, 1743. This was a mock heroic attacking the betrayal of literature by hack writers, using elements of Homer, Virgil, Dante and Milton and defending a role for the poet as a conserver of the values of society.

Colour printing was developed in Japan, *c.* 1742, with outstanding results by **Kitagawa Utamaro**, 1753-1806, who was one of the greatest exponents of the ukiyo-e school of painting. This "floating world" art form was famous for its depiction of sensuous women.
Spanish colonial architecture was executed in a baroque style, especially in Mexico. The collision with existing cultures introduced new motifs like the Puebla tiles on the Church of San Francisco, Acatepec.

Equal temperament was worked out in Germany. It made modulation to distant keys possible, as in the *Well-tempered Klavier*, 1722-44, by **J. S. Bach**, 1685-1750.

Anders Celsius, 1701-44, a Swede, devised the Celsius scale of temperature, *c.* 1744, with 0° as the freezing-point of water and 100° as the boiling-point.
The crucible method of making steel by heating scrap iron was found in England, 1740, by Benjamin Huntsman, 1704-76.
Mikhail Lomonosov, 1711-65, working in Russia, rejected the phlogiston theory and suggested the law of the conservation of mass.

1744-8

Frederick II began the Second Silesian War, 1744-5. France and Prussia defeated the Austrians and their allies at the battle of Fontenoy, 1745.
In North America, English forces took Louisburg, 1745, and made new conquests from the French in the West Indies.
In India, the Frenchman **Joseph Dupleix**, 1697-1763, took Madras, 1746. However, all these conquests were restored by the **Treaty of Aix-la-Chapelle**, 1748.

The last Jacobite rebellion in Scotland was destroyed at Culloden in 1746.

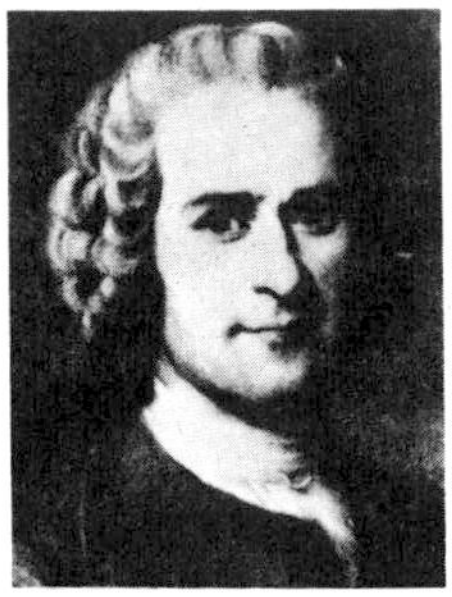

Jean Jacques Rousseau

In *The Spirit of Laws*, published 1748, the French social theorist **Charles Montesquieu**, 1689-1755, examined the relationships between a society's laws and its other characteristics such as religion and economic organization, drawing on an immense range of information about other cultures. He elaborated a study of types of governmental systems and analysed the prerequisites of their proper functioning.

Italy's greatest comic dramatist, Carlo Goldoni 1707-93, wrote *The Servant of Two Masters*, 1745. A skilful and prolific craftsman, he substituted a script and more realistic treatment of character and situation for commedia del' arte, the traditional Italian comic form in which actors playing stock roles improvised upon an outline scenario.

Chinoiserie, a taste for Chinese art and design, became popular in Europe in the 1740s.
In England, **William Hogarth**, 1697-1764, attacked the social abuses of his time in his engravings and paintings. He often followed a narrative of events in a series of paintings as in "Marriage à la Mode", 1745.

The symphony orchestra gained the basis of its present form at Mannheim court under **Johann Stamitz**, 1717-57, who trained his players to produce controlled extremes of loud and soft.

Traité de Dynamique, 1743, by **Jean d'Alembert**, 1717-83, solved problems in mechanics.
The Leyden jar, developed at the University of Leyden, 1745, was able to store a large charge of static electricity. It was used in the first investigations into the nature of electricity.
John Roebuck, 1718-94, a British inventor, developed a process for manufacturing sulphuric acid, used to bleach textiles, on a large scale in 1746.

1748-52

Louis XV, *r.* 1715-74, met united opposition from the nobility and clergy in France when he tried to introduce new taxes on their wealth to pay for his war expenses, 1751.
Robert Clive, 1725-74, seized Arcot, 1751, in search of personal power and booty, and thus established English authority over southern India, ousting the French opposition.
The Chinese invaded Tibet, 1751, following a growth in Chinese population and wealth.

Robert Clive's military and commercial activities in India, although unpopular at home, stimulated a further expansion of overseas trade.

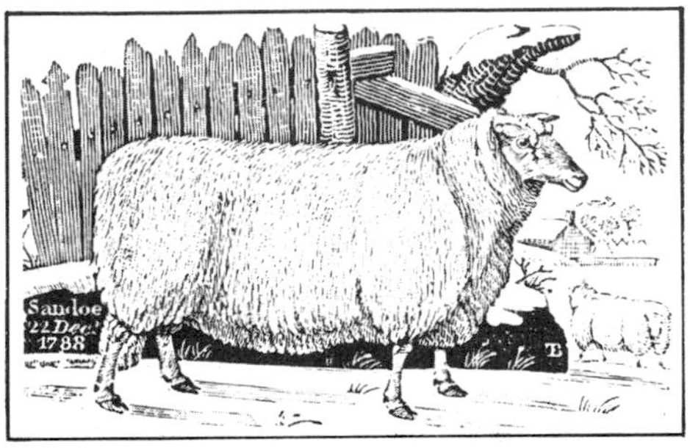

Robert Bakewell's improved sheep

The first volume of the French *Encyclopédie* appeared, 1751. Edited by **Denis Diderot**, 1713-84, and completed in 1772, this was a monument to the "philosophes" of the French Enlightenment and aimed to advance reason, knowledge and liberty. The contributors, who included **Etienne Condillac**, 1715-80, the Lockean philosopher, were deists or atheists who held liberal political views and a materialist conception of the universe.

The English novel, developed by **Samuel Richardson**, 1689-1761, in *Pamela*, 1740-1, flowered in the masterpiece *Tom Jones*, 1749, by **Henry Fielding**, 1707-54. **Laurence Sterne**, 1713-68, mastered a vein of black humour in *Tristram Shandy*; Tobias Smollet, 1721-71, the picaresque tradition in *Roderick Random*, 1748.

The "Gothick rococo" became a fashion in England with the remodelling of Strawberry Hill House, 1749, by **Horace Walpole**, 1717-97. The library fireplace combined motifs from medieval tombs in Westminster and Canterbury Cathedrals.
British and French artists such as **Joshua Reynolds**, 1723-92, and **Jacques-Germain Soufflot**, 1713-80, would revolutionize art and architecture after studying art in Rome *c.* 1750.
Pompeii was found in 1748.

American settlers began making a distinctive music with easily carried instruments. Barn dances were held as buildings were completed and hymn-singing meetings were held in homes.

Benjamin Franklin, 1706-90, working in America, flew a kite in a thunderstorm, 1752, to prove that lightning is electrical and from his results developed a lightning conductor.
Selective breeding, pioneered by **Robert Bakewell**, 1725-95, in England, improved livestock, while the experimental farming of **Viscount Townshend**, 1674-1738, improved crop rotation.
Georges Buffon, 1707-88, published the first volume of his massive *Histoire Naturelle*, 1749-88.

1752-6

Sebastião Pombal, 1699-1782, introduced Enlightenment ideas to Portugal, 1751-77, ruthlessly attacking clerical and noble privileges and stimulating industrial growth.
Dupleix was recalled to France in 1754, leaving India to the British. Delhi was sacked by Afghan invaders, 1756-7.
Moscow university was founded in 1755 to promote education among the Russian nobility.
Lisbon was destroyed by an earthquake in 1755.

Government by a regular cabinet comprising the heads of the main administrative departments was regularly adopted.

Jean Jacques Rousseau, 1712-78, published his *Discourse on Inequality* in 1755. In this work, and in *The Social Contract*, 1762, he argued that in a natural state men were equal and that it was only society that creates inequality and misery. He argued that the injustices of society could be minimized if citizens resigned their rights to a government that acted on the "general will".

The father of modern Russian literature, Mikhail Lomonosov, *c.* 1711-65, published his *Grammar*, 1755. Poet and linguist, he set up verse rules and three styles of literary diction that opened up new possibilities in Russian literature.
Romanticism was foreshadowed in France by the **Abbé Prévost**, 1697-1763, the prolific author of *Manon Lescaut*, 1731.

A torrent of publications heralded a change in taste in European art, foreshadowing **Neoclassicism**, which would be based on a detailed study of ancient Greek and Roman art. The archaeological discoveries engraved by **Piranesi**, 1720-78, in *Antichità Romana*, 1757, and such dissertations on taste as *Dialogue on Taste*, 1754, by **Allan Ramsay**, 1713-84, resulted in an ability to distinguish different phases in antiquity.

The symphony in the hands of Haydn developed greatly from 1750 to 1760, advancing its instrumentation and the form of its contrasting movements, usually four in number.

Immanuel Kant, 1724-1804, in Germany, published his views on the formation of the solar system in 1755, anticipating the work of Laplace. He also suggested that galaxies of stars exist and that the tides slow the rotation of the Earth. Both of these ideas were verified much later.
René Réaumur, 1683-1757, proved that digestion is a chemical process and invented an 80 degree thermometer scale.

1756-60

In the Seven Years War, 1756-63, Austria was at first defeated by Frederick II.
Clive won control of Bengal at Plassey, 1757.
The Marathas occupied the Punjab in 1758.
Pombal expelled the Jesuits from Portugal in 1759.
Most of Canada came under British control after the surrender of **Montreal**, 1760. This ended the need for British garrisons to defend the American colonies.

The Seven Years War greatly expanded the empire and brought a new commercial confidence in spite of political instability.

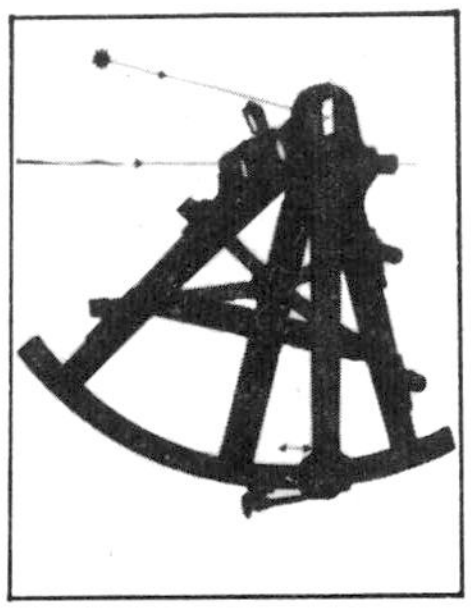

Sextant by J. Bird

The Physiocrats of the 18th century were the first scientific school of economics. They regarded agriculture rather than manufacturing as the source of wealth, and advocated the doctrine of *laissez-faire*, or free trade, against the complex trade regulations then in force. The most important Physiocrat was **Francois Quesnay**, 1694-1774, whose *Tableau economique*, 1758, was the first work to attempt an analysis of the workings of an entire economy.

Realism in Chinese fiction, exemplified in the satirical novel *Unofficial History of Scholars* by **Wu Ching-tse**, 1701-54, was further developed by **Tsao Chan**, *c.* 1719-63, in *The Dream of a Red Chamber*. In this novel, the grandeur and decline of a Chinese family was described with convincing detail and a new sense of humanity.

Russian architecture was based largely on French developments, baroque forms with rococo decoration, producing the splendour of the Winter Palace, 1754-64, in St Petersburg by **Bartolomeo Rastrelli**, 1700-71.
A positive reaction against Rococo in France was seen in the fleeting fashion of **"Le Gout Grec"** and also in a more significant dependence on antique precedents in the design of Sainte Geneviève (now the Panthéon) by **Soufflot** in Paris.

Sonata form was advanced by **C. P. E. Bach**, 1714-88, who made imaginative use of key relationships and conflicts in the development sections of first movements of his symphonies.

Carbon dioxide was discovered in 1756 by Joseph Black, 1728-99, a British chemist.
The sextant of John Bird (1758) made navigational observations far more accurate.
Lomonosov was the first man to observe an atmosphere on the planet of Venus, 1761.
John Dollond, 1706-61, produced the first achromatic lenses in 1757 in England.

1760-1800 Revolution in America and France

Principal events

The old order in Europe was fundamentally shaken by three major revolutions – in America, France and England – which changed the political and economic basis of Western society and would ultimately transform the world. The American War of Independence represented the overthrow of the old colonial and trading system and installed the ideas of liberty and democracy as the ideals of the United States. The French Revolution of 1789 swept away the privileges of the outdated *ancien régime* and established a new idea of popular right, which would be carried by Napoleon's conquests to stir the rest of Europe to revolt.

In England the Industrial Revolution began in earnest in the 1780s, providing the basis for a fundamental transformation of Western and ultimately global society by accelerating urbanization and creating new sources of wealth, new social classes and democratic demands.

1760-4

Prussia increased its military power after 1760 and an inconclusive settlement to the Seven Years War followed. **The Treaty of Paris**, 1763, confirmed English supremacy in Canada and India. **The War** left French government finances in a precarious state despite expanding trade. **The Pontiac Conspiracy**, an American Indian revolt, was suppressed by the English in Canada, 1763-6.

1764-8

The Sugar Act and Stamp Act, 1764-5, by which Britain aimed to recover revenue from the American colonies, aroused local opposition. **England ruled Bengal and Bihar** by 1765, maintaining a puppet Mogul emperor. **Ali Bey**, *r.* 1768-73, declared Egyptian independence from Turkish rule, 1766. **Catherine II** of Russia, *r.* 1762-96, consulted a convention of all social classes to reform Russian law, 1767.

1768-72

The American colonies began their westward expansion, settling Tennessee in 1769. **French trade with India** increased after the French East India Company lost its monopoly, 1769. Opposition to absolutism in France increased among intellectuals. **James Cook**, 1728-79, began the exploration of Australia in the *Endeavour*, 1768-71. In the **Boston Massacre**, 1770, British troops fought with American colonists.

1772-6

After Pugachev's revolt, a large peasant and cossack uprising, 1773-5, Catherine II reformed Russian provincial administration. **The Regulating Act** established an English governor-general in India, 1773. **Warren Hastings**, 1732-1818, reformed the Bengal administration. **Demands by the American colonists** that they be represented in the English Parliament led to the **American War of Independence**, 1775-83.

National events

The Industrial Revolution introduced factory-based machine production and resulted in the growth of a wealthy industrialist class and large new towns in the north without parliamentary representation. Radical societies for electoral reform grew up, some interested in French Jacobinism.

Overseas trade doubled between 1720 and 1760. Canals such as the Bridgwater, 1761, facilitated the movement of heavy goods around Britain.

John Wilkes, 1727-97, was thrice expelled by the Commons after winning election, 1768. He championed free reporting of Parliament.

Wilkes's elections and expulsions finally led to the establishment of freer elections. Political stability was restored by Lord North, 1770-82.

The East India Company was regulated, 1772-3. In 1775 the **American War of Independence** began.

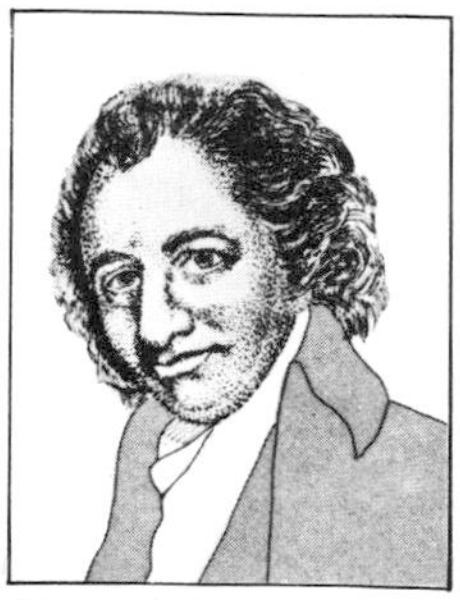

Thomas Paine

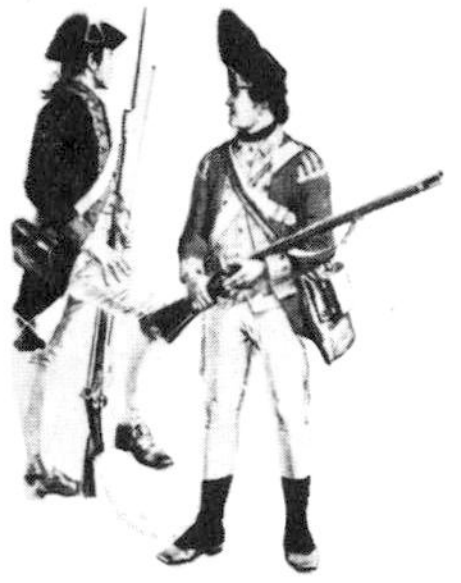

American Revolution

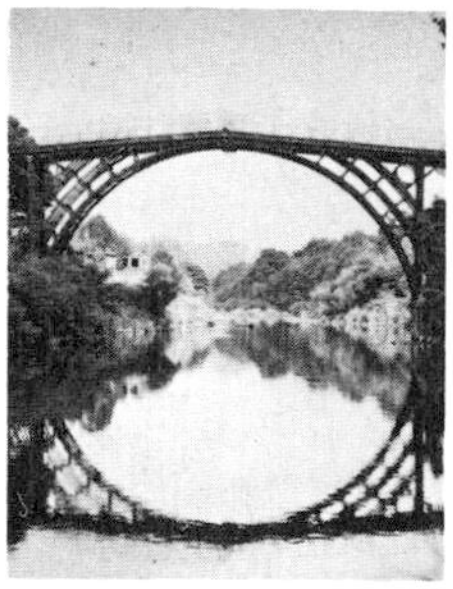

Iron bridge, Coalbrookdale

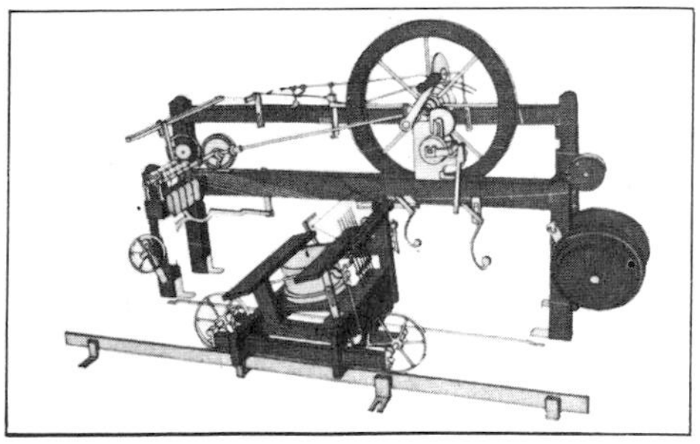

Mechanized spinning: Samuel Crompton's mule

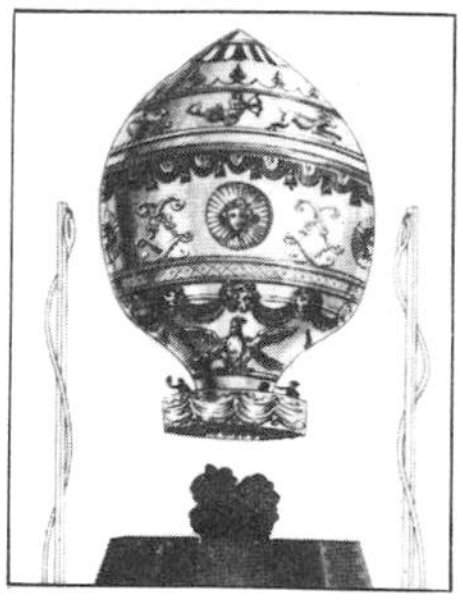

Montgolfier's balloon

Religion and philosophy

The question of the existence of God became subordinate for many European thinkers to questions of social organization.

In America the revolution was associated with ideas of democracy, liberty and equality which in turn inspired the French Revolution.

In Britain new economic thinking reflected the emergence of the industrial system. Adam Smith laid the foundation of modern economics, fostering the liberal doctrine of the free market and the absence of state encroachment on individual freedom. Bentham argued that desire for utility, avoidance of pain and pursuit of pleasure motivated behaviour. The Scottish Enlightenment advanced social thought with Ferguson's and Monboddo's work on social development and man's origins.

Kant, however, laid the basis for German idealism, with his opposition to pure empiricism, claiming that such concepts as time were innate.

The Scottish School of Common Sense Philosophy was begun by **Thomas Reid**, 1710-96, who argued in *An Inquiry into the Human Mind on the Principles of Common Sense*, 1764, that Hume's scepticism about attaining true knowledge was against common sense. **Dugald Stewart**, 1753-1828, sought rejection of fruitless metaphysical speculation and the creation of scientific philosophy.

Adam Ferguson, 1723-1816, an early British sociologist, put forward the theory that man's unceasing desire to control nature was the cause of social development, in his *Essay on the History of Civil Society*, 1766. **The Judaic religion** was interpreted by **Moses Mendelssohn**, 1729-86, in terms of the metaphysics of Leibniz, paving the way for a synthesis of Judaism and modern philosophical and scientific thought, later to develop into **Reform Judaism**.

Johann Herder, 1744-1803, German poet and thinker, was among the first modern thinkers to question the limits of reason. He emphasized the immediacy and therefore the power of feeling – ideas that were later to become the essence of the Romantic movement. **Paul d'Holbach**, 1723-1803, the most ardent materialist of the French Encyclopédists, wrote in his *System of Nature*, 1770, that man's life is determined from birth.

Lord Monboddo, 1714-99, a British anthropologist, believed man's present social state evolved from a previous animal one. This conflicted with the view then current that man was unique. He began publication of his work on language in 1773. **The "Shakers"**, a group of puritanical nonconformists led by **Ann Lee**, 1736-84, began their first colony in America in 1774. They believed total sexual abstinence was the basis of man's spiritual salvation.

Literature

Forerunners of Romanticism emerged in Germany, France and Britain. The emphasis on unity and order in literary style and the sceptical and rational attitudes of mind that marked the Enlightenment were beginning to give way to increasing respect for human instincts and emotions, sincerity of feeling and freedom and naturalism of style. This transition, initiated by Rousseau in France, was carried on in Germany by the *Sturm und Drang* movement whose greatest voice, Goethe, combined passion with discipline. The work of the British poets Gray, Cowper, Burns and Blake exemplified the transition from classicism to romanticism in English poetic style. Samuel Johnson's work advanced literary criticism.

Jean Jacques Rousseau, 1712-78, whose concept of the "noble savage" deeply influenced romanticism, published *La Nouvelle Héloïse*, 1761, a novel advocating simple relationships in a natural setting. The *Encyclopédie*, edited 1751-72 by **Denis Diderot**, 1713-84, and **Jean Le Rond d'Alembert**, 1717-83, expressed the scepticism of the Enlightenment.

Gothic themes involving the supernatural and the *crime de passion* appeared in the ultra-romantic novel *The Castle of Otranto*, 1764, by **Horace Walpole**, 1717-97. **Thomas Percy**, 1729-1811, published *Reliques of Ancient English Poetry*, 1765. **Karl Bellman**, 1740-95, a Swedish poet, began his *82 Epistles* in 1765.

Thomas Gray's *Poems by Mr Gray*, 1768, included the "Elegy Written in a Country Churchyard". Gray, 1716-71, treated themes of history and death in a sensitive, meditative manner. **Gotthold Lessing**, 1729-81 used Shakespearian models influentially in *Laokoon*, 1766.

Sturm und Drang (Storm and Stress), a German literary movement stressing subjectivity and contemporary unease, found a genius in **Johann Wolfgang von Goethe**, 1749-1832. His novel *The Sufferings of Young Werther*, 1774, began a cult of the hero ruled by the heart rather than head. Romantic pessimism was exemplified in the poems of **Novalis**, 1772-1801.

Art and architecture

The arts in Europe, and particularly in France, reflected the critical spirit of the Enlightenment by returning to an austere style based on moral and aesthetic theories. Antiquarian and archaeological investigation had transformed ideas on cultural development so that the various styles of Greek and Roman antiquity, the Middle Ages and the Renaissance, could now be distinguished. Neoclassicism, which developed towards the end of the 18th century, incorporated this knowledge, adopting Greek and Roman ideals of beauty and ethics derived from antique sculpture, architecture, painting and literature. This historical concern was also to lead to acceptance of eclecticism and the concept of a modern style.

The European colonial presence in Asia tended to paralyse the development of indigenous artistic styles, but native traditions survived in areas remote from foreign influence.

Robert Adam with his brother James introduced a new eclectic style of architecture to town and country houses in Britain, like **Syon House**, 1762-9, in which they combined elements of English Palladianism with details of Roman architecture and Renaissance palaces. **Neoclassical painting** was developed in Rome, under the impetus of the German archaeologist **Johann Joachim Wickelmann**, 1717-68, by his follower **Anton Raffael Mengs**, 1728-79.

Soufflot's church of Ste Geneviève in Paris progressed. The design combined Greek post and lintel systems and attempted to achieve the lightness of Gothic architecture. **The Royal Academy of Art**, London, was founded in 1768 under royal patronage. The first President, **Joshua Reynolds**, in "13 Discourses", 1769-1790, promoted the "Grand Manner" in English painting.

An empirical, scientific attitude to art in England was shown by **George Stubbs**, 1724-1806, in the *Anatomy of the Horse*, published 1766, and in "The experiment with the Air Pump", 1768, by **Joseph Wright** of Derby, 1734-97. **French Neoclassic architecture** was governed by the severe unadorned classicism seen in the works of **Jacques Gondouin**, 1737-1818, of which the **Ecole de Médecine**, Paris, 1769, is a fine example.

Reynold's supremacy in English portraiture was challenged in 1774 when **Thomas Gainsborough**, 1727-88, moved to London. His "William Henry, Duke of Gloucester", *c.* 1775, was deliberately glamorous and richly coloured. His later paintings introduced a more lyrical note to English portraiture. **Indian artists** in the late 18th and early 19th centuries were dominated by European techniques. An exception was the Patua paintings of east India.

Music

The classical age of European music was dominated by Joseph Haydn, 1732-1809, and Wolfgang Mozart, 1756-91. Composers pursued variety within movements, building bigger structures by manipulating musical themes and utilizing key relationships and contrasts of instrumental sound, appealing equally to the heads and hearts of their educated audiences.

The symphony and sonata grew in complexity under the hand of Haydn from *c.* 1760. The first movement had contrasting themes worked over in a development section.

Counterpoint declined in importance and the continuo disappeared. Contrapuntal forms such as fugue continued to be used but usually as part of a movement in a larger work.

Christoph Gluck, 1714-87, reformed opera in Paris, stressing the balance between the musical and the dramatic elements. He expressed his ideals in a preface to *Alceste*, 1769.

String quartets were written in large numbers. They were an ideal vehicle for the development of classical designs and allowed the composer to hear his work immediately.

Science and technology

In Britain the Industrial Revolution began to transform the face of the nation. James Watt produced the first rotary engine, which could be used to power factories anywhere in the country, while the spinning jenny and the water frame furthered mechanization of the textile industry. Agricultural improvements, including more efficient crop rotation and selective breeding, increased the amount of food and provided a surplus for the towns. Developments in hygiene and medicine, such as the water closet, vaccination and the widespread use of soap, would form the basis for substantial improvements in urban living conditions, many of which, however, were not realized until the nineteenth century.

Science was linked with liberty in revolutionary France as many academies of science were founded after 1789, while American technology worked against freedom – the success of the cotton gin helping to prolong slavery in the South.

Joseph Black, 1728-99, a Scottish chemist, defined the difference between heat and temperature, and discovered specific and latent heat, 1760-3. His basic work on heat enabled his friend **James Watt** to build a steam engine. **The spinning-jenny** was invented in England, 1764, by **James Hargreaves.** It could spin several threads at once.

The Lunar Society, an informal society of technologists, was founded in England *c.* 1765. **Neurology** was established with the work of Swiss physiologist **Albrecht von Haller**, 1708-77. Haller located nerves and showed that nerve impulses stimulate muscles. **Henry Cavendish**, 1731-1810, a British scientist, discovered hydrogen in 1766. He also made fundamental, unpublished discoveries in electricity. In 1798 he calculated the Earth's mass.

The water frame was invented in 1768 by **Richard Arkwright**, 1732-92. Powered by water, it spun cotton into a strong thread. **James Watt**, 1736-1819, patented his steam engine in 1769. This engine used a separate cylinder for condensing steam and worked quickly and efficiently. Watt's engine was the first to produce rotary motion. **Luigi Galvani**, 1737-98, an Italian, found in 1771 that two metals in contact with a frog's leg cause it to twitch. Unwittingly he had produced current electricity.

Oxygen was discovered, 1772, by the Swede **Carl Scheele**, 1742-86. He withheld his findings until after the independent discovery by **Joseph Priestley**, 1733-1804, in 1774. Scheele was also involved in the discovery of chlorine, 1774, tungsten, 1781, and other elements. **Daniel Rutherford**, 1749-1819, discovered **nitrogen** in 1772.

1776-80

The American colonies declared their independence, 1776, and allied with France, 1778, and Spain, 1779. The English overran the southern states 1778, but were weakened by a French blockade of shipping. **The French government** was ruined by this war in spite of the continued financial reforms of **Jacques Necker**, 1732-1804. **Pombal**, 1699-1782, completed the reorganization of the administration in Portuguese Brazil, 1777.

1780-4

American independence was assured by the British surrender at Yorktown, 1781, and formally recognized at the 1783 **Treaty of Paris**. A sudden growth in the English cotton industry after 1780 marked the beginning of the English **Industrial Revolution**. **Russia** occupied the Crimea in 1783. **Hastings** made an effective peace with the Marathas, 1784.

1784-8

The United States began trading with China, 1784, but suffered post-war depression through loss of contact with the West Indies, 1784-7. **The American Constitution** was signed in Philadelphia, 1787. **The aristocratic parliaments** in France blocked proposals for financial reform, 1787. **The founding of *The Times* newspaper** in England, 1788, accompanied the growth of an informed middle class in Europe.

1788-92

England established convict settlements in Australia, 1788. **Louis XVI**, *r.* 1774-92, was forced to summon the estates-general in 1789 because of the financial crisis. **The French Revolution** began when a group of middle-class radicals took over the administration with the help of the Paris mob and tried to set up a constitutional monarchy, 1789. **George Washington**, 1732-99, became the first president of the United States, 1789.

1792-6

France was declared a republic, 1792. Louis was executed, 1793, and during the ensuing terror, 1793-4, many of the nobility were also guillotined as a result of the fear of a counter-revolution backed by Austrian forces. **The French overran Holland** and established the Batavian Republic in 1795. **Revolutionary ideas** led to the freeing of slaves in the French West Indies, arousing hostility among the European powers.

1796-1800

By the **Treaty of Campo Formio**, 1797, Austria ceded Belgium to France. **Napoleon**, 1769-1821, defeated Austria, 1796, but his plans to invade England, 1798, failed and he was prevented by **Horatio Nelson**, 1758-1805, from cutting England off from India at the Battle of the Nile, 1798. In 1799 he overthrew the moderate **Directory** and established a dictatorship, 1799-1804.

Relaxation of anti-Catholic laws reflected the confidence of the government but resulted in the destructive **Gordon riots** in London in 1780.

William Pitt the Younger, 1759-1806, formed his first ministry. Further colonial expansion became necessary to replace the American colonies.

The economic boom based on coal mining and cotton production began, 1786, bringing the development of new towns in the Midlands and North.

Pitt survived the 1788 crisis of George III's temporary insanity. **Until the execution of Louis XVI**, British opinion generally backed the Revolution.

The London Corresponding Society was founded among the artisan class to campaign for electoral reform, 1792, but was suppressed by Pitt, 1796.

Payments under the **Speenhamland** system of Poor Law became common after 1795. **The Combination Acts**, 1799, banned trades union activity.

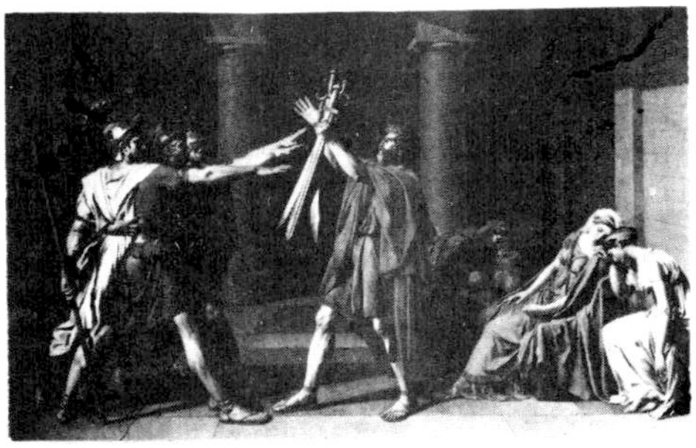

"The Oath of the Horatii" by David

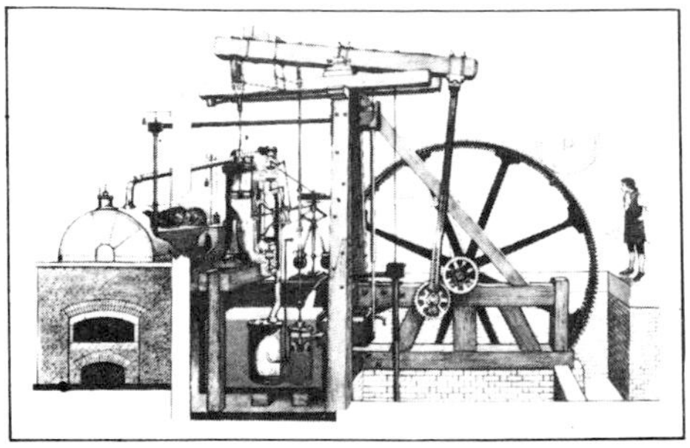

James Watt's rotary steam engine

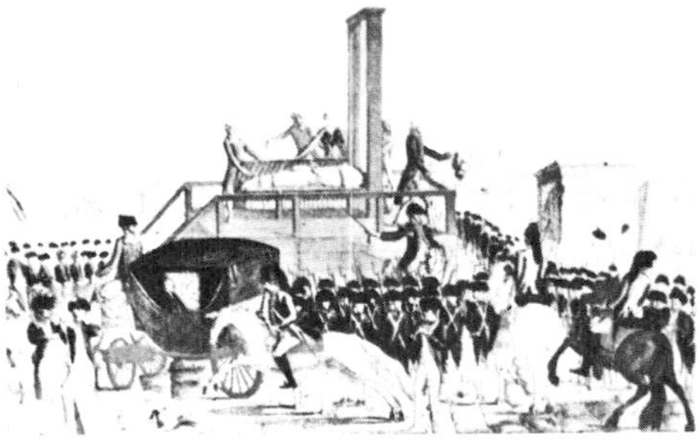

French Revolution: the execution of the king

Founder of modern economics, **Adam Smith**, 1723-90, argued that although manufacturers do not intend to satisfy the general good, they are led to do so by the "invisible hand" of the competitive market. When a producer satisfied his self-interest by selling goods for which there is a demand, he also satisfies a general social need. Smith's *Wealth of Nations* was published in 1776.

Immanuel Kant, 1724-1804, in his *Critique of Pure Reason*, 1781, wrote that although knowledge cannot transcend experience, the concepts that organize perception are innate to the human mind and prior to experience. In *Metaphysics and Morals*, 1785, he argued that man's idea of morality is *a priori* and that people act morally when the maxim on which they act is one which they can desire all men to follow.

Liberalism, the belief that the state should not encroach on individual freedom, was proposed by **Jeremy Bentham**, 1748-1832, in *A Fragment on Government*, 1776. He argued in his *Principles*, 1784, for utilitarianism, the theory that the happiness of the majority of individuals was the greatest good. This was to be achieved by allowing each individual the freedom to maximize his useful achievement by avoiding pain and pursuing pleasure.

In France, 1789-90, Church lands were nationalized and religious orders suppressed. **Edmund Burke**, 1729-97, in *Reflections on the Revolution in France*, 1790, argued that the replacement of practical politics by utopianism had led to extremism. **Tom Paine**, 1737-1809, in America, wrote *The Rights of Man*, 1791, to oppose *Burke's Reflections*. Paine believed revolution could be avoided only if the causes of the discontent were eradicated.

Equal opportunities for women to develop their talents were demanded by **Mary Wollstonecraft**, 1759-97, in her *Vindication of the Rights of Women*, 1792. Her husband, **William Godwin**, 1756-1836, published *Enquiry Concerning Political Justice*, 1793. A radical, he argued that government power over citizens inevitably bred corruption. **The Cult of Reason** and later, the **Cult of the Supreme Being** were substituted for Christianity in France, 1793-4.

The English Evangelical Movement had emerged within the Church of England, influenced by Methodism. Its followers believed in the certainty of salvation, emphasizing evangelism and social walfare. **Reverend Thomas Malthus**, 1766-1834, published his *Essay on the Principle of Population*, 1798, rejecting the possibility of infinite improvements in human conditions on the grounds that population expands more rapidly than the available food supply.

Comedy of manners, revived in England by **Oliver Goldsmith**, *c.* 1730-74, in *She Stoops to Conquer*, 1773, reached a peak in *The School for Scandal*, 1777, by the Irish wit **R. B. Sheridan**, 1751-1816. **Italian patriotism** was stirred by **Vittorio Alfieri**, 1749-1803, whose 19 verse tragedies in the classical mode opposed tyranny.

The influential French novel *Les Liaisons Dangereuses*, 1782, by **P. A. F. Choderlos de Laclos**, 1741-1803, had a savage tone in contrast to the vogue for high moral sentiment established by Rousseau. The privileges of the upper class were satirized by **Pierre de Beaumarchais**, 1732-99, in *The Barber of Seville*, 1775, and *The Marriage of Figaro*.

Scottish folk traditions found a passionate and lyrical voice in the poems of **Robert Burns**, 1759-96, whose *Kilmarnock Edition*, 1786, established him as a skilled writer of songs, satires and narratives. A deep love of nature, a major theme in romanticism, is found in the blank verse of "The Task", 1785, by the English poet **William Cowper**, 1731-1800.

A new tradition of candid biography was begun by **James Boswell**, 1740-95, in his *Life of Johnson*, 1791, bringing to life his friend **Samuel Johnson**, 1709-84. Johnson, a brilliant conversationalist, editor, poet and critic, dominated English literature after 1750 with his *Dictionary*, 1755, the Gothic novel *Rasselas*, 1759, and *Lives of the Poets*, 1779-81.

William Blake, 1757-1827, one of the most powerful, imaginative artists in English literature, published the lyrical *Songs of Experience*, 1794, complementing *Songs of Innocence*, 1789. Poet, painter, engraver and, above all, visionary, he issued prophetic warnings of the danger of industrialization and materialism in *The Marriage of Heaven and Hell*.

The Romantic movement in England began with *Lyrical Ballads*, 1798, by **William Wordsworth**, 1770-1850, and **Samuel Taylor Coleridge**, 1772-1834. **The novels of Jean Paul**, 1763-1825, including *Hesperus*, 1795, combined the idealism of Fichte with the romantic sentimentality of *Sturm und Drang*.

Classicism in Russia under Catherine the Great was led by foreign artists such as the French sculptor **Etienne-Maurice Falconet**, 1716-91; who executed the equestrian statue of Peter the Great, 1769; and Scottish architect **Charles Cameron**, *c.* 1740-1812, who went to Russia in 1779. Cameron decorated several apartments in the palace of Tsarkoe Seio (now Puskino) near Leningrad for Catherine.

Neoclassical painting was firmly established in France with "Oath of the Horatii", 1784, by Jacques-Louis David, 1748-1825, in which the subordination of colour to drawing enforces the theme of heroic self-sacrifice as exemplified by ancient Rome. "The Nightmare" by **Henry Fuseli**, 1741-1825, and the works of **William Blake**, 1757-1827, reveal an emphasis on the bizarre and supernatural in contrast with Academic aims.

The Academy on Fine Arts in Mexico City, founded in 1785, was staffed primarily by Spanish-trained artists who were largely instrumental in introducing Neoclassicism to Mexico. **English caricature** was developed by James Gillray, 1757-1815, in "A New Way to Pay the National Debt", 1786 and by **Thomas Rowlandson**, 1756-1827, who illustrated Smollet, Goldsmith, Sterne and Swift, and produced "Imitations of Modern Drawings", 1784-88.

The "Style Troubadour" originated in France when anecdotal scenes from the lives of wise kings of early French history were used by anti-royalists to accentuate the incompetence of Louis XVI. **Classicism in English architecture** was exemplified in the work of John Soane, 1753-1837, whose austere and original manipulation of the antique was seen in his **Bank of England Stock Office**, 1792, with its top-lit vaulted hall.

Painting in Revolutionary France was used as a political weapon. David's "The Death of Marat", 1793, combines classicism with an element of realism to deify a revolutionary hero and muster republican support. **John Flaxman**, 1755-1826, published his illustrations to Homer's *Iliad* and *Odyssey* in 1793. With their simple outline figures they immediately became a major model for Neoclassical painters and influenced later generations.

The success of Napoleon's Italian campaign 1796-7, galvanized French art with the public display in the Louvre of looted art treasures. This enhanced the image of Napoleon as a national hero. **The Capitol, Richmond, Va**, 1789-98, built by Thomas Jefferson, 1743-1826, was based on the Maison Carrée, Nîmes, and brought Neoclassical architecture to the United States.

African music as described by Western observers probably resembled music heard today, in which groups of instruments, such as marimbas and drums, freely explore areas of sonority.

Mozart was one of the first great composers who tried to live independently without the support of a patron, but he died a pauper. His work in opera and other fields of music shows the effects of his original thought. While others were content with the stock characters of Italian opera, he created such works of individual genius as *Don Giovanni*, produced in Prague, 1787.

Domenico Cimarosa, 1749-1801, "the Italian Mozart", composed his most celebrated opera, *Il matrimonio segreto* in Vienna in 1792.

Niccolò Paganini, the Italian virtuoso violinist, 1782-1840, made his debut in Genoa in 1793, playing his own variations on "La Carmagnole".

The violin was taken to India by British rulers. Indian musicians absorbed it into their music, utilizing its subtleties of intonation and tone colour.

A practical water closet was patented in 1778 in England by **Joseph Bramah**, 1748-1814. Bramah's many inventions introduced practical techniques that founded the engineering industry. **The spinning mule** was invented in England in 1779 by **Samuel Crompton**, 1753-1827. It was able to spin high quality thread on many spindles at once. **Cheap soap** resulted from the work *c.* 1780 of **Nicholas Leblanc**, 1742-1806, in France. He patented his process of producing soda from salt in 1791.

Uranus was discovered by **William Herschel**, 1738-1822, in 1781. It was the first planet to be discovered that was not known to ancient civilizations. **The first manned flight** took place in 1783 in a hot air balloon made and flown by the French **Montgolfier** brothers Joseph, 1740-1810, and Jacques, 1745-99. **James Watt** invented the double-acting engine in 1784.

Chlorine was first used for bleaching cloth in 1785 by **Claude Berthollet**, 1748-1822, a French chemist. **The threshing machine** was patented, 1788, by a Scotsman, **Andrew Meikle**, 1719-1811. **Jacques Charles**, 1746-1823, a French physicist, formulated **Charles's law** *c.* 1787, that at constant pressure the volume of a gas is related to its absolute temperature. **The power loom**, invented in 1785 by **Edmund Cartwright**, 1743-1823, mechanized weaving.

Theory of the Earth, 1788, by **James Hutton**, 1726-97, began modern geology by viewing all geological change as continuous. *Traité Elémentaire de Chimie*, by **Antoine Lavoisier**, 1743-94, written in 1789, founded modern chemistry with its insistence on measurement and standard nomenclature. Lavoisier stated the law of the conservation of mass; he also defined chemical reaction. In 1790 **Watt** applied his fly-ball governor to control the speed of a steam engine.

Coal gas was first produced in 1792 by **William Murdock**, 1754-1839, a British inventor. **The cotton gin**, a device used to strip cotton from bolls, was invented, 1793, by **Eli Whitney**, 1765-1825, revitalizing cotton growing in the United States. **The metric system** was adopted in France in 1795. **Scientific institutes** abounded in revolutionary France, as did prizes for scientific developments. Institutes included the Jardin des Plantes and the Ecole Polytechnique.

Vaccination, discovered in 1796 by Edward Jenner, 1749-1823, led to the eradication of smallpox. **The nature of heat**, or kinetic energy, was discovered in 1798 by the American, **Count Rumford**, who noticed that the boring of cannons produced heat and reasoned that heat is a form of motion and not a fluid. **The battery** was invented by **Count Volta**, 1745-1827, in 1800. He developed Galvani's observations into a practical idea for an electricity supply.

1800-1825 The rise of industrial power

Principal events

Inspired by a vision of himself as head of a European empire, Napoleon Bonaparte overran most of Europe but was unable to maintain his conquests. With his final defeat at Waterloo in 1815, the *ancien régime* was restored to France. His conquests, however, sparked off a multitude of constitutional and nationalist demands throughout Europe, while his occupation of Spain encouraged the Latin American countries to grasp their independence. They remained, however, unable to reorganize themselves economically or to free themselves politically from European influence.

In England, the Industrial Revolution caused the emergence of a new wealthy class and social tensions gave a greater urgency to demands for parliamentary reform, while her naval strength and leadership of the final coalition against Napoleon left her the dominant trading power in the world.

1800-2

Napoleon established the prefecture as the main instrument of local government, subject to central control. He improved education and made a compromise with the Church, 1800-1.
His aggressive nationalist campaigns led to victory over the empire and Austria, conquest in Italy, 1800, and temporary peace with England in 1802.
With the murder of Paul I, **Alexander I**, *r.* 1801-25, became Tsar of Russia.

1802-5

Nationalist feeling brought a Serbian uprising against the Ottoman rule in 1804.
Napoleon assumed the title of emperor in 1804.
Britain resumed the war against him in 1803 and was joined by **Russia, Austria** and **Sweden** in 1805. Russia was defeated at **Austerlitz**, 1805, but Britain's naval victory at **Trafalgar**, 1805, resulted in a crippling blockade of French shipping.
Napoleon proclaimed himself **King of Italy**, 1805.

1805-7

After defeating Prussia, 1806, Napoleon allied with Russia, 1807, and set up the **Continental System** (which Russia was forced to leave for economic reasons in 1810) to exclude British trade from Europe.
The Holy Roman Empire came to an end when **Francis II**, *r.* 1792-1835, who was also Emperor of Austria, renounced the title, 1806.
The slave trade was abolished in the British Empire, 1807, although slavery continued in the colonies.

1807-8

A nationalist revolt broke out in Spain when Joseph Bonaparte, 1768-1844, assumed the throne, 1808. Britain exploited this to attack Napoleon in the Peninsular War, 1808-14.
Austria and Prussia reformed their army and taxation systems to improve military capacity.
Archduke Charles of Austria appealed to the Germans to oppose Napoleon but was defeated at **Wagram**, 1809.
France assumed control of Swedish foreign affairs.

National events

Stimulated by the Napoleonic Wars, the Industrial Revolution created large, overcrowded towns centred on factories in which whole families were employed. Social and economic discontent ensued, resulting in widespread agitation for electoral reform, fostered by the growing middle classes.

Robert Owen, 1771-1858, set up a co-operative cotton mill at New Lanark, 1800.
Britain and Ireland were constitutionally united, 1801.

A Factory Act, 1802, tried ineffectually to limit children's working hours in factories.
Nelson destroyed the Franco-Spanish fleet at Trafalgar, 1805.

England declared a blockade of French ports.
Napoleon's Continental System, 1806, raised food prices and depressed the textile industry.

Parliament, based on the country's authority and agricultural constituencies, was growing increasingly out of touch with the interests of the new industries.

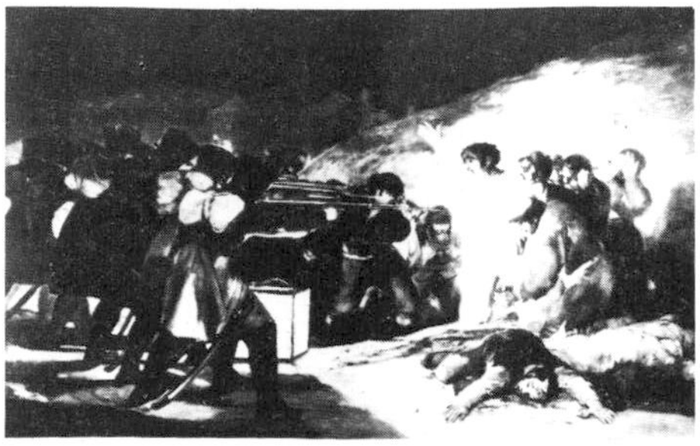

The town of New Lanark

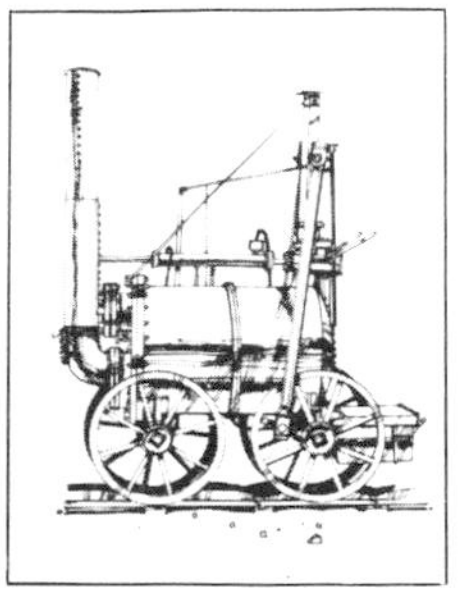

Napoleon at Eylau, 1807

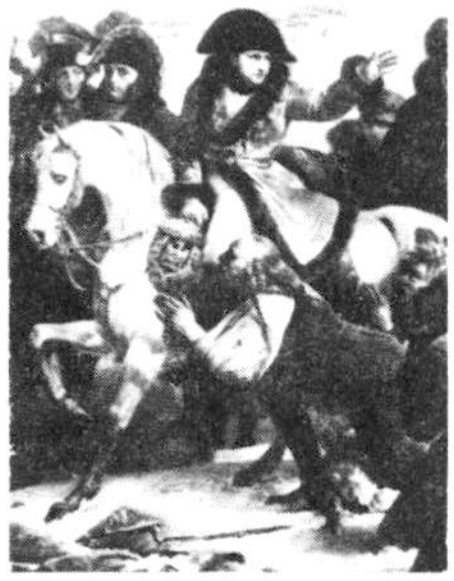

Trevithic's steam engine

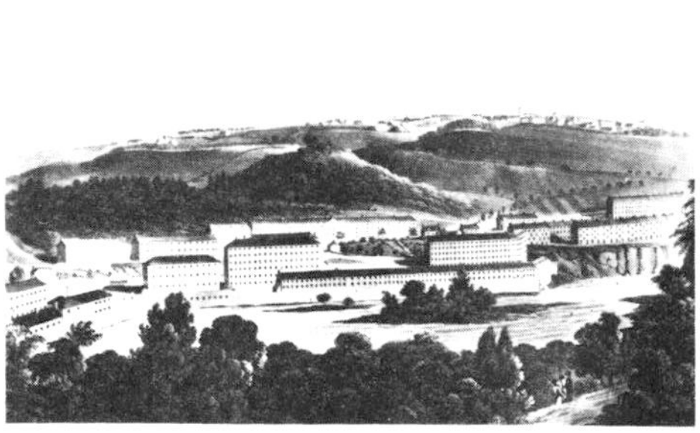

"The 3rd of May, 1808" by Goya

Religion and philosophy

Classical economic theory was developed and systematized in the work of Say in France and Ricardo in England, the latter influencing both sides of the debate about *laissez-faire* doctrines, which dominated social thought in the early 19th century. At the same time reaction to the social evils of industrial capitalism ranged from Sismondi's warning of class antagonisms to the social experiments of Robert Owen and the Utopianism of Charles Fourier.

The major philosophical school of the period, German idealism, emerged in a country as yet relatively sheltered from the major social upheavals of the time. In particular, Hegel, who would greatly influence the young Karl Marx, argued that historical progress was identical with the advancement of human consciousness, while Schopenhauer and Schelling emphasized man's darker, irrational impulses and prepared the way for Freud and existentialism.

Friedrich Schelling, 1775-1854, published his *Transcendental Idealism*, 1800, in Germany, grounding his idealism on external nature. His philosophy of man stressed the force of irrationalism which, as the source of all evil, could dominate the intellect, wherein lay the power for good.
William Paley, 1743-1805, an Anglican, advanced the idea in *Natural Theology*, 1802, that the design evident in the world implied the work of a creator.

Jean Baptiste Say published his *Traité d'économie politique* in 1803, putting forward his "law of markets", which states that supply creates its own demand with the consequence that depression is the result of overproduction in some markets and under-production in others, an imbalance that would automatically correct itself.
The *Code Napoléon* of 1804 nationalized French law and established the principle of equal citizenship.

G. W. F. Hegel, 1770-1831, the German idealist philosopher, published his first great work, *Phenomenology of Mind*, in 1807. In this and later works Hegel expressed the view that reality is essentially a whole (which he called the Absolute) comprising both mind (subject) and matter (object). The physical world would cease to be alien and objective when, with the attainment of total comprehension, object and subject merged into the Absolute.

Charles Fourier, 1772-1837, writing in France (*The Social Destiny of Man*, 1808) and **Robert Owen** in England (*A New View of Society*, 1813) advocated social reconstruction on the basis of workers' co-operatives. Owen organized mills at New Lanark, 1800-24, on principles of welfare and justice but his American experimental community at New Harmony, 1825, was short-lived, as were the communes based on the even more Utopian ideas of Fourier.

Literature

English Romanticism reached its peak with the work of the poets Wordsworth and Byron, who explored the quest for harmony with nature and stressed the independence of genius from social convention. The historical novel developed by Scott linked the interest in the past with an implicit concern for national identity – a trend echoed in the German concentration on folk-tales and mythology. In other respects, however, German Romanticism, as displayed by Goethe and Schiller, involved a less violent break with 18th-century humanism.

Chateaubriand and Madame de Staël tried to introduce the ideas of the movement to France, but met little success as classicism still reigned until the work of the poets in the 1820s.

A more subjective emphasis developed in German literature with the two unfinished novels of **Novalis**, 1772-1801, published in 1798-1800. Both were *Bildungsromans* novels on the education of the hero and the development of character and temperament, like Goethe's *Wilhelm Meister*.
William Wordsworth wrote his autobiographical poem *The Prelude* in 1799-1805.

Le Génie du Christianisme, 1802, by **Francois René de Chateaubriand**, 1768-1848, introduced to French literature a mystical Christianity which had a great influence on the French romantic writers.
The need for political freedom in Germany was the subject of the play *William Tell*, 1804, by the poet and dramatist **Johann Schiller**, 1759-1805.

The German romantic poets Brentano, 1778-1842, and **von Arnim**, 1781-1831, collected folk-poems, in *Des Knaben Wunderhorn*, 1805-8.
Heinrich Kleist, 1771-1811, published *Penthesilea*, 1808.

The humanism of Johann Goethe, 1749-1832, was expressed in his play *Faust, Part 1*, 1808.
The poetry of the Italian Ugo Foscolo, 1778-1827, extolled the past and the value of art as a permanent shrine to virtue.
The lyric dramatic poetry of **Adam Oehlenschläger**, 1779-1850, was popular in Denmark.

Art and architecture

European art in the early 19th century saw a reaction to Neoclassicism and the beginnings of Romanticism, involving a shift from formal rules to an emphasis on the subjective – feelings, impressions, imagination – and a preference for fantasy, excess and the poetic. The influence of Romanticism also inspired an interest in historical and foreign styles of architecture, while in painting it produced the freer technique and the more expressive use of colour found in the work of Delacroix. The choice of subject-matter also changed to include contemporary and historical scenes which reflected the nationalist ideals of the time – a tendency heightened in France by the exotic career and lavish commissions of Napoleon. While Neoclassicism came to be rejected by artists in Western Europe its influence spread into Russia and the New World, where it dominated architecture.

The term "picturesque" was introduced in England at the end of the 18th century as an aesthetic category, characterized by irregularity, variety and roughness of texture; it had a decisive effect on landscape painting and architecture.
British industrial architecture had developed over the 18th century to include iron frame constructions which were fireproof and functional.

The Greek revival in European architecture, *c.* 1760-1830, was now at its height. Its essence was the exact reproduction of Greek models, which were admired for their simplicity and associated with the beginnings of civilization. It was predominantly used for public buildings like the theatre at Besancon 1784, by **Claude-Nicolas Ledoux**, 1736-1806, although domestic forms, sometimes in the style of a Greek temple, were popular.

Napoleon commissioned portraits and commemorative scenes to enhance his imperial image. Canvases presented an aura of magnificence with allusions to the Roman Empire as in "Napoleon as Emperor", 1806, by **Jean-August-Dominique Ingres**, 1780-1867, and "Napoleon at Eylau", 1808, by **Antoine Gros**, 1771-1835.
Napoleonic architecture like the Paris Bourse, 1807, by **A. T. Brongniart**, 1739-1813, was similarly inspired.

Davidian ideals were questioned in France by his pupils. Some, like **Anne-Louis Girodet**, 1767-1824, in his "Entombment of Atala", 1808, used unusual light effects and mystical subjects.
The investigation of the symbolic, mystical and religious aspects of landscape took place primarily in Germany, with the work of **Caspar David Friedrich**, 1774-1840, whose "The Cross in the Mountains", 1808, was painted as an altarpiece.

Music

Romanticism in European music began to replace classicism as personal expression in the arts took precedence over ideals of formal balance. But the first romantic composers, such as Ludwig van Beethoven, 1770-1827, and Carl von Weber, 1786-1826, were trained in classical techniques and brought restraint to bear on the new, sensuous style of music.

The piano repertory was rapidly extended by **Muzio Clementi**, 1752-1832, and Beethoven, as the instrument gained a greater range of notes and sound quality.

Short forms for the piano were established by such composers as **John Field**, 1782-1837, who wrote nocturnes – one-movement lyric pieces, later made popular by **Frédéric Chopin**, 1810-49.

Beethoven straddled the classical and romantic eras, extending the range of sonata form and composing works, such as the *Coriolanus Overture*, 1807, directly inspired by literary ideas.

Programme music, interpreting the events and moods of a specific story, emerged as a feature of romantic music, using evocative sounds as in Beethoven's *Pastoral Symphony*, 1808.

Science and technology

Progress in technology and science in Europe divided between Britain and France. France became the centre of pure science while Britain forged ahead in industrial science. Although automation was invented in France, its potential was not fully exploited. Similarly, atomic theory was first proposed in England but was refined in Europe.

The most important technological innovation was that of powered transport in England and the USA, which opened new areas of industrial expansion; in the same period gas lighting transformed city life. Many scientific discoveries, too, would have subsequent importance. Electrical science developed with the discovery of electromagnetism and would stimulate enquiry into the nature of matter as well as producing new sources of energy, while modern chemistry developed under the influence of Gay-Lussac and Avogadro. The study of fossils raised new questions about the age and origins of life.

Automation using punched cards to control the production of silk fabric was invented in France, 1801, by **Joseph Marie Jacquard**, 1752-1834.
Ultra-violet light in the Sun's spectrum was discovered, 1801, by **Johann Ritter**, 1776-1810.
The interference of light was shown, in 1801, by **Thomas Young**, 1773-1829, restoring the wave theory first put forward by Christiaan Huygens. Young also studied elasticity, giving his name to the tensile modulus, or scale of elasticity.

Screw-cutting machines and lathes were developed at the engineering works of the Englishman **Henry Maudslay**, 1771-1831, who invented the screw micrometer and schooled many fine engineers.
Jean Baptiste Lamarck, 1744-1829, a French naturalist, coined the term "biology" in 1802. In his *Philosophie Zoologique*, 1809, he held that evolution occurred.
The first railway locomotive was built in England by **Richard Trevithic**, 1771-1833, and first ran in 1804.

Gas lighting was introduced in European cities *c.* 1806.
The Clermont, built by **Robert Fulton**, 1765-1815, an American engineer, inaugurated the first regular steamboat service along the Hudson River in 1807, although a short-lived service had been run *c.* 1790.
The Geological Society of London was founded in 1807.

Potassium and sodium were discovered, 1806-7, by **Humphry Davy**, 1778-1829, an English chemist.
Jean Fourier, 1768-1830, a French mathematician, discovered that a complex wave is the sum of several simple waves.
The atomic theory, stating that the same elements have the same atoms and that a compound is made up of atoms of elements combined in fixed proportions, was propounded in 1808 by **John Dalton**, 1766-1844.

1808-12

Napoleon's empire reached its greatest extent, 1812, when with Austria and Prussia he invaded Russia. French forces took Moscow, 1812, but were unable to sustain the Russian winter and were forced to retreat with serious losses. **Paraguay and Venezuela** became independent from Spain, 1811, marking the final collapse of Spanish imperial authority. **Napoleon married Marie Louise** of Austria in his search for an heir, 1810.

1812-14

The Duke of Wellington, 1769-1852, led the Allied forces into Paris, 1814. Napoleon abdicated and was exiled to Elba. **The monarchy was restored** in Louis XVIII, *r.* 1814-24. **The Congress of Vienna**, 1814-15, restored monarchs to the Austrian and Prussian thrones and the kingdom of the Netherlands was founded as a buffer against France. **Britain** won definitive control of the **Cape of Good Hope**, 1814, on the route to India.

1814-17

Napoleon returned from Elba and Austria, Britain, Prussia and Russia formed a new alliance. Louis fled from Paris to return only after Napoleon's defeat at **Waterloo** and exile to St Helena, 1815. **The Holy Alliance** aimed to crush the spread of radicalism in Austria, Prussia and Russia. **Prince Metternich**, 1773-1859, crushed similar aspirations in the German states. **Ferdinand I**, *r.* 1815-25, regained the Italian throne.

1817-20

The American and Canadian border was fixed in 1818. **The first immigrants** settled the Australian grasslands, 1817-18. **A revolt in Naples** against Ferdinand I was crushed in 1821 and Ferdinand returned with a more liberal constitution. **The British founded Singapore** to rival Dutch Malacca as the centre for Far Eastern trade. **Only Nepal, the Sikh and Sind states**, and Afghanistan were independent of British rule in India by 1818.

1820-22

Ferdinand VII of Spain, *r.* 1814-33, was captured by liberal rebels in 1820. **The nationalist Greek war** for independence from the Ottoman Empire began, 1821. The Great Powers intervened in 1827 and established a Greek kingdom in 1832. **Spain lost Mexico and Peru**, 1821, while Brazil became independent from Portugal, 1822. **Opium trade** between India and China flourished in the reign of **Hsüang Tung**, 1821-50.

1822-25

A Spanish liberal revolt was crushed with French help, 1823. **The Monroe Doctrine**, 1823, asserted that the American continent could no longer be an arena for European colonial activity. **Britain surpassed other European countries** in her industrial and trading position, but agitation began for more *laissez-faire* trading policies. **The Anglo-Burmese wars** began in 1824, following Burmese aggression.

Unemployed domestic weavers destroyed new machines in the **Luddite riots**, 1811-16, fearing the impact of mechanization on their craft.

The expansion of small country banks reached its peak, 1814, facilitating the transfer of agricultural wealth into industrial investment.

The Corn Laws, 1815, protected landowners by excluding foreign corn and keeping the price of bread high.

A Manchester reform meeting ended in the massacre of **Peterloo** in which soldiers fired into the crowd, killing several demonstrators, 1819.

The Cato Street conspiracy, which aimed to overthrow the government, was detected, 1820, and the conspirators hanged. **The post-war slump** ended.

A liberal Conservative ministry reduced duties on imports and repealed the **Combination Acts**, 1824.

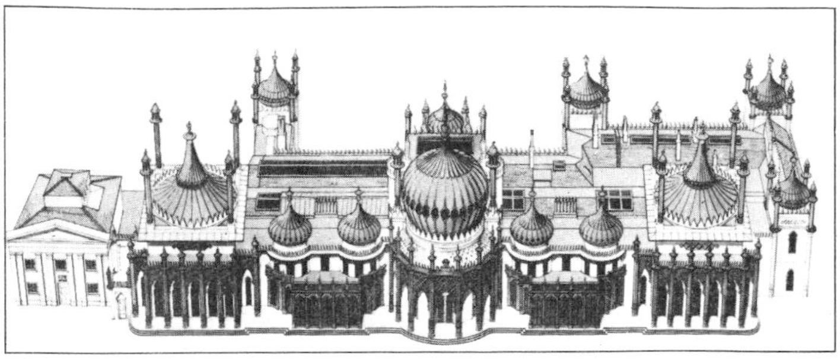

The Brighton Pavilion by Nash

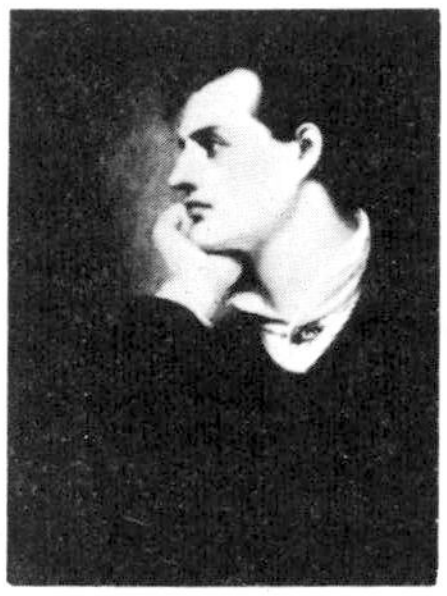

Lord Byron

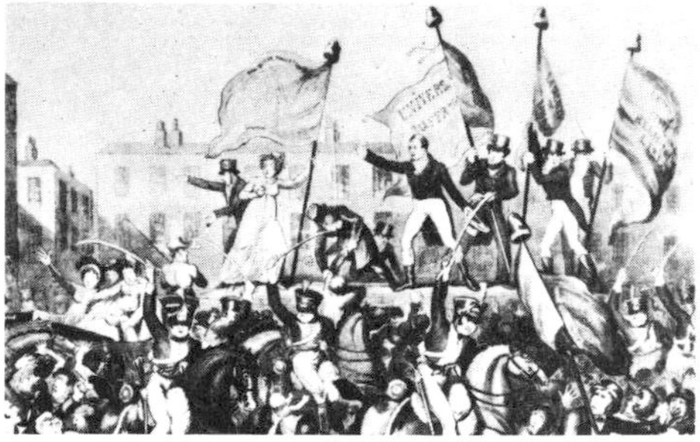

The Peterloo massacre

Hegel's *Science of Logic* was published in 1812-16. In it he developed a dialectical method of reasoning – opposing a thesis with its antithesis to establish a synthesis – with the aim of revealing the nature of the Absolute. Hegel believed history to be a dialectical progression towards the Absolute and considered the Prussian state to be the culmination of this dialectical progression.

The conservative tradition in France found exponents in **Joseph de Maistre**, 1753-1821, and **Louis Bonald**, 1754-1840, who insisted on the supremacy of Christianity and the absolute rule of the Church and pope. De Maistre published his *Essay on Constitutions* in 1814, in which he used his facility for logical argument to oppose the progress of science, liberalism and the empirical methods of the "philosophes", especially Voltaire.

The rising science of economics was systematized by **David Ricardo**, 1772-1823, in his *Principles of Political Economy and Taxation*, 1817, which aimed to set out the laws governing the division of the social product among the classes in society. The systematization of this work made him the leading exponent of the classical school in England and he was influential both among *laissez-faire* economists and their opponents, such as Robert Owen and, later, Karl Marx.

Jean Charles Sismondi, an early theorist of economic crisis, warned in his *New Principles of Political Economy*, 1819, against the effects of unregulated industrialism, predicting acute social conflict. In Germany, **Artur Schopenhauer**, 1788-1860, published *The World as Will and Idea* in 1819. His emphasis on man's will and irrational impulses prepared the way for the departure from the 18th-century idea of rational progress.

Thomas Erskine, 1788-1870, a Scottish theologian, in *Internal Evidence for the Truth of Christian Religion*, 1820, held that the meaning of Christianity lay in its conformity with man's spiritual and ethical needs. **Friedrich Schleiermacher**, 1768-1834, a German theologian and founder of modern Protestant theology, in *The Christian Faith*, 1821-2, saw religious feeling as a sense of absolute dependence and sin as a desire for independence.

The anti-union Combination Acts were repealed in Britain, 1824, after a campaign led by **Francis Place**, 1771-1854, and **Joseph Hume**, 1777-1855. Place advocated birth control as a means by which the working class could limit their numbers to improve wages. **Leopold Ranke**, 1795-1886, a German historian, wrote *History of the Latin and Teutonic Nations, 1494-1514*, in 1824, seeking a history based on scientific methods.

Madame de Staël, 1766-1817, wrote *De L'Allemagne* in 1810. **The works of Esaias Tegner**, 1782-1846, convey his belief in an ideal world and his version of Swedish national glory, as described in his poem *Svea*, 1811. **The English middle classes** were given perceptive scrutiny by **Jane Austen**, 1775-1817, in *Pride and Prejudice*, 1813 and *Sense and Sensibility*, 1811.

The English Romantic poet Percy Bysshe Shelley, 1792-1822, wrote his first major poem, *Queen Mab*, 1811-13. **The first historical novel** was the medieval romance *Waverley*, 1814, by **Sir Walter Scott**, 1771-1832. His evocations of the past had extensive influence, notably with **Manzoni** in Italy. **Brothers Grimm** made their collection of folk-tales, 1812-15.

Grotesque themes were studied by the German composer and author **Ernst Hoffmann**, 1776-1822, in his tales and in the novel *The Devil's Elixir*, 1813-15. **The psychological analysis** of a broken love affair is the subject of *Adolphe*, 1816, by **Benjamin Constant**, 1767-1830 – an ardent liberal and a political journalist, closely alligned with the French Romantics.

The spirit of the Romantic movement was epitomized in the notorious life of **Lord Byron** 1788-1824, and the tormented homeless Byronic hero became popular in European fiction. In contrast, his *Don Juan* (first two cantos, 1819), was a biting, unromanticized social satire. **William Hazlitt**, 1778-1830, commented on contemporary English life in astute essays.

Alphonse Lamartine, 1790-1869, moved from the private anguish of *Meditations*, 1820, to the mystical lyricism of *Harmonies Poétiques*, 1830. **A search for eternal perfection** is the theme of *Prometheus Unbound*, 1820, by the English poet Shelley. His friend **John Keats**, 1795-1821, wrote superlative odes, including the *Ode to a Nightingale*, 1819.

The Confessions of an English Opium Eater, 1822, was the autobiography of **Thomas De Quincey**, 1785-1859. **Thomas Peacock**, 1785-1866, skilfully used his satirical novels to attack English views, obsessions and political dogmas.

The pastiches of Indian, Chinese and Egyptian styles seen in the Prince Regent's Brighton Pavilion, from 1810, by the English architect John Nash, 1752-1835, reflected the world-wide process of exploration and colonization by the European powers. **A quasi-religious order**, the Nazarenes, was founded in Vienna, 1809, by **Friedrich Overbeck**, 1789-1869 and **Franz Pforr**, 1788-1812. They moved to Rome in 1810.

The work of Francisco de Goya, 1746-1828, combined objective reportage and a sense of personal horror at the Napoleonic Wars in "The Disasters of War", 1810-14. He later developed the new medium of lithography. **In Russia**, Alexander I commissioned classical buildings for St Petersburg and encouraged French Neoclassicism in all branches of the arts, particularly portraiture.

In France, Théodore Géricault, 1791-1824, took contemporary events as the vehicle for his themes and used large canvases to strengthen their impact in, for example, "The Raft of the 'Medusa'", 1817. **German Neoclassical architecture** first developed after the fall of Napoleon, with the emphasis on purely Grecian forms seen in the Neue Wache, Berlin, 1816, by **Karl Friedrich Schinkel**, 1781-1841.

Neo-Renaissance architecture was developed in Germany at the same time by **Leo von Klenze**, 1784-1864. His Palais Leuchtenberg, Munich, 1816, is the first German example, although the style existed earlier in France. **In 1816 Dom João VI of Brazil** invited French architects, painters and sculptors to Rio de Janeiro to "civilize" Creole taste. Their neoclassical style dominated the arts for the next hundred years.

English Romantic portraiture with its emphasis on drama and psychological investigation was exemplified in the forceful works of **Thomas Lawrence**, 1769-1830, whose portraits of the "Heads of State of Europe" in the Waterloo Chamber, Windsor Castle, 1818-20, celebrate the triumph over Napoleon.

Romantic tendencies in art were crystallized in the work of **Eugène Delacroix**, 1798-1863, where truth was no longer merely factual but a glimpse into man's soul. Delacroix set out to achieve this with the use of expressive colour and an emphasis on mood and the poetic. His work marked a decisive shift in French painting away from the importance of form and stressed violence and drama, as in his "Massacre at Chios", 1824.

Orchestral concerts became popular in London, Paris and Vienna as the middle classes began to support music. The patron and his salon declined in influence.

A greater variety of orchestral instruments allowed richer tone contrasts. There were few large orchestras so many orchestral works were published as piano transcriptions.

Lieder, a German form of lyric song, was raised by **Franz Schubert**, 1797-1828, to new heights as his piano parts provided a counterpart to the voice, echoing the mood of the lyric.

Opera centred on Paris. The light lyricism of *The Barber of Seville*, 1816, by **Gioacchino Rossini**, 1792-1868, gave way to the romanticism of **Carl von Weber's** *Der Freischütz*, 1821.

Conductors were required to marshal the expanded orchestra, as it could no longer be led by an instrumentalist. In 1820, **Ludwig Spohr**, 1784-1859, introduced the conductor's baton.

The symphony found new depths of expression, especially with **Beethoven**, as a personal creation requiring a large orchestra. His *Ninth Symphony*, 1824, is an example.

Joseph Gay-Lussac, 1778-1850, a French chemist, announced in 1808 that gases combine in certain proportions by volume and suggested that the proportions are linked to the formula of the compound formed. Gay-Lussac's work also led to the correct atomic weights of elements. **Amadeo Avogadro**, 1776-1856, an Italian, argued in 1811 that equal volumes of gases at the same temperature and pressure contain equal numbers of molecules.

Georges Cuvier, 1769-1832, a French anatomist, broadened Linnaeus' classification to include phyla and fossils, thus founding palaeontology. The hardness of materials was classified in 1812 by a German, Friedrich Mohs, 1773-1839. **Chemical symbols** as used today were introduced in 1814 by Jöns Berzelius, 1779-1848, a Swede, who later made a correct list of atomic weights. **Dark lines in the Sun's spectrum were identified**, 1814, by Joseph von Fraunhofer, 1787-1826.

The safety lamp was invented by **Humphry Davy** in 1815, to prevent explosions in mines. The optical experiments of **Jean Biot**, 1774-1862, after 1815, led to the founding of polarimetry. **The first geological map**, of England and Wales, was published, 1815, by **William Smith**, 1769-1839. **The single wire telegraph** was invented in 1816. **Photography** was born out of the experiments in 1816 of **Nicéphore Niepce**, 1765-1833.

Electromagnetism was found, 1820, by **Hans Oersted**, 1777-1851, who noticed that a compass needle was deflected by a wire carrying a current. He was also the first to prepare aluminium, 1825. **Thomas Seebeck**, 1770-1831, a Russo-German physicist invented the thermocouple, an instrument for measuring temperature as electricity, 1821.

André Ampère, 1775-1836, studied the effects of electric currents in motion, founding and naming the science of electrodynamics by 1822. He also invented the solenoid.

The electromagnet, the first machine to use electricity, was made by **William Sturgeon**, 1783-1850, an English physicist. **Sadi Carnot**, 1796-1832, published *On the Motive Power of Fire*, 1824, in which he showed that only a fraction of the heat produced by burning fuel in an engine is converted into motion, which depended only on the temperature difference in the engine. This was the basis of modern thermodynamics.

INDEX

How to use the index
Each subject is listed alphabetically. Page numbers in Roman type refer to text references; page numbers in italic type refer to illustrations or captions to illustrations.

Bibliography

General
Cambridge History of the British Empire; Cambridge U.P., 1940–59 (3 vols)
Africa
Fage, J. D.; *Cambridge History of Africa*; Cambridge U.P., 1978
Freeman-Grenville, G. S.; *Chronology of African History*; Oxford U.P., 1973
Freeman-Grenville, G. S.; *E. African Coast*; R. Collings, 1975
Hallett, R.; *Africa to 1875: A Modern History*; Univ. of Michigan Press, 1970
Oliver, R. & J. D. Fage; *A Short History of Africa*; Penguin, 1970
Wilson, M. & L. M. Thompson; *Oxford History of S. Africa*; Oxford U.P., 1969–71
Asia
Fitzgerald, C. P.; *Concise History of E. Asia*; Penguin, 1974
Luzzati, E.; *Travels of Marco Polo*; Dent, 1975
Spuler, B.; *History of the Mongols*; Routledge, 1972
    China
Schurmann, F. & O. Schell; *Imperial China*; Penguin, 1967
    Islamic Empire
Hayes, J. R. (Ed.); *Genius of Arab Civilization*; Phaidon, 1976
Holt, P. M. et al.; *Cambridge History of Islam*; Cambridge U.P., 1971 (2 vols)
Inalcik, H.; *Ottoman Empire 1300–1600*; Weidenfeld & Nicolson, 1973
Europe
Bainton, R. H.; *Age of Reformation*; Van Nost, Reinhold, 1956
Bainton, R. H.; *Erasmus of Christendom*; Collins, 1970
Bainton, R. H.; *Here I Stand: Life of Martin Luther*; New American Library, 1950
Bettenson, H. (Ed.); *Documents of the Christian Church*; Oxford U.P., 1967
Bronowski, J. & B. Mazlish; *The Western Intellectual Tradition*; Penguin, 1964
Clark, Sir G.; *Early Modern Europe*; Oxford U.P., 1966
Dickens, A. G.; *Counter-Reformation*; Thames & Hudson, 1969
Dickens, A. G.; *Reformation and Society in 16th Century Europe*; Thames & Hudson, 1966
Elliott, J. H.; *Europe Divided, 1559–1598*; Fontana, 1968
Elton, G. R.; *Reformation Europe 1517–99*; Fontana, 1969
Ganshof, F. L.; *Feudalism*; Longman, 1964
Gilmore, M. P.; *The World of Humanism*; Harper, 1962
Green, V. H. H.; *Renaissance and Reformation*; E. Arnold, 1964
Hale, J. R. et al. (Eds.); *Europe in the Late Middle Ages*; Faber, 1970
Hayek, F. A. (Ed.); *Capitalism and the Historians*; Univ. Chicago Press, 1954
Hays, D.; *Europe in the Fourteenth and Fifteenth Centuries*; Longman, 1971
Hazard, P.; *European Mind 1680–1715*; Penguin, 1973
Holmes, G.; *Europe: Heirarchy and Revolt, 1320–1450*; Fontana, 1975
Hoyt, R. S.; *Europe in the Middle Ages*; Harcourt Brace, 1976
Huizinga, J. H.; *Waning of the Middle Ages*; Penguin, 1972
Janelle, P.; *The Catholic Reformation*; Collier Macmillan, 1971
Knight, F.; *Exploration*; Benn, 1973
Knowles, D. & D. Obolensky; *Middle Ages*; Darton, 1969
Koenigsberger, N. G. & G. D. Mosse; *Europe in the 16th Century*; Longman, 1971
Lach, D. F.; *Asia in the Making of Europe*; Univ. of Chicago Press, 1965–70 (2 vols)
Leff, G.; *Heresy in the Later Middle Ages*; Manchester U.P., 1967
Parry, J. H.; *Europe and the Wider World, 1415–1715*; Hutchinson, 1966
Postan, M. M. (Ed.); *Cambridge Economic History of Europe*; Cambridge U.P., 1963–66
Smith, M. & D. Newton; *Exploration*; Schofield, 1971
Stoye, J.; *Europe Unfolding 1648–88*; Fontana, 1969
Tawney, R. H.; *Religion and the Rise of Capitalism*; Penguin, 1969
Ullman, W.; *Short History of the Papacy in the Middle Ages*; Methuen, 1972
Wendale, F.; *Calvin*; Fontana, 1965
    Britain (c.1300 – c.1500)
Barrow, G. W. S.; *Robert Bruce and the Community of the Realm of Scotland*; Edinburgh U.P., 1976
Boulay, F. R. H. du; *Age of Ambition*; Nelson, 1970
Curtis, E.; *History of Medieval Ireland*; Methuen, 1968
Dobson, R. B. (Ed.); *Peasants' Revolt*; Macmillan, 1970
Duncan, A. A. M.; *Scotland: The Making of the Kingdom*; Oliver & Boyd, 1975

Harriss, G. L.; *King, Parliament and the Public Finance in Medieval England to 1369*; Oxford U.P., 1975
Hilton, R.; *English Peasantry in the Later Middle Ages*; Oxford U.P., 1975
Knowles, D.; *Monastic Orders in England*; Cambridge U.P., 1963
Knowles, D.; *Religious Orders in England*; Cambridge U.P., 1948
McFarlane, K. B.; *Nobility of Later Medieval England*; Oxford U.P., 1973
Perroy, E.; *100 Years War*; Eyre, 1951
Roderick, A. J. (Ed.); *Wales through the Ages Vol. I*; C. Davies, 1971
Williams, G. A.; *Medieval London: Commune to Capital*; Athlone Press, 1970
    Britain (c.1500–1600)
Donaldson, G.; *James V – James VII*; Oliver & Boyd, 1965
Edwards, R.; *Ireland in the Age of the Tudors*; Crown Helm, 1977
Elton, G. R.; *England Under the Tudors*; Methuen, 1974
Hakluyt, R.; *Voyages and Documents*; Oxford U.P., 1958
Lydan, J. F.; *Ireland in the Later Middle Ages*; Gill, 1973
Mattingly, G.; *Defeat of the Spanish Armada*; Cape, 1970
Neale, J. E.; *Queen Elizabeth I*; Cape, 1967
Nicholson, R.; *Scotland: The Later Middle Ages*; Oliver & Boyd, 1973
Rowse, A. L.; *England of Elizabeth*; Macmillan, 1950
Scarisbrick, J. J.; *Henry VIII*; Eyre Methuen, 1976
Wernham, R. B.; *Before the Armada*; Cape, 1966
Williamson, J. A.; *Age of Drake*; Black, 1965
    Britain (c.1600–c.1700)
Bryant, Sir A.; *Samuel Pepys*; Collins, 1967 (3 vols)
Cipolla, C. M.; *Before the Industrial Revolution*; Methuen, 1976
Clark, Sir G.; *Later Stuarts 1660–1714*; Oxford U.P., 1956
Hill, C.; *Century of Revolution 1603–1714*; Cardinal, 1974
Hill, C.; *God's Englishman: Oliver Cromwell and the English Revolution*; Penguin, 1972
Lamont, W. M.; *Godly Rule*; Macmillan, 1969
Mitchison, R.; *History of Scotland*; Methuen, 1970
Ogg, D.; *England in the Reign of Charles II*; Oxford U.P., 1967
Stone, L.; *Crisis of the Aristocracy 1558–1641*; Oxford U.P., 1965
Wedgwood, C. V.; *King's Peace 1637–41*; Collins, 1955
Wedgwood, C. V.; *King's War 1641–47*; Collins, 1958
    Britain (c.1700–c.1800)
Churchill, W.; *Marlborough*; Harrap, 1970
James, F. G.; *Ireland in the Empire 1688–1770*; Harvard U.P., 1973
Plumb, J. H.; *Sir Robert Walpole*; Allan Lane, 1972 (2 vols)
Smout, T. C.; *History of the Scottish People 1560–1830*; Fontana, 1972
    Byzantine Empire
Nicol, D. M. (Ed.); *Last Centuries of Byzantium*; Hart-Davis, 1972
Southern, R. W.; *Western Society and the Church in the Later Middle Ages*; Penguin, 1970
    France
Goubert, P.; *Ancien Regime: French Society 1600–1750*; Weidenfeld & Nicolson, 1973
Hatton, R. M.; *Europe in the Age of Louis XIV*; Thames & Hudson, 1969
Ogg, D.; *Louis XIV*; Oxford U.P., 1967
    Italy
Burckhardt, J.; *The Civilization of the Renaissance in Italy*; Mentor, 1974 (2 vols)
Larner, J.; *Culture and Society in Italy, 1290–1420*; Batsford, 1971
    Spain
Elliott, J. H.; *Imperial Spain 1469–1716*; E. Arnold, 1963
Hillgarth, J. N.; *The Spanish Kingdoms, 1250–1516*; Oxford, 1976 (2 vols)
Parry, J. H.; *Spanish Seaborne Empire*; Hutchinson, 1966
    USSR
Auty, R. & D. Obolensky (Eds.); *Introduction to Russian History*; Cambridge U.P., 1976
Riasanovsky, N. V.; *History of Russia*; Oxford U.P., 1969
Troyat, H.; *Catherine the Great*; Aidan Ellis, 1979
Vernadsky, G.; *Kievan Russia*; Yale U.P., 1973
Vernadsky, G.; *Mongols and Russia*; Yale U.P., 1953
Vernadsky, G.; *Russia at the Dawn of the Modern Age*; Yale U.P., 1959

Major contributors and advisers to The Joy of Knowledge

Fabian Acker CEng, MIEE, MIMarE; Professor Leslie Alcock; Professor H. C. Allen MC; Leonard Amey OBE; Neil Ardley BSc; Professor H. R. V. Arnstein DSc, PhD, FIBiol; Russell Ash BA (Dunelm), FRAI; Norman Ashford PhD, CEng, MICE, MASCE, MCIT; Professor Robert Ashton; B. W. Atkinson BSc, PhD; Anthony Atmore BA; Professor Philip S. Bagwell BSc(Econ), PhD; Peter Ball MA; Edwin Banks MIOP; Professor Michael Banton; Dulan Barber; Harry Barrett; Professor J. P. Barron MA, DPhil, FSA; Professor W. G. Beasley FBA; Alan Bender PhD, MSc, DIC, ARCS; Lionel Bender BSc; Israel Berkovitch PhD, FRIC, MIChemE; David Berry MA; M. L. Bierbrier PhD; A. T. E. Binsted FBBI (Dipl); David Black; Maurice E. F. Block BA, PhD(Cantab); Richard H. Bomback BSc (London), FRPS; Basil Booth BSc (Hons), PhD, FGS, FRGS; J. Harry Bowen MA(Cantab), PhD(London); Mary Briggs MPS, FLS; John Brodrick BSc(Econ); J. M. Bruce ISO, MA, FRHistS, MRAeS; Professer D. A. Bullough MA, FSA, FRHistS; Tony Buzan BA(Hons) UBC; Dr Alan R. Cane; Dr J. G. de Casparis; Dr Jeremy Catto MA; Denis Chamberlain; E. W. Chanter MA; Professor Colin Cherry DSc(Eng), MIEE; A. H. Christie MA, FRAI, FRAS; Dr Anthony W. Clare MPhil(London), MB, BCh, MRCPI, MRCPsych; Professor Aidan Clarke MA, PhD, FTCD; Sonia Cole; John R. Collis MA, PhD; Professor Gordon Connell-Smith BA, PhD, FRHistS; Dr A. H. Cook FRS; Professor A. H. Cook FRS; J. A. L. Cooke MA, DPhil; R. W. Cooke BSc, CEng, MICE; B. K. Cooper; Penelope J. Corfield MA; Robin Cormack MA, PhD, FSA; Nona Coxhead; Patricia Crone BA, PhD; Geoffrey P. Crow BSc(Eng), MICE, MIMunE, MInstHE, DIPTE; J. G. Crowther; Professor R. B. Cundall FRIC; Noel Currer-Briggs MA, FSG; Christopher Cviic BA(Zagreb), BSc(Econ, London); Gordon Daniels BSc(Econ, London), DPhil(Oxon); George Darby BA; G. J. Darwin; Dr David Delvin; Robin Denselow BA; Professor Bernard L. Diamond; John Dickson; Paul Dinnage MA; M. L. Dockrill BSc(Econ), MA, PhD; Patricia Dodd BA; James Dowdall; Anne Dowson MA(Cantab); Peter M. Driver BSc, PhD, MIBiol; Rev Professor C.

W. Dugmore DD; Herbert L. Edlin BSc, Dip in Forestry; Pamela Egan MA(Oxon); Major S. R. Elliot CD, BComm; Professor H. J. Eysenck PhD, DSc; Dr Peter Fenwick BA, MB, BChir, DPM, MRCPsych; Jim Flegg BSc, PhD, ARCS, MBOU; Andrew M. Fleming MA; Professor Antony Flew MA(Oxon), DLitt (Keele); Wyn K. Ford FRHistS; Paul Freeman DSc(London); G. S. P. Freeman-Grenville DPhil, FSA, FRAS, G. E. Fussell DLitt, FRHistS; Kenneth W. Gatland FRAS, FBIS; Norman Gelb BA; John Gilbert BA(Hons, London); Professor A. C. Gimson; John Glaves-Smith BA; David Glen; Professor S. J. Goldsack BSc, PhD, FInstP, FBCS; Richard Gombrich MA, DPhil; A. F. Gomm; Professor A. Goodwin MA; William Gould BA(Wales); Professor J. R. Gray; Christopher Green PhD; Bill Gunston; Professor A. Rupert Hall DLitt; Richard Halsey BA(Hons, UEA); Lynette K. Hamblin BSc; Norman Hammond; Peter Harbison MA, DPhil; Professor Thomas G. Harding PhD; Professor D. W. Harkness; Richard Harris; Dr Randall P. Harrison; Cyril Hart MA, PhD, FRICS, FIFor; Anthony P. Harvey; Nigel Hawkes BA(Oxon); F. P. Heath; Peter Hebblethwaite MA (Oxon), LicTheol; Frances Mary Heidensohn BA; Dr Alan Hill MC, FRCP; Robert Hillenbrand MA, DPhil; Catherine Hills PhD; Professor F. H. Hinsley; Dr Richard Hitchcock; Dorothy Hollingsworth OBE, BSc, FRIC, FIBiol, FIFST, SRD; H. P. Hope BSc(Hons, Agric); Antony Hopkins CBE, FRCM, LRAM, FRSA; Brian Hook; Peter Howell BPhil, MA(Oxon); Brigadier K. Hunt; Peter Hurst BDS, FDS, LDS, RSCEd, MSc(London); Anthony Hyman MA, PhD; Professor R. S. Illingworth MD, FRCP, DPH, DCH; Oliver Impey MA, DPhil; D. E. G. Irvine PhD; L. M. Irvine BSc; E. W. Ives BA, PhD; Anne Jamieson cand mag(Copenhagen), MSc (London); Michael A. Janson BSc; G. H. Jenkins PhD; Professor P. A. Jewell BSc (Agric), MA, PhD, FIBiol; Hugh Johnson; Commander I. E. Johnston RN; I. P. Jolliffe BSc, MSc, PhD, ComplCE, FGS; Dr D. E. H. Jones ARCS, FCS; R. H. Jones PhD, BSc, CEng, MICE, FGS, MASCE, Hugh Kay; Dr Janet Kear; Sam Keen; D. R. C. Kempe BSc, DPhil, FGS; Alan

Kendall MA(Cantab); Michael Kenward; John R. King BSc(Eng), DIC, CEng, MIProdE; D. G. King-Hele FRS; Professor J. F. Kirkaldy DSc; Malcolm Kitch; Michael Kitson MA; B. C. Lamb BSc, PhD; Nick Landon; Major J. C. Larminie QDG, Retd; Diana Leat BSc(Econ), PhD; Roger Lewin BSc, PhD; Harold K. Lipset; Norman Longmate MA(Oxon); John Lowry; Kenneth E. Lowther MA; Diana Lucas BA(Hons); Keith Lye BA, FRGS; Dr Peter Lyon; Dr Martin McCauley; Sean McConville BSc; D. F. M. McGregor BSc, PhD(Edin); Jean Macqueen PhD; William Baird MacQuitty MA(Hons), FRGS, FRPS; Professor Rev F. X. Martin OSA; Jonathan Martin MA; Rev Cannon E. L. Mascall DD; Christopher Maynard MSc, DTh; Professor A. J. Meadows; Dr T. B. Millar; John Miller MA, PhD; J. S. G. Miller MA, DPhil, BM, BCh; Alaric Millington BSc, DipEd, FIMA; Rosalind Mitchison MA, FRHistS; Peter L. Moldon; Patrick Moore OBE; Robin Mowat MA, DPhil; J. Michael Mullin BSc; Alistair Munroe BSc, ARCS; Professor Jacob Needleman, John Newman MA, FSA; Professor Donald M. Nicol MA PhD; Gerald Norris; Professor F. S. Northedge PhD; Caroline E. Oakman BA(Hons, Chinese); S. O'Connell MA(Cantab), MInstP; Dr Robert Orr; Michael Overman; Di Owen BSc; A. R. D. Pagden MA, FRHistS; Professor E. J. Pagel PhD; Liam de Paor MA; Carol Parker BA(Econ), MA (Internat. Aff.); Derek Parker; Julia Parker DFAstrolS; Dr Stanley Parker; Dr Colin Murray Parkes MD, FRC(Psych), DPM; Professor Geoffrey Parrinder MA, PhD, DD(London), DLitt(Lancaster); Moira Paterson; Walter C. Patterson MSc; Sir John H. Peel KCVO, MA, DM, FRCP, FRCS, FRCOG; D. J. Penn; Basil Peters MA, MInstP, FBIS; D. L. Phillips FRCR, MRCOG; B. T. Pickering PhD, DSc; John Picton; Susan Pinkus; Dr C. S. Pitcher MA, DM, FRCPath; Alfred Plaut FRCPsych; A. S. Playfair MRCS, LRCP, DObst, RCOG; Dr Antony Polonsky; Joyce Pope BA; B. L. Potter NDA, MRAC, CertEd; Paulette Pratt; Antony Preston; Frank J. Pycroft; Margaret Quass; Dr John Reckless; Trevor Reese BA, PhD, FRHistS; M. M. Reese MA (Oxon); Derek A. Reid BSc, PhD; Clyde Reynolds BSc; John

Rivers; Peter Roberts; Colin A. Ronan MSc, FRAS; Professor Richard Rose BA(Johns Hopkins), DPhil (Oxon); Harold Rosenthal; T. G. Rosenthal MA(Cantab); Anne Ross MA, MA(Hons, Celtic Studies), PhD, (Archaeol and Celtic Studies, Edin); Georgina Russell MA; Dr Charles Rycroft BA (Cantab), MB(London), FRCPsych; Susan Saunders MSc(Econ); Robert Schell PhD; Anil Seal MA, PhD(Cantab); Michael Sedgwick MA(Oxon); Martin Seymour-Smith BA(Oxon), MA(Oxon); Professor John Shearman; Dr Martin Sherwood; A. C. Simpson BSc; Nigel Sitwell; Dr Alan Sked; Julie and Kenneth Slavin FRGS, FRAI; Professor T. C. Smout; Alec Xavier Snobel BSc(Econ); Terry Snow BA, ATCL; Rodney Steel; Charles S. Steinger MA, PhD; Geoffrey Stern BSc(Econ); Maryanne Stevens BA(Cantab), MA(London); John Stevenson DPhil, MA; J. Sidworthy MA; D. Michael Stoddart BSc, PhD; Bernard Stonehouse DPhil, MA, BSc, MInst Biol; Anthony Storr FRCP, FRCPsych; Richard Storry; Charles Stuart-Jervis; Professor John Taylor; John W. R. Taylor FRHistS, MRAeS, FSLAET; R. B. Taylor BSc(Hons, Microbiol); J. David Thomas MA, PhD; D. Thompson BSc(Econ); Harvey Tilker PhD; Don Tills PhD, MPhil, MIBiol, FIMLS; Jon Tinker; M. Tregear MA; R. W. Trender; David Trump MA, PhD, FSA; M. F. Tuke PhD; Christopher Tunney MA; Laurence Urdang Associates (authentication and fact check); Sally Walters BSc; Christopher Wardle; Dr D. Washbrook; David Watkins; George Watkins MSc; J. W. N. Watkins; Anthony J. Watts; Dr Geoff Watts; Melvyn Westlake; Anthony White MA(Oxon), MAPhil(Columbia); Dr Ruth D. Whitehouse; P. J. S. Whitmore MBE, PhD; Professor G. R. Wilkinson; Rev H. A. Williams CR; Christopher Wilson BA; Professor David M. Wilson; John B. Wilson BSc, PhD, FGS, FLS; Philip Windsor BA, DPhil(Oxon), Roy Wolfe BSc(Econ), MSc; Donald Wood MA PhD; Dr David Woodings MA, MRCP, MRCPath; Bernard Yallop PhD, BSc, ARCS, FRAS Professor John Yudkin MA, MD, PhD(Cantab), FRIC, FIBiol, FRCP.

(*picture credits continued*)
[Key] Fotomas Index; [1] National Portrait Gallery; [2] Fotomas Index/British Library; [3] Mansell Collection; [4] National Portrait Gallery; [5] Fotomas Index; [6] Weidenfeld & Nicolson Archives; [8] Mansell Collection; [9] Fotomas Index; [10] National Portrait Gallery. **52–3** [Key] Michael Holford/Prado Museum, Madrid; [2] Mary Evans Picture Library; [3] C. M. Dixon; [4] Musée Cantonel des Beaux Arts/André Held; [6] J. E. Bulloz; [7A] Michael Holford; [8] Mary Evans Picture Library; [9] Trustees of the National Gallery. **54–5** [Key] Mr. Simon Wingfield Digby, Sherborne Castle; [1] By kind permission of the Marquess of Tavistock; [2] Radio Times Hulton Picture Library; [4] Country Life; [5] National Portrait Gallery; [6] Fotomas Index; [8] Mary Evans Picture Library; [9] National Portrait Gallery. **56–7** [Key] Fotomas Index; [1] Mansell Collection; [2] Mansell Collection; [3] National Army Museum; [4] Weidenfeld & Nicolson Archives/National Maritime Museum; [5] Mansell Collection; [7] Fotomas Index; [8] Michael Holford/National Maritime Museum. **58–9** [Key] Mary Evans Picture Library; [1] Picturepoint; [2] Weidenfeld & Nicolson Archives; [3] Weidenfeld & Nicolson Archives/Bibliothèque Nationale; [5] Picturepoint; [6] Mansell Collection; [7] Fotomas Index; [8] Radio Times Hulton Picture Library; [9] Maggs Bros. Ltd/Geoff Goode. **60–1** [Key] Society of Antiquaries, London; [1] Weidenfeld & Nicolson Archives/BM; [4] National Portrait Gallery; [5] Mary Evans picture Library; [6] National Portrait Gallery; [7] Courtauld Institute of Art/Courtesy of the Chatsworth Settlement; [8] Mansell Collection; [9] Mansell Collection. **62–3** [Key] Radio Times Hulton Picture Library; [1] British Library; [3] Trustees of the National Gallery; [4] John R. Freeman; [6] Mary Evans Picture Library; [9] Cooper Bridgeman. **64–5** [Key] National Portrait Gallery; [1] Mary Evans Picture Library; [2] Radio Times Hulton Picture Library; [4] Mansell Collection; [5] Mansell Collection; [6] Radio Times Hulton Picture Library; [8] Fotomas Index; [9] Fotomas Index. **66–7** [Key] Weidenfeld & Nicolson Archives/BM; [1] Michael Holford/BM; [2] Weidenfeld & Nicolson Archives/V & A; [3] Mansell Collection; [4] Fotomas Index; [5] Fotomas Index; [6] National Portrait Gallery; [7] National Portrait Gallery; [8] Radio Times Hulton Picture Library; [9] Mansell Collection. **68–9** [Key] Fotomas Index; [1] Fotomas Index/BM; [2] Radio Times Hulton Picture Library; [3] Mary Evans Picture Library; [4] Radio Times Hulton Picture Library; [5] Eileen Tweedy/The London Museum; [6] National Maritime Museum; [8] A. F. Kersting. **70–1** [Key] Freemans; [1] Freemans; [2] Picturepoint; [3] Radio Times Hulton Picture Library; [4] Fotomas Index; [5] Scottish National Portrait Gallery; [6] National Portrait Gallery; [7] Freemans; [8] Art Gallery & Museum, Glasgow; [9] Freemans. **72–3** [Key] Trustees of the British Museum; [3] John R. Freeman; [4] Cooper Bridgeman/Kunsthistorisches

Museum, Vienna; [7] Rijksmuseum, Amsterdam; [10] Mansell Collection; [11] Governor & Co of the Bank of England. **74–5** [Key] Ronan Picture Library; [1] Ronan Picture Library/E. P. Goldsmith & Co. Ltd; [2] National Maritime Museum; [3] Ronan Picture Library; [5] Mansell Collection; [6] Ronan Picture Library; [7] Ronan Picture Library/E. P. Goldsmith & Co Ltd; [9] Ronan Picture Library. **76–7** [Key] Aerofilms; [1] Fotomas Index; [2] Fotomas Index; [4] Picturepoint; [5] Governor & Company of the Bank of England; [6] Radio Times Hulton Picture Library; [7] Eileen Tweedy; [8] Michael Holford. **78–9** [1] Giraudon/Louvre. [3] Snark International. **80–1** [3] Novosti Press Agency; [5] Historical Research Unit; [7] Novosti Press Agency; [8] Novosti Press Agency; [9] Michael Holford. **82–3** [Key] Novosti Press Agency; [4] Victor Kennett; [6] Novosti Press Agency; [9] Victor Kennett; [10] Historical Research Unit. **84–5** [Key] Ullstein Bilderdienst; [3] National Army Museum; [4] Archiv für Kunst und Geschichte; [5] Bavaria Verlag; [6] Amplaciones y Reproducciones Mas/Madrid Museo Municipal. **86–7** [Key] Cooper Bridgeman; [4] Mansell Collection; [6] Henry E. Huntington Library & Art Gallery; [7] Cooper Bridgeman/Victoria Art Gallery, Bath. **88–9** [Key] Mansell Collection; [1] Cooper Bridgeman Library; [2] Sun Alliance & London Insurance Group; [3] Mansell Collection; [4] Radio Times Hulton Picture Library; [5] Eileen Tweedy; [6] Mansell Collection; [7] Fotomas Index; [8] Mansell Collection; [9] Fotomas Index. **90–1** [Key] County Records Office, Bedford; [1] Museum of English Rural Life, University of Reading; [3] Museum of English Rural Life, University of Reading; [5] Museum of English Rural Life, University of Reading; [6] Museum of English Rural Life, University of Reading; [7] Museum of English Rural Life, University of Reading; [8] Mansell Collection; [9] John Webb/by kind permission of the Earl of Leicester. **92–3** [Key] National Gallery of Ireland; [1] Master & Fellows, Pembroke College, Cambridge; [2] Cooper Bridgeman Library; [3] C. M. Dixon; [4] Public Records Office of Northern Ireland; [5] Fotomas Index; [6] Radio Times Hulton Picture Library; [8] National Gallery of Ireland; [9] Mansell Collection; [10] Eileen Tweedy. **94–5** [Key] Scottish Tourist Board; [1] Mary Evans Picture Library; [2] Mansell Collection; [4] Eileen Tweedy/BM; [5] Radio Times Hulton Picture Library; [6] MB photograph; [7] Mary Evans Picture Library; [8] Studio Swain, Glasgow/Mitchell Library, Glasgow; [9] Mansell Collection. **96–7** [Key] Radio Times Hulton Picture Library; [1] National Maritime Museum; [2] By kind permission of the President & Council of the Royal College of Surgeons of England; [3] Rijksmuseum van Naturlijke Historie; [4] Akademie der Wissenschaften der DDR/George Rainbird Ltd; [5] Trustees of the British Museum/Ray Gardner; [6A] India Office Library/BM; [6B] Trustees of the British Museum/Ray Gardner; [7] Source unknown; [8]

By permission of the Royal College of Physicians of London; [9] Radio Times Hulton Picture Library. **98–9** [2] Lauros Giraudon/Musée de la Marine, Paris; [4] Radio Times Hulton Picture Library; [5] Angelo Hornak/V & A; [6] Trustees of the British Museum/John R. Freeman; [7] Ampliaciones y Reproducciones Mas, Barcelona; [8] Mansell Collection. **100–1** [Key] Fotomas Index; [2] Picturepoint; [3] National Maritime Museum; [4] Picturepoint; [5] Eileen Tweedy/India Office Library; [6] Mansell Collection; [7] National Maritime Museum; [8] Mansell Collection; [9] Josiah Wedgwood & Sons Ltd. **102–3** [Key] India Office Library & Records; [1] Ann and Bury Peerless; [3] Ann and Bury Peerless; [4] Ann and Bury Peerless; [5] India Office Library & Records; [7] India Office Library & Records; [8] India Office Library & Records; [9] India Office Library & Records; [10] India Office Library & Records. **104–5** [Key] William MacQuitty; [2] Trustees of the British Museum; [3] William MacQuitty; [4] William MacQuitty; [5] Radio Times Hulton Picture Library; [7] Trustees of the British Museum; [8] Cooper Bridgeman/National Maritime Museum. **106–7** [Key] International Society for Educational Information, Tokyo; [1] Bradley Smith; [2] Bradley Smith; [3] International Society for Educational Information, Tokyo; [4] Bradley Smith; [5] Bradley Smith; [6] Weidenfeld & Nicolson; [7] International Society of Educational Information, Tokyo; [8] Orion Press. **108–9** [Key] Werner Forman Archive; [2] Mansell Collection; [3] Mansell Collection; [4] Mansell Collection; [6] Mary Evans Picture Library; [7] Mansell Collection. **110–11** [6] By kind permission of the City of Bristol Archives/David Strickland; [7] Mansell Collection; [8] Bettmann Archive; [9] Bettmann Archive/Smithsonian Institution. **112–13** [3] Mary Evans Picture Library; [4] Metropolitan Museum of Art, New York, Gift of Mrs Russell Sage, 1910; [6] Copyright Yale University Art Gallery; [7] Mansell Collection. **114–15** [2] Ronan Picture Library; [4] A. F. Kersting; [6] Ronan Picture Library; [7] Derby Borough Councils & Art Gallery; [8] Josiah Wedgwood & Co; [9] Cooper Bridgeman/Lord Mountbatten. **116–17** [Key] Mansell Collection; [1] National Portrait Gallery; [2] National Portrait Gallery; [3] National Portrait Gallery; [4] Museum of London; [5] Radio Times Hulton Picture Library; [6] Eileen Tweedy; [7] Fotomas Index; [8] Radio Times Hulton Picture Library. **118–19** [Key] Giraudon; [4] Roger Viollet; [5] Giraudon/B. N. Estempes, Paris; [7] Giraudon/Chateau Versailles; [8] Réunion des Musées Nationales. **120–1** [Key] Roger Viollet; [2] Cooper Bridgeman/Coram Foundation; [3] Giraudon/Chateau Versailles; [5] Garanger Giraudon/Musée de l'Armée, Prague; [7] Angelo Hornak/V & A; [8] National Army Museum. **122–3** [Key] Picturepoint; [1] Radio Times Hulton Picture Library; [2] Radio Times Hulton Picture Library; [4] Robert Harding Associates; [5] Weidenfeld & Nicolson Archives/National Maritime

Museum; [6] Fotomas Index; [7] Radio Times Hulton Picture Library; [8] Eileen Tweedy. **124–5** [Key] John R. Freeman; [2] Museen der Stadt, Vienna; [3] Crown Copyright Reserved; [4] Museen der Stadt, Vienna; [5] Trustees of the National Portrait Gallery; [6] Lauros Giraudon/Louvre. **126–7** [Key] Turkish Tourist & Information Office; [1] J. E. Bulloz; [3A] Bildarchiv der Österreichischen Nationalbibliothek; [3B] Bildarchiv der Österreichischen Nationalbibliothek; [4] William Allan; [5] National Army Museum; [6] Radio Times Hulton Picture Library; [7] Bildarchiv der Österreichischen Nationalbibliothek. **128–9** [Key] Bettmann Archive; [3] Mansell Collection; [4] Douglas Botting; [5] Mike Andrews; [6] Bettmann Archive; [7] Bettmann Archive; [8] Bettmann Archive. **130–1** [Key] Mary Evans Picture Library; [4] Mansell Collection; [8] By permission of the Science Museum, London; [9A] By permission of Stanley Gibbons Ltd/Angelo Hornak; [10] Mansell Collection. **132–3** [Key] Fotomas Index; [2] Mansell Collection; [3] Weidenfeld & Nicolson Archives; [4] Aerofilms; [5] Radio Times Hulton Picture Library; [6] David Strickland; [8] Michael Holford. **134–5** [Key] Freemans; [1] National Museum of Wales; [3] Fotomas Index; [6] Radio Times Hulton Picture Library; [7] Picturepoint; [8] Spectrum Colour Library; [9] Picturepoint. **136–7** Bodleian Library, Oxford; Mansell Collection; Scala; Mansell Collection; Mansell Collection; Mary Evans Picture Library; Mansell Collection; Ray Gardner/Trustees of British Museum. **138–9** Mansell Collection; Mary Evans Picture Library; Michael Holford/V & A; Mansell Collection; Mansell Collection; Mansell Collection. **140–1** Mansell Collection; Sonia Halliday/Topkapi Palace Museum, Istanbul; Mary Evans Picture Library; Mansell Collection; Michael Holford; Mansell Collection. **142–3** Mary Evans Picture Library; Mansell Collection; Cooper Bridgeman/Rijksmuseum, Amsterdam; Cooper Bridgeman, A. F. Kersting. **144–5** Giraudon; Mansell Collection; Michael Holford/Science Museum; Mansell Collection; Michael Holford; Camera Press; Mansell Collection; Mansell Collection; Ronan Picture Library. **146–7** Michael Holford; Michael Holford/Louvre; Giraudon. **148–9** Mansell Collection; Mansell Collection; Cooper Bridgeman; Mansell Collection; Mansell Collection. **150–1** Mansell Collection; Cooper Bridgeman; Cooper Bridgeman; Mansell Collection.

The map on page 19 is based on information in *British History Atlas*, by Martin Gilbert, published by Weidenfeld and Nicolson. The map on page 2 is based on information in *The English Medieval Town*, by Colin Platt, published by Secker and Warburg Ltd. The map on page 76 is based on information in *British History Atlas*, by Martin Gilbert, published by Weidenfeld and Nicolson.

162